Romania

The principal sights:

< Lift flap for map

Edited by John Villiers

Romania

With contributions by
William Blacker, Sherban Cantacuzino,
Dudley Iles, Stephen Lloyd,
Robert Matthew-Walker, Sheila Paine,
Miranda Villiers and Sebastian Wormell

PALLAS ATHENE

Contents

Church of the Holy Archangels, Plopiş

13

Illustrations preceding title page:
p. 1 The Archangel Michael, from Monastery Church of St. George, Voroneţ
pp.2-3: Pelicans flying over the Danube Delta
pp. 4-5: The castle of Peleş, near Sinaia
pp. 6-7: The Merry Cemetery, Săpânţa
pp. 8-9: View of Sighişoara from the Clock Tower
title page: Detail of woodcarving, Church of the Holy Archangels, Şurdeşti

Stained glass arcade at Oradea

Introduction

The cultural heritage of the three former principalities of Transylvania, Moldavia and Wallachia that make up modern Romania in large measure owes its extraordinary richness to numerous outside influences: from the ancient Greeks and Romans, subsequently from Slav, Bulgarian and Hungarian invasions, later still from the Italian Renaissance and from the Byzantine, Ottoman and Habsburg empires, and most recently from elsewhere in Western Europe, particularly France. All these influences, while retaining their original characteristics, have at the same time blended with each other and with the ancient indigenous culture of the Geto-Dacians to create a culture that is uniquely Romanian.

Thus, the monumental Tropaeum Traianum at Adamclisi marks one of the highpoints of Roman imperialism, just as the painted churches of Bucovina exemplify what the eminent Romanian historian Nicolae Jorga described as 'Byzance après Byzance', the continuation of Byzantine art and religion in Romania after the fall of Constantinople. Likewise, the humanism of the Italian Renaissance found expression in the flowering of the arts that took place in all three of the principalities in the seventeenth century and gave birth to the Brâncoveanu style, while the continuity of Germanic traditions is demonstrated in the cities and fortified churches of Transylvania, and much of the architecture of the Hungarian and Szekler cities of Transylvania and the Banat, such as Cluj and Timişoara, reveals their role not only as centres of Magyar culture but latterly also as important outposts of the Habsburg Empire. By contrast, the decoration of the wooden churches of Maramureş and the glass icons with which many of them are still adorned belong to a ancient folk tradition still vigorously alive today and is to be found also in the ceramics, the textiles, stone-carving, metal-work and jewellery of the region, and no less conspicuously in Romanian music and dance.

Each of the chapters in this guide forms part of a survey that aims to provide a panoramic background to the detailed information contained in the gazetteer about the many places in Romania where the traveller can see the physical evidence of the variegated strands that have contributed to the fascinating history of Romania and the formation of its remarkable civilization.

John Villiers

Who are the Romanians?

by John Villiers

Romania and the Balkans

A glance at the map of eastern Europe as it has been at any time in the last two thousand years reveals a bewildering and shifting maze of political, ethnic and linguistic boundaries interwoven with the contours of river valleys and mountain ranges, scarcely any of which correspond with one another. More or less in the centre of this maze lies Romania. There is some difference of opinion as to whether, geographically speaking, Romania should be included in the Balkan peninsula properly so called at all. If the Danube is taken as marking the northern limit of the Balkan peninsula, then Romania lies outside it, but in that the area now covered by the modern state of Romania has shared in most of the events and developments that have occurred in Balkan history and that culturally it has a clear family relationship with Albania, Serbia, Bulgaria and Greece, it is undeniably a Balkan country. Primarily as a result of its geographical position, Romania, or to be more precise, the area covered by the three principalities of Transylvania, Moldavia and Wallachia has been subjected to as great a variety of influences, has been invaded and settled by as many different peoples and in its present form is made up of as great a synthesis of races and cultures as any of its Balkan neighbours. This is no less true of Wallachia, which is generally deemed to be the heartland of the Romanian people and for most of its history has been known as the *ţâră românească*, or Romanian land, than of the other two principalities. Before the creation of the modern state of Romania, the Romanians in all three principalities and beyond were often known as Wallachian or Vlach, and Vlach is still one of the several names given to the Arumanians, a people speaking a Latin language closely akin to modern Romanian who live in the mountainous areas on the Greek-Albanian border.

Romania, of course, shares this position of cultural crossroads or ethnic melting pot to a greater or lesser degree with many countries; it is generally only peoples living in very inaccessible or very unattractive places, on remote islands or behind impassable mountains who can maintain any great degree of racial, cultural or

Farm workers, Maramureş

19

linguistic purity. But most of the Balkan lands, and Romania in particular, have always been peculiarly accessible and peculiarly attractive, as well as strategically placed to be economic, political and cultural meeting-places. Their history has, indeed, been largely determined by this accessibility to influences from outside, which has both subjected them to the peaceful penetration of numerous different cultures and also made them the cause of almost continuous dispute among their expansionist, imperial neighbours.

The word Balkan is of Turkish origin and means a chain of wooded mountains. The mountains of the peninsula – in Greece the Pindus, in Bulgaria the Balkan Mountains and the Rhodope Mountains, in Slovenia and Croatia the Karawanken and Julian Alps, in Bosnia-Herzegovina the Dinaric Alps and in Romania the Carpathians – have all played a part in determining the historical geography of the region. They divide it roughly into four main areas: an inaccessible western area, distinguished by ancient, largely indigenous cultures and patriarchal societies, a coastal strip lying along the Adriatic Sea, with strong maritime and commercial traditions and a half-Italian, half-Slav culture, the central and eastern Balkans, which

Bran Castle

Snow on the Carpathians

includes most of modern Romania and where there are pronounced Graeco-Byzantine and Oriental elements in the culture, and Pannonia, where the Balkans and central Europe meet and which is the heartland of the Magyars. The open frontier to the south and east of the Pannonian region – Slovenia, northern Croatia, Slavonia and the Banat of Temesvar (Timişoara) – has, like the Adriatic coast, made it highly susceptible to influences from outside.

Scarcely less important than the mountain ranges in determining the character of the Balkan region are the rivers, although, unlike mountains, rivers, so far from forming barriers, positively encourage movements of population and cultural exchange. The river system of the Balkans is dominated by the Danube and its major tributaries, the Drava, Tisza, Sava, Morava, Sker, Sereth and Pruth, and it was chiefly down the Danube Valley that the migrating peoples from the Asian steppes first penetrated into the region.

However, national and ethnic frontiers seldom correspond exactly to cultural ones, least of all in the Balkans, where so many races of diverse origins have left their mark as conquerors or settlers or both – Celts, Greeks, Romans, Huns and Vandals, Ostrogoths and Visigoths, Bulgars and Avars, Slavs, Magyars, Saxons, Normans, Franks, Germans, Italians and Turks. The foreign visitor to Romania is bound, therefore, to ask himself before long who the Romanians are and in what lies their Romanianness. No doubt a good many Romanians ask themselves those questions too. The waspish comment, attributed by some to Talleyrand, *'D'être roumain, ce n'est pas une nationalité, c'est un métier'*, unkind though it is, does nevertheless contain a grain of truth, in that being Romanian means so many different things to different Romanians. The difficulty of defining the term Romanian in modern times is well exemplified by the story of the Romanian lady travelling on the Orient Express between the wars who, when asked by one of her travelling companions what her nationality was, replied that she had grown up speaking Romanian, Hungarian, Serbian, French and German, had spent some of her childhood in the Banat, which was then part of Austria-Hungary, some in Bessarabia, which is now the republic of Moldova, and some in Balchik, which is now in Bulgaria, that her mother was of the Orthodox religion, born in Kronstadt, now Braşov, and her father a Catholic, born in Temesvar, now Timişoara, so that, although her passport told her that she was Romanian, it would be more accurate to define her nationality as Wagon Lit.

A foreign visitor walking in the streets of Bucharest will gain the same impression of extreme heterogeneity. He will probably know that the Romanians are, or claim to be, a Latin people; the name of their country alone suggests this, though he may be uncertain whether it should be spelt Roumania, Rumania or Romania. He will certainly see many dark and animated faces of distinctly Latin type. At the same time he will see numerous people of more Germanic aspect, with fair hair and clear eyes, and others equally fair, with the broad cheek bones and wide-set eyes of the Slav. As for the language, the first impression that he gets is that it is a kind of dialect of Italian – *La revedere* sounds much like *A rivederla* and *bine* like *bene*. Then, however, he catches words such as *da* and *dragă*, *slab* and *bogat*, and perhaps begin to wonder whether those who maintain that the Romanians are really more Slav than Latin may not be right after all. Then, when he learns that the Romanian for rose is *trandafiri* and meets Romanians called Costache and Vasilache, he is made aware of the strong Greek element in the Romanian language.

This impression of heterogeneity is further heightened by the hybrid character of the architecture of Bucharest and other large cities in Romania. In Bucharest there are houses in Austro-Hungarian Baroque, neo-Byzantine, neo-Moorish, neo-Gothic, neo-Classical, Art Nouveau, Art Deco, and Banker's Georgian styles, miniature copies of Versailles and Venetian palazzi, adorned with Dutch gables, French mansards, Scottish Baronial turrets and Turkish balconies. Even the indigenous Brâncoveanu style, exemplified by the Palace of Mogoşoaia, is as reminiscent of Venice or Portuguese Manuelino or the Isabelline style of southern Spain, with its curly columns and Moorish arches, as of anything indigenously Romanian. Much of the city is laid out in imitation of Paris, with broad boulevards lined with trees and ending in triumphal arches or round piazzas, and before the Second World

Cantacuzino Palace (now the Enescu Museum), Bucharest

Statue of Avram Iancu,
Târgu Mureş

War, this, as well as Bucharest's tradition of good food, elegant women and brilliant night life, earned for it the epithet of 'the Paris of the Balkans', although the style of Bucharest and its inhabitants was then and still to some extent remains as much Viennese or Hungarian or Italian or even Turkish as it is Parisian.

Even a superficial study of Romanian art will reveal not only an extraordinary continuity from earliest times, but also a capacity to absorb and transmute influences from outside. The village architecture of Romania, the embroideries, the pottery, even the music and dance, as well as collectively constituting one of the few really vital and genuine folk cultures left in Europe today, reveal a fascinating blend of very ancient autochthonous styles and techniques with features that are recognizably Byzantine, Gothic, Serbian or Turkish. The sculpture of Brâncuşi provides another excellent example of this capacity of the Romanians to absorb influences from outside and graft them on to their indigenous artistic traditons. Brâncuşi is simultaneously the father of modern European sculpture and firmly rooted in very ancient Romanian traditions of folk art and craftsmanship. The fact that, like many Romanian sculptors before and since his time, he worked so much in wood is in itself evidence of this, because the Romanian peasant craftsman has always had a special feel for wood and a special skill in working it, as is well demonstrated in the architectural decoration of the wooden churches of Maramureş.

Saxon fortified church, Viscri

Who, then, are the Romanians? Without going so far as the great Romanian historian, Nicolae Iorga, who maintained that in order to study the history of the Romanians properly it is necessary to know not only the history of all their neighbours, but the history of the whole of eastern Europe, we may find at least a partial answer to this question by an examination of the history of the people and their language in the wider context of the history of the Balkans as a whole.

Geto-Dacians, Greeks, Romans and Slavs

The inhabitants of the Balkan peninsula before it was overrun by the Indo-European races have left very few traces. There is scarcely any evidence of pre-Indo-European elements in the languages of the area, nor is it known how far north the pre-Greek Indo-European languages of the *satem* group, (so called because their word for a hundred is derived from the root form *satem*), may have spread. These *satem* languages, together with the pre-Roman languages of Illyria in the west and Thrace in the east, have almost entirely disappeared, except in Albanian, that most mysterious of Balkan languages, and in certain place-names, notably the names of rivers in the region, such as Danube, Sava, Drava, Drina and Maritsa.

Evidence exists of Geto-Dacian settlements in the lower Danube area from the sixth century BC, and the Dacian language was certainly an Indo-European tongue, probably belonging to the Thracian group and linked with Albanian, although we have scarcely any idea what it was like and can only identify a handful of words in modern Romanian as being of Dacian origin, among them *barză* (stork), *brad* (fir tree), *brânza* (cheese), *bucura* (rejoice), *copil* (child), *mânz* (foal), *moş* (old man) and *vatră* (hearth). What is also certain is that by the sixth century BC Greek influences had spread north into Dacia, carried there by way of the numerous trading centres established by Greek settlers along the coasts of the Black Sea, the Aegean, the Ionian and the Adriatic, some of which had close commercial and cultural links with the populations to the north of the Danube. In Dobrogea and on the Black Sea coast of Romania the most important of these Greek settlements were at Callatis, Istros (Histria) and Tomis (Constanţa). Although Greek colonization was confined to the coasts, Greek culture penetrated deep inland, and already before the arrival of the Romans the Dacians had borrowed a number of Greek words, many of which later passed into Dacian Latin. *Martor*, from Attic Greek μάρτυς provides a particularly interesting illustration of this process. Greek 'υ', which was pronounced 'oo' before the time of Alexander the Great, was converted to a 'y' or 'i' sound in post-Alexandrian Greek and retained this pronunciation in Latin and later Western European languages. Thus, the preservation of the 'o' sound in *martor* suggests that it is a very early borrowing. Furthermore, the Romanian word has retained its original meaning of 'witness', and not 'martyr', a meaning that it only acquired in Greek and Latin after the advent of Christianity. It can therefore confidently be assumed that it was current in Dacia before the Christian era. Many other Greek words came into Romanian through Latin, which already had a large admixture of Greek vocabulary by the time of the Roman colonization of Dacia. Later, there was a further influx of Greek words into the language through Slavonic, particularly Old Bulgarian or Old Slavonic, the ecclesiatical language of Orthodox Christianity.

Latin spread from the camps of the Roman legionaries in Dacia and the garrison towns of Macedonia, along the coasts of Albania and Dalmatia into the Danubian plain. There is, indeed, evidence of emigration to Dacia even before the Roman conquest by Italian peasants made destitute by the development of the great Roman *latifundia*, which were manned largely by slaves, and by the import of corn from overseas, and this no doubt hastened the process of romanization in the region. Subsequently, the Romans attempted to gain mastery of the Balkan peninsula by the establishment of a centralized administration in the area based on the *provincia* system, partly, it seems, in order to counter threats from Illyrian pirates, so that provincial Latin became the *lingua franca* of the area. However, to some extent it had to share its linguistic dominance with Greek, and it is possible to draw a rough line from west to east, dividing Macedonia, southern Albania and Bulgaria, where Greek was spoken, from the northern Balkans, where Latin was in general use. Of the three thousand or so Dacian inscriptions so far found, fewer than forty are in Greek, and of the 2,700 names mentioned in these inscriptions, 75 percent are Roman, 13 percent are Greek, four percent are Thraco-Dacian, and four percent are Illyrian.

The modern Romanian language is the only survivor of several Latin dialects that were spoken in the eastern parts of the Roman empire. Cut off from Western Latin by the advent of the Slavs in southeast Europe in the seventh century and the Magyars in central Europe in the ninth, Romanian did not evolve from medieval Latin, but from Vulgar Latin and is therefore in many ways the most conservative of all the Romance languages. On the other hand, it was strongly influenced by the languages spoken round it and shared much of its evolution with other Balkan languages, both with Slav languages such as Serbian and Bulgarian and also with Greek, Albanian, Turkish and Hungarian.

Since the colonists of Roman Dacia came from all parts of the Roman world, they spoke many different languages as a mother tongue and only used Latin as a *lingua franca*. Consequently, the Latin they spoke was an early and probably much simplified form of Vulgar Latin and one that developed many of the same characteristics as other Romance languages, such as the elimination of deponent verbs, the replacement of the aorist by the compound perfect tense, and the abandonment of the consonant 'h' (which, however, reappeared later in Romanian in words of Slav origin). Ever

Dacians on Trajan's column, Rome

since the Roman period and in spite of all later influences, Romania has retained, at least linguistically, its character as a Latin island surrounded by a Slav ocean to the north, east and south and a German-Hungarian one to the west, and this sense of Latinity is still today one of the most potent constituents of the Romanian national identity. It was given fresh infusions in the Middle Ages by the Crusades, by the Venetians and by influences stemming from Jagellonian Poland and Angevin Hungary, and it has been reinvigorated in modern times by Romania's close cultural links with France and Italy.

By the middle of the first century AD the Romans were masters of most of the Balkan peninsula and had established a foundation for the unification of southeast Europe. In this task the achievements of the Emperor Trajan (98-117) were crucial (see Chapter IV). After conquering the Dacians and their warrior king, Decebalus, he ensured the defence of the Roman Empire in the north and its protection from barbarian attacks by constructing an elaborate defensive system of *limes* along the northern frontier. For the next two centuries the Balkan peoples enjoyed considerable prosperity under the *imperium romanum* and made a substantial contribution to the security of the empire. They provided troops for the Roman armies and many of their most capable leaders, including more than one emperor. The Emperor Aurelian (270-75) came from Moesia, the province to the south of the Danube, Diocletian (284-305) from Dalmatia, and Galerius (305-11) from near Sofia. The Byzantine Emperor Justinus I (518-27) was of Macedonian origin, and his nephew Justinian I (527-65) was born near Skopje.

The Romans' chief aim was to hold the imperial frontier along the Danube against the successive waves of barbarian invaders. It was not until 271 that Aurelian, under pressure from the incursions of the Goths, was forced to evacuate Dacia, thereby leaving the Danubian frontier open to their plundering migrations and those of the Huns. After the division of the empire in 395, Roman defence in the Balkans continued from Constantinople. In the mid-sixth century Justinian I, by moving large bodies of troops to the battlefields of Italy, north Africa and the Near East, where there was a constant threat from the Persians, accelerated the process of Roman disengagement from the region and left the imperial frontiers once again exposed to attack, first from the Avars, Slavs and Bulgars and then, in the ninth and tenth centuries, from the Magyars (Hungarians and Szeklers). Already by the second half of the sixth century the Avars had appeared in the lower Danube region in search of land and had established themselves in Dacia and eastern Pannonia. By 626 they were besieging Constantinople. For nearly two centuries thereafter southeast Europe was cut off from Byzantine rule and, by the time Byzantium had launched its counter-offensive about the year 800, most of the land had been appropriated and settled by Slavs.

Whereas the earlier Germanic migrations and the passage through the Balkans of the Visigoths and Ostrogoths had left few traces, the Slavs, the Bulgars and finally the Magyars all established permanent settlements and came to form an important element in the population over a large part of the region. The Slavs, in particular,

Street in Sighișoara

Hanul lui Manuc, Bucharest

pushed back the Greeks in the north to the coasts, the islands and the mountain regions and succeeded the Byzantine Empire as masters of most of the interior of the peninsula. Only in certain areas did the small, autonomous village communities of Latinized people known as *Romaniæ populares* survive. The memory of these communities is preserved in the name Romania, as it is in the Italian Romagna and the Romanche of the Swiss Alps, (although the spelling and pronunciation Rumania or Roumania, like that of Rumelia, suggest a common origin with Rum, the name given by the Arabs and Turks to Asia Minor and in particular to the Seljuk Turkish empire of Iconium). In this way in Romania a kind of rural Rome, comparable to the Swiss cantons in its political organization and social system, was maintained against Slav hostility.

Although the influence over the Romanians of the Slavs, an Indo-European people speaking a *satem* language, has proved to be the most profound and long-lasting of all, the social and political structure of the earliest Slav immigrant communities composed of unions of several families, and their consequent inability to form larger polities under a single ruler accounts to a great extent for the exceedingly fragmented character of their first settlements in the Balkan lands, not least in Romania. By contrast, the Bulgarians, a Turanian people who had formerly dwelt in the area between the Sea of Azov and Kuban, whence they emigrated to the area round the Danube Delta, were already recognized in 681 by Byzantium as an independent state, were converted to Christianity in 865, and, between the collapse of the Avar kingdom and the resurgence of Byzantium in the eleventh century, embarked on a policy of imperial expansion that enabled them to establish dominance over much of Romania, introducing there as they did so Slav culture and a form of Byzantine Orthodox Christianity that used Old Bulgarian or Church Slavonic as its ecclesiastical language. Church Slavonic, written in the Glagolitic, later Cyrillic, script that

had been introduced into Bulgaria in the late ninth century by the disciples of the missionary brothers SS Cyril and Methodius, became not only the liturgical language of the Orthodox Church in Romania, but also the official language of the princely courts and of administration, and remained so until the eleventh century. The earliest surviving official documents in Romanian are no earlier than the beginning of the sixteenth century, and the Cyrillic alphabet was used to write Romanian until the nineteenth century. It is one of the ironies of Romanian history that a country with a Latin language and a name that indicates its Roman beginnings acquired its Christian religion and much of its Christian culture not from Rome, but from Byzantium, and that it was transmitted to them by the Slavs.

Most of the Slav borrowings in the Romanian language occurred very early. The word for 'Yes', for example, is *da* and not, as in most other Romance languages, derived from a term of affirmation in Latin, which had no word for 'yes'. Moreover, many of the words of Slav origin found in Romanian are derived from obsolete forms that do not occur in any modern Slavonic language. There are also numerous fundamental and therefore probably very early grammatical and syntactical borrowings from Slavonic. The vocative form in '-o' for feminine nouns and the wide use of reflexive forms of the verb, which is far more extensive in Romanian than in any other Romance language and not only often has an exact counterpart in at least one Slavonic language, but also frequently occurs in association with a verb of Slav origin, are only two indications of how prolonged and pervasive Slav influence on the Romanians and their language has been. It is also noteworthy that borrowings of regional vocabulary from different Slav languages are often found in the dialects of Romanian spoken in the areas nearest to the area where that language is spoken. Thus, there are loan words from Bulgarian in the Romanian of the Wallachian plain, from Serbian in the Banat and from Russian and Ukrainian in Moldavia and northern Transylvania

In spite of obtaining a huge increase in territory after the First World War – Transylvania, including Maramureș, Bessarabia, which had been almost continuously under Russian rule since 1812, and northern Bucovina – Romania, like most of the new Balkan states, remained weak and divided, its frontiers having been determined by linguistic more than by economic considerations, and yet with substantial linguistic and ethnic minorities still enclosed within them. Ethnic minorities in Romania since 1920 have included Russians and Lipovani (descendants of adherents of certain religious sects in Russia persecuted by the Tsarist regime), Ukrainians, Bulgarians, Serbs, Slovenes, Slovaks, Greeks, Turks, Magyars, Germans, Albanians, Jews, Armenians and Roma, so that it remains as difficult today as it has ever been to answer the question who exactly the Romanians are.

Monastery Church, Curtea de Argeș

The Romans and Dacia

by Miranda Villiers

Britain and the modern state of Romania are situated at opposite ends of Europe; geography and 2000 years of history have combined, it seems, to drive them apart. In the great house of Europe their rooms have a radically different aspect; Britain looks west over the expanse of the Atlantic, Romania looks east over the great spaces of the steppe. Yet the two peoples share a considerable distinction; not only were their territories once invaded by a common foe, cultivated, developed and abandoned again, but they were the final additions to one of the most extraordinary empires the world has known, that of the Romans.

Perhaps neither of these territories should have been annexed at all; Rome's expansion had been a logical consequence of the prowess of her armies, and any rational observer would have to say with Gibbon that, by the time the Roman Republic gave way to the Roman Empire, 'the northern countries of Europe scarcely deserved the expense and labour of conquest'. The Emperor Augustus was proud of the achievement represented by so many peaceful, well-organized provinces protected by the strongly garrisoned Roman frontiers, but he disapproved of expansionism for its own sake and advised his successors through the terms of his will to confine the empire to the natural boundaries already reached, including the Atlantic Ocean on the west, and the Rhine/Danube frontier on the north.

This advice was not taken; within 100 years the bounds had been extended, and two more provinces were added to the empire: Britain in the west, and Roman Dacia, which took in a large part of modern Romania, in the east. No more were to come. Latecomers though they were, both provinces were deeply affected by the formative influence of Rome; law, administration, local government, trade, Christianity for Britain and a Latin-based language for Romania. When the frontiers receded before the barbarian invasions and the garrisons withdrew, two cultural enclaves remained, and in spite of occupation and further invasions over the centuries, much of the Roman legacy survived. The Romanians are proud of their descent from Roman settlers; they are also proud of their Dacian heritage. This is the history of how the heritage came about.

The reconstructed Tropaeum Traianum, Adamclisi

Romans attacking Dacian fortifications, Trajan's Column, Rome

It was inevitable that the expanding Roman Republic and its success in absorbing the disparate peoples of Italy should attract the attention of other power blocs around the Mediterranean. A clash with the Phoenician trading empire based at Carthage on the North African coast involved Rome in a series of wars during the third century BC culminating with the invasion of Hannibal and a long and nearly disastrous struggle on the soil of Italy itself. By the beginning of the second century Rome was exhausted. But victory over such a powerful enemy did not go unnoticed; Rome was now a power to be reckoned with in the world of the Mediterranean, and Roman military strength was courted assiduously by different elements of the Hellenistic world to the east, a conglomeration of kingdoms and confederacies, which had survived the break up of Alexander's great empire. Rome's involvement was initially reluctant; but it led to the extension of its power not only over the Balkan peninsula but also over Asia Minor and Egypt as well; the final settlement after thirty years of sporadic wars and intense diplomacy brought much needed stability to the eastern Mediterranean and set the administrative pattern for future Roman dominions overseas.

The incorporation of the Hellenistic world brought the Romans face to face with the results of five centuries of Greek colonization: with the chieftans of Thrace, and the client kingdoms of Asia. These represented an extension of power north as far as the Danube and the shore of the Black Sea. Rome's first contact with Transdanubian peoples came from the Pontic cities which ringed the Black Sea; these were Greek trading outposts, all of great antiquity, poised between the sea and the great expanse of steppe behind. They were carefully sited at strategic points on land originally leased by treaty from the chieftaincies which arose among the hitherto nomadic peoples of the hinterland, and were entrepôts from which wheat, furs and skins, fish, and salt meat as well as slaves were despatched southwards, in exchange for wine, olive oil and luxury goods such as jewellery. This trade was originally directed towards the mother cities in Greece, but there is early evidence of trading contacts with Thasos and Rhodes, and very close links were developed with Athens in particular; for centuries most of the grain needed to feed the expanding Athenian population was imported from the Pontic cities, a trade which not only enriched the cities and their cosmopolitan inhabitants, but also the Scythian tribes of the nearer steppe who, during the long period of stability in Central Asia that lasted till the first century BC, gradually abandoned their nomadic habits and warrior culture in order to produce this valuable crop. Prolonged contact with civilization could spell disaster for tribes who had acclimatized too far; by the first century AD a new and more warlike horde had appeared, known as the Sarmatians; they supplanted the Scythians, and links with the Hellenistic world had to be forged all over again.

The sites of the cities dictated their specialities: of those in modern Romania, Histria (Istros) was founded at the mouth of the Danube Delta and was a fishing port. Callatis, later Mangalia, was the centre of the grain trade, but neither was ultimately as prosperous as Tomis (modern Constanţa), which was founded well south of the Delta, a huge expanse of inaccessible marshy streams which even today presents a formidable barrier to navigation. Tomis lay at the Black Sea end of the shortest overland route to the navigable part of the Danube on its northern reach; this was the main trade route west and north to the interior.

It was therefore inevitable that a city in such a favourable position should become the main entrepôt for exports and capital of a district. Under the Roman Empire it became the principal city of the province of Lower Moesia and the seat of the hexarch, or governor, of a whole cluster of Pontic cities. Archaeological evidence from the first century AD reveals an extensive city possessing fine public buildings with mosaic floors, and, judging by the range and quality of the artefacts that have been recovered, a wealthy population. The situation of Tomis was, however, exceptional; it was a cosmopolitan city on the edge of nowhere, tucked into the farthest corner of the Roman frontiers, where the barbarian peoples of the steppe met the highly developed civilization of the ancient world.

An eye-witness account exists of just how forlorn life was in this Greek outpost on the borders of civilization. P. Ovidius Naso, the poet Ovid, was exiled to Tomis in 8 AD by the Emperor Augustus for some excess of licentious behaviour involving other members of the imperial family. Banishment was a favourite punishment and was a mark of how widely the emperor's power extended. Gibbon remarks, 'to resist was fatal and it was impossible to fly', and recalls the saying of Cicero to the exiled Marcellus, 'Wherever you are, remember that you are equally within the power of the conqueror.'

Ovid remained in Tomis until his death in 18 AD, never ceasing to lament his fate in verse or in letters to friends. His grief and longing for the society of his peers are wearisome, but it is possible nevertheless to reconstruct from his text a clear picture of what life was like in an embattled frontier city. Ovid found that the city's Hellenic culture was only a veneer, and over ten years he was obliged to learn both Getic and Sarmatian, the languages of the neighbouring steppe tribes, in order to communicate at all. 'A few people preserve traces of the Greek tongue,' he complains, 'but even this is rendered barbarous by a Getic twang.' It might seem that Ovid's skill in mastering the local languages argues a certain degree of assimilation to his uncomfortable abode, but the stream of complaints to his friends in Rome never flags. He feels the cold: 'Winter runs into winter', he writes; 'we survive here between sheets of ice and Scythian arrows.'

Above all there was fear. Ovid was wary of the Getic farmers who lived in the hinterland of Tomis (now Dobrogea), growing cash crops and coming into the city to trade; 'No fields here produce fruit or sweet grapes', he laments. Worse, these same farmers were cousins to countless fierce steppe tribesmen beyond the Danube, whose culture was based on war and plunder. Guarantees of peace and order behind the Roman frontier counted for little. The Danube did not afford much protection; whenever it froze over the city went on alert against the possibility of an invasion. Ovid describes Scythian horsemen circling the walls of the terrified city as a wolf circles a stockade full of sheep. 'I live my life amidst enemies and dangers,' he writes to one friend, and to another he expresses the hope that he may eventually be deemed worthy of a little help – to change his abode to a place free from the Scythian bow!

The power of these enemies was legendary: 'Bows and quivers give them courage, and horses capable of marches however lengthy and the knowledge of how to endure for long both thirst and hunger.' Indeed, the 'horse peoples' who frightened Ovid so much were formidable opponents, as the Roman army was to find out when it finally closed with them. Their outlandish but sonorous names fit surprisingly well into Ovid's couplets: Coralli, Getae, Sauromatae, Iazyges. These were only a few of the tribes of the steppe, that enormous expanse of plain tilting gradually downwards across Central Asia from Siberia and the confines of China into Central Europe, till it expends itself against the rampart of the Carpathians.

Trajan with his staff officers before the walls of Sarmizegetusa,
Trajan's Column, Rome

Northwards the plains continue through the Ukraine into Poland and Germany.

These steppe peoples were cattle breeders, nomads originally from the east who gradually spread out across the plain in response to climatic changes in the eighth century BC, which destroyed grazing grounds and displaced local peoples, putting pressure in turn on others so as to create a great westward movement of population. The tribes were diverse, many speaking languages of radically different origin. But there were also considerable similarities born of a vast network of inter-tribal contacts: in their distinctive art forms, many bearing motifs revealing their eastern origins, and in their burial customs and religious observances. To the Greek world such peoples were considered the very paradigm of barbarity, and all the more fascinating on that account. The writer Herodotus in the fifth century BC devoted almost an entire book of his *Histories* to an account of the Scythians, their customs and beliefs; much of what he says was dismissed as legend embellished by a fertile imagination. until the findings of modern archaeology started to bear him out.

Most of these hordes were made up of small hierarchical societies led by a chieftain and nobility, the criterion for excellence being riding and fighting skills,

37

particularly with the bow and the sword. All these tribes were known generically as Scythian, and despite long contact with the civilizations to the south and east, they remained contemptuous of urban peoples.

This was true of the Dacians, a collection of Scythian tribes who around 700 BC had been attracted into the Carpathians by sources of iron in what is today Transylvania, and who had colonized the plains within the semicircular ring of mountains known as the Carpathian arc. The tribes settled there with their flocks, deforesting the land to produce grazing, and gradually over the centuries came into close contact with the Danubian people, with their outlets to the south and with the trading ventures of the Pontic cities to the east. A combination of circumstances – contact and trade with highly developed civilizations, the security that comes from settlement in easily defended territory, reserves of wealth from the gold mines as well as the plentiful iron ore that they discovered – all these transformed an agglomeration of allied steppe tribesmen organized in small-scale units; it brought about at least a partial detribalization, and the gradual development of larger and more complex societies with service industries – metal-workers, miners, interpreters and others – serving a mounted elite.

Thus it was that, during the second century BC, after the Roman conquest of Greece and Macedonia, the Dacian peoples north of the Danube came into contact with the Romans. Initially the Romans' trading interests across the Danube lay more in slaves than in wheat; the Dacians quickly established themselves as a useful source of slaves, traded in exchange for Roman goods and know-how, technical and military. While the Dacians remained merely a group of Transdanubian tribes among many another chiefdom and client kingdom, the Roman commanders of the first century BC, who were heavily occupied in consolidating their territorial gains in Gaul and in establishing the Roman frontier on the Rhine, were content to maintain trade links with them, to make treaties with the chieftains, and to pay them to provide auxiliary troops for battles elsewhere.

It only required the existence of a charismatic military leader, a Napoleon-like figure who could forge an alliance of the neighbouring peoples and lead them successfully to conquest, for Dacia to coalesce into a state which could constitute a threat to Rome and the might of its army. That such a person could emerge twice in just over 100 years must go far to explain why the Romans went to such trouble to find a final solution: to subdue the Dacians at considerable cost and to annex their lands. The threat was all the greater because Dacia commanded a weak spot in the Roman frontiers, the steppe corridor at the southeastern corner of the Carpathians through which, for invading hordes, there could be easy access by the shortest route to the Adriatic and to the Roman heartland.

The first leader of genius was Burebistas, who in 63 BC united the Carpathian peoples to defeat the Celts and to drive them westwards, who sacked several of the Pontic cities and made incursions over the Danube into Roman territories that brought him to the northeastern corner of Italy. He seems to have had the personal authority to forge the disparate peoples within the Carpathian arc into a powerful fighting force that impressed all those who encountered it. He was clearly a disciplinarian, and we get a glimpse of his methods from the Greek geographer Strabo who, writing within a hundred years of these events, tells us that he achieved his results 'by exercises, by abstention from wine and obedience'.

The arts of peace seem to have flourished too. The large number of coin hoards found north of the Danube dating from this period indicates that the Dacian 'state' under Burebistas had a domestic coin economy, perhaps as a result of the slave trade with Rome, which would have flourished the more after Pompey's suppression of piracy in the Mediterranean in 67 BC. Burebistas also seems to have established a state religion and the office of high priest at Sarmizegetusa in southwest Transylvania, which henceforth combined the status of capital and major shrine. There is some evidence that, so powerful was the priestly caste, the Dacians operated a dual rulership – king and priest. In any case it is with Burebistas that the first indications appear of the religious dynamic of the Dacian state.

By the time of the Roman civil war the empire of Burebistas was large and powerful enough for Pompey (in 48 BC) to include him in his list of client kings with whom he had diplomatic relations so as to raise levies of auxiliaries for his army. And we know from at least two sources that Caesar was sufficiently provoked in 45 BC to plan a diversion from his journey to the east in order to campaign against him on the Danube frontier. This plan was frustrated in 44 BC, as both Burebistas and Caesar were assassinated in that same year.

Burebistas demonstrated what the presence of a leader of genius could do for the able, warlike Dacians. Without his vision the Dacian 'state' could not continue, and after his death it broke up. The lesson was not lost on the Romans, however; they had been assailed before by such people. Perhaps the energy and competence of Burebistas recalled folk-memories of Hannibal. In the principate of Augustus the northern frontiers of the Roman Empire were completed and consolidated along the Rhine and the Danube by the creation of two garrisoned provinces, Pannonia and Moesia, the gap between the courses of the two rivers being fortified with an artificial *limes* or frontier garrisoned by forts manned by auxiliaries. When the republican legions were broken up and reformed in 30 BC, in order to prevent further invasions from beyond the frontiers and to extend Roman influence in remote areas, 100,000 veterans were settled with gratuities in the Danubian borderlands, while in 13 BC Aelius Catus transported 50,000 Getae from the north bank of the Danube and settled them in Moesia behind the frontier.

The terrible defeat in 3 AD of a Roman army in the Teutoburg Forests at the hands of German tribesmen led by their chieftain Hermann put paid to any attempt to settle the German frontier as far north as the Elbe – the 'lost legions of Varus' were to haunt commanders and to influence military thinking throughout the first

DECEBAL

century AD – and it seemed that, as Augustus had decreed in his will, the Roman Empire had reached its furthest extent. Such advice is usually made to be ignored, but until Britain was invaded in 45 AD the frontiers remained as they had been for nearly a century.

The threat of invasion from over the Danube receded but did not disappear; the Dacians themselves, despite the potential danger they represented, were always in contact with the Romans and watched events closely. 69 AD, the 'Year of the Four Emperors', saw an invasion of the Dacians in alliance with the Roxolani from the Moldavian plains into Moesia while the Emperor Vespasian was preoccupied with events in Germany. The invading forces were finally defeated and order restored, but only after a Roman force under Fonteius Agrippa had been cut to pieces – a foretaste of things to come. The Flavian emperors acknowledged a weak place in the frontiers and carried out further measures of consolidation: forts were built on the Danube at Novae (Şistov), Oescus (Ghigen) and Durostorum (Silistra), and at Troesmis (Igliţa) in the Delta, while a wall and vallum were dug across the Dobrogea from the Danube to the Black Sea. The three legions permanently garrisoned in Moesia were strengthened with two more.

The return of activity on the northern frontier was closely associated with the rise of a new Dacian leader, the second in fairly short succession, who was capable, as Burebistas had been, of unifying the Dacian tribes to recreate an effective Dacian state and, motivated by hatred of the Romans, of pursuing a damaging forward policy which would eventually require the full force of Roman military might to destroy. This was Decebalus, who emerged as chieftain of Dacia around 70 AD. From this point the position on the Danubian frontier was to become increasingly unsatisfactory. We have seen how it was Roman policy to treat with the independent kings and chieftains and to be prepared to pay subsidies or even to provide military and technical 'know how' in return for levies of auxiliary troops to supplement the heavy armed infantry of the legions. Decebalus was a good politician as well as a general, and during the Flavian principate he derived what benefit he could from the Romans in return for defending the northern frontiers so that the emperor could make war elsewhere. In 85 AD he struck.

In another incursion into Lower Moesia, again in concert with the Roxolani, he defeated a Roman army, killing its general, Oppius Sabinus, and destroying several of the newly established forts and the legionaries' camps, though at Novae he was successfully beaten off. Punitive measures were called for, but a large force under Cornelius Fuscus that was sent through the Carpathians, probably by the Jiu Gorge, to attack Decebalus in his fastnesses beyond the mountains was trapped and annihilated in the heavily wooded valley of the Mureş below Sarmizegetusa. Fuscus was killed and, worse still, the standards were captured and remained in Dacian hands

Opposite: Statue of Decebalus, Deva

for nearly twenty years. A legion was destroyed, and only a very few fugitives escaped pursuit to reach the far bank of the Danube. Decebalus contemptuously offered to return the prisoners for a ransom – almost the greatest shame of all.

Revenge could not be long delayed. The Emperor Domitian, though Cassius Dio notes that he was too pleasure-loving to accompany his army, was a tried commander and had fought successful campaigns in Germany. In 88 AD he sent another force against Decebalus under Tettius Julianus, who turned the flank of the Carpathians rather than risk ambush in any of the Carpathian passes. It was also a sensible move to use the western approaches to Decebalus's domains, since the Iazyges, the people whose territories lay to the west, were friendly to Rome at the time. At Tapae (Caransebeş) Tettius defeated Decebalus in a hard-fought pitched battle, in which the carnage was to be a portent of the style of battles to come. Unfortunately for the Romans, Decebalus and his lieutenants escaped.

The peace terms were not as harsh as they might have been. There was no triumph. Domitian forbore to take the honorific 'Dacicus' as a mark of his success. Decebalus's capture of many Roman prisoners gave him considerable bargaining power. The prisoners were returned, but the annual subsidy was restored and, amazingly, Roman engineers were seconded to help Decebalus with defence works, assistance of which he was to make very good use. The court poets sang Domitian's achievements, but the historian Tacitus was humiliated. A further expedition of reprisal was decreed for the following year, which could have followed up more successfully the Tapae victory and carried the war right up to Decebalus's citadel, but this had to be postponed when civil war broke out on the western frontier. Such a pre-emptive strike would have saved Rome much trouble; Decebalus used the time he had gained to exercise his considerable diplomatic ability in inciting his neighbours to revolt, even making overtures to the king of Parthia on the eastern frontier to combine with him against their common enemy.

In 96 AD Domitian succumbed to a palace plot; his death brought the Flavian dynasty to an end. Despite their achievements, the family had won their way to the principate by violently unconstitutional means, and there was much relief when the Senate and army between them chose as the next emperor M. Cocceius Nerva, an elderly senator of noble family and unimpeachable reputation, who adopted as his heir another worthy man, M. Ulpius Traianus, and began a tradition that was to serve Rome well for the next century. Trajan did not have to wait long; he succeeded in 98 AD and soon turned his attention to the unfinished business in Dacia.

Nerva had made a good choice; Trajan was an able and experienced general who had already served on the Danubian frontier, and both he and his wife Plotina were modest people: Dio reports her comment on the huge marble palace she inherited as empress: 'It is my wish that I should leave this place the same person as I enter it.' Trajan was a follower of Stoic philosophy, with its emphasis on good government and high personal morality; his fellow Stoics had been much persecuted during the last 30 years. From his experience on the Danubian frontier he knew with Tacitus that 'the Dacians were never a trustworthy people'. Like Ovid, he knew that even as wide a river as the Danube was an unreliable frontier against a warlike and determined foe, and that any final solution would have to include the Carpathian salient and the lands in the Carpathian arc behind.

In 100 AD Trajan moved against Decebalus, adding another four legions to the nine already stationed on the Danube frontier. 'This memorable war,' says Gibbon of Decebalus, 'approved himself a rival not unworthy of Trajan, nor did he despair of his own and the public fortune till, by the confession of his enemies, he had exhausted every resource both of valour and of policy.' Dio tells us that Trajan did not make war so much to avenge the defeats of Sabinus and Fuscus, but rather because of the Flavian settlement, by which the Roman taxpayer paid ever larger subsidies to Decebalus, who became ever more insolent and treacherous.

The course of the First Dacian War, as Trajan's campaigns of 100 and 101 AD are known, is not easy to follow in detail; there is indeed much room for conjecture as to what exactly happened and where. The period at the turn of the first and second centuries AD is very poorly covered by written sources; we know that the third-century historian Cassius Dio covered the period thoroughly in his monumental history of Rome, but the later books are lost, and are only known to us through somewhat arbitrary selections made by epitomists centuries later, who tended to pick out the good stories and ignore the detail that would have been so valuable to later historiography. There are no records from the Dacian side: this extraordinary people, so skilled in so many ways, were non-literate. Of course much information can be pieced together from inscriptions; we know much about the movement of legions from soldiers' tombstones which list their military posts, but it is from the reliefs on Trajan's Column in Rome that the most information can be gained as to what the course of events may have been.

This 100-ft high column, which marked the centre of Trajan's enormous Forum, survives in an excellent state of preservation today. Between pedestal and upper plinth it displays a winding ribbon of low reliefs carved in Parian marble, which cover the entire surface of the column from top to bottom and which represent Trajan's Dacian wars in a series of separate scenes. The workmanship is uniformly fine, and many details, large and small, have triumphantly survived exposure to the wind and weather of 2000 years.

Tantalizingly, it is not possible to identify with certainty any but a few of the places, or the battles, still less the personnel, with the exception of the Emperor Trajan himself, who is present in nearly every scene addressing or reviewing the troops, watching the legions at work, surveying the battle and accepting the surrender of the conquered. The Column was not intended to chronicle the course of the wars; it was dedicated by the Senate and people to glorify the army and the Roman fighting machine. The most valuable information it yields – and in some cases it is our chief source of knowledge – is about the life and work of the legionary, how forts, camps and signalling stations were constructed and of what materials, about the cavalry, about the dress and armour of the legionary, whether on the march, in camp, at work or in battle, about the appearance and role of the auxiliary troops, about their weapons and fighting skills. We learn from the evidence of the Column that, in the Dacian campaigns at least, the auxiliaries bore the brunt of the fighting, while the legionaries operated the machinery and did the heavy construction work.

We also learn much about the Dacians; they are portrayed consistently as strong, bearded men with hair cut short; they have high cheek bones and dignified expressions; they wear belted tunics and trousers; the distinguishing caps of the nobility and the robes of their priests are faithfully represented. They fight hand to hand to the death, with oval shields and small curved swords similar in appearance to the Gurkha kukri. As befits a rich people, the buildings of Sarmizegetusa, as depicted on the Column, are palatial. Moreover, judging by the remains and the extent of the temples and stone circles that survive on the site to this day, the city itself clearly remained the great spiritual centre that Burebistas had founded.

But the scenes do represent actual battles and actual places: of that there can be no doubt. In the placing of the scenes a certain progression can be observed, and it is tempting to use the evidence of the Column to fill in what is already known from other sources of the course of the Dacian wars.

In 101 AD Trajan crossed the Danube; there is some evidence that he crossed in two places, splitting his army. This would seem to be a sensible strategy and one which he was later to pursue in 115 AD in Parthia, especially in light of Decebalus's proven strategy, used so successfully against Fuscus, of luring the army into the deep woods and valleys where it could be surrounded and destroyed. Trajan's force is thought to have followed Tettius's route round the Carpathians, taking advantage of the friendly Iazyges on his left flank. The Dacians gave ground before him, but stood to fight at Tapae, where another Roman victory was won.

There is evidence from the scenes on the Column to suggest that during the winter Decebalus, blockaded on the west, joined with the Roxolani once more to make incursions into Lower Moesia in order to besiege the Danube forts. Trajan is pictured disembarking at a well-fortified place on the Danube at the head of the relieving force of cavalry and light troops and fighting a battle with the Dacians among enemy waggons – the only point at which these waggons appear. The waggon – the 'ship of the steppe' – played a very large part in the economy of the steppe population, and its appearance on the Column is a convincing indication of the presence of steppe tribes. The scene is also interesting for the engagement of Sarmatian heavy cavalry among the besieging forces the helmet and all-over scale armour lends the rider an uncanny resemblance to a medieval knight.

The Dacians were repulsed, which must have been a setback for Decebalus, for in the next campaigning season, in 102 AD, Trajan closed on Sarmizegetusa and its

Trajan attacks the Dacians who beg for mercy; soldiers show the severed heads of Dacian chieftains, from the Arch of Constantine, Rome

ring of defending forts with a pincer movement, sending a column through the mountains to the east up the valley of the Olt, while he himself approached from the west. The evidence of the Column suggests that, at this point, Decebalus, ever cunning, sent embassies to sue for peace, but that these were rejected, either because the terms were too severe or because Trajan was in no mood to spare so determined an enemy. The Roman army used all its might to capture the forts one by one, dividing the army into three so as to avoid Decebalus's favourite tactic of entrapment in the valleys below the citadel. The battles for the forts are reproduced on the Column and are portrayed as having been fought with the utmost ferocity and great loss of life. It is quite clear from the solid construction of the forts how much the Dacians had benefited from Roman engineering skills; in one of them a lost standard of Fuscus is clearly visible resting beside the sinister dragon banner which always marks the Dacian host. In another, above the Roman-type battlements and against a backdrop of Roman-style houses, the impaled heads of Roman prisoners lend a touch of barbarity.

The fortresses fell, and Decebalus, forced back to his capital, surrendered. The old

Roman ideal was *'Parcere subjectis'* – 'spare those you have subdued'. Decebalus was spared and re-installed as a client king. Dio lists the terms: he was forced to accept a Roman garrison in his capital and to pull down the fortifications. Any remaining prisoners were to be returned, and all captured territory restored. A Dacian embassy was sent to Rome to walk *'en posture d'esclave'* in Trajan's triumph. The title of 'Dacicus', which had eluded Domitian, was bestowed on Trajan by a grateful people.

By 105 Decebalus was breaking the clauses of his treaty with Rome one by one. He attacked and besieged Roman camps, rebuilt his fortifications, started a campaign of incitement amongst his neighbours and annexed the territory of his western neighbours, the Iazyges, always so friendly to Rome. The other old Roman ideal was *'debellare superbos'* – 'defeat the proud utterly', and Trajan did not miss the opportunity to put him down for ever.

In order to destroy this enemy, who had for so long threatened Rome's most vulnerable borders and who refused to retire into the background with the status of client king – a status which had been in the past so beneficial to many frontier rulers – Trajan called on the might of the Roman army – thirteen legions, auxiliaries from all over the Empire and fresh household troops from Rome. To mobilize this great host he decreed that a bridge should be built over the Danube at Drobeta, designed by his architect, Apollodorus of Damascus. This huge structure, which in the opinion of Dio deserved to be a Wonder of the World, had twenty piers, fragments of which still survive, each sixty feet apart, and was built without need to drain the water or divert the river. The upper works were of wood, with forts at each end. On the Column there is a very detailed picture of the dedication of the bridge by the emperor himself.

Despite frantic attempts by Decebalus to postpone the inevitable, at first by conciliation and by treachery, and finally by desperate resistance, Sarmizegetusa was taken. In the corresponding scenes on the Column – the citadel was so large that there are scenes showing action on several sectors of the wall – the Dacians on the battlements fight off the attacking Roman troops with every available weapon: bows, spears, stones, and huge rocks. Trajan and his suite look on, implacable. The walls themselves are obviously of new construction – barely finished, in fact – and the hammers and pile drivers remain outside the walls, mute witnesses to Decebalus's treachery.

Although nothing can be concluded with absolute certainty, the Column is reasonably clear from this point. Decebalus and his family escape northwards into Transylvania, but are pursued, surrounded and captured by Roman cavalry. Decebalus commits suicide; a cavalryman cuts off his head (we have the inscription from the tombstone of this particular man); it is shown to the troops and presented to the emperor. Little illustrates more clearly how much Decebalus was feared, and how important his death was to the whole Roman state, than the silver coins that

Sarmizegetusa today

were struck in 106, showing Victory sitting with her outstretched foot resting on Decebalus's severed head.

A further proof of how important the successful conclusion of these five-year long campaigns was considered to be is provided by another imposing monument to Trajan's generalship and to the military might of Rome. This is the Tropaeum Traianum, or Trajan's Trophy, which stands at Adamclisi on a windy upland a short way east of the Danube in the Dobrogean hinterland of Constanţa.

The trophy itself was a stone representation of armour, a full suit facing each way, raised sixty feet high on three layers of hexagonal drums forming the core of a huge brick and concrete mound 100 feet in diameter. Core and mound have survived nearly 2000 years to confront the traveller and to convey at least some idea of the size of this great monument when it was complete. Exposure to nineteen centuries of cold and frost have gradually denuded the mound of its cladding of masonry and sculptures, which have fallen off the drum on to the ground surrounding the base, often face downwards, a fortunate chance that accounts for their survival, many of them in a remarkable state of preservation.

The unrestored Tropaeum Traianum, Adamclisi

The sculptures were rescued in the nineteenth century by a team of Romanian archaeologists, and sufficient of them remain to give scholars a good idea of how to reconstruct the monument. General consent seems now to have been given to the following arrangement: a layer of 54 'metopes' or sculptured plaques approximately 6' by 3.5' were set into the masonry cladding of the drum, probably two or three courses below the rim. Above and below the metopes were bands of decorative friezes, acanthus leaves above, wolves' heads below. Stone pilasters separated the individual scenes. Above the drum rose a stone balustrade at the edge of the roof, which sloped up to the trophy itself. This balustrade had 26 wide crenellations, on which were sculpted various chained prisoners, the detail of their dress distinguishing them beyond possible doubt as Getic tribesmen of the steppe, Roxolani and Germans from the northern plains. The trophy itself is weathered almost beyond recognition; other remains, almost as indistinct, point to the existence of life-size stone figures, grouped symmetrically at the foot of the trophy. An inscription survives, which dedicates the monument to Mars the Avenger; the dedicator is the Emperor Trajan in his thirteenth tribunate, thus dating the monument effectively to 109 AD.

A 'trophy' by its very nature celebrates a victory; the practice of making a triumphant display of victorious arms goes back to the Greeks, who raised a trophy after Marathon. That the Roman armies celebrated their victories on the German frontier in this way we know from references in Suetonius and Tacitus. Without the testimony of a written source, however, the purpose of the Adamclisi monument is not so clear. Trajan's structure shares the site with two other monuments. One is another great mound within an outer circle of stone and the remains of a central drum rather like the Tropaeum, which has always been known as the Mausoleum, although there are few signs that it ever had a funerary purpose. It is made of the same stone as the third monument: a Roman altar dedicated 'to the fallen'. This is sometimes taken to refer to those who fell in the defeat of Oppius Sabinus and his army at the hands of a confederation of steppe tribes in 85 AD very close to the Adamclisi site, though the title and birthplace of the commanding officer make it unlikely that he was Oppius Sabinus – or even Cornelius Fuscus, whose defeat in 86 AD, it is suggested, might also have made him a candidate for commemoration. Research into the names and particulars of the troops listed on the altar have indicated that the legion was most probably recruited on the northern frontiers, and the most convincing explanations group both monuments together; the 'Mausoleum' bears all the signs of being another, less permanent trophy, earlier by several years than the Tropaeum, and superseded by it, while the altar commemorates the dead of a legion such as I Minervia, that had fought successfully in the Dacian Wars, and was, we know, stationed to guard captured territory in Lower Moesia.

It certainly seems reasonable to suppose that the Tropaeum Traianum, with its dedication to Mars Ultor and built as it was on a site visible northwestwards over the Danube, celebrates not only the defeat of the Dacians, many miles to the west beyond the mountains, but also the acquisition of new territory. There are good reasons, however, for assuming that the Monument was not the equivalent in the field of the Column in Rome; the captured enemies are recognizably representatives of the local tribes and bear no resemblance to the Dacians and their allies as shown on the Column; the battle scenes depict the traditional enemies of the inhabitants of Lower Moesia. In other words, the Tropaeum has a local significance and may have been executed, as we shall see, in local military workshops by craftsmen whose rudimentary skills did not permit them to venture far from the familiar.

The metopes, on which the battle scenes occur, are well worth scrutiny for their sculptures as well as for clues as to the purpose of the Monument. These are clearly the work of local craftsmen; by comparison with the exquisitely sophisticated modelling of the reliefs on the Column this is rustic work, almost certainly executed by the corps of military funerary craftsmen to be found in or near every camp of the legions: stonecarvers responsible for military tombstones and the accompanying inscriptions. Yet their work has the strength and vigour of simplicity. Like the craftsmen who carved the Column, they seem to have worked from eye-witness sketches of action; their most successful scenes are those in which the subject fits well into the frame of the metope. They are good too on arms and armour. But some of the more complex scenes are almost beyond their skill altogether, and the craftsman's struggle against the limitations of his technique produces some strange effects. Indeed, it has been plausibly suggested that the metope form was devised so as to spare the sculptors the technical problems involved in working a continuous band.

The exact sequence of metopes is uncertain, although all arrangements of the

Metopes from the Tropaeum

order allow that at some point an engagement with the enemy takes place; the action itself and the troops of both sides are delineated in sufficient detail to show that this is not a stylized battle, part of an ideal representation of war, but a depiction of actual warfare. The result of the battle is a victory for the Romans, and it ends in a massacre of the tribesmen with their women and families among their waggons.

Some commentators have pointed to a similar battle among the wagons shown on the Column, possibly as the culmination of a punitive expedition eastward led by the emperor himself against Decebalus's diversionary forces of Roxolani. It is tempting to identify the battle on the Monument with this one on the Column; the ingredients are there, but it should be emphasized that there is no solid evidence which would attach the action beyond doubt to a particular time or place.

So, as with the Column, it is best, perhaps, not to impose too categorically on the reliefs of the metopes the status of a chronicle in stone. For those who prefer to look at the detail of each picture, there are many interesting points of clothing, armour or weaponry that are found nowhere else; examples of this are the legionaries' greaves and elaborate vambrace armour to protect the sword-arm against the great curved two-handed yataghans of the tribesmen, which could lop off an arm or a leg with one blow. All this is very well depicted, the tribesmen's swords standing up like murderous hockey sticks. The legionaries' scale armour, the horns and the hornblowers, the banners and standards, the different ways different soldiers wear the *sagum* or military cloak, and details of the officers' field-service uniform – tunics, cloaks and boots – in which they paraded, or marched if there was no danger

Metopes from the Tropaeum

of hostilities en route, are all worthy of study.

The metopes also reveal a small piece of social history, so little noticed that it is worth mentioning here; it is interesting to observe from the costume of the Roman officers on the metopes and from the costume of the emperor and his suite on the Column, how far the wearing of breeches had become acceptable by the end of the first century AD. It was for centuries one of the distinguishing marks of Graeco-Roman civilization that male dress consisted of tunic or toga worn without any leg covering; only barbarians wore trousers. The classical authors deride the wearing of any kind of leg-garment as un-Roman, even as effeminate. Medical writers suggest delicately that the wearing of tight nether garments undermines masculinity. Tacitus reports the arrogance of one of Vitellius's generals, who shocked Italian country-men by making speeches to toga-clad audiences, while he himself wore 'exotic garb' – a parti-coloured cloak and trousers. Suetonius reports Caesar's boast that 'they had got the Gauls out of trousers and into the *latus clavus*' (toga with a broad stripe). Any tribe within the frontiers that took full advantage of the Roman civiliz-ing mission had to obey this dress code.

It is mildly surprising therefore to see from the metopes how every officer, down to the centurions and the standard bearers wear breeches; these appear below the hem of their tunics reaching to a point well below the knee. Owing to the sculptor's lack of skill an impression is given that these are cloth or wool leggings, and as such might be a protection against the cold. On the Column, however, these garments are depicted much more clearly; the emperor and his suite wear them on virtually all occasions beneath their ceremonial armour. In one relief it is possible to see that they are laced at the side and are cut a little wider above the knee. It seems therefore that they are most probably made of leather and are riding breeches, the equivalent, perhaps, of the jodhpurs worn by the General Staff of many armies even today. No legionaries wear them, whether on the Monument or on the Column, leading to the conclusion that breeches had at some point during the century become acceptable as part of officers' formal dress and were a mark of rank.

Whatever the particular reason for building the Tropaeum, the message it conveys can be discerned even today. It was to proclaim the might and majesty of an emperor who was also a successful general and who had put a signal mark of his virtue and his achievements on an often beleaguered corner of the frontiers to give the people of Lower Moesia his pledge of support. Indeed, with the conclusion of the Dacian wars, the position of that part of the frontiers was transformed.

After the death of Decebalus, Trajan was faced with the need to reorganize Dacia into a province. First, Sarmizegetusa was dealt with once and for all. As in Britain, the rites and cults of Druidic religion were considered deeply un-Roman, and the place was razed to the ground, groves and temples alike. It was never inhabited again, and the ruins of temples and of the strange circular ritual buildings can still be seen, the only remains of the spiritual power-house of the Dacian peoples. The Romans' policy of wholesale destruction may not have arisen only from dislike of what they perceived as barbaric practices. Throughout the history of Roman relations with the Dacians, from the emergence of Burebistas to the fall of Decebalus, there is some indication that the Romans feared the priestly element that was so mingled with the Dacian idea and practice of kingship. The size and power of the Trajanic victory monuments convey, even after 2000 years, some sense of the formidable energy that the Dacians brought to their wars, reinforced by their priestly caste, and the relief of the Romans at having defeated them.

Yet very little is known about Dacian religion; Herodotus gives descriptions of the human sacrifices and the live burials that the Dacians' Scythian ancestors practised, but no evidence has survived to show convincingly that such rituals took place regularly in Sarmizegetusa. A certain amount is known about the priests. As the steppe peoples, despite differences of language and origin all had some aspects of culture in common, so the priesthood called 'druidic' was found in slightly varying forms all over northern Europe, from Ireland to the steppe. We know that some may have been transvestites, or at least have shown some female elements, such as the *enarees* or 'women-men' mentioned by Herodotus as being characteristic of the Scythian priesthood. This, and much more, is conjecture. But the huge site certainly has atmosphere. The size and number of the terraces that contained the priests' dwellings are impressive, as is the citadel at the top of the hill. Remarkably little excavation has taken place beyond the ritual buildings, though there is an archaeologists' reconstruction of a Dacian house copied from the Column, and the debris of a film that was shot on location a few years ago on the life of Burebistas, in which Ceauşescu himself played the main part. Thick woods and the proximity of the encircling mountains contribute to the atmosphere of the site, and the most prosaic traveller might be forgiven for thinking that Transylvania had its strange places long before the advent of Dracula or Vlad the Impaler.

Whatever the reason for the abandonment of the site, Trajan founded a new city some thirty miles away: Ulpia Traiana, which would become the capital of his new province. He decreed a programme of road building to link it with the other Dacian cities – Apulum (now Alba Julia) and Potaissa (Turda), and set in train the final settlement of the 'Dacian Question'.

The Dacians themselves fell apart once more after the death of their leader. Many had been killed over five years of nearly continuous fighting. Many of the remnant felt that their sanctuary had been violated, and preferred to trek northward to the furthest extremities of the Carpathian arc and beyond rather than treat with their conquerors. Some 50,000 went as prisoners to Rome. Some joined the Roman army as auxiliaries. In order to populate the abandoned territories Trajan initiated an immense movement of peoples; he settled veterans and imported colonists from all over the Roman Empire in as large an operation of its kind as any emperor had hitherto achieved. A particularly large number of settlers were transferred from the Empire's eastern dominions; they brought their household gods and their skills with them; they intermarried with what remained of the Dacian population and with each other. Gods from the east, Mithras and Cybele, replaced the Dacian Sabadius and Salmoxis; some of the statues and artefacts that the newcomers brought with them have found their way into the museums of Cluj, Bucharest and Constanţa. Latin was their lingua franca and over the centuries evolved into Romanian. The new province became from its very inception the most cosmopolitan of all the Danubian provinces.

It was also one of the richest. One of the most fortunate results of the collapse of all resistance in Dacian lands was the Roman annexation of the Dacians' enormous wealth. A huge sum both in gold and silver was sent to Rome and financed for years to come the great public building projects of the emperor as well as the games and lavish amusements which were so much part of Roman life. Much was done to develop the new province: salt, iron ore and cattle breeding. The gold mines were also systematically exploited, and a *procurator aurariarum* was put in charge of them.

The new province of Dacia extended over the territory within the Carpathian arc – what is now Transylvania – eastward to the valley of the Olt and southward to the Danube. The steppe between the eastern wall of the Carpathians and the Danube was never either completely pacified or fully incorporated. After the death of Trajan in 117 AD Rome only exercised nominal control over the steppe parts of the Lower Danube. However, in recognition that this territory was, as always, a danger point in the perimeter, three legions were left in Lower Moesia to guard the approaches between the Olt and the Black Sea.

These legions were established in the strategically placed forts of Novae and Durostorum on the Lower Danube, and Troesmis in the Delta. Between them they surveyed the plain and its shifting population, fully aware that this was the gateway through the Roman frontier defences. Behind them Dobrogea entered into a long period of peace and prosperity; farming communities grew up which served the legionary camps as well as the trading cities on the Black Sea coast; these entered into a period of great wealth and enjoyed a building boom. A small settlement 'known asTropaeum Traianum' was established in the shadow of the great monument. It seems to have survived well into the fifth century, and the ruins of its fortifications and public buildings give a good impression of a small prosperous frontier town.

As for the rest of the Danubian military settlement, nothing shows more clearly how completely Dacia had been pacified than the new arrangement of legions. Two legions were left to garrison Upper Moesia, and one only – the XIII Gemina – was assigned to the province of Dacia itself. When Trajan turned his attention to war with Parthia the remaining seven legions were redeployed on the eastern frontier.

The creation of Dacia was the second and last exception to the precepts of Augustus. It was an extension to the frontiers that could be easily justified both in terms of defence and because of the wealth it had brought to the coffers of Rome. Trajan's settlement had created a well protected buffer zone on the most vulnerable section of the northern frontiers. Yet, in spite of the inbuilt stability of the new province, the dangers that lurked always beyond the Danube were never forgotten. We know from Dio that Trajan left the bridge of Apollodorus standing so as to afford a retreat for any military units trapped on the north bank, while his successor Hadrian had the upper works of the bridge dismantled so as to deny a passage to any hostile invading tribes. Hadrian and the Antonine emperors revived the habit of paying subsidies to the plains tribesmen so as to discourage them from migrating south and westward in search of plunder. This was to hold off the threat of invasion for some time.

In spite of those who feared that the creation of Dacia was a province too far and that it could not long be maintained, the wise government of four strong emperors in succession, who ceaselessly monitored the frontiers and who would not tolerate provincial misgovernment, enabled the Trajanic settlement to survive for 170 years. There were changes; Hadrian, always concerned to consolidate the imperial frontiers, divided Dacia into two – Upper and Lower Dacia. The lower half was never easy to defend and, when the Emperor Aurelian withdrew the Danubian legions in 275 AD, the eastern half of Trajan's province was left to fend for itself. Around 300 AD Diocletian fortified Dobrogea and the Black Sea coastal strip in a new province of Scythia, but this in turn was eventually swept away in successive invasions of Goths and Vandals, followed by the Avars in the fourth century. Upper Dacia in its mountain stronghold not only survived but was even, from its position on the flank of the invading barbarian hordes, able to give assistance to Rome, now fighting for its life.

Over the centuries, the enclave of Dacia, with its heterogenous population settled in a strong defensive position and enjoying the legacy both of Rome and of Decebalus on the fertile plains within the bastions of the Carpathian arc, was to suffer invasions of Slavs and Magyars, waves of Tatars and other steppe peoples breaking over the Carpathians, and finally the imposition of Turkish hegemony, but it would survive them all and has survived to this day.

Roman tomb, Turda

The Principalities of Transylvania, Wallachia and Moldavia

by John Villiers

The emergence of states in the Balkans

During the Middle Ages numerous Balkan states emerged from the struggle for power among the different peoples in the area bounded by the Adriatic, the Danube and the Black Sea. In the thirteenth century three expansionist imperial powers vied for supremacy: in the south and southeast, Byzantium and the Bulgar-Slav kingdom ruled by the Asen dynasty, and in the north and west, the Hungarian empire formed by the Magyars, who had arrived in the Pannonian plain in the late ninth century and extended their rule under the Arpad dynasty over a vast area stretching from Slovakia to Croatia. All three strove unsuccessfully to revive the Roman imperial idea in the region and to gain control of the two great trade routes that from earliest times had existed in southeast Europe, one running southwards to the Aegean and Byzantium and the other eastwards to the Black Sea and the Crimea. Already in the ninth century small states had emerged in Transylvania and the Banat of Temesvar (Timişoara), over which the Hungarian kings had established suzerainty within a century of their arrival in Pannonia. At the beginning of the thirteenth century Andrew II of Hungary (r. 1205-35), assisted by the Teutonic Knights, had embarked upon a policy of extending Hungarian rule and the Catholic religion into the area south and east of the Carpathians. Meanwhile, other powers became involved in the Balkan conflict: Venice, which had already largely superseded Constantinople as mistress of the Adriatic and the Aegean; Poland, which became powerful and united in the fourteenth century under the later Piast and early Jagiellonian kings; Kiev under the Riurikid dynasty; the Grand Duchy of Lithuania, united dynastically with Jagiellonian Poland; and Serbia, which rose to power in the late thirteenth century under the Nemanjich dynasty.

Woodcut of Vlad Ţepeş dining before his impaled enemies outside Braşov, while his servant boils heads in a kettle, from Dracole Wayda, *(Strasburg, 1500). Vlad's spectacular cruelties, inspired perhaps by the Turks amongst whom he lived as a child, but surpassing them, was the stuff of pulp publishing even during his lifetime. The connection with vampirism – a popular folk superstition in Romania and the Balkans – was not made until Bram Stoker's novel of 1890.*

It is therefore scarcely surprising that by the beginning of the fourteenth century the Balkans had broken up into a welter of small warring states, incapable of offering a united resistance to the attacks of the Ottoman Turks, who were already beginning to assume the mantle of Balkan imperialism left to them by Rome and Byzantium. Among these warring states were the two Romanian principalities of Moldavia and Wallachia, both of which came into existence as a consequence of the break up of the Tatar empire after the death of Nogai Khan and the decline of Hungary after the extinction of the Arpad dynasty. Both were in an area exposed to attacks from the steppes of central Asia and particularly from the Tatars of the Golden Horde and their successor khanates, and it was chiefly to protect their eastern frontiers from invasion that the Hungarians had initially established them as vassal states under their suzerainty. The principality of Wallachia emerged in the area between the Carpathians and the Danube, including Oltenia, when the Wallachian nobles (boyars) elected one of their number, Basarab (r. 1317-52) as reigning prince or voivode. Basarab's capital was first at Câmpulung and then at Curtea de Argeş. In November 1330 he defeated his suzerain Charles Robert of Anjou, king of Hungary at the battle of Posada. He also incorporated into his principality and gave his name to Bessarabia, the lands north of the Danube Delta between the Prut and the Dniester rivers, which now form the republic of Moldova. His son and successor Nicolae Alexandru (r. 1352-64) continued Basarab's policy of aggrandizement, married his daughters to neighbouring rulers in Bulgaria, Serbia and Hungary, and in 1359 founded the first metropolitan church in Wallachia at Curtea de Argeş, while his son and successor Vladislav Vlaicu (r. 1364-c.1377) promoted trade and the arts, minted the first Romanian silver coins (bearing a Latin inscription), and in 1370 gained permission from Constantinople to found a second metropolitan church at Turnu Severin. At the end of the century, Mircea the Old of Wallachia (r. 1386-94 and 1397-1418) won a series of victories against the Turks, as a result of which he was able in 1404 to wrest control over the Dobrogea from them.

Moldavia emerged in the area east of the Carpathians slightly later, when Dragoş, a prince of Maramureş, having failed to gain independence from Hungarian suzerainty for Maramureş, transferred his activities to Moldavia, where in 1352 he was elected voivode by the Moldavian boyars. In 1359 Bogdan I, another Maramureş prince, removed Dragoş's successor, Balc from the Moldavian throne and became the first ruler of a truly independent Moldavian state. He continued Moldavian resistance to Hungarian suzerainty, compelling King Louis I to abandon his attempts to subjugate the principality and instead to compensate himself by confiscating Bogdan's lands in Maramureş and bestowing them on Balc. Ştefan I, who became voivode of Moldavia in 1394, decisively defeated Louis I's son-in-law, Sigismund of Luxemburg, at the battle of Hândău.

The Romanian principalities after the fall of Constantinople

During the first half of the fifteenth century, the Ottoman Turks, under a succession of exceptionally able sultans, continued their inexorable advance into the Balkans, culminating in the conquest of Constantinople in 1453. For three centuries after the fall of Constantinople, the struggle between the Turks and the Hungarians for control of the Romanian lands was a dominant feature of Balkan history. Transylvania was only under Turkish rule until 1688, after which it came under Habsburg control, and the Hungarian and Romanian populations there became inextricably intermixed; Wallachia and Moldavia remained under Ottoman suzerainty until the nineteenth century and were consequently subjected to stronger and more lasting Turkish influence. It is therefore not surprising that there are so many Hungarian and Turkish elements in Romanian traditional culture and so many words of Hungarian or Turkish origin in the Romanian language. Many of the words borrowed from Hungarian have to do with trade and economic activity or abstract ideas and concepts, while most of the Turkish terms are concerned with warfare and military organization or with food and cooking. Thus, when a Romanian celebrates his reconciliation with an enemy (*dușman* – Turkish) by dining with him off *ciulama* (a chicken and mushroom dish – Turkish) and a *baclava* (sweet cake -Turkish) he is, as it were, spiritually located to the east of the Romanian cultural crossroads, but when he begins trading (*meșteșug* – Hungarian) with him and agrees to spend (*cheltui* – Hungarian) a sum of money on purchasing merchandise (*marf* – Hungarian) from him to be delivered in the next city (*oraș* – Hungarian), he is placed to the west of those crossroads.

*Iancu of Hunedoara in 1444
(Augsburg, 1553)*

The principalities of Moldavia and Wallachia, in spite of their dangerous position between the Tatars to the northeast, the Poles, Lithuanians and Hungarians to the northwest, and the Ottoman Turks to the south, managed to maintain a precarious independence and by means of frequent changes of alliance to avoid the collapse that overtook many of their Balkan neighbours. All three of the Romanian principalities engaged in sporadic warfare against both Turks and Hungarians in the period immediately after the fall of Constantinople. Iancu of Hunedoara, voivode of Transylvania from 1441 to 1456, was the most prominent opponent of the Turks in this period, and in 1456 inflicted a decisive defeat on the Ottoman armies under Mohammad II before Belgrade. Iancu was followed by Vlad Țepeș (the Impaler) in Wallachia (1456-62) and Ștefan the Great in Moldavia (1457-1504). The latter won a famous victory over Matthias Corvinus of Hungary at Baia in 1467, and eight years later in 1475

Mihai the Brave in 1601: engraving by Egidius Sadeler made on the occasion of Mihai's visit to the court of Rudolf II in Prague

successfully repelled a Turkish advance across the Danube at the battle of Podul Înalt.

The princes of Moldavia and Wallachia were nevertheless forced to make some concessions to the Porte, especially after the series of military triumphs won by Suleiman the Magnificent in the 1520s. In 1521 the Turks conquered Belgrade, and in 1526 they defeated the Hungarians, then under the ineffectual rule of Louis II, at the battle of Mohacs, after which the Hungarian lands were divided, with one part passing under the rule of Ferdinand of Habsburg, brother of the Emperor Charles V, and the other under János Zapolya, prince of Transylvania. In 1528 they reached the gates of Vienna, but were unable to take the city.

Wallachia, which had been paying regular tribute to the Porte since 1411, accepted Ottoman suzerainty during the reign of Radu of Afumați (1521-29), and in 1538 Petru Rareş of Moldavia was defeated by the Turks, who installed Ştefan Lăcustă (Grasshopper) as ruling prince in his place. In the same year, under the terms of the Treaty of Oradea between Suleiman and Emperor Charles V, the Habsburgs were designated as heirs of John Zapolya, king of Hungary. After John Zapolya's death in 1540, Charles V's brother, Ferdinand became king of Imperial Hungary, Transylvania became a vassal of the Porte under the rule of Zapolya's son, John Sigismund, and the rest of the Hungarian lands were divided up into pashaliks. In 1552 the Turks annexed the Banat and created another pashalik, with its capital at

Mihai the Brave as seen in the 19th century: Memorial to the unification of Wallachia, Transylvania and Moldavia in 1600, by Cartier Belleuse (1876) Piaţa Universitătii, Bucharest

Timişoara. Not until the battle of Lepanto in 1571 did the tide of Turkish expansion in Europe at last began to turn.

When Moldavia and Wallachia accepted Ottoman suzerainty, both had been able to wring important concessions from the Porte, including the right freely to elect their own princes as governors or hospodars, to make their own laws and to enjoy administrative autonomy, in return only for recognition of Turkish supremacy and the payment of tribute and supplies of foodstuffs to the Ottoman armies and the city of Constantinople. The two principalities thus acquired a special position within the Ottoman Empire, with a tripartite system of government in which power was divided between the native hospodars, the boyars and the Porte.

In 1593 Mihai the Brave came to the throne of Wallachia and in the next year, with Aaron of Moldavia and Sigismund Bathory, prince of Transylvania, he joined an alliance of European states that included the Papacy, Tuscany, Spain, the Empire and many of the German princes, and that aimed to drive the Ottoman Turks out of Europe altogether. In 1599 Mihai defeated Andreas Bathory of Hungary at the battle of Şelimbăr and thus became ruler of Transylvania, and, when in the next year he also defeated Ieremia Movilă, hospodar of Moldavia and builder of Suceviţa, he united all three principalities under his rule. However, the union was to be brief in the extreme, for in 1601 Mihai was murdered on the orders of the Imperial general, Georgio Basta. His death led to the reimposition of Ottoman rule over the three principalities: in Transylvania in 1606 after the Peace of Zsitvatorok, and in Wallachia and Moldavia in 1611.

During the fifteenth and sixteenth centuries the rulers of all three principalities encouraged the development of a historical literature in order to glorify their deeds and to keep alive a spirit of national resistance to foreign invasions. In Wallachia and Moldavia it was written in Slavonic, in Transylvania in Latin. The earliest of these historical texts were composed in Moldavia in the reign of Ştefan the Great and include the *Putna Chronicle*. In Transylvania the most important of the early chronicles is the *Dubnik Chronicle*, composed about 1474-79. The first Wallachian chronicles are somewhat later and include the *Chronicle of Chancellor Theodosie Rudeanu*, produced in 1597 and dedicated to Mihai the Brave. Printing was not introduced into the Romanian principalities until the early sixteenth century, and the first book printed in Romanian, a catechism, only appeared in 1544.

Perhaps because of this continuing resistance, both active and passive, Ottoman rule in the Romanian principalities in the seventeenth century seems to have been on the whole less oppressive and the burdens of tribute less onerous than in the previous century. Moldavia and Wallachia continued to be ruled by their native princes and Transylvania by Hungarian princes, though the former were given shorter terms of office and there was an increasingly tendency for the Porte to appoint them directly instead of permitting the boyars to elect them. Transylvania, in particular, enjoyed a wide measure of autonomy during the period it was under Ottoman control. Under its Hungarian Calvinist prince, Gabriel Bethlen, it had played an important part in the Thirty Years War, fighting against the Catholic Habsburgs; and it sent its own independent delegates to the Peace of Westphalia in 1648. The Porte recognized it as containing three nations, Hungarians, Szeklers and Saxons (but not Romanians), and four religions, Catholic, Lutheran, Calvinist and Unitarian (but not Orthodox), and these were all represented in the Transylvanian Diet. The Szeklers, a Hungarian-speaking, Magyar people, had arrived in southeast Europe a little later than the Hungarians and had settled principally in the eastern Carpathians. The Saxons were German immigrants, chiefly from the Rhineland, most of whom arrived in the twelfth century and settled in the area between Braşov (Kronstadt) and Sibiu (Hermannstadt), and around Bistriţa (Bistritz). At an early date, both Szeklers and Saxons had received charters from the king of Hungary confirming their privileges and giving them self-government in the areas where they settled. Both were commercially active and tended to form their own urban communities separate from the Romanian peasantry around them; the Saxons in particular were highly exclusive and would not allow Romanians to own any property in their territory or to intermarry with them. At the Reformation, the Hungarians had adopted Calvinism and Lutheranism and the Saxons Lutheranism, while the Szeklers had either remained faithful to Rome or adopted Lutheranism and Unitarianism. Clergy of all four religions were represented in the Transylvanian

Diet and enjoyed the same privileges and status in it as the nobility. The Romanian population, which consisted largely of enserfed peasants, Orthodox in religion and working on Hungarian, Szekler or German estates, had no representation in the Diet, and the metropolitan see at Alba Iulia was under the jurisdiction of the metropolitan of Ungro-Valachia in Bucharest. As for the members of the small Romanian nobility in Transylvania, they tended naturally to associate with their Hungarian peers, whose views and aspirations they shared more readily than those of their fellow Romanians.

Transylvania under Habsburg rule

In 1688 after the defeat of the Turks at Belgrade, the Transylvanian Diet met at Făgăraş and declared an end of Ottoman rule, and in 1691 Emperor Leopold I issued a charter formally separating Transylvania from Hungary and confirming the continuation of the system of government based on three nations and four religions under Imperial authority. In 1699 the Treaty of Carlowitz briefly brought to an end a series of wars between the Ottoman Empire, Austria and Poland. Under the terms of this peace, Austria regained the whole of Hungary and Transylvania except for the Banat, and most of Croatia and Slavonia. In 1711, under the terms of the Peace of Satu Mare, direct Habsburg rule was established in Transylvania, but before the end of that year hostilities between Austria and the Porte had broken

Cloşca, Horea and Crişan , the leaders of the 1784 Romanian revolt, painted by Johann Martin Stock in the prison at Alba Iulia (Bruckenthal Museum, Sibiu)

out yet again, ending in 1718 with the addition of the Banat to the Habsburg dominions.

In 1784 a revolt against Habsburg rule led by three Romanian serfs named Horea, Cloşca and Crişan broke out in Transylvania. Although the Emperor Joseph II suppressed it with great severity (Horea and Cloşca were broken on the wheel), he nevertheless abolished serfdom in Transylvania in the following year. He was also responsible for a number of fundamental reforms in Transylvania, as in other parts of the Habsburg dominions. In 1781 he had issued the Edict of Toleration, which allowed freedom of worship in private and permitted the building of churches and schools in communities consisting of more than a hundred families belonging to any one Christian faith, including Orthodoxy. In the same year he issued a decree on *Concivilität*, by which equal rights of ownership of property and admission to guilds were granted to all the inhabitants of whatever nationality, including Romanian and Hungarian, in areas hitherto reserved by the Saxons exclusively for themselves. In 1784 he introduced new administrative divisions for the whole of Transylvania, to be headed by officials appointed in Vienna, and declared that German was to be the language of government. After his death in 1790, however, his successor, Leopold II revoked these administrative changes, and Transylvania returned to its former regime of three nations and four religions.

The main opposition to the rule of the Catholic Habsburgs in Transylvania came from the Hungarian nobility and from the Diet, both of which were largely Protestant. It was this that prompted the authorities in Vienna to try to convert the Transylvanian population, the vast majority of whom were Orthodox, to Roman Catholicism, thus making them, it was hoped, more dependent on Vienna and more likely to oppose the aspirations of the Hungarian nobility. In 1693 the Society of Jesus was invited back to Transylvania, and shortly afterwards the Uniate or Graeco-Catholic Church was established. In order to qualify for membership of the new Church, converts were hardly required to accept any fundamental changes of doctrine or liturgy, but only had to agree to the main articles of the Council of Florence of 1439, which included recognition of the pope as head of the Church, and acceptance of the doctrine of the Descent of the Holy Spirit from both the Father and the Son (the famous *filioque* clause) and of the doctrine of Purgatory. The majority of the Orthodox clergy accepted these changes at a synod held at Alba Iulia in 1697. An Act of Union followed in 1698, and in 1699 and 1700 Leopold I issued two Diplomas recognizing Metropolitan Atanasie Anghel as head of the Uniate Church and giving the Uniate clergy the same rights and privileges as their Roman Catholic brethren, including freedom to levy tithes and exemption from corvée services. Not surprisingly, the creation of the Uniate Church aroused strong opposition from the other nations and churches in Transylvania and from senior clergy throughout the Orthodox world, including the patriarchs of Jerusalem and Constantinople, as well as from the metropolitan of Bucharest, the Romanian princes and, not least, the mass of the Romanian Orthodox peasantry, who either did not understand or were indifferent to the religious changes that were being forced upon them and quite rightly suspected the political motives behind them.

There was, however, one beneficial result of the creation of the Uniate Church, and this was in the field of education. Within a few years it had become the focus of Romanian intellectual life in Transylvania and its influence began to spread into Wallachia and Moldavia. This was in large part owing to the endeavours of the gifted Bishop Ioan Inocenţiu Clain (also known as Klein or Micu), who was in office from 1724 to 1751 and believed that acceptance of the Diplomas and cooperation with the Habsburg government was the only sure way of gaining recognition for the Romanians as the fourth nation in the Transylvanian Diet and of thus bringing about social reforms. Like many later Romanian nationalists, Clain based his arguments on the assertion that the Romanians were of Roman descent, that their ancestors had completely exterminated the Dacian population in the region, and that, when the Hungarians first arrived in the region, they had shared the land equally with the Romanians who were already there. The centre of this Romanian cultural activity was Blaj, which published its first printed book in Romanian in 1753 and opened its first Romanian secondary school in 1754.

The Phanariot regime in Wallachia and Moldavia

Meanwhile, in Wallachia and Moldavia, the Turks were increasingly interfering in the election of the hospodars. In 1711, the same year that Transylvania passed under Habsburg rule, both Moldavia under Dimitrie Cantemir, author of the *Descriptio Moldaviae*, and Wallachia under Constantin Brâncoveanu supported Peter the Great's unsuccessful campaign against the Turks on the Prut. As a result of this, the Porte withdrew the right of the boyars in both principalities to elect a native prince from among their number and began to appoint foreign hospodars in Constantinople to govern them. Thus was initiated the rule of the Phanariots, so called because all the hospodars appointed by the Porte were Greeks from the Phanar, the Greek quarter of Constantinople. The long reign of Constantin Brâncoveanu, the last of the native princes in Wallachia (1688-1714), was marked by political stability, economic progress and notable cultural and artistic achievements. However, although in 1699 the Porte had bestowed upon him the office of hospodar of

Dimitrie Cantemir in 1745

Audience given in 1794 in Bucharest by Prince Alexandru Moruzi
to the British ambassador to the Porte, Sir Robert Ainslie

Wallachia for life, Brâncoveanu was deposed in 1714 on a trumped up charge of conducting treasonable negotiations with Austria and taken to Constantinople, where he was beheaded with his four sons.

The imposition of the Phanariot regime, even though the boyars retained their estates and their control over the peasants who worked on them, marked a profound change in the relationship between the principalities and the Porte. Unlike the native princes, who were elected by their peers and to that extent at least represented their people, the Phanariot hospodars were merely agents of the Ottoman government, to which they were directly responsible, and they could be removed and summarily executed if they failed to carry out the duties of their office satisfactorily. Their position was thus similar to that of the pashas in other parts of the Ottoman Empire, with whom, although the principalities were never officially designated as pashaliks, they were considered to be equal in rank. The office was sold to the highest bidder, and the successful candidate consequently had to amass as much wealth in as short a time as possible in order to make a profit for himself, while at the same time fulfilling his primary duty of supplying the Porte with huge quantities of money and foodstuffs, before he was removed from office on one pretext or another. As a result, Phanariot rule was extremely corrupt. Already in 1709, out of a total of 649,000 thalers collected in tax revenue in Wallachia, 514,000 thalers, or twice as much as the official tribute, was paid to Constantinople. During the 110 years of Phanariot rule there were altogether 74 hospodars in the two principalities chosen from among only eleven families, and the average length of their reigns was less than three years. So aware were they of the precariousness of their position that they kept their treasures permanently packed in trunks, so that, if necessary, they could flee at a moment's notice. This need to accumulate wealth rapidly and at the same time keep Constantinople supplied inevitably encouraged ruthless exploitation and crippling taxation of the peasants, the majority of whom were serfs, and many fled to Transylvania, where conditions were less harsh.

Some of the Phanariot princes tried to introduce reforms, notably Constantin Mavrocordat, who ruled from 1735 to 1741 in Wallachia and from 1741 to 1743 in Moldavia. After the Treaty of Belgrade that ended the Russo-Austro-Turkish war of 1736 to 1739 and restored Oltenia, which had been under Habsburg administration since 1718, to Wallachia, Constantin Mavrocordat introduced a number of reforms of the tax and judicial systems in both principalities and simultaneously tried to curb the power of the boyars over their peasantry by abolishing serfdom. These measures, however, had no lasting success, as the Porte continually increased the number of levies it imposed upon the principalities and so compelled the Phanariot rulers to undo most of their own attempts at reform.

The development of Romanian nationalism

As the eighteenth century advanced, the Romanian boyars increasingly looked to St Petersburg and Vienna for support in their opposition to Ottoman rule and their demands for independence. Their principal grievances were political and economic, for under the *pax ottomana*, even during the Phanariot period, the Romanians of Moldavia and Wallachia always enjoyed greater cultural and religious freedom than did the Romanians in Transylvania under the *pax hungarica*. Except in Bosnia and Albania, the Turkish conquests in Europe had not been followed by forced mass conversions to Islam, and Moldavia and Wallachia remained the principal guardians of the Graeco-Byzantine religious and cultural traditions to which the Romanian historian Nicolae Iorga gave the epithet of 'Byzance après Byzance'. The great monasteries of Moldavia – Putna, Neamţ, Moldoviţa, Suceviţa and the rest – many of which were adorned both inside and out with magnificent wall-paintings and possessed rich collections of manuscripts and embroideries, as well as providing a refuge for fugitives from other countries overrun by the Turks, played a crucial part in the preservation of this Byzantine cultural heritage and may even have helped to spread it among the eastern Slavs as far as Kiev and Moscow. Under the Phanariot hospodars, who modelled their rule on that of the Byzantine despots, this Graeco-

Byzantine heritage was still further enhanced, and both the Romanian Orthodox Church and the native boyars became markedly hellenized, while, in contrast to what happened in Transylvania after it had become an integral part of the Habsburg Empire, the mass of the people underwent a degree of orientalization and isolation from western influences as a result of Turkish domination. Unlike Transylvania, therefore, Moldavia and Wallachia remained largely untouched by the humanism of the Renaissance, while the Reformation never penetrated much beyond Slovenia and Hungary, and, later, the events of the French Revolution seem to have aroused little interest in Iaşi or Bucharest.

This attachment of the Romanians in Wallachia and Moldavia to their Byzantine heritage and the politically pan-Romanian sentiments which it engendered was, however, not accompanied by any strongly nationalistic religious sentiments among the Orthodox faithful. During the centuries of Muslim Turkish domination, nationalism and religious fervour were, of course, closely allied, the forces working for political independence and religious autonomy tended to be the same, and Orthodox monasteries in Wallachia and Moldavia, as in Serbia and Bulgaria, were centres not only for the preservation of national traditions, but also for the fostering of new political ideas. Nevertheless, this development of nationalism in the political field does not seem to have extended to the organization of the Orthodox Church itself, and it was only in 1865, four years after the unification of Moldavia and Wallachia, that the authority of the Greek patriarch was sought for the proclamation of an autocephalous Romanian Orthodox Church.

Nor was there any significant development in any of the three principalities during this long period of foreign domination of an ethnically Romanian urban

Open-air school in Bucharest, 1842

middle class that might have provided leaders for nationalist movements. Indeed, at least until the mid-seventeenth century, towns in Romania remained essentially foreign organizations. In Wallachia and Moldavia they were based on Byzantine or Turkish foundations and were usually built round princely courts or caravanserai, such as Suceava, Iaşi and Bucharest, while in Transylvania they either originated in Saxon urban settlements, such as Braşov, Sibiu and the other towns of the Siebenbürgen, or were Hungarian foundations, such as Cluj (Kolozsvar), Arad and Timişoara (Temesvar). As we have already noted, the very word for town in Romanian, oraş, is of Hungarian origin. In Moldavia and Wallachia, moreover, the rise of Ottoman power accelerated the process whereby trades and crafts in the cities passed out of the hands of the native, largely rural native population and became the preserve of Turks, Greeks, Armenians and Jews living in the cities.

It was the predominantly rural character of the vast majority of the subject populations everywhere in the Balkans that made any concerted opposition to Ottoman rule so difficult, at least so long as the Turkish military machine functioned efficiently and there was therefore a real fear of harsh reprisals. The brief achievement of independence by the Albanians under Skanderbeg in the fifteenth century, the courageous and prolonged resistance of the Montenegrins under the kings of the Crnojevich dynasty, who won their freedom from Turkish suzerainty in 1516, and the fleeting unification of the Romanian principalities by Mihai the Brave in 1600 were all exceptional episodes and had no sequels or permanent results. It was left to the other powers in central and eastern Europe – Habsburg Austria, Venice, Poland and Russia – to intervene against the Turks in the Balkans, not usually from any altruistic desire to liberate the subject peoples of the region from the Ottoman yoke, but in order to further their own political ends, and seldom with any lasting success.

In any case, during the eighteenth and nineteenth centuries it was still the interests of the great powers that determined the degree of freedom and autonomy achieved by any of the Balkan countries. Each power exploited the readiness of the Balkan peoples to rise up against Turkish rule when they thought it would serve their own expansionist or strategic aims in southeast Europe. In this connection, it is interesting to note that it was in Habsburg Transylvania, and not in Moldavia or Wallachia, that the first concerted declaration of Romanian national aspirations was made, when in 1791 the Romanians of Transylvania addressed a petition to Leopold II entitled *Supplex libellus Valachorum transylvaniensium* (notice the use of the word *Valachus* to mean Romanian), asking that the Romanians be given representation proportionate to their numbers in the Transylvanian administration and their own national Orthodox assembly comparable to that of the Serbian Orthodox Church at Sremski Karlovci, on which the Transylvanian Romanians who had remained faithful to Orthodoxy had been dependent since the defection of their bishop, Atanasie, to the Uniates in 1698. Leopold passed the petition on to the Transylvanian Diet, where inevitably the Hungarian, Szekler and Saxon members rejected it out of hand.

Russia, Turkey, the 1821 revolution and the Règlements Organiques

In 1768 the Porte declared war on Russia. The war ended in a Turkish defeat, and under the terms of the Treaty of Kuchuk Kainarji of 1774 Russia replaced the Ottoman empire as the most influential power in the principalities. Russian interest in them was, however, exclusively military and strategic, and not, as with the Turks, as a source of tribute and supplies. From the Russian point of view, they stood on the road to Constantinople and the Dardanelles, and at the same time provided the Turks with a gateway for expansion against Poland, the Ukraine and the Tatars of the Crimea.

In 1821, during yet another Russo-Turkish war, there was a revolt inspired by the Greek revolutionary organization Filiki Etairia in Greece (Peloponnese and Rumeli) and in the Danubian principalities. The main objective of the Filiki Etairia was to bring Ottoman rule to an end throughout the Hellenic world and to re-establish a Greek imperial state with its capital in Constantinople, in other words not merely to create a national Greek state but to revive the Byzantine Empire. To achieve this end it looked to Russia, in vain as it turned out, for active support. Its founders were a group of Greek merchants, and its leader was Alexander Ypsilantis, who was both an aide de camp to Tsar Alexander I and the son of Constantin Ypsilanti, a former Phanariot hospodar of Wallachia. It also had the tacit support of Ioannis Capodistrias, a native of Corfu and at that time joint Russian foreign minister with Count Nesselrode.

At the same time a revolutionary movement began independently in Oltenia (Wallachia) under the leadership of Tudor Vladimirescu. Vladimirescu was born in 1780 into a family of free peasants, had served in the local militia or *pandours* that had been raised in the recent wars to assist the Russian army in the defence of Wallachia, and had then become sub-prefect of Cloşani and a successful businessman trading in livestock. He was widely travelled, having even spent some time in Vienna at the time of the Congress of Vienna in 1814. Vladimirescu and his associates had no particular sympathy with the Etairia and certainly not with their plans for a pan-Hellenic revival in the Balkans, which would inevitably involve collaboration with the Phanariots, but he was willing to fight with them in order to achieve his own aims. Like the Romanian boyars, Vladimirescu aspired to independence for the principalities under Russian or Austrian protection or, failing that, restoration of the rule by native princes under Ottoman suzerainty, but he shared with the Romanian peasantry the belief that the first objective was to achieve land reform and a lightening of the crushing burden of taxation. In short, Vladimirescu's aims were primarily social and only secondarily political. Indeed, in his first public address, delivered in February 1821 in the Oltenian village of Padeş, he said nothing about Romanian, still less Greek national liberation but simply called upon the peasants of Wallachia to rise up against the 'dragons that swallow

*Wallachian round performed by gypsies and danced
by troops before Prince Alexandru Ghica, 1837*

us alive, those above us, both clergy and politicians'. Social and economic conditions in the principalities were certainly desperate at that time, as two recent hospodars, Ioan Caragea in Wallachia (1812-18) and Scarlat Callimachi in Moldavia (1812-19) had been more than usually corrupt and incompetent. Caragea's misgovernment, indeed, had been so scandalous that he had had to flee the country and had been replaced by Alexandru Suţu, who was almost as bad and arrived in Bucharest with a suite of eight hundred people and an Albanian guard. Yet, in spite of this, Vladimirescu, so far from calling upon the Romanians to throw off the Ottoman yoke, remained in touch throughout the revolt with the Ottoman authorities, sending them frequent requests to take steps to remedy the abuses of their government in the principalities

Vladimirescu had been promised the support of the Etairia, who had decided to begin their rebellion in Moldavia and, if successful there, to cross the Danube and march into Greece. But in the event the revolution, both in Moldavia and Wallachia, soon petered out in a welter of looting and anarchy. This was primarily because of the failure of Russia, then under the autocratic rule of the deeply conservative Tsar Alexander I, to support either Vladimirescu or the Etairia, in spite of numerous atrocities committed by the Turks against Greek Christians as reprisals for their killing of Ottoman civilians, including the hanging of the Patriarch of Constantinople and several of his bishops by Janissaries on Holy Saturday 1821. The furthest that the Russian government was prepared to go was to break off diplomatic relations with the Porte in August 1821, after the revolution was already over. Vladimirescu, who was known by the Greek leaders to have been engaged in what they considered to be treasonable negotiations with the Porte, was kidnapped, tortured and killed, whereupon his followers simply deserted and returned home, and the Ottoman army was able to inflict a series of crushing defeats on the disordered and ill-armed Greek forces and to regain control of the principalities.

The 1821 Revolution was not, however, a total failure, as it succeeded in bringing about the abolition of the Phanariot regime and the restoration of the rule of the native princes, with the election of Ioniţa Sturdza in Moldavia and of Grigore Ghica in Wallachia. After the end of yet another Russo-Turkish War in 1829, the Peace of Adrianople gave the Russians occupation of Wallachia and Moldavia, and instituted the so-called Règlements Organiques, which provided the two principalities with their first constitution and called for their eventual union.

The principal terms of the Règlements Organiques were that each province was to be ruled by a prince elected for life from among their number by a special assembly of 150 boyars, that legislative powers were to be exercised by assemblies of boyars, which the prince could prorogue with the approval of the Porte and of Russia, but not dissolve, and that the boyars were to be designated as owners of all the land, while the peasants were allowed a share of that land according to the number of cattle they owned. Corvée duties were fixed at twelve days a year, but in practice came to much more than this, reaching as many as fifty days in Moldavia, where the landowners usually managed their estates themselves, in contrast to Wallachia, where they often preferred to rent out their land to the peasants and get stewards to manage their estates, while they lived in Bucharest or elsewhere.

Turkish suzerainty was reduced to the payment of a tribute of three million piastres and to confirmation by the Porte of the appointment of the ruling princes. The first two princes, in fact chosen by the Russians and not elected, were Alexandru Ghica in Wallachia and Mihai Sturdza in Moldavia. The Russians also appointed General Count Pavel Kiseleff, an able commander and administrator, as president of the Divans of the two principalities. Kiseleff remained in office until 1834, when he and all the Russian forces withdrew. In 1842 in Wallachia, the hospodar Alexandru Ghica, a brother of Grigore, was deposed and replaced by a constitutionally elected prince, George Bibescu.

The principalities after the 1848 revolution

During 1848 revolts and uprisings occurred all over Europe. They particularly affected the Habsburg Empire, as well as many of the German and Italian states, and were to have important repercussions in the Romanian principalities. Only in

Wallachia, however, was there a serious attempt at revolution. Its leaders were Ion and Dumitru Brătianu, Nicolae and Radu Golescu, C. A. Rosetti and Nicolae Bălcescu. Like Tudor Vladirimescu, their aim was not to overthrow Ottoman rule but to restore what they believed to be the ancient rights of the Romanians. Unlike the 1821 revolution, however, this was not a peasant uprising and was not backed by any armed force. In June 1848 the revolutionaries issued the so-called Islaz Proclamation, which declared an end to the Règlements Organiques and to the Russian protectorate. Prince George Bibescu at first agreed to these terms, but then, after an attempt on his life, abdicated and retired to Transylvania, and a new government was formed under Metropolitan Neofit, of which Bălcescu, Ion Brătianu and some of the other revolutionaries were also members. The ultimate result of these events was a joint invasion by Russian and Turkish forces in September 1848, the flight of the revolutionary leaders and the establishment of another government under Constantin Cantacuzino. By the Convention of Balta Liman, concluded in May 1849, it was agreed that both in Moldavia and in Wallachia the hospodar should once again be chosen by Russia and the Porte, and appointed for only seven years, and that the boyars' assemblies should be replaced by Divans the members of which would be nominated by the ruling prince in consultation with the Porte. Russian forces remained in the principalities until 1851 and then withdrew, only to be recalled at the outbreak of the Crimean War in 1853.

In Transylvania, ever since it had been administered directly from Vienna, the Diet had ceased to have any political influence and only met occasionally. Its members continued to be appointed by the Imperial authorities from the three nations and the four religions, so that the Ro-manians were still not represented. In the 1830s and 40s the Romanian national movements that developed in Transylvania placed great emphasis on the Latinity of the Romanian language and sought the removal from it of all words of Slav and other foreign origin (e.g. *amic*, 'friend' for *prieten* and

Proclaiming the Constitution of 11 June

inamic, 'enemy' for *duşman*), and the replacement of the Cyrillic by the Roman alphabet. At the same time the Hungarians in the Transylvanian Diet were agitating to replace Latin by Hungarian as the language of their proceedings. After the outbreak of the revolution in March 1848 the Hungarian Diet in Buda unilaterally proclaimed the full union of Transylvania with Hungary, the abolition of the Transylvanian Diet and its replacement by an allocation of 69 seats to the Transylvanians in the Diet in Buda. The Romanian peasantry under Avram Iancu, the intellectuals under Simian Bărnuţiu, and the Orthodox clergy under their bishop, Andreiu Şaguna united against this decision and attempted to bypass Buda by petitioning Vienna directly for the Romanians to be given a position commensurate with their numbers, for Romanian to be an official language and for other liberal measures, including freedom of speech and of the press.

Although serfdom was abolished in both Hungary and Transylvania after the 1848 revolution, hopes of achieving greater independence were dashed by the incorporation in 1867 of Transylvania into Hungary only three months before the Emperor Franz Joseph I went to Budapest to be crowned king of Hungary. At the same time the Banat was united with Serbian Voivodina to form an imperial province with its capital at Timişoara, while Bucovina became a grand duchy, also under the rule of Vienna. The only crumb of compensation that the Romanians were able to derive from all this was the separation in 1864 of the Romanian Orthodox Church in Transylvania from the authority of Sremski Karlovci and the creation of its own metropolitan see at Sibiu. The Transylvanian Romanians now more or less abandoned political activity and adopted a policy of passive resistance.

Romanian independence, Alexandru Ioan Cuza and King Carol I

In the later nineteenth century it was only by accepting the protection of Austria, Germany or Russia and, in most cases, only by accepting a foreign ruler selected for them by these powers that the Balkan states were able to achieve full independence. At the end of the Crimean War in 1856 the Russian protectorate of Moldavia and Wallachia was superseded by a return to nominal Turkish rule, this time under the joint guarantee of the European powers, and the Règlements Organiques were replaced by the so-called Ad Hoc Divans. The powers were in disagreement on the question of union and the nomination of a foreign prince; the peoples of the two principalities however voted in favour of union and a foreign prince. In 1859 the special assemblies set up in Moldavia and Wallachia helped to resolve the problem of union by both electing the same person, Alexandru Ioan Cuza, prefect of Galaţi, as temporary prince until such time as the guaranteeing powers consented to the complete union of Wallachia and Moldavia and the election of a foreign prince to rule them.

Cuza's reign was notable for three achievements: the passing of an agrarian law in

1864 which gave every peasant free ownership of a plot of land according to the number of cattle he possessed, the amalgamation of the legislative and administrative institutions of the two provinces, the compilation of a civil code based on the Code Napoléon, and the establishment of a primary and secondary education system and of universities in Bucharest and Iaşi. Meanwhile, Ion Brătianu found a candidate for the Romanian throne in Prince Karl of Hohenzollern-Sigmaringen, who, as son of the head of the Catholic branch of the ruling royal house of Prussia and a cousin of Napoleon III, was considered eminently suitable, and who, following the forced abdication of Alexandru Ioan Cuza in 1866, became Prince Carol, and in 1881 King Carol I of Romania.

Alexandru Ioan Cuza, Prince of Moldavia and Wallachia

The reign of Carol I was marked by major economic advances. Agricultural development was encouraged in part by grants of land to the peasants, which, combined with improvements in farming methods, led to a great increase in the export of grain. There were also rapid increases of production of textiles, leather goods, timber and salt, and expansion of mining, of crude oil extraction and of oil refining, and these industrial developments were associated with the development of the road and rail networks, and of sea and river navigation, notably by making the Danube navigable as far as the Iron Gates and by modernizing the port of Constan_a. Electricity came to Bucharest in 1882, telephones in 1894, and by 1904 there were 64 private cars registered in the capital.

These developments in industry and agriculture brought a new prosperity and coincided with a flowering of talent in intellectual and artistic life. In literature, the work of such writers as the poet Mihai Eminescu (1850-99), the prose writer Ion Creanga (1839-89) and the playwright Ion Luca Caragiale (1852-1912) was of particular importance because it marked the emergence of the modern Romanian language and thereby contributed to the forging of a Romanian national identity. Parallel developments took place in the visual arts and in music. Romanian music and literature at this time owed much to the influence of King Carol's wife, Queen Elisabeta, herself a writer and musician of distinction, who wrote under the name of Carmen Sylva. Romanians also made notable contributions during this period to the sciences, especially in mathematics, aeronautics and medicine.

In 1907 a peasant uprising broke out in Moldavia and Wallachia. Its principal cause arose from the tendency of the peasants to divide their newly acquired land among their children and grandchildren into ever smaller parcels with the result that each holding became too small to provide a livelihood, and this in turn led to the peasants being forced to lease land, often under very unfavourable terms, from the owners of large estates. The uprising was put down with the utmost severity:

in only three days as many as 10,000 peasants were killed, and entire villages were razed to the ground. Its immediate result was the government's acceptance of the need to carry out a radical programme of land reform, but this was not finally achieved until 1921, when a long-promised law was passed and over 12 million acres of land were expropriated and redistributed.

After the Second Balkan War in 1913, which brought about the final demise of Ottoman rule in the Balkans and as a result of which Romania acquired southern Dobrogea (the Cadrilater) from Bulgaria, Romania attempted to maintain neutrality. At the outbreak of the First World War the following year, the royal family was, not unnaturally, pro-German, but they were well aware that the great majority of the population wanted a rapprochement with France, not least because they wished to see Transylvania rejoined with Wallachia and Moldavia, at a time when the Romanian population of Transylvania was becoming increasingly restive under Habsburg rule. The Liberal prime minister, Ionel Brătianu, son of Ion Brătianu, succeeded in persuading the Crown Council that Romania should remain neutral, but in a state of armed preparation to enter the war on the side of the Allies at the right moment. An agreement was reached with Russia whereby not only Transylvania but also the Banat and Bucovina should be ceded to her in return for her joining the Allies in the war. In August 1916 Germany declared war on Romania, and Brătianu brought Romania into the war on the side of the Allies.

Things went badly for the Romanian forces from the outset, and by the end of December 1916 German troops had occupied Bucharest and had gained control of most of the rest of the country. Romania's gold reserves and the crown jewels were sent to Russia, most of them never to be returned.

Russian withdrew from the war in consequence of the Revolution in 1917, and so, although during the summer of that year the Romanians won victories against Germany and Austria at Mărăşeşti and Oituz, Romania was forced to cease hostilities, and in May 1918 concluded a peace treaty with the Central Powers. However, the reversals later suffered by Germany and Austria-Hungary and their defeat reversed the situation. By the treaties of Saint Germain (1919), Neuilly (1919) and Trianon (1920) concluded with Austria, Bulgaria and Hungary respectively, Romania gained Transylvania and all the other territories to which she had laid claim, including Bessarabia, which had already declared for union with Romania. Thus did 'Greater Romania' come into being. This seems to have been as much the achievement of Ferdinand's remarkable queen, Marie, who went to Paris to plead the Romanian cause at the Peace Conference, and won all hearts there as of the Romanian delegation at the Conference, whose leader, Ionel Br_tianu, Harold Nicolson considered 'could not have been more foolish, unreasonable, irritating or provocative' and who 'so mishandled the Romanian case that he estranged the most ardent friends of Romania'.

From Unification to the European Union

by John Villiers

The great increase of territory which Romania gained after the First World War together with the introduction of universal suffrage in 1917 and the land reforms of the same year, which greatly improved the lot of the peasantry and limited the power of the great landowners, led to a period of sustained economic development under a series of Liberal governments. Whereas the Conservative Party drew much of its support from the great landowners, the Liberal Party, which adopted as its slogan 'By ourselves, alone', was espoused by the civil service and the urban middle class, who were in favour of agrarian reform and state promotion of business and were opposed to foreign investment in industry. The relative stability and prosperity of the country during these years also led to a flowering of intellectual and artistic life.

During the 1920s Romania became the fifth largest producer of oil in the world and a major producer of agricultural products, including wine and grain. Education also developed rapidly, with the extension of compulsory education to the seventh grade and the foundation of four universities. In 1923 a new Constitution was promulgated, which declared all citizens of Romania of whatever race to be equal before the law, although, since its first article insisted that the state was 'unitary, national and Romanian' and since it provided no safeguards to protect ethnic minorities against discrimination, the inter-war period was marked by overt discrimination against the Jews, the Transylvanian Hungarians and Germans (Saxons) and the Roma (gypsies), who still to this day are a despised and persecuted people.

A symbol of post-First World War national pride: Mausoleum built in 1930 at Mărășești to commemorate the Romanian victory against the Central Powers in 1917

In March 1921, the heir to the throne, Crown Prince Carol married Princess Elena of Greece, and on 25 October 1921 she gave birth to a son, the future King Mihai (Michael). However, Carol, who had already caused a scandal before his marriage to Princess Elena by eloping with a girl named Zizi Lambrino, now began a new affair with a divorcée of Jewish-Hungarian extraction known variously as Magda Wolf and Elena Lupescu. In November 1925 he renounced his succession to the throne and went into exile with Elena Lupescu, and in 1928 his marriage to Princess Elena was dissolved. On 19 July 1927 King

King Carol II

Ferdinand died of cancer, aged 61, and was succeeded by his five-year-old grandson Mihai. Only a few months later the Liberal prime minister, Ion Brătianu, also died, and a new government under Iuliu Maniu, leader of the National Peasant Party, was appointed by the Regency Council and subsequently elected with a large majority. Maniu's government abolished censorship of the press, ended martial law and abandoned the economic protectionism of the previous Liberal governments by lowering tariffs and encouraging capital investment from abroad. However, two events occurred in 1929 which had important consequences for Romania. The first of these was the economic depression that followed the crash of 1929 and led to a serious decline in manufacturing and in oil production, which in turn caused widespread strikes and a steep rise in unemployment. The second was the acceptance by Prince Carol of Maniu's rash invitation to him to return to Romania, not as king, but as regent for King Mihai, and on condition that he break off his relationship with Elena Lupescu and remarry Princess Elena. As soon as he arrived in Bucharest, Carol declared that he was still king and had been ever since the death of his father, whereupon Maniu resigned, and the Romanian parliament repealed the act excluding Carol from the throne and bestowed on Mihai the resounding but meaningless title of grand voivode of Alba Julia.

Having once regained his crown, Carol began to bypass parliamentary government and to rule through a small group of friends. He founded the Royal Scouts, which he used as a kind of private police force to intimidate his political opponents, and in response to this an extreme right-wing movement emerged, led by Corneliu Codreanu, son of a German mother and a father of Polish-Ukrainian origin. Codreanu believed that the parliamentary democracy established in Romania was part of a Jewish conspiracy aimed against the Romanian people. In 1922 he established the National Christian Defence League and in 1927 the Legion of the Archangel Michael. The leadership of the Legion was limited to thirteen members, who were sworn to obey the six precepts of discipline, work, silence, education, mutual love and honour. In 1930 Codreanu set up a military wing of the Legion, known as the Iron Guard or Greenshirts from the colour of their shirts. From the outset the Legion and the Iron Guard established links with the Nazis in Germany and the Fascists in Italy and received support from both of them. Codreanu himself indulged in an extravagant personality cult. Styling himself 'Capitanul' (the captain), dressed in a white peasant costume and mounted on a white horse, Codreanu would ride about holding an icon of the Archangel Michael, whose representative on earth he declared himself to be. The similarities of all this with the personality cults of Hitler and Mussolini, not to mention later with Antonescu and Ceauşescu, are striking. The credulous peasants, disillusioned with the government of the National Peasant Party, were strongly attracted to the Legion and its extreme nationalist, anti-Communist and anti-Semitic policies and flocked to join the Iron Guard. At the same time Codreanu was violently hostile to King Carol and his Jewish mistress Elena Lupescu.

The king attempted to outflank the Legion by imposing martial law and inviting Ion Duca, the leader of the Liberal Party, to form a government, and after his election in November 1933, Duca obtained the permission of the king to outlaw the Legion. The immediate result of this was the assassination of Duca on Codreanu's orders and his replacement as prime minister by another Liberal leader, Gheorghe Tătărescu. Tătărescu held this position until 1937, when another election was held in which the Liberals won 36 percent of the votes, Iuliu Maniu's National Peasants Party 22 percent and Codreanu's Everything for the Country Party (i.e. the Legion) 16 percent. Maniu was returned to office as prime minister in an

Corneliu Zelea Codreanu

uneasy alliance with Codreanu. At this, the king immediately dissolved Parliament before it had even assembled and invited the poet Octavian Goga, leader of the extreme right-wing, anti-Semitic National Christian Party to form a government. After a few weeks, partly as a result of the protests of the French and British ministers in Bucharest, Carol dismissed Goga, suspended the Constitution, abolished all political parties and established the Front of National Rebirth under his own command, assisted by, among others, the Orthodox Patriarch Miron Cristea, Gheorghe Tătărescu and the eminent historian Nicolae Iorga, who as long ago as 1910 had founded the National Democratic Party, one of whose principal tenets was the 'solution of the Jewish question by the elimination of the Jews'. A new Constitution was drawn up modelled on the Constitution of Fascist Italy, with the king as absolute ruler, and imposing strict limits on the freedom of speech and assembly.

Popular endorsement of the new regime was given in a referendum held in February 1938. Meanwhile, the conflict between the king and the Legion continued, and a series of riots and mass rallies ensued, terminating in the arrest of Codreanu on a charge of high treason, for which he was sentenced to ten years of hard labour, and the murder of 252 members of the Legion.

In spite of these political upheavals, the Romanian economy continued to grow during the 1930s, partly as a result of the government's policy of subsidizing manu-

facturing industry, and guaranteeing the price of agricultural produce and encouraging grain exports. In the field of foreign policy, Carol attempted to remain on good terms both with the Western democracies and with Nazi Germany. In November 1938, with the outbreak of war already on the horizon, Carol visited London and Paris in order to try to strengthen commercial links with the Western Allies, but he only received vague assurances of support. On his way back to Romania the king stopped at the Berghof in Bavaria for a meeting with Hitler, who told him that as far as he was concerned there was only one ruler in Germany and that was Codreanu. On hearing this, the king, while still on the train to Bucharest, ordered Codreanu to be eliminated, and on 30 November the government announced that Codreanu and thirteen members of the Iron Guard had been shot while trying to escape from prison. In fact they were garrotted, acid was poured over their

Iuliu Maniu

dead bodies, and they were buried in the prison under a concrete slab.

Soon after these events, in March 1939, Romania was dragooned into concluding an unequal treaty with Germany, which placed the Romanian economy, and in particular its oil industry, firmly under German control. The French and British responded by concluding commercial agreements with Romania, which, however, were too limited to counteract the effects of the German treaty, and by issuing a guarantee of the independence of Romania, but not of its territorial integrity. In March 1939 the Iron Guard, in revenge for the death of Codreanu, assassinated Carol's chief adviser, Armand Călinescu.

When war broke out, Romania, in expectation of a speedy victory by the Western Allies, declared itself neutral, but the fall of France in June 1940 left Romania alone and defenceless, and Carol accordingly turned to Hitler in the hope that thereby he would secure both his throne and the territorial integrity of his country. In June 1940 Romania renounced the useless French and British guarantees and a month later left the League of Nations. Tătărescu was replaced as prime minister by the pro-German Ion Gigurtu, and the Legion was incorporated into the Front of National Rebirth, which was renamed the National Unity Party.

In August 1939 Molotov and Ribbentrop signed the German-Soviet Pact, one of the provisions of which was the division of Eastern Europe between them into spheres of influence. In June 1940 Stalin issued an ultimatum ordering Romania to hand over Bessarabia (now the republic of Moldova) and northern Bucovina, while Hitler not only advised the king to comply with the Soviet demands, but by a diktat issued in Vienna on 30 August 1940 also demanded that Romania cede northern Transylvania to Hungary, At the same time, by an agreement signed at Craiova on 7 September, the southern part of Dobrogea, known as the Cadrilater, which had been ceded to Romania in 1913 after the Second Balkan War, was returned to Bulgaria. Romania thus lost a third of its territory (36,000 sq kms) and a third of its population (6,000,000), of whom fifty percent were not ethnic Romanians. It is said that the Romanian delegate was so appalled by the terms of the Vienna diktat that, when he heard them, he fainted at the conference table.

King Carol, at the suggestion of Iuliu Maniu, now asked General Ion Antonescu, who had already served briefly in the Goga government of 1937-38, to form a new government. Antonescu accepted and promptly demanded that the king abdicate and leave the country. On 6 September, as soldiers fired shots at the departing train, Carol left Romania, taking with him Elena Lupescu and a large and valuable collection of pictures and other treasures, and leaving in his place as king for the second time his son Mihai, now eighteen years old. Carol went first to Mexico, where he married Elena Lupescu, and then to Estoril in Portugal, where he died in 1953.

Antonescu declared himself head of the Romanian state and president of the Council of Ministers and, having failed to gain the support of the Liberal and National Peasants parties, allied himself with the Legion. Romania was named a National Legionnaire State, Horia Sima, Codreanu's successor as leader of the Iron Guard, was appointed deputy prime minister, and other ministries were given to members of the Iron Guard. Antonescu surrounded himself with a personality cult almost as extreme as that adopted by both Codreanu and Sima and later by Ceauşescu; he was known as 'Conducatorul' (the leader) and, among other extravagant epithets, as 'father-saviour... personification of the Daco-Roman tradition and superman of dizzying simplicity'. But he exercised little control over the activities of the Legion and dissensions soon arose in the alliance.

Before deciding to assume dictatorial powers and to form a government in alliance with the Legion, Antonescu had consulted the German minister in Bucharest, and it was on the minister's advice that he had got rid of King Carol and his entourage. This now committed him irrevocably to supporting Germany against the Allies. Moreover, unlike King Mihai, who believed that the Allies would win the war, he was firmly convinced that Germany would win, and this led him, as a matter of expediency, if for no other reason, to declare war on the Soviet Union in the vain hope that after Germany's final victory Romania would be able not only to claim back the territories she had lost to the Soviet Union, but also to persuade Hitler to restore northern Transylvania to her.

No less fundamental than Antonescu's differences with the young king in the field of foreign policy, were the deep seated disagreements between him and the Iron Guard over domestic policy. Antonescu was considered by the Iron Guard to be dangerously conservative in outlook, to represent what Horia Sima called the 'old world', in which political parties were still allowed to function, albeit unofficially, the press was only loosely controlled and the economy was still run on liberal lines, whereas the Iron Guard wanted to establish a completely new political and social order. The language that they used to promote these views was strikingly similar to that employed before and since by the Communists, and indeed by many revolutionaries of all political shades.

Antonescu was alarmed by the high-handed activities of the Legion and in particular by their establishment of the Commission for the Romanization of Companies, which licensed the Iron Guard to confiscate factories, businesses and farms managed by Jews and other non-Romanians and even by Liberals. He also deplored the personality cult surrounding Horia Sima, who in language as extravagant as that he used of himself, was described, among other epithets, as 'God's own Choice' and 'our Thought, our Sentiment, our Will and our Arm'. Relations became even more strained when in November 1940, the historian Nicolae Iorga, the economist Virgil Madgearu, secretary general of the National Peasant Party, and 65 of the people who had been involved in Codreanu's assassination were murdered by Legionnaires. In January 1941 Antonescu, with Hitler's permission, abolished the Commission for the Romanization of Companies and dismissed several Legionnaires from government posts, whereupon the Iron Guard in retaliation barricaded the radio station and other public buildings in Bucharest and sacked the Jewish quarter. After three days of fighting the uprising was put down, leading Legionnaires were either sent to Germany or received heavy sentences, the National Legionnaire State was formally abolished by royal decree, and a military dictatorship under Antonescu was established.

In October 1940 the first German troops had arrived in Romania, and a month later Antonescu signed the Tripartite Pact with Hitler and Mussolini. In June 1941 Antonescu ordered the Romanian army to cross the River Prut, and by the end of July both Bessarabia and northern Bucovina had been won back from the Soviet Union. Antonescu then foolishly decided, in spite of the opposition of King Mihai and most of his own political and military advisers, to cross the River Dniester and press on into Soviet territory that had never belonged to Romania. Hitler continued to support Romania and entrusted Antonescu with the administration of Transdniestria. On 1 December 1941 Britain issued an ultimatum demanding the withdrawal of Romanian troops to the Dniester, and, when this was ignored, Britain

King Mihai celebrates his nameday in 1941; his mother is to his right and Antonescu at the far left

declared war on Romania on 7 December, followed six months later by the USA.

At this time the Communist party in Romania was in its infancy, with fewer than a thousand members, and most of its leaders were either in prison in Romania or in exile in the Soviet Union. In June 1944, with the approval of the king, all the parties opposed to Antonescu, including the Communists, formed a union of democratic parties aimed at forcing Antonescu to resign. Meanwhile, in April the Soviet ambassador in Cairo had delivered to Prince Barbu Ştirbey the text of an armistice agreement, but this had been rejected by Antonescu. The king now demanded that Antonescu accept the terms of the armistice and, when he still refused, organized a coup d'état, with the assistance of the palace guard and a group of opposition political leaders, among them a young Communist named Gheorghe Gheorghiu-Dej, who had recently escaped from prison in Târgu Jiu. Antonescu and all his chief ministers were arrested, and the king then issued a royal proclamation ordering the Romanian army to cease hostilities against the Soviet Union and instead to attack the German lines. Antonescu was taken to Russia as soon as the Soviet army entered Bucharest, and General Constantin Sănătescu was appointed prime minister in a new government, which included four members of the National Peasant Party, four Liberals, three Social Democrats and one Communist, Lucreţiu Pătrăşcanu, who was made minister of justice. Pătrăşcanu later became a minister in Groza's government; he was executed in 1952.

An armistice, the terms of which were much less favourable to Romania than those given to Prince Barbu Ştirbey in Cairo, was finally concluded in Moscow in September 1944. By then the Red Army had occupied the whole country, and Romania was not only made responsible for maintaining the occupying army but was also obliged to pay huge reparations. Although Britain and the USA were nominally members of the Allied Commission of Control in Romania, in practice this was run by the Russians, and after the Yalta Conference, which placed the whole of Eastern Europe except Greece under Soviet control, the British and Americans had no alternative but to accept Soviet dominance in Romania and to leave the task of policing the country in the hands of the Soviet army.

During its brief existence Sănătescu's government concentrated on finally eliminating the Legion and the Iron Guard, on repealing anti-Semitic legislation and bringing about the return of the territories that Romania had ceded to the Soviet Union. The latter policy naturally did not find favour in Moscow, and, after a visit to Bucharest by the Soviet deputy foreign minister, Andrei Vishinsky, in November 1944, Sănătescu was forced to resign. He was succeeded briefly by another general, Nicolae Rădescu until the Soviet nominee, Petru Groza, leader of a phantom party called the Ploughman's Front, became prime minister. Although not a card-carrying member of the Communist Party, Groza was acceptable because he was willing to

Nicolae Iorga

do as he was told by Moscow in return for the perquisites of office. The other key government posts were all filled either by Communists or fellow-travellers. Britain and America refused to recognize Groza's government, and the king, confident of their support, demanded his resignation. When Groza refused, the king retaliated by refusing to sign any decrees or laws presented to him, a futile gesture of defiance, which the government simply ignored.

However, in December 1945 the Russians agreed to allow a number of non-Communists to be brought in to Groza's government, including the former Liberal leader, Gheorghe Tătărescu, described by the British ambassador in Moscow and British member of the Three Power Commission in Bucharest, Sir Archibald Clark-Kerr, as 'steeped in deceit and treachery', who became deputy prime minister and minister of foreign affairs. As a result of this apparent compromise, Britain and America recognized the Groza government, and the Soviet Union finally agreed to the return of northern Transylvania to Romania. The way was now clear for Moscow to begin the process of imposing a thoroughgoing Communist regime. Romanian companies in all the major industries, including oil, timber and shipping, were expropriated under the guise of being converted into joint Soviet-Romanian enterprises, all land belonging to Germans, to collaborators, to war criminals and to absentee landlords, and all estates larger than fifty hectares were confiscated and distributed among the peasantry, while lands belonging to the Crown, to churches and monastic foundations and to charitable institutions were converted into state farms. These measures were popular among most of the rural population, and the government therefore considered it would be safe to call a general election, which resulted in the government party, the National Democratic Front, winning 80 percent of the votes. In May 1946 Antonescu, after almost two years in exile in Russia, was brought to trial by a people's court in Bucharest with seven of his associates. Their sentence had already been decided in Moscow, and after a trial lasting only eleven days they were all condemned to death.

Despite clear evidence that in the election of 1946, which was to be the last until 1990 in which any democratic party participated, all manner of fraudulent, violent and unscrupulous devices had been used to ensure a Communist victory, both Britain and America signed a peace treaty with Romania in February 1947, thus bringing about the demise of the Allied Commission of Control and removing the last impediment to a Communist takeover of the country apart from the monarchy. In July 1947, the National Peasant Party was declared illegal and its leaders sentenced to life imprisonment. The same fate befell the leaders of the Liberal Party, while the Social Democrats were absorbed into the Communist Party. During 1946 and 1947 a methodical purge of all those elements deemed to be hostile to the Communist regime took place. It is reckoned that 60,000 people were executed and many thousands more imprisoned, and that as many as 300,000 people died in labour camps. Church property was confiscated and clergy arrested; the Uniate Church was forcibly incorporated into the Orthodox Church; and the 1927 concordat with the Vatican was repealed. The final nail in the coffin of democratic Romania was hammered in when King Mihai went with his mother to London to attend the marriage of his cousins, Princess Elizabeth and Prince Philip. While in London he met Princess Anne of Bourbon-Parma and before his return to Romania became engaged to her. During the king's absence the packing of the Groza government with Communists continued: Gheorghe Gheorghiu-Dej was appointed minister of the economy, Anna Pauker minister of foreign affairs, and Emil Bodnăraş defence minister. On the day that the king and his mother left for England Iuliu Maniu had been sentenced to solitary life imprisonment. On 21 December 1947 King Mihai and Queen Elena returned to Romania and went to Sinaia, where they spent Christmas. On 29 December Gheorghiu-Dej and Groza requested them to come to Bucharest in order, they said, to discuss 'an intimate family matter'. The next day the king and his mother obediently went to the Kiseleff Villa in Bucharest, which had been surrounded by troops, and there, while Groza threatened Queen Elena with a pistol, King Mihai was forced to sign a declaration of abdication. Three days later he followed his father into exile, and Romania became a People's Republic.

By 1960 everything from mines to restaurants and banks to cinemas had become the property of the state, and five-year plans were imposed upon all economic enterprises. By 1963 the collectivization of Romanian agriculture had been completed, and only six percent of the agricultural land remained in private hands. The education system in Romania was reorganized to discriminate in favour of the urban proletariat and peasant classes, and anyone deemed to be a class enemy or in any way politically unsound was denied higher education.

As in other East European Communist regimes, the Party became a kind of parallel government, with its leading role enshrined in the Constitution, so that the Central Committee of the Party and the Party Secretariat became the principal organs of government and the First (later General) Secretary the most powerful person in the country. The armed forces and the judiciary were controlled by the Party, and the secret police (Securitate), which by 1980 is thought to have employed 20,000 full-time personnel, penetrated every aspect of daily life in Romania. All cultural activity was strictly controlled and circumscribed.

Gheorghe Gheorghiu-Dej

During the years after 1947 there was much infighting among the various factions within the Party, which finally came to an end when the Stalinist faction, many of whom had spent time in Romanian gaols during the war, came to the fore, and Gheorghe Gheorghiu-Dej, who was one of their number, gained Stalin's approval and became both first secretary of the Party and then in 1952 prime minister. The death of Stalin in 1953 was followed by a brief period of relative freedom, and it was not until 1955 that Romania joined the Warsaw Pact, but Gheorghiu-Dej was determined to resist the reformist programme which Khrushchev attempted to impose on the Romanian Communist Party and which was being adopted in other Eastern European countries and instead adopted a policy of nationalist 'independent Stalinism', which gained him a measure of popular support.

Many Romanians demonstrated in support of the Hungarian uprising of 1956, and one of the people who was most prominent in crushing the demonstrations was the then head of the National Students' Union, Ion Iliescu, later to become one of Ceauşescu's right-hand men, until in 1989, having judiciously distanced himself from the centre of power, he became first president of post-Communist Romania.

The sudden death of Gheorghiu-Dej in 1956 led to the appointment of Nicolae

Ceaușescu, as leader of the Party in his place. Ceaușescu was the son of poor peasants with almost no education who had met and been befriended by Gheorghiu-Dej in prison. At first he had to share power with the prime minister, Ion Maurer, and the president, Chivu Stoica, but by 1969 he had succeeded in sidelining both. One of his first acts as Party leader was to change the name of the Party from Workers' Party to Communist Party, and of Romania from People's Republic to Socialist Republic, changes that were intended to suggest that a new era was now about to begin in which Romania would become a fully-fledged socialist paradise.

Ceaușescu at first pursued a policy of moderation, rehabilitating a number of politicians who had been arrested in the 1950s and were now dead or very old, publicly distancing himself from the repressive domestic policies of Gheorghiu-Dej, denouncing abuses of the security police, allowing shops and restaurants to operate under private ownership, relaxing the insistence on socialist realism in the arts and allowing young writers and artists to enjoy a measure of freedom of expression and to make contacts abroad. He encouraged investment in the production of consumer goods at the expense of heavy industry and thereby greatly

The young Nicolae Ceaușescu

improved the supply of foodstuffs and other essential commodities in the shops. New apartment blocks were built in Bucharest and other cities, and the number of cars and electrical goods in private ownership increased.

Like Georghiu-Dej, Ceaușescu, while maintaining a Stalinist regime of repression internally, pursued an independent line in foreign policy. This earned him the good opinion of Western governments and led to frequent visits by Western leaders to Bucharest and by Ceaușescu and his wife to the USA and other Western countries, culminating in 1978 in a state visit to Paris and then to London as guests of Queen Elizabeth II. In 1966 Romania concluded a commercial agreement and the next year established diplomatic relations with the German Democratic Republic; in 1967 she did not break off relations with Israel after the Six Days' War; in 1968 she refused to take part in the Soviet invasion of Czechoslovakia, which Ceaușescu declared before the Grand National Assembly to be a 'flagrant transgression of the national independence and sovereignty of the Czechoslovak Socialist Republic'; she remained neutral in the Sino-Soviet dispute; and she joined GATT, the World Bank and the International Monetary Fund.

Ceauşescu acclaimed on one of his foreign trips

Having secured his position as unchallenged ruler of Romania and asserted his independence of Moscow, Ceauşescu now reverted in his domestic policy to more traditional Communist principles and policies. In 1971 he issued the notorious July Theses, in which he denounced 'cosmopolitanism' and liberalism in the arts and called for a return to socialist realism, and at about the same time he launched a programme of rapid industrialization based on economic ideas first implemented in the Soviet Union in the 1930s. This caused him to attempt to create a larger workforce by introducing a programme of demographic engineering, in which all forms of birth control and abortion were prohibited. As a result, huge numbers of unwanted pregnancies occurred and this in turn led to the creation of the orphanages that so shocked the world when the horrifying conditions in them became known after the fall of the Ceauşescu regime.

The industrialization programme also resulted in a huge increase in Romania's national debt. By 1982 this had reached US$10 billion dollars, which Ceauşescu paid off by exporting everything that could be exported and reducing imports to the barest minimum. This led to steep price rises and serious shortages and rationing of food, fuel, medical supplies, soap and other basic commodities. Electricity and gas supplies were reduced until it only became possible to cook in the middle of the night, and only one 40-watt bulb was permitted per room. A black joke circulating

Ceauşescu visiting a butcher's shop in Bucharest in the later 1980s

in the capital during the 1980s that demonstrates how desperate the situation had become by then concerns a group of friends sitting and smoking in a flat on a freezing January night, and when one of their number proposes opening a window to let out some of the smoke, the others hasten to prevent him, saying that, if he did that, a passer-by might catch cold. Meanwhile, Ceauşescu and his family lived in ostentatious and tasteless luxury in their many palatial houses and hunting lodges.

At the same time Ceauşescu created a highly eccentric brand of nationalist socialism that declared the Romanian Communist Party to be the means by which Romania's national destiny would be fulfilled and the embodiment of the spirit of Romanian history, even to the extent of being seen as the direct heir of the ancient Dacian state. In 1971 Ceauşescu and his wife Elena visited China and North Korea. They were deeply impressed by what they saw of the Cultural Revolution in China and the role played in it by Chairman Mao's wife, Jiang Qing, and by the personality cult surrounding Kim Il Sung in North Korea. This not only prompted the promulgation of the July Theses on their return to Romania, but resulted in June 1973 in Ceauşescu placing his wife on the Executive Committee of the Party. A year later Maurer was removed from his position as head of the government, and Ceauşescu was proclaimed president of the Socialist Republic of Romania by the

Nicolae and Elena Ceauşescu at the very end

Grand National Assembly; at his inauguration ceremony he was handed not only a sash of office but also a sceptre. He now launched a personality cult for himself and his wife reminiscent of the excesses of the Iron Guard. Like Antonescu he styled himself 'Conducatorul' (the leader), and was described by his eulogists as 'a Danube of Thought', 'Genius of the Carpathians', 'Son of the Sun', 'Secular God' and other designations similar to those once lavished on Codreanu and Sima, while his wife, whose intellectual powers and academic attainments were extremely limited, was styled 'Comrade Academician Doctor Engineer Elena Ceauşescu, outstanding activist of the party and state, eminent personage of Romanian and international science'.

In 1977 the earthquake that devastated parts of Bucharest in 1977 gave Ceauşescu the idea of indulging his megalomania to the full by destroying even more of the city in order to build his gigantic People's Palace and a vast boulevard leading up to it (see p. 184ff). This project necessitated the destruction of 26 churches and two monasteries and the displacement of 40,000 people in the old Uranus-Antim quarter of the city. Estimates of the eventual cost of the building range from US$950 million to US$3.3 billion.

In 1977, 1981, 1983 and 1987 there were strikes of miners and factory workers for more pay and better working conditions, all of which were brutally suppressed. One particularly unpleasant means employed by the Securitate to break these strikes, which they used during the 1977 miners' strike in the Jiu valley, was forcibly to expose the leaders to chest x-rays lasting for five minutes, thereby ensuring that they developed cancer.

In the 1980s Ceauşescu embarked on his insane policy of 'systemization', in which it was planned to destroy 8,000 of Romania's villages, particularly in the Hungarian speaking areas of Transylvania, and to house their populations in so-called agro-industrial centres in an attempt to destroy the traditional way of life of the rural population. This led to a belated realization in the West of the horrors of his rule and to outspoken protests within Romania, of which perhaps the best known was that made in 1988 by a university teacher named Doina Cornea in an open letter, and in another open letter composed by six former leaders of the Communist Party attacking Ceauşescu and his family and accusing them of betraying socialist ideals. King Mihai likened the systemization policy to what Pol Pot had done in Cambodia in the 1970s. At the same time the adoption by Gorbachev of his policy of perestroika and glasnost led the Soviet Union to abandon support of Ceauşescu, along with other hard-line Communist leaders, such as Zhivkov in Bulgaria and Honecker in East Germany, and to seek ways of removing them.

Popular uprisings during 1989 in Poland, Czechoslovakia and East Germany prompted the Romanians to follow suit. In the same year a Hungarian Protestant pastor in Timişoara named László Tökés was expelled from his parish for voicing criticism of the regime and forcibly evicted by the Securitate when he refused to leave. This led to a full-scale revolt in Timişoara, which was brutally suppressed. However, partly because of the extensive coverage given to it on foreign radio and television, as well as to the overthrow of Communist regimes then taking place in other East European countries, the revolt soon spread to other cities, including Arad, Cluj, Constanţa and Târgu Mureş, and then to Bucharest, where on 21 December 1989 a large crowd of about 100,000 persons, composed chiefly of workers and students, assembled in the great square in front of the Central Committee Building to hear Ceauşescu, newly returned from an official visit to Teheran, make one of his interminable speeches. In the middle of his speech there were cries of 'Murderer' and 'Timişoara' and throughout the rest of the speech, during which he promised increases in wages and pensions in a futile attempt to placate the crowd, he was continually interrupted. Afterwards the militia were only able to disperse the crowd with water cannon and tear gas, and finally by opening fire.

During a meeting summoned by Ceauşescu that evening in the Central Committee Building it became clear that his rule was already crumbling. It emerged that several units of the army had failed to obey orders to fire at the demonstrators and that some had already defected, and it seems that the formation of the National Salvation Front, which was to constitute the new government, had already begun among senior army officers, leaders of the Securitate, members of the old guard of the Communist Party who had fallen out with Ceauşescu for one reason or another, and some younger members, including Petre Roman, who was to become prime minister in the new government. During the night General Vasile Milea, the defence minister, who had already incurred Ceauşescu's anger by failing to issue live ammunition to the troops at Timişoara, instructed his army commanders in Bucharest and elsewhere not to carry out Ceauşescu's orders to shoot on demonstrators and reinforce the defences of the Central Committee Building. As a result, the following morning he was summoned by Ceauşescu to the Central Committee Building and then taken out of the room and shot by members of the president's personal bodyguard. This was probably the turning point of the revolution: the demonstrators stormed into the Central Committee Building, without the soldiers making any attempt to stop them, while Ceauşescu and his wife, and two of his henchmen, Manea Manescu and Emil Bobu, made their escape by helicopter from the roof. The helicopter landed near Boteni military airport, where the Ceauşescus hijacked a car. They were spotted by two militiamen, who pursued them as far as Târgovişte, where they were stopped and arrested. On Christmas Day they were charged with numerous crimes, including genocide, and in a secret trial lasting only three hours conducted by a small group of members of the NSF, were condemned to death and summarily executed.

Immediately after the Ceauşescus' flight, a course of action had been agreed between Ion Iliescu and General Nicolae Militaru, both of whom were former high-ranking Party members who had been dismissed from the Central Committee, Militaru in 1984 and Iliescu in 1978. Militaru went to the radio station and broadcast an appeal to the chief of staff of the army, General Guşă, and the other generals to order the army back to barracks and to obey the orders of the National Salvation Front, which had just been set up by Iliescu in the Central Committee Building and which, having telephoned the Soviet embassy in Bucharest, he claimed had Soviet backing. A manifesto was drafted which included the establishment of multi-party democracy, free elections, radical reforms of industry, agriculture and education, and restoration of the rights of national minorities. Membership of the Council of the NSF included such prominent dissidents as Doina Cornea, László Tőkés and the poet Ana Blandiana.

Although the majority of the members of the NSF were former members of the Communist Party, they lost no time in repealing most of Ceauşescu's repressive measures. The laws against abortion were repealed, the systemization programme was stopped, the Securitate was placed under the Ministry of Defence, rationing was abolished and the free market in farm produce reinstated, and supplies of gas and electricity for domestic use were doubled. The discrimination which the Hungarian Transylvanians had suffered under Ceauşescu in education, language and culture was officially abandoned. All these and other measures won Iliescu immediate acclaim. At the same time some of the worst excesses and extravagances of the Ceauşescu family were revealed, to such an extent that the Ceauşescu personality cult was transformed into an anti-cult, and an Iliescu cult began to emerge. Ceauşescu ceased to be a demigod and became a devil, and Elena Ceauşescu was transformed from a brilliant scientist into a promiscuous illiterate. Ceauşescu's four principal henchmen – Bobu, Dincă, Postelnicu and Manescu - were given public trials preceded by press conferences at which their guilt was announced in advance. At the ensuing trials the four defendants incriminated themselves and each other in well-rehearsed confessions, and they were all sentenced to life imprisonment.

Nevertheless, it did not take long for disenchantment with the new regime to set in, as it became clear that there were still many ex-Communists in the government and as the system of food distribution began to break down, largely through the incompetence of local officials, until the situation became as bad as it had been before the revolution. Although the NSF retained much of its popularity simply by virtue of having overthrown Ceauşescu, it was increasingly accused of having betrayed the revolution. Iliescu himself did nothing to dispel these feelings of disillusion by publicly declaring in conventional Communist language his belief that multi-party democracy was an outdated system, that 'democratic centralism' should be the basis of good government, and that the NSF was the only legitimate heir to the revolution and the only true reflection of the will of the broad masses of the people. Furthermore, although he had stated that the NSF would only remain in government temporarily until free elections could be held, he now announced that it would compete in the elections after all. This produced protests from, among others, Doina Cornea, who promptly resigned from the Council of the NSF, and the next few months saw numerous protests and demonstrations in Bucharest and elsewhere. There were also protests and demonstrations among the Romanian population of Transylvania, notably in Cluj and Târgu Mureş, alarmed at the re-emergence of Hungarian language and Hungarian educational and cultural institutions in areas where the Hungarians predominated, and at the wholesale emigration of the Transylvanian Saxons back to the Federal Republic of Germany and the occupation of their villages by the hated Roma.

By the time the first elections after the revolution were held in May 1990, there were over 80 political parties, of which only four – the National Salvation Front, the Hungarian Democratic Union of Romania, the National Liberal Party and the National Peasant's Party commanded a substantial degree of support. In the election campaign there were numerous instances of intimidation and fraud and even one murder, but there was never any doubt that the NSF would win, if only because of its revolutionary credentials in bringing about the fall of the Ceauşescu regime. The result was that in the presidential election the NSF received over 12 million votes, or 85.07 percent of the poll, and the NLP, the next largest party, only one and a half million or 10.6 percent, while in the election for the Chamber of Deputies the NSF received 66.3 percent of the votes and the NLP only 2.6 percent.

The years following the revolution were marked by a deteriorating economic situation, with high inflation, unemployment, falls in industrial and agricultural production and the re-imposition of rationing. One cause of these problems was the privatization of agriculture, which made it difficult to introduce mechanization on a large scale and so increase efficiency. Another was the civil unrest in former Yugoslavia, which seriously hampered Romania's use of the Danube as a trade route and a source of hydroelectric power. At the same time Romania found it difficult to attract foreign investment, in spite of regaining most favoured nation status with the USA in 1995. These woes led to a great increase in emigration, not least among the Roma, many thousands of whom crossed illegally into Hungary and Czechoslovakia. The general situation remained grave until 1994, when inflation began to fall, albeit accompanied by a continuing increase in unemployment, which reached one million by 1998, and by further decreases in industrial output.

Internationally, Romania began the slow process of rejoining the European family of nations, becoming a member of the Council of Europe in 1993 and of NATO in 2004.

In the elections of 1996 Ion Iliescu was ousted from power and was replaced as president by Emil Constantinescu, leader of the Romanian Democratic Convention, which had been formed by a coalition between the National Peasant Party and the Christian Democrats. It was this event rather than the revolution of Christmas 1989 that really marked the end of Communist rule in Romania. Constantinescu's prime minister was Victor Ciorbea, a union leader who initiated a programme of privatization, liberalization and other measures designed to meet the economic and civil rights requirements demanded for admission to the European Union, which was finally achieved in 2007. Constantinescu remained in power until 2000, but failed to tackle corruption effectively and did little to revive the economy, and in that year Ion Iliescu was re-elected with a landslide majority. Iliescu remained in power until 2004, when he was succeeded by Traian Băsescu, who had been one of the original Communist members of the National Salvation Front, and later became mayor of Bucharest and then leader of the Democratic Alliance, consisting of a coalition of the Liberal and Democratic Parties. In April 2007 Băsescu was suspended by Parliament on a charge of abuse of power. The real reason for his suspension may have been that he was at loggerheads with the prime minister, Călin Tăriceanu, a right-wing millionaire businessman who was largely responsible for achieving the transition to a market economy and for a number of other reforms necessary for Romania to qualify for admission to the European Union. Whether or not this was the case, in a referendum the following month the electorate voted against Băsescu's impeachment, and he was reinstated on the all too familiar agenda of reform and the eradication of corruption, which is still evidently endemic in much of Romanian public life.

The Romanian Economy: Overcoming the Legacy

by Stephen Lloyd

Although far slower than some of its neighbours in making the transition from a socialist system to a capitalist economy, and in achieving a clear level of political stability and transparency in government institutions such as the judiciary, Romania's recent economic performance suggests that she may finally be on her way to catching up with her richer neighbours.

The key event was accession to the European Union, achieved in 2007. There was great joy throughout the country at this confirmation that the Communist period, and the unfortunate 1990s that followed, were now entirely behind it.

Of course, the legacy of Ceauşescu has been difficult to overcome. Few people understood the appalling state of the economy until the floodgates of freedom were opened. For all Ceauşescu's success in maintaining an independent foreign policy and a ruthlessly imposed quiescence at home, he understood nothing about economic policy and markets. Forced investment in the 1980s produced widespread poverty and misery. There was no private sector. Old equipment and machinery were not replaced. Prestige projects, widespread corruption and a collapsing infrastructure were the main features of the Romanian economy. At the same time a shibboleth was made of paying off foreign debt, an exercise that made little economic sense.

After Ceauşescu's overthrow in December 1989 optimism could be felt everywhere, but the new President was his former close associate Ion Iliescu, to whom the concepts of a stock exchange, private property and foreign investment were not exactly familiar. His government failed to commit to economic reform or provide the dynamic leadership required to bring about fundamental change in basic government institutions. Consequently, the image of Romania from 1990 to 1996 was negative, and foreign investors and financial institutions remained wary.

Evidently the government faced substantial difficulties. A full-scale programme of privatization was the highest priority – in Communist days it was difficult even to find a privately owned typewriter. Unfortunately neither the financial institutions nor the framework were adequate to their task. In particular, a consistent investment law with the correct mix of incentives was required to attract capital inflows. In any case most state companies were bankrupt. Industry required training at all levels and investment in key economic sectors. During this period the government's policies had limited success in responding to these deep-seated economic problems.

For example, the State Ownership Fund (SOF) was established in 1992 to sell off state-owned companies. Foreign investors correctly complained about delays in processing tenders, massive bureaucracy and constant changing of the rules. Indeed, I remember one meeting in 1996 with the SOF to discuss a minor matter on behalf of a British company. Fifteen employees of the SOF were present. Few had read the background material; even fewer understood the financial statements. Added to this was the Romanian tendency to ask unrealistic prices for companies with large debts and machinery dating back to the 1970s.

Under Iliescu's successor, Emil Constantinescu, some progress was made with the privatization programme, and Romania's image abroad with a young leader seemed to improve. But the underlying statistics showed negative growth in 1997 (-6%) and 1998 (-7%). Inflation reached a high point of 155% in 1997.

On Iliescu's return to office in 2000 he appeared to have learned from his earlier failures and carried out some significant economic reforms. Indeed, in 2003 the Romanian Government successfully concluded an IMF (International Monetary Fund) stand-by agreement for $370 million, tied to specific financial reforms and inflation targets. President Traian Basescu, who was elected in 2004, has continued on this promising road. In 2006 real economic growth was 7.8%, and inflation was reduced to 6.6%. However, Romania is still behind its richer neighbours. For example, the GDP per head in that year was $13,400 in the Czech Republic, $11,100 in Hungary and only $5,400 in Romania.

Foreign investors recognize that Romania offers substantial opportunities. Its undeveloped resources, large potential markets, price advantages in certain industries and highly trained workforce are important factors. Romania must continue its commitment to economic reform and transparency. This means cooperation with the IMF, completion of the privatization programme, responsible borrowing on the international markets and good relations with the EU.

However, the renewed instability of 2007 shook the confidence of some investors, and while the EU has judged that the independence of the judiciary and the fight against corruption are satisfactory, in reality much remains to be done.

Nonetheless, the IMF recently said that Romania will remain attractive to foreign investors despite its recent political problems. Indeed, they estimated growth rates in 2007 to be around 6.5%. The European Bank for Reconstruction and Development announced a programme of $672 million in 2007. The World Bank is extremely active with projects in many key economic sectors. Together this represents a vote of confidence in the future of the Romanian economy.

Meanwhile, many major western banks, law firms and consultants have established offices in Bucharest. Almost every week sees the announcement of another international firm with plans for participating in the future growth of Romania. Restaurants, residential developments, hotels, clubs and new factories are springing up in Bucharest as well as other large cities such as Cluj and Timişoara. All these signs seemed to portend a transition to a successful capitalist economy.

СФНТЯЛ. Н. ГЕОРГЕ

St George, painted glass icon from Arpașul de Sus, 1872

Maramureş, interior of peasant house

Maramureș farmers in traditional costume

Arnota, the monastery

Oradea, the Roman Catholic Cathedral by F. A. Hillebrandt

Oradea, the town centre, with statue of Michaël the Brave

Alba Julia, the citadel and Cathedral of Unification

Sighişoara, the Clock Tower

Sighişoara, street in the old town

Mediaş the main square

Viscri: interior of the church fortifications

Biertan: Saxon church and village

Bistriţa: the monastery church

Voroneţ: wall paintings

The Painted Churches of Moldavia

by John Villiers

The principality of Moldavia was first formed during the fourteenth century by the fusion of several small polities that had grown up along the commercial river routes which joined Cetatea Albă (Moncastro, now Belgorod Dnestrovskiy, Ukraine) at the mouth of the Dniester and the other ports on the west coast of the Black Sea to the great inland markets of Kiev, Halych and Ľviv. This commercial growth was encouraged by the arrival of Greek, Armenian, Italian and Saxon merchants and artisans to settle in the area. The most numerous of the settlers were the Saxons, who already by the mid-fourteenth century had their own episcopal see at Siret in northern Moldavia. Successful wars against the Tatars of the Golden Horde in Crimea and other neighbouring states were followed by an equally successful attempt to throw off Hungarian suzerainty, so that in 1359 the Moldavian boyars were able to elect Bogdan of Cuhea, a prince of Maramureş, known as the Infidel, as the first fully independent voivode of Moldavia.

Moldavian independence was threatened from the outset by the expansion of the Ottoman empire, and from the mid-sixteenth century Moldavia was forced to recognize Turkish suzerainty. The hostility to the Turks which this engendered and which is vividly reflected in the art of the painted churches, remained a fundamental feature of both Moldavian and Wallachian social and political life from that time right up until the late nineteenth century and the achievement of Romanian independence, and, particularly in Moldavia, the militant Orthodox Church played a crucial role both as a bulwark and defence against the Muslim Turks and as a focus for the preservation of national artistic and cultural traditions.

The reign of the Voivode Petru I Muşat (1374-91) was a period of political consolidation in Moldavia, of reorganization of the defences of the principality and of important developments in religious life. Petru Muşat appointed the first metropolitan bishop and built a princely court and fortifications at Suceava. Unfortunately few buildings and no paintings of his time have survived. Under Petru Muşat's brother and successor, Roman I (1391-94), Moldavia's eastern boundaries reached the Black Sea, and the next voivode, Petru's son Ştefan I (1394-99) defeated the Hungarian forces sent against him under the command of Sigismund of Luxemburg at Hândău, near Târgu Neamţ, and thus finally and definitively threw off Hungarian suzerainty.

Ştefan I's son, Alexandru the Good (1400-32), was a skilful diplomat and pursued a policy of alliance with Poland and Lithuania against the Teutonic Knights and Hungary. He was also a patron of the arts, and both icon painting and embroidery flourished during his reign. He made two major monastic foundations, at Bistriţa and Probota, both of which have yielded fragments of painting on the interior walls that date from his reign and are the earliest surviving mural paintings in Moldavia. It seems unlikely, however, that they are the first to have been commissioned by a Moldavian ruler, as churches with painting on the interior walls of an earlier date than these are found in several places in southeast Poland, notably Cracow and Sandomierz, as well as in Transylvania and in Wallachia. Indeed, the earliest wall paintings anywhere in Romania, dating from about 1360, are to be seen in the princely Church of St Nicholas at Curtea de Argeş in Wallachia.

Among the artists who enjoyed the patronage of Alexandru the Good was Gavril Uric, one of the great Romanian painters of the Middle Ages. Uric worked at the Monastery of Neamţ, where in 1429 he produced for Alexandru's wife, Princess Marina the exquisitely illuminated *Four Gospels* which are now in the Bodleian Library in Oxford. Notwithstanding its small scale, Uric's work combines hieratic Byzantine formality and rigidity with a freer, more expressive and personal style in a manner that foreshadows the monumental work of the Moldavian mural painters of the early sixteenth century.

Alexandru's death was followed by 25 years of disputed succession and political instability that were only ended in 1457 when Ştefan III the Great succeeded as voivode of Moldavia. Ştefan was described by a contemporary chronicler as a 'well-balanced man, not slothful, who knew how to cope with his work and had a capacity for appearing where he was least expected. Master of the craft of war, he would go wherever he was needed, and his men, having once seen him, would never retreat. As a result, there was seldom a war that he did not win. When he was defeated, he did not lose hope, but instead would rise above his conquerors.' Ştefan made Moldavia for a short time one of the strongest powers in eastern Europe. In 1453 Constantinople had fallen to the Turks, the Byzantine empire had come to an end, and the Balkan peoples had begun five hundred years of subjection of varying degrees of severity to the Ottoman yoke. Not surprisingly therefore, Ştefan's reign was marked by almost continuous hostilities against the Sublime Porte, culminating in his defeat in January 1475 of a huge Turkish army under Suleiman Hadân Pasha, beglerbeg of Rumelia, at Podul Înalt near Vaslui, a hundred miles south of Iaşi.

Ştefan also restored several of his predecessors' princely courts and built or rebuilt numerous citadels and fortifications. He constructed a new stronghold at Roman, improved and extended the citadels at Suceava, Neamţ and Cetatea Albă,

Monastery Church, Neamț: south façade, above; plan, below left; vaulting, below right

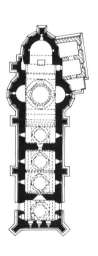

99

and between 1479 and 1481 made the Church of St Nicholas at Rădăuţi, founded a
hundred years before by Bogdan I (1359-65), into a dynastic pantheon. The wall-
paintings of Ştefan and his family in this church, which date from about 1480, are
the earliest surviving votive paintings in Romania.

During the first phase of the formation of the Moldavian state, both secular and
religious buildings were still made of wood. Stone and brick only began to be used
in the mid-fourteenth century, and then only for buildings of exceptional importance. The first of Ştefan's major religious monuments in brick and stone was the
Church and Monastery of Putna, which he built between 1466 and 1469 and
endowed with rich gifts. Unfortunately, both church and monastery burned down
twice in the next fifty years. They were restored by the Voivode Alexandru
Lăpuşneanu in 1559, and then pulled down and rebuilt between 1654 and 1662. The
monastery was again destroyed in 1739, this time by an earthquake, and restored
soon after by the Metropolitan Iacob Putneanul. Further restorations were carried
out in the nineteenth and twentieth centuries, most recently in 1977. Consequently,
almost none of the original buildings or of the mural paintings survives.

Between 1487 and 1504, Ştefan and his boyars built or rebuilt over thirty more
stone and brick churches and monasteries, including Neamţ, Voroneţ, Pătrăuţi,
Bălineşti, Dobrovăţ and Probota. In accordance with the traditions of Byzantine
and southern Slav Orthodox ecclesiastical architecture, all the churches were constructed on a rectangular or tricuncial plan or a combination of the two. The earliest
surviving stone and brick church in Moldavia built on a tricuncial plan is the
Church of the Holy Trinity at Siret, which is traditionally ascribed to the reign of
the Voivode Sas (1354-58), and by the late fifteenth century, although not universal,
this plan had been widely adopted both in Moldavia and in Wallachia. The interior
was divided into four clearly defined sections – a semi-circular domed apse (*altar*)
containing the altar at the east end, with side apses sometimes consisting only of
niches in the thickness of the wall, a nave (*naos*) and a burial chamber (*gropniţa*) in
the centre, and a narthex (*pronaos*) at the west end. A complicated system of arches
peculiar to Moldavian architecture was sometimes adopted for the vaulting of the
nave in which the four principal arches that crossed in the centre were surmounted
by pendentives, thus making the square base of the vault into a circle. Above these
were four smaller skew arches, which made the upper part of the vault into a square,
and a further series of pendentives creating another circle above the square and supporting the base of the tower. This arrangement shows on the outside of the church
as a series of false storeys of diminishing size at the bottom of the tower. However,
although Byzantine in general plan and in much of their decorative detail, these
churches also have Romanesque and Gothic features, notably the door and window
frames, the tracery of the windows, the buttresses and the ribbing of the vaults. The
buttresses served little or no structural purpose, but were added primarily as architectural decoration.

Putna: Tomb of Ştefan III the Great

The interior walls of most of these early churches were painted soon after they were built. The exterior walls, however, were not painted, but, in addition to the buttresses, were decorated with tall, slender blind arches on the curved wall of the apse and, running right round the upper part of the building, thus forming a frieze above the tops of the buttresses and beneath the cornice and wide eaves, one or two rows of shallow niches framed by semicircular arches. The Moldavian builders further embellished the exterior walls by juxtaposing bricks and stones of different colours and setting circular tiles of glazed earthenware embossed with various heraldic devices into the spaces between the tympana of the niches and on the crowns of the window arches. Excellent examples of these decorative features can be seen on the Church of the Ascension at Neamţ and the Church of the Holy Trinity at Siret. The various surfaces created in the spaces enclosed by the many blind arches were later to be exploited by the Moldavian mural painters. One of the finest of the painted interiors of this early period is in the Church of St Nicholas in Bălineşti, which was founded by the Logothete Tăutu in 1499 and painted before 1511 by Gavril Ieromonah, one of the outstanding Romanian painters of the time.

To encourage manuscript painting and embroidery, Ştefan the Great established scriptoria and embroidery workshops at Suceava, Putna, Neamţ and elsewhere. Through their work, together with that of the stonemasons and painters, the princely monasteries preserved and fostered Moldavian culture, and in particular those elements of it for which Byzantium provided the model, during a time of almost continual warfare.

The death of Ştefan the Great in 1504 was followed by another period of disorder, which was brought to an end in 1527 by the succession of his illegitimate son, Petru III Rareş. The most important of the few mural paintings belonging to this troubled

101

Humor: Monastery Church

period are those in the Church of St Nicholas at Dorohoi, which were executed between 1522 and 1525, but they have been so blackened by centuries of candle smoke that it is difficult to discern their true quality.

Petru Rareş restored many of the churches and monasteries that had been ravaged during the previous 23 years, notably the Church of the Holy Spirit at Dobrovăţ, the interior of which was painted in 1529. He also built several entirely new churches and monasteries, including Humor and Moldoviţa, and it was during his reign that churches began to be decorated with paintings on the outside as well as on the inside walls. The earliest of these exterior paintings to survive are a few fragments on the walls of the monastic Church of St Nicholas at Probota, which date from 1532. In 1993 a programme of restoration was undertaken at Probota by UNESCO, with financial assistance from Japanese sources.

Much better preserved are the exterior paintings on the Church of the Assumption at Humor, which date from 1535, only three years after Probota. Humor is of special interest because it was certainly painted by a group of artists headed by one of the greatest of the early Moldavian painters, Toma of Suceava, whose signature appears on the outer west wall of the church and who is described in a document dated 1541 as 'the painter of Suceava, courtier of Petru [Rareş], the glorious and mighty prince of Moldavia'. It is also remarkable in two other respects: it was the first Moldavian church to have no glazed ceramic decoration and instead to be entirely covered on the outside with paintings, and the first to be built with the narthex in the form of an open porch with four arches, creating an exonarthex.

This arcaded exonarthex is also a feature of the Church of the Annunciation at Moldoviţa, a fourteenth century church that was destroyed in an avalanche, rebuilt in 1532 by Petru Rareş and painted in 1537, two years after Humor. Slightly later again is the painting of the Church of All Saints at Părhăuţi, dating from 1540, and of the Church of St John Beheaded at Arbore, which was built in 1502 and painted by Dragoş Coman in 1541. The latter church and its paintings are now urgently in need of restoration. The Church of St Nicholas at Râşca was founded in 1542 and painted a few years later by a Greek painter from the island of Zakynthos named Stamatelos Kotronas. The Church of St George at Voroneţ was built in 1488 and the interior painted before 1500, but its magnificent exterior paintings were not completed until 1547, a year after the death of Petru Rareş. The last of the major Moldavian painted churches is the Church of the Resurrection in the Monastery of Suceviţa, which was built between 1582 and 1586 for the Voivode Ieremia Movilă and his family and painted in 1595-96 by two artists named Ion and Sofronie. The painting of Suceviţa is of the highest quality, and the buildings are greatly enhanced by being set in a landscape that, even by Moldavian standards, is of quite exceptional natural beauty. Finally, there is the curiously proportioned Church of the Descent of the Holy Spirit at Dragomirna, which was founded by the Metropolitan Anastasie Crimca in 1602 and painted in 1608-9. The paintings in the apse and nave of this tall, narrow church are in an elaborate and highly decorated style reminiscent of the miniature manuscript paintings of the period, and it may be significant in this

Humor: votive portrait of Anastasia, wife of the founder Toader Bubuiog, in the burial chamber

*Sucevița : votive portrait of Ieremia
Movilă and his son*

connection that Anastasie Crimca was himself an accomplished miniaturist and cal-
ligrapher.

The idea of decorating the outside walls of a church with pictorial representations
of religious subjects is not, of course, unique to sixteenth-century Moldavia. Mosaic
is used in a similar way on the outside of Italian churches, and there are some
Gothic churches in Transylvania that have paintings on the outside walls. But the
idea of covering the entire wall with painting from the foundations to the roof does
seem to be peculiar to Moldavia and to have originated in the reign of Petru Rareş.
Moldavian wall paintings were executed *al fresco* on a base of fresh lime plaster, and
on the interior paintings distemper was used for details and finishing touches. The
problem of fragmentation of large surfaces and the consequent loss of architectural
unity caused by the painting of numerous small scenes all over them was brilliantly
overcome by the use of a single colour for the background, for example blue at
Voroneţ and Moldoviţa and green at Sucevița. There was even a kind of primitive
colour coding: scenes of Paradise and the Garden of Eden, for example, were always
depicted on a white background. The painting was not usually done until four or
five years after the completion of the building, in order to allow time for the foundations to settle and the mortar to harden. The murals inside have suffered badly
from centuries of candle smoke, but the exterior paintings have withstood the

Moldoviţa: monastery and church

extreme variations of the Moldavian climate quite extraordinarily well and, without ever having been restored, most of them are still glowing and vivid. This is partly because most of the colours are of mineral origin (cobalt blue, for example) and therefore resist atmospheric changes and do not fade in strong sunlight, and partly because of the very wide eaves of the roof that protect them from the elements. The paintings nearer the base of the walls have as a rule lasted less well than those higher up, largely because of the effects of damp rising from the ground.

The principal purpose of the mural paintings, both inside and out, was to illustrate religious stories from the Old and New Testaments and the lives of the saints, but they also had a propaganda function. They were intended to assert the legitimacy and authority of the voivode's rule, particularly if, as in the case of the bastard Petru Rareş, his claims to the throne were somewhat shaky, and at the same time to inspire the Christian Moldavians to assist him in his struggle against the Muslim Ottoman Turks. After the Fall of Constantinople, Ştefan the Great and his successors saw themselves as the heirs of the Byzantine emperors, upholders of the Byzantine tradition and champions of Greek Orthodox Christianity. Ştefan strengthened this claim by marrying a Byzantine princess, Maria of Mangop, and sought to enlist the support of other Christian rulers in eastern Europe, declaring to them that, if Moldavia, 'which is the gateway of Christianity, is lost, which God forbid, then all Christendom is in danger'.

The main cupola of the nave is always dedicated to the Celestial Church, so the centre of the dome is occupied by Christ as Pantocrator or Universal Ruler, surrounded on the walls of the drum by celestial cohorts, winged seraphim, prophets, evangelists and apostles. On the upper pendentives are the four Evangelists, symbolizing the link made by the Gospels between the Celestial Church and the Church on earth. The same symbolic role is performed by the paintings in the area between the cupola of the nave and the semi-dome of the apse, where the Hetimasis or Throne of the Last Judgement and Jesus as the Ancient of Days are depicted.

The apse is devoted to the theme of Redemption, beginning with the Incarnation, here represented by the Virgin in her guise as the Platytera or All-embracing One, enthroned as the Queen of Heaven, holding the Infant Jesus in both arms and surrounded by angels. In the apse at Moldoviţa she is shown accompanied by her parents, St Joachim and St Anne. The theme of Redemption is further illustrated by scenes associated with the Sacrament of the Eucharist, particularly episodes from the Last Supper such as the Washing of the Disciples' Feet and the First Eucharist of the Apostles. On the lower part of the walls are figures of saints, among them the most important doctors of the Church. The theme of Redemption is sometimes illustrated here by a representation of Jesus in the Tomb leaning against the Virgin, a subject found also in Serbian painting of this period.

The walls of the nave and the vaults surrounding the cupola illustrate the New Testament and the Life of Christ, from His Baptism to the Descent of the Holy Spirit from the Tomb, with special emphasis on the Passion and Crucifixion. The paintings of scenes from the Passion provided Moldavian artists with a wider choice of subject matter and gave them an opportunity to paint in a more naturalistic and dramatic style, creating thereby a stronger sense of spirituality than was possible in the votive paintings and depictions of saints, in which iconographic correctitude was of prime importance. This greater naturalism became increasingly apparent during the 1520s and 1530s. In the paintings of the Passion in the Church of the Holy Spirit at Dobrovăţ, for example, which date from 1529, although the Byzantine legacy is still clearly evident, the style of the painting is remarkable for its freedom, liveliness and even humour, and shows a number of iconographic innovations and features borrowed from the West that contrast srikingly with the formal and idealized treatment of the votive portraits of Ştefan the Great, Bogdan III and Petru Rareş and his family in the same church. Furthermore, the subject matter includes episodes that are seldom found elsewhere in European religious art at that time, such as Pilate washing his hands, Peter cutting off Malchus' ear, Peter denying his Master with the cock that crew twice, Judas Iscariot hanging himself, Joseph of Arimathaea before Pilate, the Preparation of the Cross, Christ mounting the Cross, the Distribution of Christ's Clothes among the Soldiers, and the Descent into Limbo.

The votive portraits of the founder and his family offering up a model of the church to the ecclesiastical authorities or to the Virgin Mary are always painted on the south side of the west wall of the nave. This scene is always very grand and solemn. The kneeling figures of the donor and his family are portrayed against a background of golden stars, clad in sumptuous costumes derived directly from the imperial Byzantine court, with tall gold crowns and brocaded caftans. One interesting feature of these votive scenes is the accuracy with which the artist renders the architectural details of the model of the church being offered. This makes them valuable sources of information on the architectural history of the building.

The narthex is dedicated to portrayals of the Virgin and scenes from her life. In the lunette over the doorway into the narthex she is portrayed, often with great spirituality, as the Eleousa, the Virgin of Compassion. In the dome she is portrayed as the Vlacherniotissa (praying with a medallion of the Infant Jesus on her breast) surrounded by the four saints who wrote hymns to her – St Joseph, St Cosmas, St Theophanus and St John Damascene. On the walls of the narthex is the Menologos, a religious calendar that shows for each day of the ecclesiastical year, beginning on 1 September, a miracle or the martyrdom of the saint whose feast falls on that day. It is seldom complete, and certain scenes seem to be particular favourites regardless of the days to which they refer, notably the numerous miracles of St Nicholas, a major saint of the Greek Orthodox Church, St Luke painting the icon of the Virgin, St Marina brandishing the hammer with which she defended her virginity in the monastery into which her father had smuggled her dressed as a boy (there is a particularly fine example of this scene at Arbore) and St John Chrysostom, who preached that the Gospel was the 'spring of life' and is shown with engaging literalness holding an open Bible from which a stream of water flows out towards his listeners.

Also on the walls of the narthex immediately beneath the dome are portrayals of the seven Œcumenical Councils and the Acts of the Apostles. The depictions of the Councils are particularly notable for the skilful use they make of the curvature of the wall to create in a restricted space the impression of a vast concourse of people. These paintings were intended to demonstrate the role of Moldavia as guardian of the doctrinal purity of Orthodox Christianity at a time when the Eastern Church, like the Western, was threatened by the Reformation and, once again, to mobilize the spiritual forces of the Moldavians against the Ottoman Turks. The same militant idea is conveyed by the Procession of Soldier Saints on horseback, which is also often found in the narthex. The Soldier Saints are led by the Archangel Michael, who is generally portrayed pointing out a luminous cross in the sky to the Emperor Constantine the Great. This is a reference to the story of the Battle of the Milvian Bridge in 330 AD, at which Constantine defeated his pagan rival Maxentius. On the night before the battle a luminous cross appeared in the sky carrying the inscription 'In hoc signo vinces', and this led Constantine after his victory to proclaim

Christianity as the official religion of the Roman Empire. Among the saints escorting St Michael are St George, St Demetrius, St Procopius, St Theodore Tiron, who is credited with having killed a dragon before St George, St Theodore Stratilas, St Nestor, St Artemius, St Eustachius and St Mercury, who is believed to have been sent from Heaven in 363 AD to kill the Emperor Julian the Apostate in Persia. The earliest portrayal of the Procession of Soldier Saints is at Pătrăuţi, where the Archangel Michael is depicted himself wearing the crown and dalmatic of a Roman emperor. The whole scene may be interpreted both as a general illustration of the Church Militant overcoming paganism and more specifically as a call to the Moldavians to take up arms against the infidel Turks and Tatars.

The paintings in the burial chamber are devoted principally to scenes from the Old Testament, such as the Driving Out of Balaam and the Ascension of the Prophet Elijah, who at Voroneţ and elsewhere is shown ascending seated in a rustic cart of clearly Moldavian manufacture drawn by two horses. In the burial chamber at Suceviţa is a delightful series of scenes from the story of Moses and the Exodus painted in a naive but naturalistic style. One of these shows horse-drawn carts full of people in Moldavian dress fleeing before the Pharaoh's mounted soldiery, with a column of dogs and pigs marching beside them in the foreground of the picture. This is generally taken to be a reference to the Romanian expression *cu căţel şi cu purcel*, 'with puppy and with piglet', which means 'with all one's goods and chattels', or 'lock, stock and barrel'. New Testament subjects, such as the Nativity, are also sometimes represented in the burial chamber, as, for example, at Humor, where there is a particularly charming scene of the Bath of the Infant Jesus.

The paintings on the outside walls generally illustrate four or five main themes. The first of these is the theme of the Celestial Hierarchy, which is found on the walls of the main apse and side apses and on the east and west walls of the nave adjacent to the apse. At the summit is Christ Enthroned as Pantocrator. Beneath this is a figure of the Virgin Platytera and then representations of the Deisis or Intercession, together with portrayals of the Holy Mandylion, the Sacrificial Lamb or St Simeon with the Infant Jesus in his arms, the Host on a Paten, the Archangel Michael and St George. On either side of these are rows in several registers of winged seraphim, angels, prophets, apostles, doctors of the Church, martyrs and hermits, portrayed standing or marching purposefully against a starry background, holding books, scrolls or other attributes. At Suceviţa the Celestial Hierarchy occupies no fewer than seven registers. The detailed and elaborate portrayal of this vast subject seems to have been intended to serve as a veiled warning by the voivode, in particular Petru Rareş, to the boyars, many of whom were opposed to his autocratic rule and were plotting with the Turks to overthrow him, to submit obediently to his rule in the same way as the members of the Celestial Hierarchy

Humor: Christ in glory, surrounded by angels

submitted themselves to the Christian God, the Pantocrator.

Sometimes scenes from the lives of individual martyrs and hermits are found else-where on the exterior walls. On the south front of Voroneţ, for example, there are numerous depictions of martyrs and hermits and other holy men and women, among them Grigore Roşca, the metropolitan of Moldavia, who was the second founder of the monastery in the early sixteenth century and commissioned the painting of the exterior of the church, and Daniel the Hermit, a counsellor of Ştefan the Great who had been the priest of the wooden church that originally stood on this site. On the west façade of Arbore is a magnificent scene of the reception of St George at the imperial court in Constantinople. We have already noticed that the many miracles of St Nicholas are also popular subjects, as is the Martyrdom of St John the New, the patron saint of Moldavia, and the removal in 1402 of his relics, accompanied by a procession led by the Metropolitan Iosif Musat, to Suceava, where they were ceremonially received by the Voivode Alexandru the Good and his entire court, is naturally given a special place in the painted churches. The finest and most complete depiction of the story of St John the New is on the south façade of the exonarthex of Voroneţ.

Suceviţa: Birth of St George, and his reception by the Emperor at Constantinople

Voroneţ: east end of the
Monastery Church

On the exterior of some churches the Miracle of St Sabbas of Jerusalem, St Peter the Athonite and the Vision of St John Climax ('of the Ladder') at Mount Sinai are portrayed. These subjects were chosen to represent Jerusalem, Mount Athos and Mount Sinai, the three spiritual centres of the Christian East, which by the sixteenth century had all fallen under the Ottoman yoke. The most dramatic representations of the Vision of St John Climax are on the south side apse at Râşca and on the north façade of Suceviţa. Each rung of the ladder in the saint's vision represents a stage in the spiritual development that is attainable in the monastic life. On one side are the devils, who have tails, wings and second faces in their stomachs, arguing and struggling with the monks in an attempt to gain their souls as they climb the ladder. On the other side are the angels hovering behind the monks and holding crowns above their heads. At Suceviţa the ladder is surmounted by a group of delightful scenes from Genesis and from the life of St Pachomius, the founder of Christian monasticism in the fourth century.

Another major theme illustrated on the exterior walls of the painted churches is the Tree of Jesse, which is always either on the north or the south façade of the burial chamber or the narthex. This subject is rarely found outside Moldavia,

111

Moldoviţa: detail of the Tree of Jesse

although not quite unknown – it occurs, for example, in the early sixteenth-century
Monastery of Lavros on Mount Athos – and the reason for its frequent occurrence
on churches painted during the reign of Petru Rareş may no doubt be that it offered
him yet another opportunity to assert his right to rule, in this case on grounds of
heredity. The two most notable depictions of the Tree of Jesse in Moldavia are at

Moldoviţa and Voroneţ. The tree emerges from the side of Jesse, who lies recumbent at the bottom, and its branches, which are painted with an abundance of vegetal and floral motifs, spread both vertically and horizontally to cover the entire wall, creating the effect of an enormous and intricate tapestry. The central branch ascends to David and the kings of Judah, and so to the Virgin Mary and Jesus. On either side are figures of the prophets and the leaders of the twelve tribes of Israel, among whom are interspersed various scenes illustrating prophecies and predictions of the Birth of Christ and the Redemption, including Moses receiving the Tablets of the Law, the Queen of Sheba visiting Solomon, the Benediction of Egypt, the Curse of Jerusalem, Jacob's Ladder, the Dream of Nebuchadnezzar, Shadrach, Meshach and Abednego in the Burning Fiery Furnace, Gideon's Fleece and the Vision of Ezekiel. One branch leads, rather unexpectedly, to a group of sibyls and pagan Greek philosophers and poets, including Homer, Socrates, Thucydides, Plato, Aristotle, Pythagoras and Plutarch.

Usually also on the south front is the Acathistic Hymn, a canticle in 24 strophes that is traditionally believed to have been composed on the occasion of the Persian and Avar siege of Byzantium in 626 and is so called because it was sung standing. One scene is devoted to each strophe. The first twelve strophes are concerned with the Immaculate Conception and the Birth and Childhood of Jesus, and include dramatic portrayals of such scenes as the Annunciation, the Arrival of the Magi, the Flight into Egypt and the Presentation in the Temple. The twelve other strophes deal with mystical visions associated with the Adoration of the Virgin, who is generally portrayed here as a princess wearing the crown of Moldavia, signifying that she will defend the Moldavians against the Turks and other enemies.

On some of the painted churches, beneath the Acathistic Hymn. is a depiction of the Siege of Constantinople by the Turks in 1453. The south façade of Moldoviţa has the best preserved version of this theme. It is placed below the Acathistic Hymn because there is a clear connection between the two subjects. The Hymn was composed at the time of the siege of Constantinople in 626, and the idea of linking it with a portrayal of the siege of 1453 was to make both paintings into a single prayer to the Virgin for help in the struggle against the Turks. Both at Moldoviţa and Humor the artillery and cavalry of the besieging army are clearly Turkish, and the architecture of the towers of Constantinople is equally clearly Moldavian. At Humor the meaning of this juxtaposition is further underlined by the iconographically highly eccentric depiction in the Acathistic Hymn of the icon of the Virgin Hodogitria (Guide or Teacher), which the Byzantine emperors took into battle, issuing on a long pole from the emperor's left side. It is significant that at Arbore, which was painted in 1541 after Petru Rareş had capitulated to the Turks, the Turkish army is replaced in the portrayal of the siege by the Persian army, and that in later Moldavian painted churches the siege is not portrayed at all, and is usually replaced by scenes illustrating the Birth of the Virgin.

The fourth great theme illustrated on the outside is the Last Judgement. This is usually on the west wall of the exonarthex inside the porch, or occasionally, as at Râşca, on the south façade. The earliest representation of the subject is at Probota, the best preserved are at Humor and at Voroneţ. Here are portrayed Jesus Christ, the Supreme Judge seated on the Throne and flanked by Adam and Eve. On the left of the Judge are the elect on their way to Heaven and on the right are the damned, who include Jews, Turks, Tatars, Armenians and other heretics and infidels. Here also are scenes of devils trying to falsify the weighing of souls and being repulsed by the Archangel Gabriel, angels blowing on horns to announce the resurrection of the dead, tombs opening to release their corpses, still swaddled in bands, animals vomiting out the people they have eaten, the sea, symbolically represented by a woman holding a boat in her hands and seated on the back of a dolphin, the doors of Paradise guarded by St Peter with a key, the Garden of Paradise planted with trees and the Patriarchs Abraham, Isaac and Jacob with souls on their knees, King David playing the lute (at Voroneţ shown as a Moldavian *cobza*), the Virgin Mary seated between two angels by the side of the Good Thief carrying his cross. At the bottom the Signs of the Zodiac are usually also shown and, uniquely to Moldavia, the Celestial Customs, in which 24 devils, each one responsible for a different sin, are portrayed assaulting souls as, escorted by their guardian angels, they ascend a high tower towards Heaven. Unfortunately none of the depictions of this scene, which is usually painted on the north or west façade, is well preserved.

A return to the the theme of Redemption is made on the exterior of some churches, for example the west façade of Moldoviţa, with depictions of scenes from Genesis, the Creation of the World, Adam and Eve in the Garden of Eden and the Expulsion from Paradise. On the north façade at Voroneţ there is a remarkable series of scenes illustrating stories of Adam and Eve after the Fall, some of them taken not from the Bible, still less from traditional Byzantine iconography, but from Moldavian folk Christianity, and painted with a vigorous, rustic simplicity that owes little to any Byzantine model – Adam ploughing, Adam signing a pact with the Devil, Eve with her distaff, and Cain reaping while Abel guards sheep.

The stylistic variations evident in this vast array of wall paintings are attributable as much to differences in the iconography and general treatment considered appropriate for the different subjects they depict as to the date at which the painting was executed or to the fact that often, if not always, several artists were employed simultaneously on a single church. It is this happy combination of Byzantine formality, used for the portrayal of exalted themes, with a more naturalistic and popular style reserved for homelier topics that makes these wall paintings so remarkable. It is also an extraordinary achievement to have produced works of art of such richness and

Voroneţ: King David playing a Moldavian cobza

splendour on the walls of such relatively small buildings, where the restricted size of most of the surfaces to be painted precludes any very large scale conception of design. The period spanned by the painted churches is brief – scarcely two hundred years separate the paintings at Bistriţa and Probota from those at Dragomirna – but, during that brief period, the Moldavian artists who worked on them created a highly distinctive art form that has had an effect on the style and subject-matter of much subsequent Romanian art, not least the painting of icons on glass. The Moldavian painted churches have no exact parallel elsewhere and, with the sculptures of Brâncuşi, they constitute Romania's most important and original contribution to the European heritage in the visual arts.

The Brâncoveanu Style: Art and Architecture in Romania in the Seventeenth Century

by Sherban Cantacuzino

There are two great periods in the history of the Romanian people, both of which, not unusually, coincided with a flowering of the arts. The first of these periods, which is covered above, is the reign in Moldavia of Ştefan the Great and of his illegitimate son, Petru Rareş, roughly one hundred years after the Fall of Constantinople in 1453. The second period, the subject of this chapter, witnessed the ascendancy in Wallachia of the Cantacuzino and Brâncoveanu families from the beginning of the seventeenth century to 1714 when, on orders of the sultan, Constantin Brâncoveanu (r. 1688-1714) was deposed, and he and his four sons were taken to Constantinople and beheaded. Two years later Brâncoveanu's successor, Ştefan Cantacuzino and his 77-year-old father, the high steward (*stolnic*) Constantin, took the same road, only to be imprisoned and strangled, while Constantin's brother, Mihai, founder of the Sinaia Monastery and Colţea Hospital in Bucharest, and commander-in-chief of the army (*mare spătar*), was beheaded in Constantinople.

Constantin Brâncoveanu and his four sons

Not that there is anything final in these dates as far as art and architecture were concerned. The art and architecture which reached maturity during these two high periods continued in Moldavia under Alexandru Lapuşneanu (1552-61 and 1564-68), the Movilâs (1600-11) and Vasile Lupu (1634-53) into the middle of the seventeenth century: and in Wallachia as the Brâncoveanu style (*stil brâncovenesc*) throughout the hundred years of Phanariot rule, until the arrival of imported eclectic styles in the nineteenth century.

Constantin Brâncoveanu's reign in Wallachia marks the climax to a century of cultural renaissance following Mihai the Brave's military and political achievements (1593-1601), which for a brief moment brought the three principalities under one

117

rule and first aroused a latent nationalism in the Romanian people. It is in the light of these achievements that the campaigns in Transylvania of Mihai the Brave's successor in Wallachia, Radu Şerban (1602-10), the attempt by Gabriel Bethlen (1613-29) in Transylvania to proclaim himself king of Dacia by uniting all three principalities, the repeated efforts of Vasile Lupu in Moldavia to annex Wallachia, and the courageous anti-Ottoman rebellion in 1659 of the Wallachian reigning prince, Radu Mihnea III, can be better understood. The seventeenth century prepared the ground for the future union by developing a national consciousness and by establishing a cultural and artistic base common to all three nationalities.

Before examining these trends it would be as well to make some general observations about the nature of the Romanians. National traits are determined by race, climate and topography. Frequent raids and invasions have made Romanians tough, brave and resilient. Political instability, the uncertainty of what the future holds, has made them intensely resourceful and practical, but also wily and corruptible. Romanians are neither mystical nor dreamers by nature. Hence Romanian art does not suffer from an excess of fantasy, but is firmly rooted in rationalism and based on observation. Architecture is generally a response to practical needs and is hardly ever extravagant; decoration, with the one exception of the painted churches, is rarely done to excess.

The topography of Romania is dominated by the Carpathian Mountains, the crests of which are ever in view from all three principalities. The Carpathians have played an important part in the ability of the Romanian people to retain their independence and to sustain that love of freedom and sense of pride which are innate characteristics. Wallachia and Moldavia were never formally made pashaliks of the Ottoman Empire, unlike Serbia or Bulgaria and, for more than 150 years, the greater part of Hungary. Wallachians and Moldavians were vassals of the Turks, never their subjects. Villagers would take refuge in the heavily wooded mountains and only return when the danger had passed, to find their village devastated and in need of reconstruction. Hence the Romanian saying: 'the tree is man's friend'. Hence perhaps also the fact that there are in Romanian as many as three different words for tree: *arbore, copac* and *pom*.

Until the middle of the twentieth century Romania was predominantly a peasant society and, like all peasant societies, traditionalist and conservative by nature. Romanians hold on to their traditions, not like the English, because these traditions are enshrined in antiquity, but because they provide a stable factor in an extremely unstable world. One would therefore not expect to find innovation in Romanian art, and the work of Brâncuşi in the twentieth century must be regarded as an exception, just as that of Henry Moore is an exception for England, which had never before produced a sculptor of significance, let alone greatness.

The Romanians are also a religious, God-fearing and superstitious people. All their religious zeal, their more primitive superstitions and fatalistic streak, and their

Monastery church, Cozia

political aspirations are expressed, given the total proscription by the Orthodox Church of three-dimensional representational art – in other words sculpture – in the great mural paintings of Moldavian and Wallachian churches. At the same time they are a Latin race – an island surrounded by a sea of Slavs and Magyars. This latinity explains why, in the declining years of Byzantium – for which we must of course read Eastern Empire and Second Rome – Romanians embraced the Orthodox Church and the Byzantine style in art and architecture, making it into something of their own over the next 500 years. The continental climate of cold, dry winters and hot summers, with plenty of sun and light of a Mediterranean quality, must have reinforced this sense of belonging to the heart of the antique world.

It is hardly surprising, therefore, that in the first half of the seventeenth century the humanism of the Italian Renaissance should have reached the three Romanian principalities by diverse routes. The history of the ancients became the model for writing contemporary chronicles, and there were printing presses at Govora, Târgoviște, Bucharest, Iași and Alba Iulia which made their dissemination possible.

119

The first such example in Romania was a history of Mihai the Brave's exploits, *The Chronicle of the Buzescu Family* (1602-10), so-called because of the important part played by that family at the time. Similarly, at the court of Matei Basarab in Wallachia (1632-54), at which the lord chamberlain (*postelnic*) was Constantin

Matei Basarah

Cantacuzino, son of Mihai the Brave's intimate counsellor, Andronic, and the first member of this Constantinopolitan family to settle in Wallachia, a history of the principality from its beginnings in the fourteenth century was compiled and later continued to the end of the seventeenth century, extolling the part played by the Cantacuzinos during these later years and called *The Chronicle of the Cantacuzino Family*.

The boyar Udrişte Nasturel, whose wife was the sister of Matei Basarab, in the foreword to his translation into Slavonic of the *Imitatio Cristi* (1647), examined the relationship between Romanian and Latin. At about the same time he built himself on the banks of the River Argeş at Herăşti, some 40 kilometres south of Bucharest, a manor house in late Renaissance style, constructed entirely of dressed stone and L-shaped in plan, consisting of two apartments, each with its entrance and staircases leading to the first floor and cellar.

Nicolae Milescu was a Moldavian boyar and commander-in-chief of the army (*mare spătar*), but he was also a mathematician, who wrote the *Aritmologion* (the first book on mathematics by a Romanian), and the translator into Romanian of the Old Testament. Between 1675 and 1678 he travelled to China as the envoy of the tsar of Russia and later wrote two books, *Journey through Siberia* and *Description of China*, which were published in Paris and which brought him European fame. Radu Greceanu, chancellor (*logofăt*) of Wallachia, who in 1714 wrote the chronicle of Constantin Brâncoveanu's reign, was responsible, with his brother Şerban, for incorporating Milescu's translation of the Old Testament into the first Romanian Bible, published in Bucharest in 1688 under the auspices of the reigning prince, Şerban Cantacuzino. His brother Constantin, *stolnic* of Wallachia and man of letters, who had studied in Padua, published the first map of Wallachia in 1700 in Venice and wrote the first history of all the Romanians, of which only fragments survive.

In 1643 at Iaşi in Moldavia, the Metropolitan Varlaam wrote and published his sermons in a language that rose above regional differences so that it could be understood by Romanians everywhere: and two years later the same metropolitan printed his response to the Calvinist catechism, in the foreword of which he asserted the

*Iaşi: south apse of
the Church of the
Three Hierarchs*

national unity of Romanians in Moldavia, Wallachia and Transylvania. It took
another thirty years for one of his successors, the Metropolitan Dosoftei, to introduce the Romanian language into the Church, replacing Slavonic, and in 1679
Dosoftei consolidated this achievement by explaining why it had been necessary to
do this in a foreword to his translation of the Missal from the Greek. The first great
chronicler of Romanian history, who also asserted the Latin origins of the
Romanian people, Grigore Ureche, was a Moldavian. At his death in 1647 he had
drawn up the *Chronicles of Moldavia* from its origins to 1595. They were continued
in 1675 by Miron Costin, *logofăt* of Moldavia, who also wrote *Concerning the*

People of Moldavia, whence came their Forebears, a brief work on the Latin origin of the Romanians and on the glory of their ancestors.

The first Moldavian philosophical work, printed in Iaşi in 1698, *The Wise Man's Counsel or Quarrel with the World, or the Trial of Soul and Body*, was written by Dimitrie Cantemir, a scholar and man of letters who had briefly reigned in Moldavia in 1693 and was to reign there again in 1710-11. Cantemir also wrote a treatise on Turkish music, the *Descriptio Moldaviae* and, audaciously in Constantinople where he spent many years, the *Hieroglyphic History*, an allegory of Romanian political life and of its connections with the political realities of the Ottoman Empire, in which the personalities of the times were disguised as birds and animals. Following his defeat by the Turks in 1711 at the Battle of Stălineşti-Fălciu on the River Prut, Cantemir took refuge in Russia, where he became an intimate counsellor of Peter the Great and where he was able to indulge his intellectual pursuits. He was elected a member of the illustrious Berlin Academy in 1714 and died in 1723.

The first Romanian chronicle in Transylvania was written by the Archimandrite Vasile of Schei (the Romanian quarter of Braşov) between 1629 and 1633. It included an historical account of the Romanians in Braşov and their relations with Wallachia. The outstanding chronicler of Transylvania, however, was Johannes Bethlen (1613-78), who wrote *Rerum Transylvanicarum libri quatuor* (1629-67) and *Historia rerum Transylvanicorum* (1662-73). The metropolitan of Alba Iulia, Simion Ştefan, under whose aegis the first complete translation of the New Testament was published in 1648, in his admirable *Preface* emphasized the importance of using a literary language which could be understood by all Romanians. The first codes of law appeared in print in the three principalities within a few years of one another, in Moldavia in 1646, in Wallachia in 1652 and in Transylvania in 1653, as the *Compillatae Constitutiones*, a great collection of laws, the publication of which was not complete until 1669.

The first Romanian philosophical work in Transylvania, which preceded Cantemir's in Moldavia by nearly half a century, was the *Logics* of Gavril Ivul, published in 1654 and followed closely by *Philosophia* (1655) and *Philosophia Novella* (1661) by the same author. In 1666 Johann Tröster published in Nuremberg *Das Alte and Neue Teutsche Dacia*, in which he examines the origins, language and customs of Transylvania's inhabitants and explains the Latin origin of the large number of Romanians living there. The following year in Lyons appeared the *Origines et ocassus Transylvanorum* by Laurentius Toppeltinus of Mediaş, which included a history of Transylvania up to 1622 and which was used by Miron Costin and Constantin Cantacuzino to prove the Latin origin of the Romanians. In 1686, however, three years after the siege of Vienna, at which the Turks were decisively repulsed, Transylvania by the Treaty of Vienna accepted the protection of the Habsburg Empire: and in 1691, by the Leopoldine Diploma, the principality was subordinated to the Emperor, who confirmed the rights of the three privileged 'nations' (Hungarians, Saxons and Szeklers, excluding Romanians), recognized the old legislation and obliged the inhabitants to pay heavy yearly tribute. In 1692 the Emperor Leopold took the first steps to establishing the Uniate or Graeco-Catholic Church by extending the rights given to the Roman Catholic clergy to those of the Romanian Orthodox clergy who would accept union with Rome.

'Roumania', Sacheverell Sitwell states in his *Roumanian Journey*, 'has . . . no buildings upon the heroic scale. All its architecture is sensible and small.' In the Middle Ages in the Romanian principalities there were basically two kinds of building activity. There was the peasant who built and rebuilt his own house and village church; and there was the reigning prince, or sometimes one of his boyars, who ordered the construction of fortifications and founded churches and monasteries which were then built and decorated through the agency of the corporations and guilds. There was practically no civic architecture until the nineteenth century, and of the manor houses built by the boyars very few remain. Monasteries were invariably fortified, providing the local peasant population with a place of refuge from raids and incursions. Monasteries, therefore, represented not only religious architecture, but also military architecture and, given the community of monks that lived there, domestic architecture as well. In the course of the seventeenth century the influence of the Italian Renaissance on art and architecture, as on science and literature, increasingly made itself felt, whether directly or via France, Austria or Russia. At the same time former characteristics specific to one principality began to cross borders, and the different styles tended to merge in an attempt to produce a synthesis and a single Romanian style.

In Transylvania Gábor Bethlen (1613-29) introduced the Renaissance by inviting Italian architects to design a new type of fortification with bastions. The citadel of Oradea was entrusted to Giacomo Resti of Verona, while Iernut Castle in the *judeţ* (administrative district) of Mureş was designed by Agostino Serena of Venice on a rectangular plan enclosing a courtyard, with all but detached and diagonally pointed corner bastions, which, like the main body of the castle, have classical cornices supporting hipped roofs, giving the whole a charming domestic air. Of similar spirit and date (1615-24) is the Castle of Balta in the *judeţ* of Alba, an outward-looking rectangular block with bulky circular corner towers and steeply pitched roofs reminiscent of the main keep at Chambord, the plans of which are also attributed to an Italian architect. It was on Gábor Bethlen's initiative that a new citadel on this same pattern was built at Alba Iulia (rebuilt 1715-35 by Giovanni Visconti on Vauban principles) and that the Castle of Făgăraş was remodelled into a powerful fortress encircled by ramparts and bastions, and by a deep moat, which could be flooded when required with water brought from the River Olt by a canal specifically built for the purpose. The Renaissance is felt in the two-tier arcaded loggia of the inner court, a feature which is brought to the outer face of the building fifty years later in

the Bethlen castle at Sânmiclauş (1668-73), designed with axial symmetry and perfect regularity by its owner, Nicolas Bethlen, who had had occasion on his visits
abroad to study Italian influence on French castles.

Fundamental in the construction of a church where the interior spaces are relatively large is the way these spaces are spanned and roofed. In Byzantine churches
the vaults are carried by massive internal piers or columns. In Gothic churches they
are carried by internal piers or columns and external buttresses. The rational and
practical side of the Romanian character demanded that the interior of the church be
kept free of columns and projections so that people could circulate more easily and
walls could have uninterrupted surfaces for the painting that formed such an essential part of the decoration. The most common type of church plan, of Byzantine
origin but brought to Wallachia and Moldavia via Serbia, was the combination of a
rectangular narthex (*pronaos*) with a trefoiled nave (*naos*). Externally, there was no
articulation of the parts: the side walls were straight and continuous until they
broke out into the semi-circles of the trefoil. A tower rose invariably over the *naos*
and, from the sixteenth century onwards, a second smaller tower over the narthex
sometimes made its appearance. Such a plan had the advantage of being flexible in so
far as it was easy to expand lengthwise by the addition of extra bays to make the
narthex or *naos* larger, or of extra compartments, such as entrance porches or the
burial chambers (*gropniţa*) in Moldavian monastery churches. The prototype is the
Monastery Church of Cozia, built in the last quarter of the fourteenth century and
consisting of a barrel-vaulted narthex of rectangular plan, and a trefoiled *naos*
divided into three bays, the central bay carrying a cylindrical tower, and the bays on
either side barrel vaults and the three apses of the trefoil half-domes.

Examples in Moldavia, where the type was most common, include the painted
churches of Voroneţ (1488), Humor (1530), which have an internal dome instead of
a tower, Moldoviţa (1532) (see p. 97ff) and, in the eighteenth century, the Church of
St Theodore at Iaşi with its narthex opened up to the *naos* and its entrance porch
carrying a west tower. Examples of the expanded form are the monastery churches
of Neamţ (1497), Suceviţa (1582-84), Probota (1530), Slatina (1554) and Galata, Iaşi
(1583): and in the seventeenth century Vasile Lupu's great foundation at Iaşi, the
Church of the Three Hierarchs (Trei Ierhari) (1636-39), which was largely reconstructed between 1882 and 1904 by the French architect, A. Lecomte du Noüy.

Examples in Wallachia include the late fourteenth-century church of Brădet in the
judeţ of Argeş; the mid-sixteenth-century Church of the Old Court (Curtea Veche)
in Bucharest, in which the fine mouldings of the stone plinth and cornice, as well as
other details recalling Moldavian churches, may be attributed to the wife of the
reigning prince and founder of the church, Mircea the Shepherd, who was the
daughter of Moldavia's reigning prince, Petru Rareş. Other examples in Wallachia
include the Monastery Church of Mihai Vodă (1591) and the Stavropoleos Church
after its enlargement in 1730, both in Bucharest (see pp. 190, 196); and the

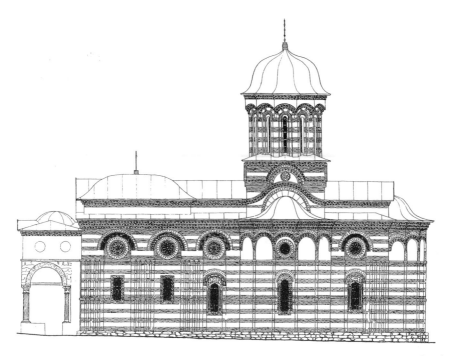

Cozia: Monastery Church

monastery churches in Oltenia of Căluiu (1588) and Polovragi, the latter a reconstruction of an older church dating from the reign of Matei Basarab, which was
completed and embellished by Constantin Brâncoveanu in 1703.

Examples in Transylvania are few because the rural, impoverished and largely
enserfed Romanian Orthodox population built either wooden churches, few of
which earlier than the eighteenth century have survived, or the simple type of
monastery church with a rectangular plan extended at the east end with an apse.
Examples of masonry churches with trefoil plans include the sixteenth-century
Orthodox Church at Vad in the *judeţ* of Cluj, though the apse of the choir is pentagonal rather than semi-circular, and the vaulting of the narthex and *naos* Gothic;
and St Nicholas Schei at Braşov, where the early eighteenth-century trefoiled *naos*
survived the alterations made between 1733 and 1750, which greatly extended the
church westwards, adding a west tower and side chapels on the north and south
sides.

A second type of church plan, purely Byzantine and exclusive to Wallachia, was
the inscribed Greek cross: four barrel-vaulted bays and four heavy piers around a
central space, over which rose a cylindrical or polygonal tower. To this was added

125

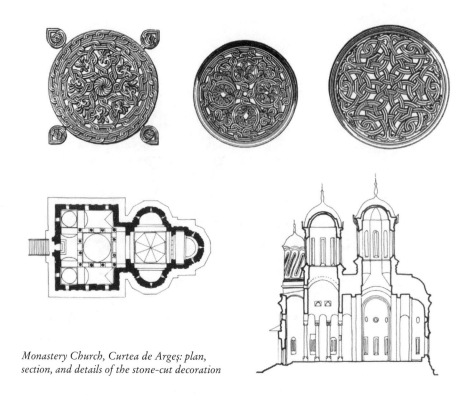

Monastery Church, Curtea de Argeş: plan,
section, and details of the stone-cut decoration

an apsidal choir and an entrance porch. The earliest example is the Princely Church at Curtea de Argeş, built around the middle of the fourteenth century by Greek masons brought over from the Constantinople region by the first ruler of Wallachia, Basarab I (c. 1310-52) . We find the same plan type again during the reign of Neagoe Basarab (1512-21) in the Monastery Church of Snagov north of Bucharest and in the old Metropolitan Church at Târgovişte, but it was not popular in its pure form, only in combination with a trefoiled *naos* and only in Wallachia.

The enlargement and elaboration of the narthex, a precondition of this combination, was first seen in the Church at Dealu (1500) near Târgovişte, built by Radu the Great (1495-1508) within an existing monastery. The narthex is still the same width as the trefoiled *naos* but is given two bays, the second bay nearest the *naos* supporting two corner towers, which defer in height to the graceful main tower over the *naos*. More remarkable for such an early date is the external treatment of the walls, made entirely of fine dressed stone and divided by an elegantly moulded string course into two tiers of classically proportioned blind arcading, which rises from a plinth and is topped by a bold cornice. This is no longer Byzantine, but it is too early to show Renaissance influence. The exclusive use of stone and the decorative stonework on the west front and window surrounds of the towers may be due to Armenian masons belonging to one of the emigrant colonies established in Moldavia since the fourteenth century, who are believed to have been responsible for the decorative stonework at, among other monuments, the Monastery Church of Curtea de Argeş (begun 1512), on the tower of the Monastery Church at Dragomirna (1602) and at the Church of the Three Hierarchs at Iaşi.

The enlargement and elaboration of the narthex at Dealu occurred, as we have seen, within the traditional rectangular and trefoiled plan. However, a few years later at the Monastery Church of Curtea de Argeş, because the founder and reigning prince, Neagoe Basarab, wanted the building to serve as a family mausoleum as well as a church, the narthex was greatly enlarged and made much wider than the *naos*, so that externally the two parts, rectangular narthex and trefoiled *naos*, were now strongly articulated. The narthex itself consisted of two unequal central bays, the entrance bay, which was barrel-vaulted, and the larger bay on the *naos* side, which was defined by twelve columns supporting a tower that was a little shorter than the main tower over the *naos*. The corner bays flanking the entrance bay carried smaller towers, making a total of four towers, which was only equalled by the contemporary Monastery Church of Snagov and, 150 years later, by the Patriarchal Church in Bucharest (1655). The plan adopted at Curtea de Argeş became the model, albeit with a reduction in the number of towers to three or two, for the church of the former Monastery of the Trinity in Bucharest (*c.*1570), known today as the Radu Vodă Church; for the Church of St Nicholas (1571-1572) formerly of the Cobia Monastery in the *judeţ* of Dambovita; for the monastery churches of Cotroceni in Bucharest (1679, destroyed 1984), Hurez (1690-93) in the *judeţ* of Vâlcea, Antim in Bucharest (1715) and Văcăreşti, south of Bucharest (1716-22, destroyed 1985); and for the Fundenii Doamnei Church (1699) and Creţulescu Church (1720-1722) in Bucharest.

Nothing has been said so far, and not a great deal need be said, about a third type of church plan, the simplest and most common, consisting of an external rectangle containing both narthex and *naos*, with a choir in the form of a single semi-circular or polygonal apse. From the seventeenth century onwards there was sometimes a tower over the narthex, but this type of church was mostly without a tower or belfry, especially when it was a modest village church or a chapel. The prototype can be said to have been the Church of St Nicholas at Rădăuţi (*c.*1360), the oldest surviving masonry church in Moldavia, which Stefan the Great made into a mausoleum for the first Moldavian princes. It is essentially a Romanesque basilica with barrel-vaulted nave and aisles, adapted to the Orthodox rite by the lateral subdivision into narthex, *naos* and choir. Among the more important examples of this type of plan in Moldavia are the churches at Piatra Neamţ (1497-98) and Arbore (1502) with their crypto-trefoiled plans (the side apses are scooped out of a very thick straight wall) and internal domes over the *naos* substituting for a tower, the belfry of the Church of St John the Baptist, Piatra Neamţ being in the form of a free-standing tower, and at Arbore a monumental recess of the west front, with the bell suspended from the overhanging roof and a stone seat for funerals and feast days, the feature as a whole anticipating the open porch, which appears some thirty years later and which came from Serbia via Wallachia. In the seventeenth century the type became popular in Wallachia, but with the addition of a belfry over the narthex, which is reached either by a straight staircase contained in the thickness of the wall, as at Goleşti in the *judeţ* of Argeş, where the belfry has disappeared, and at the Princess's Church (Biserica Doamnei) in Bucharest (1683), or by a spiral stair contained in a turret, as at Matei Basarab's foundation, the Oltenian Monastery Church of Strehaia (1645), with its imposing belfry or west tower, and at the Church of St Nicholas in Făgăraş, a Brâncoveanu foundation and a weak imitation of the Strehaia Church.

The plain types which have been considered are a response to practical needs. The porch is a protection against the sun and the rain; the narthex houses the women; the burial chamber is for the tombs and treasure of the church. The nave is for the men and for the offices; and the sanctuary is for the use of the priest only, and is screened from the nave by the iconostasis. Each space is for a specific use and is divided by a wall with only a small opening in it, though from the late sixteenth century onwards a tendency to open up one space to another made itself felt.

If we look at a typical plan and section of a Moldavian church such as Voroneţ, we find a rectangular narthex and a trefoiled *naos* of the same width as the *pronaos*. In French Romanesque architecture such a space would be uninterrupted by lateral subdivisions and would be covered with a barrel vault. In Gothic architecture it would be spanned by a quadripartite or sexpartite vault, as indeed are many of the medieval Saxon churches of Transylvania. The Byzantine tradition, however, required lateral subdivisions and the resulting rectangular spaces to be covered by arches and domes. But domes do not sit easily over rectangular plans, so a way had to be found of reducing the rectangle to a square. Looking at the nave of Voroneţ, we see that this is done by throwing very wide arches laterally across the nave and only very narrow arches longitudinally. The result is a square which is still too large to form the circular drum of a tower. So an intermediate circle is formed, over which a further set of diagonal arches are thrown to reduce the opening to a size which can comfortably carry the tower above it, the total reduction being exactly half the width of the nave.

Sometimes, as in the narthex of the church at Arbore, a single dome is supported on four pairs of arches, each pair being tiered. A variation of the same principle, which produces a more decorative effect, is when the four initial arches that reduce

Dintr'un Lemn: porch of the Monastery Church

the rectangular plan to a square, carry a series of interlaced arches, which in turn provide a base either for a dome or for an octagonal or circular tower. An early example with a dome is the Church of St George at Hârlău (1492), while a fully developed version with dome and tower is to be found in the Monastery Church of Dragomirna.

Another system is illustrated by the narthex at the monastery churches of Suceviţa and Slatina, where the rectangular plan is divided into two bays by a transverse arch. Wide longitudinal arches, which take their support from the cross-wall at one end and the transverse arch at the other, reduce each bay to a square so that it can be covered with a dome.

In Wallachia vaulting remained essentially Byzantine. Domes and towers, whether over the rectangular narthex or trefoiled *naos*, were supported on arches, the transition from square to circular being made by means of pendentives or squinches. The inscribed Greek cross plan consisted of nine bays, four of which were barrel-vaulted and supported, with the help of four piers, the dome or tower over the central bay. The four square corner bays were domed. The inscribed Greek cross plan, as we have seen, survived in the nave of the Metropolitan Church of Târgovişte and of the Monastery Church of Snagov. It also survived in the narthex of the much later Monastery Church of Văcăreşti. In the enlargement and elaboration of the narthex, however, the number of bays was reduced to six, and what had been the central domed bay in the inscribed Greek cross plan, giving this part of the church centrality and separateness, was pushed off-centre towards the nave, creating unity out of two disparate parts.

The principle of the roof treatment over these different forms of vaulting, however, is the same in both Wallachia and Moldavia: to express and articulate each vaulted or domed bay as in a Byzantine church. This is manifestly clear in the more Byzantine of the Wallachian churches, which have inscribed Greek cross or combined inscribed Greek cross and trefoiled plans. The Church of Curtea Veche in Bucharest, for example, has separate roof forms, which follow the lines of the vaults beneath for the narthex, for each of the side apses of the *naos*, for the apsidal choir and even for the *diaconicon* (for vestments and books) and the *prothesis* (for the eucharistic elements), two very small rooms appended to the sides of the choir. The tower over the nave consists of two distinct parts, each with its own roof: the square base and the cylindrical drum of the actual tower.

In Moldavia the climate demanded steep roofs, which are more inclined to conceal the form of the vaulting beneath, as is evident in churches without towers such as St Nicholas at Rădăuţi or St John the Baptist at Piatra Neamţ. In the case of churches with towers nineteenth-century restorations rode roughshod over the evidence provided by the votive paintings inside the churches. Usually situated in the narthex, these show the founder and patron holding the church in his hands as an offering to God. In nineteenth- and even twentieth-century restorations the roofs were made

*Suceava: Chapel of St
John the Baptist*

with a continuous ridge, engulfing the base of the tower and ironing out as much as possible the difference between the roof forms. The votive painting at Voroneṭ, for example, shows the church with separate roofs over the narthex (the porch is a later addition), over each of the three apses of the trefoiled nave and over the tower. More recent restorations have sought a return to the original articulated roof-forms, completely altering the appearance and proportions of these churches by breaking up a single roof into a number of separate roofs and by exposing the base of the towers, which consequently appear taller. An example is Vasile Lupu's delightful little court Chapel of St John the Baptist (1643) at Suceava, where the tower rises from a two-tiered base consisting of an eight-pointed star sitting on a square block with blind arcading. The absence of side apses means that there are separate roofs only over the narthex and choir.

The seventeenth century, as we have already noted, witnessed the development of a national conscience and the establishment of a cultural and artistic base common to the three principalities. Already in the reign of Petru the Lame (Schiopul) (1574-79 and 1582-91), one of several reigning princes of Moldavia who were of Wallachian origin and who kept close links with the neighbouring principality, there is the example of the Monastery Church of Galata at Iaşi (1583), which, though Moldavian in its plan and general appearance, has some specifically

Wallachian features, such as the opening-up of the tomb chamber to the nave and the system of arches in the narthex derived from the Monastery Church at Curtea de Argeş. Externally, the decoration of the wall, with blind arcading of narrow, slender proportions, which diminishes in height as it rises, is divided horizontally by a string course, recalling the division into two of the wall decoration at the Monastery Church of Dealu near Târgovişte.

The Church of St Nicholas in the village of Aroneanu near Iaşi, part of a monastery which has disappeared, built in 1594 by the reigning voivode, Aaron the Tyrant (1591-95), incorporates both principles of construction and decorative features derived in equal measure from Moldavian and Wallachian practice. It is the reverse of Galata: its plan, with an open entrance porch and square, domed narthex opened up with a triple arch to the trefoiled nave, is thoroughly Wallachian, while the system of arches supporting the tower over the nave remains Moldavian. The treatment of the external stuccoed wall, a combination of coloured ceramic tiles and incised patterns in broad horizontal bands, is interesting for the way it incorporates elements of popular art and at the same time anticipates the stone-carved floral and geometric patterns of Armenian origin which cover the walls of the Church of the Three Hierarchs at Iaşi.

The third church which, together with the monastery churches of Galata and Aroneanu, points to the future and to what was to become the national characteristic of seventeenth-century architecture, is the beautifully sited Monastery Church of Dragomirna. Founded in 1602 by the Metropolitan Anastasie Crimca, it was given strong defensive walls in 1629 by the reigning prince, Miron Barnovski-Movilă. The church is unique for its elongated plan and extreme height, resulting in interior spaces of vertiginous proportions. The apse of the choir at the east end of the church has its equivalent form in an apsidal entrance porch at the west end, reminiscent of certain Wallachian churches. Also Wallachian is the horizontal division of the façades by a string course carved with an over-scaled twisted cord motif – Armenian influence again, no doubt – to be found also inside the church on the pilasters and arches of the narthex and nave, and used later at the Stelea Church in Târgovişte (1645), and in a more elegant version at various monuments of the Brâncoveanu period. The octagonal tower sits on a three-tiered base consisting of a square block and two fourteen-pointed stars. Tower and base are faced with elaborately carved stonework of oriental, possibly Islamic influence, for which Armenian masons may have been responsible. Inside the narthex and nave the system of arches and domes – pendentives and plenty of interlacing – is Byzantine, but the dense rib vaulting of the entrance porch is late Gothic from Transylvania.

The appearance towards the end of the sixteenth century of reigning princes in Moldavia who were of Wallachian origin has already been noted. In the seventeenth century it was not unusual for the same reigning prince to move from one principality to the other. The Wallachian Radu Mihnea reigned in Wallachia from 1601 to

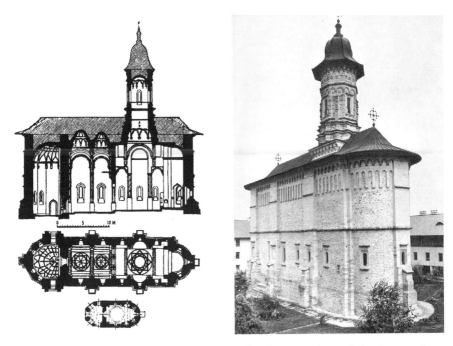

Dragomirna, Monastery Church: section, plan, and view from southeast

1602 and again from 1611 to 1616. He then reigned in Moldavia for three years (1616-19) before becoming prince of Wallachia for a third time (1620-23) and, finally, again of Moldavia (1623-26). The Moldavian Gheorghe Ghica was briefly reigning prince of Moldavia from 1658 to 1659, and of Wallachia from 1659 to 1660; and the Moldavian Gheorghe Duca reigned twice in Moldavia (1665-66 and 1668-72), then in Wallachia (1673-78) and, finally, again in Moldavia (1678-83). Before being appointed by the Porte in 1716, the first Phanariot reigning prince of Wallachia, Nicolae Mavrocordat, had twice been reigning prince of Moldavia (1709-10 and 1711-15). In Phanariot times the alternation sometimes reached ludicrous proportions. Constantin Mavrocordat, for instance, had no fewer than six short reigns in Wallachia and four in Moldavia.

Such alternation, however, did not happen when there were strong men at the helm, and, in the second quarter of the seventeenth century, both Wallachia and Moldavia were fortunate in having at about the same time reigning princes of exceptional ability. Matei Basarab in Wallachia (1632-54) and Vasile Lupu in Moldavia (1634-53). It was during these two reigns that the first generation of Cantacuzinos took wing. Sons of Mihai the Brave's counsellor, Andronic, they had arrived in

Iaşi, Church of the Three Hierarchs: section, plan, and view from southeast

Wallachia and Moldavia from Constantinople via Crete during one of the reigns of Radu Mihnea, whose policy had been to encourage the immigration of Greeks to the principalities. In Wallachia Constantin Cantacuzino, who had married the daughter of the former reigning prince of Wallachia, Radu Şerban (1602-19) of the Basarab family, became *postelnic* and intimate counsellor of Matei Basarab. In Moldavia Iordache Cantacuzino, whose influence with the Porte helped Vasile Lupu to bcome reigning prince of Moldavia, was married to the sister of Vasile's wife and became Vasile's trusted treasurer (*vistiernic*).

Vasile Lupu's ambitious and imperious nature, however, made him Matei Basarab's lifelong rival. He saw himself as a second Mihai the Brave, destined to unite the principalities as the successor to the Byzantine Empire. In the early years of his reign he invaded Wallachia twice, the first time to install his son as reigning prince and the second, after obtaining a sentence of banishment from the Porte for Matei Basarab, to seize the throne himself. In 1645 a truce was established, and Vasile Lupu, in token of his reconciliation with Matei Basarab, raised the Stelea Church at Târgovişte in a thoroughly Moldavian style, but with the typically Wallachian horizontal subdivision of its façades by a string course. The truce lasted nearly eight years, but in 1653, the year of his deposition, Vasile Lupu again attacked Matei Basarab's army and was again defeated.

During his relatively long reign Vasile Lupu endeavoured to revive some of the splendours of the imperial Byzantine court and promoted cultural and artistic activity. He introduced the printing press and commissioned printed books, illuminated manuscripts, icons and much sumptuous embroidery and silver for his many religious foundations. In addition to the Church of the Three Hierarchs at Iaşi, the Stelea Church at Târgovişte in Wallachia and the court Chapel of St John the Baptist at Suceava, he founded many other churches. Among these St John the Baptist and the Vovidenia Church at Iaşi, St Paraschiva, Stefăneşti, SS Voievozi, Scânteia, and the Church of the Blessed Virgin, Galaţi, built by the merchants of that huge river port that lies at the entrance to the Danube Delta, have massive west towers over the entrance porch, like Matei Basarab's foundation in Oltenia, the Monastery Church of Strehaia. Like Strehaia, St John the Baptist and the Church of the Blessed Virgin were conceived in the manner of the fortified Saxon churches of Transylvania, with a *chemin de ronde* above the vaulting.

If the construction of the Church of the Three Hierarchs is a notable achievement of the first years of Vasile Lupu's reign, that of the monastery church of Golia marks a fitting close. Named after its first founder, Ioan Golia, a Moldavian boyar who built a small church on the site around 1560, Golia was rebuilt between 1650 and 1653 as a large monastery church with an elongated rectangular plan consisting

Golia, Monastery Church

135

Târgovişte: Stelea Church

of entrance porch, narthex, burial chamber, nave and apsidal choir, the narthex being opened up to the burial chamber with a triple arch, and the burial chamber to the nave with a single high arch, effectively eliminating the wall. The apses of the nave, and the *prothesis* and *diaconicon* in the choir, are contained within very thick side walls, made necessary by the extreme height of the church and the absence of any cross walls between the tomb chamber and the choir.

What is quite new at Golia is the monumental treatment of the exterior come straight out of Italy. The first view of the church as one enters through the imposing gate tower and belfry is of the long south façade, which consists of pairs of giant Corinthian pilasters rising the full height of the wall and carrying a full-blown Classical entablature: between the pilasters are aedicule-type windows set in monumental blind arches. Above the entablature there are no high-pitched roofs; instead, set back and disposed more or less symmetrically, as if from a flat roof, rise six towers; in the middle a pair of low structures, not really towers at all, concealing the domes over the tomb chamber; on either side, the main towers of almost equal height, over the narthex and nave; and, at each end, square towers, again of roughly equal height, over the entrance porch and choir. Every part is faced with dressed stone and would reveal late Renaissance influence were it not for a fire in 1735 and an earthquake in 1738, which led to a reconstruction of the towers in an inappropriate Russian Rococo style fashionable at the time. Paul of Aleppo, who accompanied Macarie, patriarch of Antioch, on his journey to Moldavia and Wallachia between 1653 and 1658, visited Golia when it was barely finished. In praising the monastery he also remarks that 'nobody in the world has distinguished himself in the art of building churches and monasteries out of carved and hewn stones as Prince Vasile, who called on masters from Poland for the purpose'. It is true that Vasile Lupu fostered links with Ľviv and that he probably summoned masons from there who may have been of Italian origin. An Italian traveller, Cornelio Magni, on the other hand, who was with the Turkish army when it occupied Iași in 1672, in his description of Golia noted that the master builders definitely included Italians who came from Rome itself.

In Wallachia Matei Basarab proved himself to be as great a patron of the arts and founder of churches and monasteries as Vasile Lupu, building at least nine new monasteries and rebuilding another six: all his monasteries were surrounded by massive curtain walls, which was a way of building fortifications without attracting the attention of the Turks, who had forbidden the construction of town walls or citadels. Of the fortified monasteries the first was Arnota (1633-36), where only the church survives from Matei Basarab's time, the monastic ranges having been reconstructed in the neo-Gothic style between 1852 and 1856. The plan of the church consists of a trefoiled nave with an octagonal tower, and a modest rectangular narthex, which nevertheless slightly exceeds the width of the nave, bringing it closer to the second plan type discussed above, combining the inscribed Greek cross with the trefoil and articulating the parts. The fortified monasteries were either built on a rectangular plan, for example Arnota, Brâncoveni (begun 1640) and Dintr'un Lemn (1646) in Oltenia and Căldărușani (1638) near Bucharest, or on an irregular polygon to fit the irregular topography, for example Câmpulung (1635-1636) in the *judeţ* of Argeș, Brebu (1650) in the *judeţ* of Prahova, Plumbuiţa (1647) outside Bucharest, and Gura Motrului (1653) and Strehaia in Oltenia.

The form of the churches was generally derived from the Dealu Church, sometimes with Dealu's three towers, as at Căldărușani and Brebu, but more often with one tower only, as at Arnota (the entrance porch with its tower was added by Brâncoveanu in 1694) and Plumbuiţa. The stucco wall treatment, also of the Dealu type, consisted of a string course dividing the façade horizontally into two unequal parts, each part decorated with mouldings describing rectangular panels or blind arches. This became standard practice in the seventeenth century, continuing throughout the eighteenth and until the second half of the nineteenth century.

The most notable feature of Matei Basarab's fortified monasteries, however, was the robust gate-tower which served also as belfry, and which was decorated not only with panels and blind arches, like the walls of the church, but also with round, coloured ceramic tiles, the most remarkable examples being found at Brâncoveni, Brebu, Strehaia and at the Negru Vodă Monastery in Câmpulung, where the use of coloured ceramic tiles made this ancient Moldavian practice fashionable for a while locally.

Of the monasteries that Matei Basarab rebuilt, none was more important than Govora in Oltenia, where he repaired Radu the Great's church (seventy years later Brâncoveanu built the church we see today), and added on the west side a range of cells and on the east side a workshop for the printing presses, brought from Kiev, which in 1640 printed the first book in Romanian in Wallachia, the Pravilă or Code of Laws of Govora. In reconstructing the abbot's house, he added an extra floor, incorporating an arcaded loggia or belvedere, a feature which was to become the hallmark of the new domestic architecture.

In Transylvania, where Wallachian influence on a rare example of masonry construction had already been made explicit in Mihai the Brave's church at Ocna Sibiului (c.1600), Matei Basarab helped build the Church of St Nicholas at Turnul Roşu (1653), while in the last years of the century Constantin Brâncoveanu renewed the church of the ancient hermitage of Sâmbăta de Sus near Braşov and built St Nicholas Church at Făgăraş, for which the model, as has already been noted, was Matei Basarab's Monastery Church at Strehaia, both churches having rectangular plans with towers over the narthex and spacious, open-sided entrance porches; in the case of Strehaia, these were added by Brâncoveanu.

To understand fully the synthesis in the arts associated with the reign of Constantin Brâncoveanu, which has come to be known as the Brâncoveanu style, it is necessary first to examine briefly the relationship of popular art with high art. Historically the Romanians have been a predominantly peasant agricultural society with a rich popular culture. They have always sought a close relationship with nature, knowing instinctively how to set their buildings in a landscape which is nearly always beautiful and often idyllic. An essential part of this landscape and of this peasant culture has been the age-old well which, with its great variety of forms, constitutes a rich vernacular treasure. To express the notion 'Romania' in a simple diagram, the architect and writer G. M. Cantacuzino (1899-1960) would draw a long horizontal line to denote a field, and a short diagonal to represent a well, in this case the *cumpănă*, a primitive type of well with a long wooden lever arm and a weight at one end to bring up the bucket of water at the other. For him the *cumpănă*, which is still found all over Romania and which predates the wheel, is the first machine and part of the natural landscape, whereas the *puţ*, the more usual type of well with a wheel, which is compact enough to be roofed or wholly enclosed, is the first social structure and part of the built landscape.

If, as is rightly claimed, popular art is at the root of high art, it becomes necessary to understand vernacular building before considering the development of domestic architecture in the latter part of the seventeenth century. Time is unimportant for vernacular building because its survival depends on constant renewal. The peasant's house is made of ephemeral materials found locally, mainly wood, earth and thatch, and is whitewashed every spring, its whiteness softened by the shaded balconies and porches, which are filled with plants and covered with creeper, so that the house disappears into the landscape. Whether it is a low-lying house in the plains or a tall

Măldăreşti: Manor house (Cula Duca)

house in the mountains, its basic parts are the same: plinth, porch and roof, all of which can be developed for larger houses. The plinth, which is usually built of stone, may be quite low, merely to raise the living quarters above the ground or, more commonly, it may be high enough to accommodate storage space. Access to the living quarters is by means of external steps up to a porch or balcony, which can extend the full length of one, two or even three sides of the house. In larger houses, such as the Cartianu House in the village of Cartiu near Târgu Jiu, the ground floor is still used for storage, but there are two floors of living accommodation above, with balconies running continuously around three sides of the house and generous external staircases. The core of the house is built of masonry finished with stucco, and only the roof and surrounding balconies are timber.

Much longer and built entirely of masonry is the Oltenian *cula* (from the Turkish *kule*, meaning 'tower'), Like the Border castle in England, the cula was a fortified house in which a family with its modest retinue and worldly goods, including even its cattle, could resist raiders with guns of limited firing power. Archaeological evidence suggests that the nobility were not in the habit of taking elaborate defensive measures on their estates in the first half of the seventeenth century. But the Turco-Tatar invasions in 1658, which resulted in the enslavement of Romanians of all classes, brought a period of relative stability to a sudden end.Walled enclosures with towers were built again, while the cellars of the more modest houses were raised above ground level to provide a high base on which to seat the living quarters. Such a house survives, at Glogova on the banks of the Motru, and it marks a significant step in the development of the cula.

Two of the earliest culas, both dating from the late seventeenth or early eighteenth century, are in the village of Măldărești. A dozen others survive, among them the culas at Broșteni and Curtișoara, and many more are known to have existed. The type, moreover, is not unique to Oltenia, but is also found on the right bank of the Danube in Serbia and Bulgaria. They were built throughout the eighteenth century and during the first two decades of the nineteenth as a result of the decline of the Ottoman Empire, which produced that familiar sequence of ruthless exploitation, violent uprising and equally violent oppression, a sequence which culminated in a series of Turkish raids (1800-1806) of such horror that they remain to this day part of the local folklore. During this period of anarchy the high nobility of Wallachia tended to leave their large country estates in the hands of tenant farmers and go to live in the towns. It was left to the small landowners to carry on some of the traditions of life in the country; and they were able to do this by building themselves culas.

The typical,white, tower-like form of the cula, often enhanced by its dominating situation and not at all forbidding despite its defensive nature, stands out memorably, whether in the open landscape of the plain with its willows and poplars, or in the wooded foothills with their richer texture of oak, beech, walnut and wild

Mogoșoaia: the Palace

cherry. Culas are roughly square in plan and usually three storeys high, with store rooms on the ground floor and living quarters on the first and second floors. The most distinctive feature is a spacious arcaded verandah at the top which, though useful for observation and signalling, was primarily a concession to a style of life, a place to catch the breeze in summer, to admire the view from, and to rest unobserved by the outside world. The cula walls, which are largely blank in the lower storeys, are dotted about with loopholes. They are built of brick, or a mixture of stone and brick, stuccoed and whitewashed. Windows have often been enlarged or added. The staircase is of oak with one side built into the masonry walls. External decoration is limited to simple mouldings dividing the façade into panels which correspond to the three storeys and sometimes incorporates a bold string course at first-floor level. Although evidence is scant, oral tradition has it that there was often an underground tunnel from the ground floor to the well outside, or even an internal well, as in a Norman keep.

The rough and ready character of the culas relates them back to their peasant roots and gives them their charm. No longer rough and ready, but expertly constructed of thin Roman-type bricks, stuccoed and whitewashed are the manor houses and palaces which Constantin Brâncoveanu built for himself and his large family on his many estates, for example at Potlogi for his elder son Constantin, at Doiceşti for his son Mateiaş and at Mogoşoaia for his son Ştefan. Other examples are the manor houses at Obileşti and Stoeneşti, the palace at Sâmbăta near Făgăraş, the princely residences at Braşov and at the monasteries of Hurez, Brâncoveni and Dintr'un Lemn. All these buildings retain in essence the elements of the peasant house – plinth, porch, balcony and roof – and make wide use of popular art in their decoration.

Domestic architecture, hitherto secondary to religious and military architecture, evolved greatly under Constantin Brâncoveanu and began to compete in importance with religious architecture. This is evident not only in the houses and palaces bult by Brâncoveanu himself, but also in the domestic buildings of monasteries, which grew larger and took a more prominent part in the monastic group. In so far as every well-defined artistic period has its typological building, that of seventeenth-century Wallachia was unquestionably the palace. The growing ambitions of the boyars and their tendency to use the church as a subtle means of propagating a spirit of nationalism with which to fight the Turks contributed to the development of secular architecture and to the corresponding decline in the spiritual role of the Church. Very few of these palaces survive – Stoeneşti, Potlogi, Mogoşoaia – and they were in any case small by western standards. But their most characteristic features – the projecting loggia and the arcaded balcony – were adopted by the monasteries, providing them with a plastic force that the earlier buildings often lacked. Entrance porches to churches also became longer and grander, a striking example being the spacious porch of Brâncoveanu's New Church of St George (Sf. Gheorghe Nou) in Bucharest. In many cases fine new churches were added to older churches, as at the monastery of Cozia, where the porch also protects the painting of the Last Judgement on the west wall, which was added at the same time.

It is in domestic architecture, however, that the porch and balcony came fully into their own, whether in the residential part of a monastery or in the houses and palaces of the time. They are the most insistent and characteristic features of seventeenth-century Wallachian architecture, and it is not surprising to find that there are at least four words denoting them in Romanian – *pridvor, cerdac, prispă, foişor* – and that these do not include words borrowed from other languages such as *balcon, verandă, loggia, belvedere*. Even if the open church porch was introduced from Serbia into Wallachia and then into Moldavia, it is not unreasonable to suppose that the peasant's house has always had an outdoor room covered by the roof to protect it against the sun and rain. It was, after all, a wonderful way of giving a building light and shade, while at the same time creating a space within the structure from which the view could be admired.

It was in the porch and loggia, too, that much of the decoration was concentrated. Colonnades and arcades became more elaborate. The trilobe arch of supposedly Venetian Gothic origin appeared at this time. Stone columns, arches and balustrades became richly carved, the finest examples being found at Potlogi and Mogoşoaia, in

Hurez: detail of the loggia

Dionisie's loggia (1752-53) at Hurez and in the porch of the Stavropoleos Church (1724) in Bucharest. At Mogoşoaia the entrance porch is also domed and the pendentives of the dome are decorated with paintings.

There were essentially four kinds of decorations – stonecarving, woodcarving, plaster ornament and mural painting. The decoration, though florid and sumptuous, was all of a piece, well-disciplined and always subordinate to the architecture. Stone-carving was not only applied to the columns, arches and balustrades of the porches and loggias, but also to the columns of the narthex, of which the two finest examples, at the monastery churches of Cotroceni and Văcăreşti, were destroyed by Ceauşescu; to church portals such as those at Hurez and especially Colţea (1704) in Bucharest, where the Renaissance-inspired design consists of engaged columns supporting a full entablature, which is enlarged disproportionately to contain the carved inscription commemorating the foundation of the church; to window surrounds, of which good examples are at the Monastery Church of Cozia, added at the same time as the porch (1704-07), and at the Chapel of the Patriarchate (1724) in Bucharest; to string courses as at the Creţulescu Church, Bucharest (1722) and, exceptionally, because they are normally of carved wood, to iconostases, as at the Antim Monastery (1715), also in Bucharest.

Some of the finest wood iconostases of the time, such as those from Arnota Monastery and the Metropolitan Church of Târgovişte, are now in museums, where they are out of context but more clearly seen than in the dark, candle-lit churches. Still *in situ* and also very fine are the iconostases at the Stavropoleos Church in Bucharest, and at the monastery churches of Hurez and Govora. Iconostases are monumental structures which screen the choir from the nave. They consist of an elaborately carved and gilded wooden frame in tiers of arches or lunettes containing icons of the great feast days, the apostles and the prophets. The bottom tier contains the imperial doors and large icons, and at the top is a crucifix flanked by icons of the Virgin and St John the Evangelist. Other examples of fine wood-carving are the stalls in the Church of the Princess (Biserica Doamnei) in Bucharest (1683), and the entrance doors to the Church of St Nicholas at Făgăraş and to the monastery churches of Hurez, Arnota, Tismana and Antim.

The plaster decoration is probably oriental in origin. It depicts mainly flowers and birds, and the most remarkable example is the Church of Fundenii Doamnei, with its seventeen stucco relief panels decorating, most unusually, the external walls. Plaster decoration is found more commonly inside houses, and delightful examples exist in the Potlogi Palace and in the Cula Duca at Măldăreşti.

Mural painting was usually reserved for the inside, and only sometimes the outside, of churches, sketes and chapels, and occasionally also for the porches, halls and reception rooms of manor houses and palaces, though very little indeed survives in the few palaces that have come down to us. In the case of churches, mural painting inside the building continued an older tradition in both iconography and style. Externally, however, the subject matter became almost entirely secular and filled with popular themes, as for example on the arches of the entrance porch of the Church at Hurez, on the baldachin which stands in front of this porch, and on the arches of the Church of Fundenii Doamnei. A characteristically Romanian aspect of this painting, both in the seventeenth-century Wallachian revival and in the earlier Moldavian manifestation, is the importance given to the votive painting of the donor or founder in the narthex. The difference in the Wallachian revival is the great expansion of the subject to include the whole Brâncoveanu family, as at Hurez, or a dynasty of Cantacuzinos, as at Sinaia. This, among other things, was a way of making clear who was master both over rival boyars and over rival foreign powers, in particular the Ottoman Empire.

Despite the deep political antagonisms between the Romanian principalities and Constantinople, it is important to remember that the Muslim Turks were far more tolerant of their Christian subjects than were Catholic Austrians of their Orthodox communities, that Constantinople remained an important and much-visited cultural centre ,where east and west met, and that the Greek world as a whole provided an historical link with Byzantium and its glories. But if the ruins of the Eastern Empire continued to educate and inspire, the Romanian boyars, many of whom had grown rich and powerful by the middle of the century, also looked towards western Europe, especially Italy. Constantin Cantacuzino, Matei Basarab's *postelnic*, sent

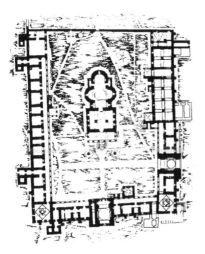

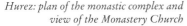

*Hurez: plan of the monastic complex and
view of the Monastery Church*

two of his sons, Constantin and Mihai, to study in Italy, while Brâncoveanu himself chose an Italian, Antonio-Maria del Chiaro, as his private secretary.

At the same time the Cantacuzino family maintained strong links with Constantinople, whence they originated, so that the *stil brâncovenesc*, which is epitomized at Hurez, remains essentially autochthonous but modified as much by a Renaissance feeling for order as by an oriental love of ornament.

Hurez Monastery was built just before the turn of the seventeenth century and is Constantin Brâncoveanu's first major foundation as reigning prince of Wallachia. It lies in the wooded foothills of the southern Carpathians in an area that was well endowed with religious foundations from the earliest times and that could boast two printing presses by the middle of the century. With its surrounding hermitages it ranks today as the largest group of conventual buildings in Romania. Work began in the summer of 1690 under the direction of Pârvu Cantacuzino, first cousin of the reigning prince, who was succeeded on his death the following year by Cernica Stirbey. The church was completed in 1693, its frescoes two years later, and the whole monastery in 1697, when the reigning prince and his court came to celebrate the occasion, occupying the princely residence in the south range. To the east and within the outer precinct, the reigning prince's wife in 1696 built a range of cells (later turned into a hospital and today in ruins), a chapel and a most unusual free-standing belvedere, where it was perhaps intended that the sick monks should convalesce while enjoying the wonderful landscape all around. The hermitages of the Holy Apostles (northeast) and St Stephen (west and on the other side of the river) were built in 1698 and 1703 respectively by the Archimandrite Ioan and consisted of a chapel in a walled precinct with living quarters appended to one side. The Chapel of the Holy Apostles, the most impressive of the outlying buildings, has a full complement of parts like the main monastery church – a porch, narthex and nave. Except for a nineteenth-century wing, which forms an unhappy projection of the south range, two other additions complete the monastery as we see it today. The Archimandrite Ioan converted the space under the chapel in the west range into a vaulted refectory in 1705-06, and in 1752 the Archimandrite Dionisie Bălăcescu added a delightful loggia to the same range. Entry into the inner precinct is through a vaulted space under the belfry in the south range. It is no accident that this tower is off-centre, for the oblique views provide the visitor with an interest that no axial entry ever could. On the right, the church, seen at its best against the mountains, dominates by its mass and height; on the left, the richly carved stone columns of Dionisie's loggia and the slender forms of the chapel rising above the roof provide an important but secondary point of interest; further to the right the princely residence attracts attention by its slightly forward position and its two projecting loggias; and all around the double arcade, seen in almost every degree of perspective, provides a sense of movement and an essential unifying element. In fact the layout is rectangular and roughly symmetrical about an east-west axis, along which lie the church and chapel of the inner precinct, the Princess's Chapel of the outer precinct and, more remotely, St Stephen's Hermitage. A free-standing church surrounded by conventual buildings was quite traditional; what was new, indicating Italian influence, was this geometric discipline, which we will find again at the monasteries of Antim and Văcăreşti, and at the Palace of Potlogi.

The inner precinct comprises the usual monastic repertoire of cells in the north range; kitchen and bakehouse disposed dymmetrically about the axis in the northwest and southwest corners and roofed interestingly with a series of diminishing diagonal arches crowned by an octagonal lantern; refectory, chapel and guest rooms in the west range; and the library, belfry and princely residence with its impressive vaulted cellars and fine staterooms above, now used as a museum of church art, in the south range. A curious feature of the north range is that lines which are normally horizontal, such as ridges, eaves and parapets, here follow the slope of the ground in the manner of terrace-houses in Welsh mining villages. Another feature which distinguishes Hurez from earlier monasteries is the frequent use of loggias which project into the central space and provide direct access to the first-floor gallery. These together with the lofty and outward-looking balcony (really the porch) of the chapel, and the Princess's Belvedere are further evidence of that communion with the outside world which first began in Renaissance Italy and later developed in Baroque palaces and gardens all over Europe.

There is nothing new, however, in the monastery church, and innovation, indeed, is rarely to be found in the churches of the period. The five arches of the porch, which stretch across the full width of the narthex, bear no relation to its interior, which is divided into three domically vaulted compartments. The combination of a broad rectangular narthex with a trefoiled nave continues a tradition established at the Monastery Church of Curtea de Argeş nearly 200 years earlier. It is an attempt to bring together two centrally planned forms – one square, the other apsidal – both surmounted by central towers. The interest lies in the way these two disparate forms are made to integrate both internally and externally. The wide arched opening between the two at Argeş has become a mere doorway at Hurez, while the complex rhythm of the four towers at Argeş, building up from the small western pair to the tallest over the nave, has been reduced at Hurez to the much simpler statement of one tower behind the other, like the divided interior. But if the church at Hurez does not break new ground, its two separate spaces result in a pronounced verticality that makes a powerful and exciting contrast to the insistent horizontal lines of the surrounding buildings.

The building materials, too, were traditional. By the seventeenth century many earlier brick buildings had been rendered over, and rendering, or stucco, with its integral decoration of round mouldings, dog-tooth or twisted-cord patterns and floral bands, had become standard Wallachian practice. The Palace of Mogoşoaia and the manor house at Stoeneşti were originally stuccoed and whitewashed before having their fine brickwork exposed in modern restorations. Door and window surrounds, columns and balustrades were often, as at Hurez, finely carved stone. The iconostases of gilded carved wood in the church and chapel at Hurez, and the carved wood entrance door to the church, are the work of the Wallachian master carpenter Istrate. The master mason, Vucaşin Caragea, was a Serb, and the master painter of the frescoes, Constantinos, a Greek. That these two key figures in the creation of the *stil brâncovenesc* were foreigners is less significant than the fact that, as a result of their work at Hurez, they established national schools, and that Constantinos became a proud Wallach, signing himself Constantinos of Wallachia.

Some of these master craftsmen are represented in the frescoes of the porch, and it is revealing that their portraits are far more realistic in style than those of the donor and his family. There can be no doubt that the hieratical procession of Brâncoveanus and Cantacuzinos in the narthex and portraits of the Emperor Constantine and his wife in the chapel had clear political motives in addition to their artistic qualities. The *stil brâncovenesc*, moreover, especially the decorative aspect, was easily copied and easily debased. This had political advantages too, for the style spread rapidly throughout the principalities and survived a hundred years or more. One way of fighting the Turks was with arms: the other, and in the long run more effective, way, was to consolidate the foundations of a national culture.

Towns of Transylvania and the Banat

by Sebastian Wormell

At the time of their incorporation into Romania at the end of the First World War Transylvania and the Banat had already been integrated into Hungary for fifty years, since the Compromise of 1868. In the nineteenth century the Habsburg government had struggled to cope with the aspirations of the various nationalities, who were no longer satisfied with the old regime. The clash between resurgent Magyar nationalism and the newly militant assertion of Romanian rights brought increasing bitterness.

Transylvania has a special significance for both Romanians and Hungarians. For Hungarians it is where the Magyar spirit was kept alive during Turkish and Habsburg domination. It was the cradle of the Rákóczi uprising of 1703-1711, and where the Revolution of 1848 achieved brilliant but short-lived military success, in which Sándor Petöfi, the greatest Hungarian poet, died fighting for Hungary in the battle of Sighişoara. Transylvania is also where the Romanian national revival began in the eighteenth century. The peasants' revolt in Transylvania in 1784 (see Chapter III) created early martyrs for the cause of Romanian liberation, and here the Romanians found a voice in the Revolution of 1848. For much of Transylvania's history the Romanians had made hardly any impression in the towns; in urban life the Hungarian nobility and the German settlers held sway. It was not until the nineteenth century that a significant urban Romanian population emerged. Although today only a tiny German community remains, and the Hungarians no longer dominate as they did a hundred years ago, the towns of Transylvania still preserve reminders of the past.

Romanians look back to the period when the area around Haţeg in southwest Transylvania was the centre of Dacian and Romano-Dacian power. Archaeological excavations in and around the site of the Dacian royal capital Sarmizegetusa in the Orăştie mountains (near Grădistea Muncelului) have revealed evidence of Dacian urban life. The Roman *colonia* founded by Trajan in AD 110 after his conquest of Dacia was called *Colonia Ulpia Traiana* (but was also confusingly known by the name of the old capital Sarmizegetusa, although it

Cluj: Church of St Michael: door to the sacristy

149

was situated on the Hațeg plain some 30 km west of the old site). Further north, the Dacian settlement of Napoca, on the site of present-day Cluj, was also developed as a *colonia* under Roman rule.

There is little archaeological or documentary evidence for the centuries after the Roman withdrawal from Dacia in AD 271, yet this was a crucial period that saw the emergence of the people who would later be called the Romanians. Cities and towns do not appear again until the Magyar penetration of Transylvania, beginning in the tenth century. In the twelfth and thirteenth centuries, as the region was gradually incorporated into the Hungarian kingdom, the Hungarian kings of the Arpád dynasty invited settlers to the borders of their Transylvanian territory and granted them privileges in return for colonizing the land and defending the kingdom from attack. The vanguard of the Hungarian advance was formed by the Szeklers, Magyar frontiersmen who were given land on the eastern edge of the territory. The German settlers, who arrived from the mid-twelfth century onwards, became known as Saxons (see p. 157ff). They were concentrated on the southern frontier, though there was also a settlement in the north and also in the southeast (Burzenland), where the Teutonic Knights established a colony in 1211-24. The Szeklers and Saxons lived in specially designated territories – Szekler Land and King's Land respectively – and each group was answerable to a count appointed by the king to govern it. The rest of Transylvania was divided up into counties and occupied by Hungarian nobility. These three groups – Hungarian nobles, Szeklers and Saxons – were henceforth to play a major role in the history of Transylvania.

The foundation of new towns was an essential part of the colonizing process and began in earnest after the Tatar invasion in the thirteenth century. The main Szekler town was Târgu Mureș (*Novum Forum Siculorum*, Marosvásárhely, Neumarkt). Sibiu (Hermannstadt) became the most important of the Saxon towns, and there were also important Saxon centres at Sighișoara (Schäßburg) and Sebeș (Mühlbach) in the southern King's Land; Bistrița (Bistritz) in the northeast; and Brașov (Kronstadt) in Burzenland. Hungarians were the dominant group in Alba Iulia (Gyulafehérvár). Germans also played a part in the foundation of towns outside Saxon territory: Cluj (Kolozsvár, Klausenburg) and Oradea (Nagyvarad, Großwardein) for instance. Cluj had been a Hungarian settlement in the eleventh century on a Romano-Dacian site, and German influence came in the thirteenth century, but by the seventeenth century was much diminished and by the nineteenth had vanished.

The fourteenth century was a time of great prosperity for the Transylvanian towns, as their merchants made the most of their position on major trading routes. However, as the Turkish threat grew stronger, the Angevin kings of Hungary granted further privileges to the towns, including the right to build fortifications. The victory of the Turks at Mohács in 1526 spelt the end of the kingdom of Hungary, and in 1541 an autonomous principality of Transylvania was established

The Castle of Criş

under the suzerainty of the Ottomans. For the next century and a half it was ruled by a succession of elected Hungarian princes, usually holding court at Alba Iulia. There were frequent civil wars as the princes fought to hold their own against the Habsburgs and the Ottomans, while the Saxon burghers and peasants jealously guarded their privileges.

Yet this was also a period of cultural achievement. The Reformation left Transylvania with a variety of different religious denominations, adherence to which generally followed national lines. The Saxons adopted Lutheranism and many Hungarians became Calvinists, though there was also a significant Unitarian minority and some Roman Catholics. All the religious groups promoted education: a celebrated school was founded by the Saxon Lutheran Honterus at Braşov, where under Lutheran influence the first Romanian school was also founded in the sixteenth century; in Ceauş a Unitarian academy was established, followed by a Jesuit college founded by the Catholic Prince Stephen Báthory in 1580; and a Calvinist academy was founded at Alba Iulia by the Protestant Prince Gabor Bethlen. The Romanians stayed with their Orthodox faith and, except for the school at Braşov, remained largely untouched by this religious and educational activity.

Since the fifteenth century the affairs of Transylvania had been decided by the three privileged 'nations' represented in the Transylvanian Diet: the Hungarian nobles, the Szeklers and the Saxons. The Romanians, although comprising the largest group in the population, were not granted any political rights until 1849. Predominantly serfs tied to their masters' land, they played little part in urban life until the nineteenth century. The Roma gypsies who have lived in the region for centuries were, of course, even more marginalized.

At the end of the seventeenth century the defeated Turks surrendered their suzerainty of Transylvania to the Austrian Habsburgs. Although the Emperor

Leopold II promised in 1691 that the old rights and laws would be maintained, the Imperial government continued to exert considerable control. The Hungarian nobility resisted, rising in rebellion under the leadership of Ferenc Rákoczi in 1704 and securing by the Treaty of Szatmar (1711) the confirmation of their privileges.

The Banat of Timişoara had a rather different history from that of Transylvania proper. Extending southeastwards, it had been part of the Hungarian kingdom and after its conquest by the Turks in 1552 became an Ottoman pashalik. Thus it did not have the autonomy that Transylvania enjoyed, nor the old political institutions and the network of privileges and rights that had determined the relationship between the Transylvanian 'nations'. When the Austrians took it from the Turks in 1718, the Emperor Charles VI placed it under military rule and set about draining marshes and building roads. Germans and Serbs were encouraged to settle the depopulated region by Charles and his daughter Maria Theresa. The Germans, called Swabians, founded villages and towns. The Serbs came into conflict with their Orthodox brethren the Romanians, who, as in Transylvania, formed the largest ethnic group, by claiming precedence over them.

Under the Habsburgs Catholic activity increased throughout the region, particularly the Banat. Protestantism was tolerated in Transylvania, and Calvinism remains the dominant faith of the Transylvanian Magyars today. The Habsburgs had more success with their scheme to bring the Romanian Orthodox into the Catholic fold by arranging union with the Roman Church. The establishment of this Uniate Church, with its headquarters at Blaj, split the Romanian community, but through the efforts of its clergy, particularly Bishop Ion Inocenţiu Micu, created a powerful lobby for Romanian rights and national aspirations.

Saxon houses in Sighişoara,
by Károly Kós

Sighişoara in the seventeenth century

Townscape

The architecture and townscapes of Transylvania and the Banat reflect the area's ethnic and religious variety. The Saxons, Szeklers, Hungarians and Romanians all have distinctive vernacular styles. In the mid-nineteenth century Charles Boner noticed that many German or Hungarian villages had a large Romanian settlement of humbler buildings attached: 'Where the houses of the German or Hungarian end, there the others begin, – differing from them so much in build, arrangement, and general appearance, that it is impossible to mistake one for the other.'

In the Middle Ages the Romanians, who formed the majority of the Transylvanian population, did not have the resources to build many stone buildings of any architectural merit. The few exceptions are in the Hunedoara district in the southeast of the region. They include the remarkable fourteenth-century village church of Denşus built with stone from the nearby Roman colony of Ulpia Traiana, and churches such as Strei and Strei-Sângeorgiu founded by Moldavian and Wallachian princes. An Orthodox church was built in stone in the Romanian suburb of Braşov in 1512-21, but this was exceptional. Romanian timber architecture in the region is often impressive, as can be seen in the peasant houses and churches in villages in the north and northeast (see p. 167ff).

As urban life developed and the aristocracy prospered, architects trained in the workshops of west and central Europe were employed to create impressive stone churches in villages and towns. The early buildings of the settlers had been built of

153

wood. The first stone churches date from just after the Tatar invasion of 1241. The Romanesque basilica of Sebeş is well preserved, but the most impressive is the cathedral of Alba Iulia with its fine sculpture. The early churches of the Saxons clearly show the influence of western European architecture, particularly the Burgundian Gothic of the Cistercian Order, which had a foundation in Transylvania at Cârta.

The wealth and political power of the towns in the fourteenth and fifteenth centuries is expressed in such town churches as the hall-choir of Sebeş (completed in 1382), St Michael in Cluj (1350-1444) and the Black Church of Braşov (1385-1476). Craftsmen from the Parler workshop in Prague worked in Transylvania. In the Saxon towns the great houses of the patricians and merchants are unmistakeably German in style, while the palaces, castles and luxurious townhouses of the Hungarian nobles reflect their status.

In frontier territories defence was always a priority. Towns received royal permission to strengthen their walls as Turkish raids increased in the fifteenth century. The town walls and bastions were usually paid for by the rich and powerful guilds which gave their names to the towers. The citizens of Braşov maintained the castle

Bran: the castle

A romantic view of the castle at Hunedoara, c. 1950

of Bran (Törzburg), which defended the trade route to the town. The Saxon villagers built their own elaborate fortifications around their churches. Of the feudal castles the greatest is at Hunedoara, largely the creation of Iancu of Hunedoara (Janos Hunyadi) and his son Matthias Corvinus, with additions by Gabor Bethlen in the seventeenth century.

The brief efflorescence of the Renaissance at the Hungarian royal court of Matthias Corvinus at the end of the fifteenth century left its mark on Transylvanian art and architecture. An example of Matthias' patronage of Italian art can be seen in the fresco above the south door of Braşov church and the paintings he commissioned at Hunedoara. A pioneering Renaissance building is the Lászay Chapel (1514-24) on the north side of Alba Iulia Cathedral. Later examples are the windows and doors inserted in the parish church of Bistriţa in 1560. There are few well-preserved Renaissance townhouses from the period, though the Haller House in the main square of Sibiu (*c.* 1550), built for a powerful patrician family originating from Nuremberg, the Market Hall in Braşov and the Goldsmiths' House in Bistriţa (*c.* 1560) are good examples. There are also some fine Renaissance castles, notably Criş (1550), with its impressive round tower and arcaded galleries, adorned with plaster reliefs of warriors.

Austrian rule brought Baroque architecture to the region. Its most prominent achievement in Transylvania is the Citadel of Alba Iulia (1714-38), which combines strong defence with Baroque iconography lauding the Habsburg emperor. Jesuit churches were built at Cluj (1718-24), Sibiu (1726-33) and Braşov (1785). Baroque made a greater impact in the Banat with the new Catholic cathedrals built at Timişoara (1736-54) by Johann Emmanuel Fischer von Erlach, and Oradea (1752-60) by Franz Anton Hillebrandt, who also designed the large Viennese-style Bishop's Palace. Baroque churches were built for the Romanian community: the Uniate cathedral in Blaj (1738-65) and the Orthodox cathedral in Oradea (1784-86). Great Baroque town palaces were built by the Austrian-appointed governors of Transylvania, such as the Bánffy Palace in Cluj (1774-85) by Eberhard Blaumann for György Bánffy, and the Brukenthal Palace in Sibiu (1778-85) by Anton Martinelli for Samuel von Brukenthal.

There is much that is typically Austro-Hungarian in the architecture of the nineteenth and early twentieth centuries. In 1906 at Cluj, for instance, the architects Fellner and Helmer built one of the many theatres they designed throughout the empire. At the same time the creation of distinctive national styles of architecture was an important element of nineteenth-century nationalism. Here the nationalist architecture is mostly Magyar. Buildings in a distinctively Hungarian Art Nouveau style can be found, particularly at Oradea and at Târgu Mureş Town Hall (1907-8) and in the Cultural Centre (1911-13), which is by Marcell Komor and Dezsö Jakab.

The new confidence of the Transylvanian Romanians was expressed above all in the building of imposing new Orthodox churches in the towns. The Metropolitan Cathedral at Sibiu (1902-6) by Josef Kamner and Virgil Nagy boldly took Hagia Sophia in Istanbul as its model. In the years after the First World War new cathedrals were built at Alba Iulia (1921-22), Cluj (1923-33) and Timişoara.

Arms of Jancu,
Hunedoara

The Transylvanian Saxons and their Fortified Churches

by William Blacker and Sebastian Wormell

The Saxons of Siebenbürgen

The presence of the first settlers from northern Europe was attested in southern Transylvania in 1143. They became known as Saxons, although, judging by their language and the layout of their villages, they seem to have come not from Saxony but from around Luxembourg, the Mosel and the Lower Rhineland, and Transylvania came to be known in German as Siebenbürgen ('Seven Castles') after their seven principal towns. In return for special privileges and a large measure of autonomy granted to them by King Geza II of Hungary (1141-62) they had agreed to colonize and guard the southern and eastern borders of the Hungarian kingdom. A frontier people, like the Hungarian Szeklers who had settled on the eastern side of Transylvania from the tenth century onwards, the Saxons were among the first Germanic settlers to make their home in eastern Europe and they have preserved their distinct identity to this day.

In the green and rolling countryside just to the north of the southern Carpathian mountains they prospered. There, although islanded for centuries amongst Hungarians and Romanians and subjected to repeated raids from Turks and Tatars, they resolutely defended themselves and their old way of life and traditions against all encroachments; so much so that they never lost their distinctive 'Saxonness' and continue to speak in their old northern European dialect, which is related to the Mosel Frankish dialect. As a result, despite being very much in southeastern Europe, the Saxon lands have a feel of southern England about them. Walking across the wooded hills between the villages, one is guided by the tall towers and steeples of their old Gothic churches, and the hymns sung in those churches are all familiar.

In 1990 the vast majority of Saxons decided to take advantage of a law of the Federal Republic of Germany which granted German citizenship to anyone who could demonstrate German ancestry. They laid down their scythes, sold their horses, carts, ploughs and traditional costumes and made the journey to northern Europe, 850 years after their ancestors first departed from there. It took just a

couple of years to destroy a community whose life had undergone little change since less than one hundred years after the Norman Conquest of England. In some villages there are now no Saxons left. In others just a few elderly people remain valiantly looking after the church, still ringing the bells and winding up the clock. According to legend, the Saxons were the descendants of the children of the town of Hamelin who were led through the mountain to Transylvania by the Pied Piper. Today that legend has been uncannily reversed: almost all the young have now left Transylvania and only a few old people remain sitting out on benches in the sun in their old peasant clothes watching bemused the changing scene. When asked where everyone else has gone they reply sadly: 'They have all left.' And will they go too? 'We do not want to go, this is our homeland,' they say, 'but if we stay, who will bury us?'

The Saxon villages are some of the most beautiful and unspoilt in Romania. There are almost no modern buildings. More often than not the streets are untarmacked, dusty in summer, muddy in winter, with ducks and geese wandering about freely, and in the mornings and evenings filled with cattle, horses, sheep and goats being taken to or from pasture. The villages are generally compact settlements built on a radial plan with defence in mind. In the centre looms a vast medieval fortified church, around which stand solid Saxon houses washed in blue, green or golden ochre yellow, with steep hipped roofs and old decorative plasterwork. In villages where there are no Saxons left, or only a very few, many of the fine old houses have been vandalized and are falling into ruin. The fortified churches, with their tall defensive walls and towers, village strongholds that protected generations of Saxons for hundreds of years, are threatened.

The Transylvanian Saxons were renowned for their self-sufficiency and well-ordered community life. The English traveller Charles Boner in the last century noted that 'the Saxon peasant acts in all according to system. Strictly ordered, admirable arrangement has ever been the groundwork of his existence. It was so of his political well-being and of his social life, in times when, but for this, surrounding inimical influences would have destroyed him.' Indeed, cooperation within the community was essential for survival in villages constantly under threat. The characteristic Saxon institution of *Nachbarschaft* (neighbourhood, community), by which every member of a neighbourhood would come to the assistance of an individual if he suffered damage to his property or other misfortune, survives into modern times.

As late as 1990 the fields in summer were full of Saxons in their broad-brimmed straw hats scything the meadows and loading up carts with hay. In the evening in the villages the yards would be full of noise and activity, the horses and carts

Opposite: A typical Saxon town, Viscri (Deutsch-Weisskirch), seen from the church tower

returning, the pigs being fed. Everywhere could be heard the Saxon language. Their life was very traditional and old-fashioned; sometimes the people, their clothes, almost every detail seems to come out of a painting by Breughel or one of the Flemish old masters.

Nowadays the noise and the children tend to be Roma. Before 1990 the average Saxon village was composed of approximately 70 per cent Saxons, 25 per cent Romanians, and 5 per cent Roma. Now the statistics are more nearly 5 per cent Saxons, 40 per cent Romanians and 55 per cent Roma.

History

In 1224 King Andrew II of Hungary recognized the Saxons' important role in developing the country by confirming and extending their privileges in his 'Golden Charter', which determined the character of Transylvanian Saxon communities for centuries to come. It granted the members of the settlements established in the region around Sibiu (Hermannstadt), the most important of the Saxon towns, the status of free peasants, not subject to feudal lords, but under the direct authority of the king. They had the right to choose their own magistrates and priests, and were granted trading privileges and exclusive farming rights in their territory, which was called the 'Königsboden' ('*Terra Regalis*', 'King's Land').

Further privileges were granted under the Angevin kings of Hungary in the four-teenth century, when the administrative districts, *sedes* or '*Stühle*', were created

Sibiu town church

around Sibiu and in the south of Transylvania. The merchants of the Transylvanian towns were much favoured by King Louis the Great (1345-82), and during his reign their trading contacts extended across central Europe to the Netherlands and the Hanseatic cities of the Baltic. The prosperity of the burghers of Braşov and Sibiu can be seen in the great merchant houses and the big new town churches which were built at this time. The royal privileges remained of fundamental importance to the Saxon communities right up until the First World War, and they were jealously guarded.

In the fifteenth century came the menace of the Ottoman Turks, who invaded Transylvania fifteen times. It was in response to such attacks that the village churches were fortified and a sophisticated early-warning system was developed. Much of the work of fortification was done in the middle of the century, when the campaigns of the governor of Transylvania,

Sibiu, the Town Hall

Janos Hunyadi, known in Romania as Iancu of Hunedoara, gave the Saxon communities some respite from Turkish attacks. From then on the fortifications remained in readiness, and they were needed in the seventeenth and eighteenth centuries when the land rarely enjoyed peace for long.

During these perilous times, in the first half of the sixteenth century the Saxons adopted Luther's Reformation. One of the main centres of the Reformation in Transylvania was Braşov (Kronstadt), where its leading light was the humanist Johannes Honterus. Among the chief concerns of Honterus was the improvement of education throughout the Saxon communities. His legacy survived, for right up to the early 1990s the Saxon schools were the best in Transylvania.

Transylvanian Protestants travelled to western Europe to study – some even came as far as England, prompting Milton to remark in his *Areopagitica*: 'Nor is it for nothing that the grave and frugal Transylvanian sends out yearly from as far as the mountainous borders of Russia and beyond the Hercynian wilderness, not their youth, but their staid men, to learn our language, and our theologic arts'. Saxons studying for the ministry made their way to Lutheran centres of learning in Germany. This certainly broadened their horizons: in the mid-nineteenth century the English traveller Charles Boner observed that the 'Saxon schoolmen and clergymen are undoubtedly the best-informed men in the country'. However, increased contact with Germany also encouraged a strong sense of German identity, which contributed to the catastrophe which overtook the Saxons in the twentieth century.

The collapse of the Hungarian kingdom after the fateful defeat at Mohács in 1526 led to the creation of a principality of Transylvania in 1541. The Turks never actually conquered Transylvania, but in 1553 the principality accepted the suzerainty of the Ottoman sultan. For many generations the Saxons suffered in the struggles for power between the Habsburgs, the Ottomans and the Transylvanian princes. Their fortified churches, built against Turkish attack, now provided a defence against the various bands of mercenaries which swept through the land. The destruction wrought by the campaigns of Gabriel Báthory, prince of Transylvania (1608-13), was particularly severe, while the rule of his successor, Gabriel Bethlen (1613-29), was more benign, though Bethlen upset the Saxons of Hermannstadt when he attempted to reduce their precious privileges. In 1658 the Turks sent a punitive expedition against the troublesome Prince George II Rákóczi, and during the destructive civil war that followed the Saxons had to tread a delicate path, sometimes fighting on the side of the Turks, who were able to install an amenable nobleman, Michael Apafi, as prince.

In general, the later seventeenth century was a period of decline, but with their defeat at Vienna in 1683 the Ottomans' power in Europe was broken, and the Habsburgs were soon able to take control of Transylvania. This was confirmed by the Peace of Karlowitz in 1699, but there was resistance to Austrian rule, and during the Hungarian Kuruz Uprising at the beginning of the eighteenth century the Saxons were again caught in the crossfire. Following the Peace of Szathmar in 1711 Transylvania enjoyed a prolonged period without serious conflict. The fortifications of the towns were mostly demolished in the nineteenth century, though notably the impressive walls and bastions of Sighişoara and sections of those of Braşov are still there, and most of the fortified village churches survived.

The Fortified Churches

The history of individual fortified village churches generally follows a recognizable pattern. The church building usually dates back to the thirteenth century, and its austere style often shows the influence of Cistercian architecture (Prejmer, Sebeş, Hărman). Occasionally the Romanesque village church remains intact (as at Cisnădioara and Drăuşeni), but it was usually remodelled on a grander scale in the fifteenth century. The west tower and chancel were heightened and fortified, and ring walls with towers and wooden galleries were built round the church. Within the walls each village family had a small room in which they lived in times of siege, and the family's provisions were kept permanently inside the fortress in case of sudden attack. Today the few Saxons who remain still keep their flitches of bacon in the *Speckturm*, hanging from ancient rusty hooks and carefully labelled with the owner's name and house number. There are no weapons left now, though in

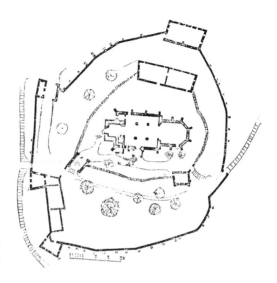

*Plan of a typical Saxon church and
its fortifications: Apold*

the 1850s Charles Boner saw swords and spears, and even a huge drum to warn villagers of approaching trouble, still hanging in the fortress at Saschiz (Keisd). The last Turkish invasion of Transylvania had taken place only sixty years before, in 1788.

Although the threat of external attack diminished after the defeat of the Turks at Vienna in 1683, the Saxons remained vigilant. Right up until today in fact, the fortified churches have been maintained almost in their original condition by generations of Saxon masons, tilers, joiners and smiths and they remain medieval fortresses ready to repel an attack. The wooden galleries and rickety old ladders that the Saxons used to reach the battlements survive; even the wooden flaps of the arrow slits that swivel open and shut on firing and loading are still there.

Each village administered its own affairs as a small and efficient peasant democracy, and consequently the fortresses were built entirely by the villagers themselves; they were not the creations of feudal barons, the Saxons having vigorously maintained their independence from the Hungarian aristocracy from the fourteenth century onwards. Nonetheless, the fortifications are highly sophisticated, if unusual, examples of military architecture. Round the church itself there are sometimes two or even three concentric encircling and bastioned walls filled with gun- and arrow-slits pointing in every direction, chutes for rolling rocks down on to attackers, and portcullises. Patrick Leigh Fermor wrote of them: 'These defensive rings are amazing, even in a border region that bristles with castles . . . they are as full of purpose as bits of armour.' Even the upper storey of the church above the nave and the church tower are brimming with defensive mechanisms. Often you can see painted or carved on the church door the first line of Luther's famous hymn 'Ein' feste Burg ist unser Gott' ('A Mighty Fortress is Our God'). For the Saxons on the front line of defence of Western Christendom, these lines were more than metaphorical.

Yet, perhaps surprisingly, the interiors of the churches are charmingly decorated and peaceful places, quite at odds with their warlike surroundings. Up above there is often Gothic vaulting, and the windows (as at Saschiz) may be traceried. They are characteristic Lutheran interiors, retaining pre-Reformation furnishings, such as the font and the sacrament house (good examples at Moşna and Apold). Some medieval wall paintings have survived, notably at Mălâncrav. Over the altar there is often a fine, many-panelled late Gothic or Renaissance altarpiece, carved and painted; outstanding among these are the altarpieces at Biertan, Mediaş, Prejmer, Mălâncrav, Cincu and Beia. The galleries, which were usually added in the seventeenth or eighteenth century, and the side pews are prettily painted with simple designs of flowers, trees, birds or primitive views of villages. No bright modern restorations offend the eye. A distinctive feature of some churches are the Turkish rugs of distinctive 'Transylvanian' pattern, which are hung from the walls and galleries (Cincu, Dealu Frumos, Sighişoara, Braşov, Mediaş, Biertan).

Today some of the churches are not used at all, even though there may be a few old Saxons still living in the village. At others there is a service perhaps only once every three weeks and then the church is almost empty; a few years ago it would have been full, with each person, depending on whether they were a boy or a girl, married or unmarried, middle-aged or village elder, given their allotted place.

In 1990 there were altogether 90,000 Saxons in Transylvania. Now there are fewer than 20,000. In 1990 there were approximately 250 pastors; now there are only about forty. Previously every Saxon village had a school; now there are almost none. The reasons for this precipitate departure of the Saxons after the borders opened in 1990 had been maturing throughout this century. Transylvanian Saxon culture is in reality one of the later casualties of the Second World War.

The Saxons had fought either in the Romanian army or, as *Volksdeutsche*, with the Waffen SS. Immediately after the war, in 1945, the Russians demanded human labour as reparations, and the Romanian police, perhaps understandably scapegoating the ethnic Germans who had been the most enthusiastic supporters of Hitler, rounded up all Saxon men between the ages of 18 and 45 and women between 17 and 35, and delivered them into the hands of the Russians, who deported them to the Soviet Union for hard labour. Many mothers were separated from their young children. At the same time all Saxon lands and houses were confiscated and given to Romanians and Roma.

A couple of years later all land was in any case collectivized when the Communists took over. From then on for the next forty years the Saxons, like everyone else, had to live under the Communist dictatorships of Gheorghiu-Dej

Inside the fortifications,
Prejmer

and Ceauşescu, during which time their self-sufficiency and Saxon individuality were not appreciated. When in the 1970s the West German Chancellor Helmut Schmidt came to an agreement with Ceauşescu to buy exit visas for ethnic Germans (each costing around 8,000 DM, later 12,000 DM) there were many Saxons who were only too happy to get out.

This created a psychology of emigration that had not existed before, so that when the borders opened in 1990 the trickle of emigrants became a flood. The previous fifty years had proved so difficult for the Saxons that most were not even interested to see if things would improve. Those who remained, hoping for better days, were disillusioned. They still felt themselves to be 'foreigners' in their own homeland. They protested, for example, that in the resdistribution of lands they were not given their old ground back, but only the plots that were least fertile and furthest from the village. So they gave up hope and left too.

In most villages, where the last few elderly Saxon inhabitants struggle to keep the church in repair, the Saxon exodus has brought a centuries-old way of life to an end. In other villages, such as Viscri (Deutsch-Weisskirch), the reduced Saxon population is making brave attempts to keep the community alive. Many of those who have left the villages to seek a new life in Germany are homesick and disappointed; but only a very few are returning to Transylvania.

The fortified churches have always been at the centre of Saxon village life, and their preservation poses difficult problems for the future.

The Wooden Churches of Maramureş

by John Villiers

History

The remains of stone churches and monastic buildings dating from as early as the mid-fourteenth century have been found in many places in Romania, not least in Transylvania and especially in the area that today constitutes the *judeţ* (administrative district) of Maramureş. One of the best preserved of these stone churches is at Sarasău, a few miles west of Sighetu Marmaţiei, where the pentagonal apse and the east end of the nave of a fourteenth-century Gothic stone church are still intact. However, until the fifteenth century virtually all the churches in Maramureş, as elsewhere in the Romanian world, were built of wood. Even after stone had replaced wood during the nineteenth century as the principal material for both ecclesiastical and secular buildings, this tradition of building wooden churches was maintained in many parts of Transylvania, especially in Maramureş proper (Ţara Maramureşului), parts of which are now in Ukraine and Slovakia, in Lăpuş and Chioar, two regions lying immediately to the south, in Năsăud and Bistriţa in the northeast of Transylvania bordering on Moldavia (Bucovina), in the plateau between the Someş Mic and the Someş Unit rivers northeast of Cluj-Napoca (Podiş Transilvano-Someşan), and in the area further south and west between Cluj and Huedin. This chapter is confined to a discussion of the wooden churches in the modern *judeţ* of Maramureş, which includes the valleys of the Mara, Cosău, Iza, Vişeu and Tisa rivers in Ţara Maramureşului, and Lăpuş and Chioar.

In the fourteenth century the princes of Maramureş of the Dragoş dynasty obtained for the Orthodox Church in Maramureş a number of important liberties and privileges, culminating in 1391 in the grant to the monastery of the Archangel in Peri, now in the Ukraine, by the Patriarchate of Constantinople of the status of *stavropighie* (σταύροπηγιον), which placed it directly under patriarchal rather than episcopal jurisdiction. This established Peri as the most important monastic centre in northern Transylvania for at least the next hundred years and led to the building of large numbers of churches, the majority of them in wood, throughout the region. From the early sixteenth century Romanian Orthodoxy in northern Transylvania

Late seventeenth-century Calvary, Berbeşti

Farmhouse at Silsig Codru, Iza Valley

was further strengthened, and the building of churches given further encouragement by the establishment of two bishoprics with their sees at Vad, between Chioar and Dej, and at Feleac, immediately south of Cluj. Both these places were within the domain of the voivodes of Moldavia, who at that time had extensive territories in northern and central Transylvania in the area of Ciceu and Cetatea de Baltă and were anxious not only to protect their Romanian subjects and Orthodox Christianity in that region against the assaults of the Ottoman Turks and the Tatars, but also to counteract the growing influence of Hungarian Catholicism and, later, Calvinism in the region. Although these ecclesiastical links with Moldavia were weakened with the loss by the Moldavian voivodes of their Transylvanian possessions at the end of the sixteenth century and the consequent translation of the metropolitan see of all Transylvania, 'including the Hungarian parts', to Bălgrad (now Alba Iulia) in 1571, Moldavian influence on the religious art and architecture of northern Transylvania remained strong.

The establishment by two imperial diplomas of 1699 and 1701 of the Uniate or Graeco-Catholic church in Transylvania, Orthodox in liturgy but in communion with Rome and recognizing papal authority, in an attempt to bring the Orthodox Romanians in Transylvania more closely under the control of the Habsburg government in Vienna, brought about a resurgence of church building in the region and contributed to the increase in the use of stone as a building material which took place at that time. It also led to the adoption of some Renaissance and Baroque elements derived from Catholic models in church architecture and interior decoration. The conclusion of the Peace of Satu Mare in 1711, which re-established Habsburg rule in Transylvania after the rebellion of the Hungarian and Transylvanian nobility led by Francis Rákóczi II, and the cessation of Tatar invasions after 1717 gave further encouragement to the construction of churches for both Orthodox and Uniate communities in towns and villages throughout the principality. In many Transylvanian villages today there are at least two churches, one serving the Orthodox community and the other the Uniates, and often the only way the casual visitor can distinguish one from the other is by the picture of the Pope hanging in the Uniate church. Since the reinstatement of the Uniates after the overthrow of Ceauşescu in December 1989 the ownership of some of their churches, which had reverted to Orthodox use under the Communist regime, has been in dispute.

Architecture

Although some of the wooden churches of Maramureş, like some of the painted churches of northern Moldavia, were originally attached to a monastic foundation (e.g. Călineşti Căieni, Cuhea [now Bogdan Vodă], Giuleşti [Mânăstirea], Moisei), the majority were parish churches built to serve the spiritual needs of small, somewhat isolated, agricultural communities. They are usually to be found situated picturesquely in the middle of the village, often on a hill or small eminence, surrounded by a cemetery and by apple orchards and groves of plane trees, and they tend to be modest in scale and relatively simple in form, while the woodcarving and wall paintings with which they are decorated are often unsophisticated and even naive in style. Both their architecture and their decoration owe as much to ancient indigenous folk traditions as to borrowings from post-Byzantine, Gothic or Western European religious art, and, indeed, the wooden churches of Maramureş and the carvings and paintings that adorn them represent one of the last as well as one of the finest truly living traditions of folk-art still remaining in Europe.

The churches are built of pine, spruce or oak, and few of those built before 1700 survive, at least not in their original form, while many of the older churches have been moved at one time or another from their original site to another village, some, such as the early eighteenth-century Church of the Assumption at Cărpiniş, more than once, and have undergone various modifications with each move. Some have been removed from their villages in recent times and placed in open-air museums,

Budeşti Josani Church, plan and elevation

most notably the Church of the Archangel in Dragomireşti in the Iza valley, which is now in the Village Museum in Bucharest. Some have been demolished, such as the monastery church of Cuhea that was brought to Văleni in 1787 and was pulled down in the 1940s, and others have, not surprisingly, been destroyed by fire: the magnificent seventeenth-century church of St Paraschiva (Paraskevi) in Libotin, for example, which had been brought there from Remetea in 1811 for the use of the Uniate community, was burnt to the ground as recently as 1973. All the churches are liable to attack from termites and from the woodpeckers that eat those termites, and their lack of foundations, although it makes them easy to move, also renders them prone to subsidence and the effects of rising damp. During the last ten or twelve years of Ceauşescu's rule, after he had abolished the Commission for Historic Monuments because they had attempted to thwart his plan for the demolition of central Bucharest, the villagers were left to maintain their churches as best they could from their own resources, and this led in some cases to their abandonment and in others to the construction of concrete walls round them to prevent their collapse and the replacement of the wooden shingles on their roofs by sheet-metal. Since the fall of Ceauşescu there has been a remarkable revival of religion in Maramureş, as elsewhere in Romania, and this has led to severe overcrowding in these small wooden churches, which in turn has caused further damage to the wall paintings and in some places resulted in the building of new concrete churches to accommodate the larger congregations. Inevitably since this chapter was written some of the churches described in it will have been moved, demolished or substantially altered.

Almost all the wooden churches have the same basic plan derived from the early Byzantine basilica, and similar to, but simpler than that of the stone churches of northern Moldavia. It consists of an apse at the east end, usually pentagonal with a semi-dome or a barrel vault, but occasionally square (e.g. Onceşti, Poienile Izei,

Woodcarving on Sârbi Susani Church

Rona de Jos, and the Church a Nistoreştilor at Săliştea de Sus), a rectangular nave (*naos*) with a barrel vault in the centre, a narthex (*pronaos*) with a simple vault occupying the whole width of the west end, and sometimes a porch or exonarthex. Very occasionally, as in the Church of the Archangel at Plopiş, which was built in the first years of the nineteenth century and has many unusual features, the nave has a trilobate and not a barrel vault. The church of Călineşti Susani, built in 1784 to replace an earlier church dating from 1712, is equally unusual in being built on the trefoil plan characteristic of many Moldavian churches, with a polygonal apse at the east end and two subsidiary apses on the north and south sides of the nave, and a pentagonal narthex with an entrance in the south wall. One reason for this may be that it was built during the incumbency of Filip Opriş, who seems to have spent several years in Moldavia and was, indeed, ordained in Iaşi by the metropolitan of Moldavia before beginning his ministry in Maramureş.

The church of the former monastery of Călineşti Căieni at Călineşti Josani, which was built before 1663, was enlarged in the nineteenth century by the addition of an entrance with a large open porch in the south wall. A few other churches have simi-

Şurdeşti, porch of the Church of the Archangel

lar south entrances with porches (e.g. Hărniceşti, Lăpuş, Sârbi Susani and, as noted above, Călineşti Susani). The tiny, very plain Church of the Archangel in Cupşeni, which was built before 1733 in Peteritea and brought from there to Cupşeni in 1847 for the use of the Uniate community, also has a south entrance, but without a porch. In most Transylvanian wooden churches, however, the main entrance is at the west end and is preceded by an open porch (e.g. Glod, Poienile Izei, Rozavlea, Şieu), sometimes with an upper storey (e.g. Borşa, Botiza, Onceşti, Rona de Jos, the church a Bălenilor at Săliştea de Sus). Occasionally, as in the Church of the Dormition of the Virgin in Lăpuş, the porch is used also to house the offerings table (*masă pomenilor*), which in most churches is placed in the nave. In several churches (e.g. Vălenii Şomcutei), the entrance has been moved from its original place in the south wall of the narthex to the west end, where a porch has also been added.

The walls are built on a stone base and constructed of round or squared wooden beams fixed with wooden nails and laid horizontally one above the other in such a way as to project at the corners where they intersect. The steeply-pitched roof is supported inside not by columns, but by massive beams that transfer the weight on to the walls, and outside by a combination of joists and brackets, and is covered with shingles made in a wide variety of shapes, sizes and patterns, which give it a distinctively frilly appearance. The brackets are sometimes decorated with carved motifs, as, for example, in the large and imposing Church of St Nicholas in Costeni.

Notable for the exceptionally steep pitch of its roof is the Church of the Birth of the Virgin Din Şes (in the plain) at Ieud, which dates from the early eighteenth century and is one of the finest of all the Maramureş wooden churches. The nineteenth-century additions to the church of the former monastery of Călineşti Căieni at Călineşti Josani consist not only of the south entrance with its open porch mentioned above, but also, most unusually, of an aisle with a separate barrel vault on the north side of the nave, with which, however, it shares a roof. In the larger and more elaborate churches the nave and the apse sometimes have separate roofs. Some churches have a secondary lean-to roof below the main roof, with eaves that run parallel to the upper eaves round the entire body of the church, including the polygonal apse. In the wall between the two rows of eaves small windows with round panes of glass are sometimes placed, as, for example, in the Church of the Archangel at Şurdeşti, built in 1738. Likewise, the porch at the west end is frequently covered by a continuation of the lower eaves (e.g. Botiza, Rozavlea, Şieu), and sometimes, particularly in the smaller churches, the main roof is extended to cover the porch (e.g. Bârsana, Borşa, Onceşti, Rona de Jos, the Church a Bâlenilor at Săliştea de Sus). The west porch of the church of Şurdeşti not only has a double roof, but is embellished beneath the roofs with two rows of arches one above the other, and a door with a richly carved frame, over which is an inscription reading 'the carpenter of this church was Macarie Ioan,

Church of the Archangel, Plopiş, during re-roofing works, c. 1960. For the church as it is today, see frontispiece

1766', one of the very few wood-carvers who worked on these churches whose name has been recorded. Grigore Both, who built the Church of the Archangel, Răzoare in 1706, is another.

At or near the west end of the church there is a square bell-tower, usually surrounded by an arcaded and balustraded gallery decorated with fretwork and surmounted by a tall, slender Gothic spire, sometimes with a turret at each of the four corners of its base (e.g. Budeşti Josani, Coruia, Costeni, Cupşeni, Plopiş, Răzoare, Rogoz, Stoiceni, Şurdeşti). The balustrade of the gallery surrounding the tower is sometimes so high that it almost meets the base of the spire and obscures the gallery arcade, as in the church of Sârbi Josani, which dates from 1703. The spire is constructed from a central wooden column against which are fixed horizontally or diagonally, somewhat like the branches of a fir tree, beams of progressively diminishing length, and these beams support the shingled roof. The tower of the Church of St Elia at Cupşeni, the date of which is uncertain, is specially notable for its richly carved and fretted balustrade and the elegance of the spire and four corner turrets that surmount it. Even more striking is the Church of the Archangel at Şurdeşti, built in 1738. This church is 54m high, which makes it the tallest wooden building in Romania, and the disproportionate height of the tower and the spire above it in relation to the body of the church gives it an exaggerated, albeit impressive verticality. Similar in profile to Şurdeşti but more harmoniously proportioned is the Church of the Archangel at Plopiş. The dramatic effect of the tall tower of this magnificent church, with its slender spire and four corner turrets, is enhanced by the beautiful natural setting. The Church of the Archangel at Strâmtura, which was brought there from Rozavlea in 1661 and extended in 1771, is exceptional among wooden Maramureş churches in having a bell-tower surmounted by a bulbous spire. In all these churches, the weight of the tower, like the weight of the rest of the roof, is transferred on to the walls by means of wooden beams in the ceiling.

Woodcarving

The churches contain numerous external surfaces and architectural features for the woodcarvers to decorate, using a wide repertoire of ancient motifs and patterns, many of which can also be seen in the stonecarving, the textiles, the ceramics and the metalwork and jewellery of the region, as well as in domestic buildings and in wooden furniture and utensils. The projecting ends of the beams at the corners where they intersect are often carved and serrated in the form of spread wings, and the sides of the walls are also sometimes decorated with carving, one common motif being a twisted rope moulding or cabling that runs like a belt at about waist-level round the entire building, in a manner reminiscent of the stone mouldings that girdle the exteriors of some Moldavian churches. The small but richly ornamented church of Sârbi Susani, which dates from 1667, and the slightly later Church of the Archangel at Dobricu Lăpuşului have particularly fine examples of this motif, which can also be seen at Bârsana, Bogdan Vodă, Botiza, Săcălăşeni, Sat Şugatag, Sârbi Josani and Vălenii Şomcutei. Wooden doors and dorways, whether at the west end or in the south wall, window frames, balustrades, brackets and columns often carry an abundance of decoration, incised, fretted or carved in relief, and composed of rosettes, roundels, crosses, and a great variety of zoomorphic, floral, foliate and geometrical motifs. The Church of the Assumption of the Virgin at Săcălăşeni, which is traditionally believed to have been built in 1442 and, if so, is the oldest surviving church in Maramureş, but appears to have been extensively altered in the seventeenth century, has woodcarving of exceptional richness and elaboration, notably on the south door, which is set in a Gothic frame with a rope moulding surmounted by an accolade ornament. Equally fine is the west door of the Church of St Paraschiva (Paraskevi) at Sat Şugatag, which dates from 1642. This church is one of the most charming in Maramureş. Its ceme-

tery contains an unusually large number of fine wooden crosses, while the village of Sat Şugatag has several houses with magnificent carved wooden doorways. In the church of Sârbi Susani both the south doorway and a window in the south wall framed in a semicircular arch are elaborately ornamented with rosettes, crosses and twisted rope. The west doorway of the eighteenth-century church of Deseşti is decorated with a particularly fine rope moulding, and the south entrance of the Church of the Archangel at Drăghia, which was probably built in 1706, also has fine carved decoration consisting of cable moulding, dentils, rosettes and sun motifs. The church of Culcea, which was erected in 1721, remodelled in 1860 and again in 1900, has an entrance at the west end preceded by a porch with elaborately carved pillars. We have already referred to the richly carved door-frame dating from 1766 by Ioan Macarie in the double-roofed west porch at Şurdeşti. The late eighteenth- or early nineteenth-century Church of St Demetrius at Remetea Chioarului, which

Wood-carver at work in Bârsana

Details of timber construction at Cupşeni

was renovated in 1960-62, has a most unusual west porch with an arcade of shallow arches supported by massive pillars adorned with carving. In many instances, particularly in the older churches, both the form of the frames of the doors and windows and the decorative motifs carved on them are strongly reminiscent of the architecture of Romanesque and Gothic stone churches elsewhere in southeast Europe.

It may be noted in passing that wrought iron was used for certain elements on both the outside and the inside of the wooden churches, such as the crosses at the tops of the spires, roof ridges, window lattices, and the grilles that in some churches divide the narthex from the nave (e.g. Budeşti Josani, Rozavlea) and that these often demonstrate a high degree of craftsmanship and employ many motifs similar to those used in the woodcarvings.

Within the church, a doorway separates the narthex from the nave, and the nave is in turn separated from the sanctuary in the apse by an iconostasis, a high wooden screen on which icons are fixed. In most iconostases there are two doors providing access to the sanctuary, the *uşă împărătească* (imperial) on the south side and the *uşă diaconească* (diaconal) on the north. The iconostasis and the doors provide both woodcarvers and painters with opportunities for elaborate decoration. For example, the small Church of the Dormition of the Virgin at Lăpuş, which dates from 1661, although it has scarcely any carved decoration on the outside, is notable for the extraordinary richness of the woodcarving in the interior, especially on the beams of the vaults, the panels and frames of the doors between the narthex and the nave and the imperial doors leading to the sanctuary. These last are also painted and carry the date 1742. The church of Sârbi Josani has equally magnificent carved doors dating from 1764 and attributed to Alexandru Ponehalschi.

The art of the Maramureş woodcarvers is further demonstrated on the wooden crosses that stand in the cemeteries surrounding the churches. The Merry Cemetery at Săpânţa is the best known of all the many Maramureş cemeteries, but the memorials there, all of them carved and painted by one man, Stan Patrăş, in the 1970s, are more noteworthy for the charm of their naive and brightly coloured scenes illustrating the occupations and characters of the deceased than for the intrinsic quality of their woodcarving. By contrast, on the northern outskirts of Berbeşti, a village in the north of the Mara Valley, is a late seventeenth-century wooden Calvary carved in high relief, which is one of the most refined examples of wooden sculpture of any period in Maramureş and is remarkable for the naturalistic rendering of human figures and draperies.

During the nineteenth century the use of stone for the construction of churches as well as the adoption of Baroque and Renaissance or neo-Classical elements in their design became increasingly widespread in northern Transylvania, but this did not lead to the abandonment of wood as a building material or to the disappearance of traditional architectural forms or decoration in the region. On the contrary, most of the new stone churches, whether destined for Orthodox or Uniate congregations, were still constructed according to the conventional tripartite ground plan of apse, nave and narthex, and many retained the shingled wooden roofs and arcaded towers with fretted arcades and balustrades surmounted by tapering Gothic spires characteristic of the entirely wooden churches that they superseded. Examples of these half-stone, half-wood churches in Maramureş include Trestia (c.1850), Coruieni (1867) and, most notably, Fânaţe, near Cerneşti (1840), which has a strictly traditional wooden tower with a gallery and four corner-turrets and a Gothic spire of exceptionally elegant proportions.

Wall painting and icons

The traditional medium for the paintings on the walls and vaults is tempera on a thin layer of plaster, usually pure gypsum (hydrated calcium sulphate). Strips of cotton or linen are laid in the gaps between the timbers to provide a flat surface. As with the Moldavian churches, only vegetable and mineral dyes are used, including malachite for green, cobalt for blue and iron oxide for yellow, bound with egg yolk or glue. The interior of at least two churches in the Chioar district – Vălenii

Şomcutei and Remetea Chioarului – were decorated in the second half of the nineteenth century with paintings executed on canvas fixed to the walls. At Remetea Chioarului, the canvas covered earlier mural paintings and was removed when the earlier paintings were restored in 1960-62. At Vălenii Şomcutei, the paintings on canvas, which were executed in the last decade of the nineteenth century and show strong western influence, also cover earlier wall paintings, but of these only a few traces remain.

The paintings in the vault of the nave usually depict the Holy Trinity surrounded by portraits of the Evangelists and on the walls scenes from the Old Testament, especially Genesis, together with representations of the Miracles, Passion, Crucifixion and Resurrection of Christ. The apse is generally devoted to the Virgin Mary, and in particular her Coronation (as at Budeşti Josani). The walls of the sanctuary, which are often arcaded, contain depictions of the Holy Hierarchs and also of the Virgin, Jesus Christ, the Eucharist and the Apostles. In the narthex the principal subject is the Last Judgement. The paintings in the narthex of the modest little early eighteenth-century Church of the Archangel at Ungureni, which are attributed to Radu Munteanu, depict, in addition to the Last Judgement, several subjects seldom found in other churches, such as illustrations of the Parables, and scenes from the life of St John the Baptist and the life of King David.

The majority of these wall paintings have undergone several restorations and in their present form are seldom earlier than the late eighteenth century. On the other hand, the icons, which are painted either on wood or on glass, are usually in their original state, and in those cases where an icon has been replaced, the old frame has usually been retained. A few Maramureş icons dating from the late fifteenth century have survived. Two of these, one of St John the Baptist and the other of St Nicholas, are in the church of Budeşti Josani, while a third, depicting the Virgin and Child, was formerly in the collection of icons belonging to the wooden church brought to Văleni from the monastery of Cuhea (Bogdan Vodă) in 1787 and, when that church was demolished in the 1940s, was moved with the rest of the collection to the Sighetu Marmaţiei Museum. In the church of Budeşti Susani are three important icons of the Nativity, Christ Enthroned and St Paraschiva, painted by an anonymous Moldavian master in about 1550.

The icons, whether painted on wood or glass, are either placed in the iconostasis or hung on the walls elsewhere in the church, particularly the narthex. The iconostasis is usually sumptuously decorated, in the eighteenth century often with the addition of much Baroque and Rococo ornament. The Church of St Nicholas at Bogdan Vodă, which was built in 1718 on the site of an earlier church burnt down in a Tatar raid, contains an early eighteenth-century iconostasis of unusual elaboration, with six icons in the lower register depicting the Annunciation, the Virgin and Child, the Infant Jesus and SS Demetrius, Nicholas and George, and twelve in the upper register depicting the twelve Apostles. The Church of the Archangel at

Şurdeşti, wall painting of the Last Judgement in the Church of the Archangel

Rozavlea, which was built between 1717 and 1720, also to replace an earlier church destroyed in a Tatar raid, has an equally fine Baroque iconostasis, containing some early nineteenth-century icons by Toader Hodor of Vişeu de Mijloc.

Many icon painters painted on the backs of old icons, thus creating a double-sided icon with a painting of a different date on each side. A striking example of this is the iconostasis of the church of Budeşti Josani, where the backs of the original early seventeenth-century icons were painted with new icons in 1760. In some churches, where there are no dated inscriptions or documentary records, the icons may provide the principal evidence of the date of the church which contains them.

In the first half of the seventeenth century the monastery of Moisei became an important centre of icon painting, and when in 1637 the bishop, Dumitru Pop, established his see there it became the cultural centre of northern Transylvania, with close links with Moldavia. The work of Moisei artists can be seen in the churches at Borşa, Botiza, Breb, Cupşeni, Mănăstirea (Giuleşti), Poienile Izei and Vişeu de Mijloc, as well as at Moisei itself. In their composition and iconography the icons of

179

this school adhere to Byzantine traditions, but Renaissance and Baroque elements, derived in some cases from illuminated manuscripts and the illustrations of printed books that were being produced in Romania at that time, are already discernible in the treatment of details of costume, architecture and landscape, as well as in the ornamentation of the frames. These elements became more pronounced both in icons and wall paintings as the seventeenth century advanced, and Western European, Catholic influences began to make themselves increasingly felt in the religious art of Transylvania. Attribution of the icons of this period is not easy, not only because most of the painters were anonymous, but also because their work was frequently copied, as for example Luca of Iclod, who was active in northern Transylvania in the last quarter of the seventeenth century and whose famous icon of the Virgin and Child painted for the church at Nicula in 1681 was widely copied throughout the region.

Another somewhat similar school of painters was established in the early seventeenth century in the villages of the Mara and Cosău valleys. The work of these artists is firmly based on Byzantine models, but has some features derived from the late Gothic art of Transylvania, Slovakia and Poland, as can be seen in the seventeenth-century icons in the churches at Budeşti Josani, Şieu and Sârbi Susani.

Rogoz, wall painting of the Creation of Eve in the Church of the Archangel

At the same time, yet another group of Maramureş artists looked towards Moldavia and the more conservative post-Byzantine style of Moldavian religious painting as their model and were influenced by the woodcuts used to illustrate Moldavian printed books. It seems that many of the itinerant painters working in Maramureş during this period were either of Moldavian origin or had trained in Moldavia. Early examples of paintings of this school include the paintings on the imperial doors at Onceşti (1621) and at Budeşti Susani (1628). The icon of the Martyrdom of St Paraschiva from Sârbi Susani contains decorative motifs that appear to be derived directly from woodcuts in the *Cazania lui Varlaam*, an early Romanian printed book of homilies published in Iaşi in 1643, of which the Church of St Nicholas at Budeşti Josani and the Church of the Archangel at Strâmtura both possess copies. In the remarkable icon of the Descent of the Holy Spirit from the Church of the Archangel at Sărata, south of Bistriţa, which is thought, however, to be the work of a late seventeenth century Maramureş artist, the human figures are grouped round the Virgin against the background of an unmistakeably Renaissance building. Also belonging to this Moldavian school is the painting of the Last Judgement on the north wall of the narthex of the Church of St Paraschiva at Poienile Izei, which includes gruesome depictions of the tortures of Hell. This church is thought to have been built in 1604 and possesses several icons from the early seventeenth century, but the wall paintings appear to belong for the most part to the early eighteenth century, when the church was restored.

In the eighteenth century there was a great flowering of icon painting and wall painting in Maramureş. As in previous centuries, many of the artists who worked in the region at this time came from Moldavia or had trained in Moldavia, and their painting combines features of the post-Byzantine tradition of Moldavian Orthodox art with elements derived from the Renaissance-Baroque style that was still prevalent in the religious art of much of Catholic Europe. Most of the painters are anonymous, but in some cases they signed and dated their work, or their names are recorded in an inscription. Often only their first name is given, followed by Zugrav or Zugravul ('painter' or 'the painter'), and sometimes the place from which they came. Arguably the most important of these painters, and certainly one of the most prolific was Alexandru Ponehalschi of Berbeşti, also known as Alexa Zugravul, whose work spans a period of over forty years and is to be found all over Maramureş, especially in churches in the Cosău and Iza valleys and in the Năsăud area. The earliest wall paintings known to be by his hand date from 1754 and are in the nave and narthex of the church of the former monastery of Călineşti Căieni at Călineşti Josani. This church also contains several of his icons, including a fine triptych. A group of icons dated 1755 in the small, early eighteenth-century Church of St Nicholas at Corneşti and the exceptionally fine carved and painted imperial doors in the early eighteenth-century church of Sârbi Josani are attributed to Ponehalschi, and it is certain that he executed the wall paintings at Budeşti Susani,

Budeşti Josani (1762) and the Church of St Nicholas, Fereşti. His work at Fereşti was unfortunately heavily restored in the early nineteenth century. In 1768 Ponehalschi carried out work in Năsăud, in 1772 he painted several icons for the Church a Nistoreştilor at Săliştea de Sus and in 1779 for the monastery of Giuleşti (Mânăstirea). In 1782 he executed a series of wall-paintings, including a notable Last Judgement and scenes from the life of St Paraschiva, in the Church of the Birth of the Virgin Din Deal (on the hill) at Ieud. Like many itinerant church painters at this time, Alexandru Ponehalschi sometimes worked with one or more assistants, among them Iosip Iacovu, who in 1760 collaborated with him on painting the icons and the murals in the nave and narthex in the church of Sârbi Susani. The paintings in the apse of this church, however, are by Nicolae Famokevici and are thought to date from the last years of the eighteenth century.

Among the religious painters working in northern Transylvania later in the century were Gheorghe Vişovan, several of whose icons, including one depicting the Virgin and another St Nicholas, both dated 1785, are in the church of Sat Şugatag, and Radu Munteanu, who came from Ungareni in the east of Lăpuş, and whose wall paintings and icons can be found in churches all over the region. Radu Munteanu's earliest known work is at Ungureni, where in 1767 he executed the paintings in the nave and an icon of the Holy Trinity. Other early works include the icons in the seventeenth-century Church of the Dormition of the Virgin at Lăpuş, and it is possible that about the same time he or one of his pupils painted the interior of the Church of the Archangel at Libotin, which was burnt down in 1973. The murals in the old church at Botiza, which date from 1771 (the present parish church was brought to Botiza from Vişeu de Jos at the end of the nineteenth century), are attributed to him, and the icons that he painted for the Church of St Nicholas at Glod, including a fine depiction of the Three Hierarchs, belong to the same year. In 1775 he painted two icons for the church of Sârbi Josani, and the interior of the Church *a Bâlenilor* at Săliştea de Sus, where, however, only fragments of his work remain. In 1780 he worked at Deseşti with Gheorghe Zugravul, and from June to September 1785 in the Church of the Holy Archangel at Rogoz with Nicolae Man of Poiana Porcului. In the last decade of the century he painted murals and icons in the churches of Dobricu Lăpuşului, Budeşti Susani and Sârbi Susani, and also at Chiueşti and Rugăşeşti near Dej on the Someş Plateau (Cluj *judeţ*). Radu Munteanu's style draws more than that of most of his predecessors on folk traditions and it contains naive elements that are reminiscent of the glass icons then being produced in Gherla, at the nearby monastery of Nicula, and elsewhere in northern Transylvania (see p. 234f).

The westernizing tendency and the use of Baroque and Rococo motifs that had already become characteristic of much of the religious painting of Transylvania by the late eighteenth century can be seen in the work of several Maramureş painters of this period. Among these are Nicolae Cepschin Zugrav, who in 1788 painted part of the interior of the church of Călineşti Susani, Ştefan Zugravul of Şişeşti, whose work can be seen at Baia Sprie, Baia Mare, Şurdeşti (1783), Cetăţele, Tăuţii de Sus (1810) and Plopiş (1811); Toader Hodor of Vişeu de Mijloc, who executed the wall paintings at Corneşti (1807) and Năneşti (1809); and Ioan Plohod of Dragomireşti, who in 1806 worked with Toader Hodor at Bârsana, painted at Bocicoel in 1810, at Rona de Jos in 1817 and at Săcel in 1826, and was also responsible for the icons in the fine Baroque iconostasis at Rozavlea.

The school of painters of murals and icons on wood and glass centred on Nicula remained active throughout the nineteenth century. Among the important artists of this school were Filip Şanţner, who painted the apse of the church of Rozavlea in 1823. The interior of the church of Stoiceni was painted in 1872 by two icon painters from Nicula, Toader Tecariu and Dionisiu Iuga, and in 1899 Dionisiu Iuga and his daughter Aurelia painted the interior of the old church at Botiza. The churches of Budeşti Susani and Ieud Din Şes contain important collections of glass icons from Nicula, Gherla and other centres in northern Transylvania.

Since the overthrow of the Ceauşescu regime, a number of agencies both within and outside Romania have become interested in the conservation of the wooden churches of Maramureş. Among these is the Maramureş Project, which includes a conservation programme based on seven churches – Bârsana, Budeşti, Călineşti Căieni, Deseşti, Ieud Din Deal, Rogoz and Surdeşti. The Romanian government has also proposed restoration programmes for several other wooden churches in Transylvania; those in Maramureş include Costeni, Hărnicesti, Lăpuş, Răzoare and Săcălăşeni.

Bucharest and its architecture

by Sherban Cantacuzino

Bucharest became the capital of Wallachia in the middle of the sixteenth century in preference to the earlier sub-Carpathian capitals of Câmpulung, Curtea de Argeş and Târgovişte. It then became the capital of the united Romanian principalities of Wallachia and Moldavia after their union in 1859, and in 1918 the capital of Greater Romania, so-called because of the addition of Transylvania and Bessarabia after the end of the First World War. Bessarabia was annexed by the Soviet Union in 1940 and is now the independent republic of Moldova, with a Romanian population of over 2.5 million, constituting 64 per cent of the total. From its beginnings in the early part of the fourteenth century to the mid 1980s Bucharest developed gradually, without undergoing any sudden or dramatic change. It is true that it suffered destruction repeatedly, whether by fire, earthquake or the sword, and that its population was decimated often enough by the plague, but it recovered from these disasters time and again. Despite the considerable increase in the rate of change and the modernization which took place after the Union and again after the First World War, when it suddenly found itself the capital of a country more than twice its former size, it remained recognizably one city.

Today, however, Bucharest consists of two distinct cities. This change was brought about in his last years of power and in the most brutal manner possible by Nicolae Ceauşescu, dictator and tyrant, general secretary of the Communist Party from 1965 until 1974 and president of Romania from 1974 until 1989, when he was deposed and executed.

Ceaşescu's twofold ambition was to restructure Bucharest by providing services worthy of a modern capital, and to immortalize the 'Golden Age' of his rule in the construction of a monumental civic centre. Unfortunately he pursued the latter aim at the expense of the former. Only the Metro was built: water and electric power

I am greatly indebted to the late Professor Grigore Ionescu, whose *Bucureşti ghid istoric şi artistic* (Bucharest, 1938) and *Architectura pe Teritoriul României de-a Lungul Veacurilor* (Bucharest, 1981) have proved invaluable in the preparation of this chapter.

'The Paris of the East': Belle époque roof decoration, Bucharest

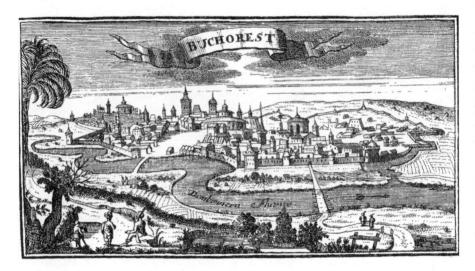

An early 18th-century view of Bucharest

supplies, sewerage and roads were neglected, so that at the time of his fall Bucharest looked like a Third World city. While there is no denying that Ceauşescu continued the comprehensive planning policy of earlier Communist governments (they called it 'systemization'), which resulted in the construction of vast industrial complexes such as Berceni (south of the city), satellites with populations of 150,000 or more such as Titan-Balta Albă (southeast of the city), and centres for sport and culture comprising stadia and theatres such as the 23 August Park (east of the city), the peripheral location of such developments meant that they made little or no impact on the city itself. Ceauşescu's centre, on the other hand, to which he devoted all his energy in the last decade of his rule, introduced a new component that was alien in both scale and character to the larger urban whole.

A severe earthquake struck Bucharest on 4 March 1977, leaving over 1500 dead and destroying or damaging a great many buildings. The area selected for the new development, however, was part of Bucharest's historic centre: the Uranus quarter and parts of the adjoining Antim and Rahova quarter located in the hilly area south of the Dâmboviţa River, where the buildings had barely been affected by the earthquake thanks to this area's natural anti-seismic properties. Ceauşescu therefore could not make the poor structural conditions of the buildings an excuse for demolition, but he no doubt appreciated the fact that the anti-seismic properties of the area would also benefit the new centre. Still under construction when Ceauşescu met his end and unfinished even today, the new centre consists of a 120-metre-wide boulevard (one metre wider than the Champs-Elysées) three kilometres long and lined along its western half with ten-storey apartment buildings. This boulevard, which is now called Bulevardul Unirii, runs east-west and leads nowhere, cutting across at least five old-established north-south routes, one of which, Calea Rahovei, one of the five main radial arteries of old Bucharest, is totally cut off. At its western end stands the Casa Republicii, 84 metres high and covering more than 265,000 square metres, the largest building in the world after the Pentagon, since 1996 housing both the Chamber of Deputies and the Senate, and renamed Palace of Parliament. It stands isolated from the city it is meant to serve by acres of waste-

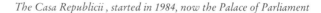

The Casa Republicii , started in 1984, now the Palace of Parliament

Early 20th-century house and apartment building in central Bucharest, demolished with the surrounding area in 1987

land, intended no doubt to be landscaped, but now awaiting a decision following the international architectural competition 'Bucharest 2000', held in 1996, which required competitors to weaken the new centre's symbolic properties by, for example, building closely around the Palace of Parliament and so absorbing it into the city.

The Boulevard opens out with sweeping crescents of government buildings facing the Palace across a vast square. The Palace appears overpoweringly dominant on its gentle acclivity, which is all that is left of a large hill on which stood at the river end until 1984 the Monastery of Mihai Vodă, founded in 1589 by Mihai the Brave, the reigning prince of Wallachia, who in 1600 briefly succeeded in uniting all three principalities under his rule. The monastic buildings and the prince's residence, rebuilt at the beginning of the twentieth century to house the State Archives, were demolished, but Ceauşescu gave his consent to the relocation of the church and eastern gateway, and these can now be seen in a back yard off the Strada Sapienţei between the Boulevard and the river, overshadowed by tall buildings. They were moved bodily, first by being lowered vertically down a shaft to the level of the new site and then horizontally on rails.

On the larger southern part of the hill, called Spirea after a famous eighteenth-century doctor who lived there and built the Church of Spirea Veche (also demolished in 1984 to make way for the new centre), stood the ruins of the New Court (Curtea Nouă), which was built in 1776 to replace the ruined Old Court on the other side of the river, and which served as the Phanariot princes' residence until its destruction by fire in 1812, after which it became known as the Burnt Court (Curtea Arsă).

The Boulevard extends eastwards across the old Piaţa Unirii and over the river on to the left bank, ending in another large square, which Ceauşescu hoped would provide the setting for a monument to the Victory of Socialism, the Boulevard's full name having originally been 'of the Victory of Socialism'. Along this eastern section of the Boulevard, one of the buildings for which foundations were laid was a grandiose opera house that was intended to replace the charming and more than adequate opera house built as recently as 1945.

To make way for the new centre, most of the Uranus quarter and parts of the Antim and Rahova quarters had to be destroyed. 10,000 dwellings were demolished and more than 40,000 people displaced. To prevent organized resistance little or no warning was given. With only a few hours' notice of the bulldozer's arrival, people were unable to take with them all their belongings, barely having time to collect their most treasured possessions and flee to their new abode, which was more often than not an unfinished block in a remote part of the city.

The areas which were demolished had a special urban character typical of old Bucharest: streets meandering, capricious, sylvan: each house having its spacious courtyard with trees: a concentration of trees heralding a church, usually free-standing or, if monastic, surrounded by walls – not a long perspective view but as often as not a sudden surprise effect. It is still possible to experience this character on the edge of the demolished areas, south of the Patriarchate Hill or in the neighbourhood of the Radu Vodă Monastery, for example. The houses which have been lost ranged from nineteenth-century neo-Classical, through early twentieth-century

Demolition underway in central Bucharest, c. 1987

The Mihai Vodă Monastery in 1794

National-Romantic, to the Art Deco and Modernist style of the 1930s. But the interest of the area lay not so much in its individual houses as in the total effect, the whole being greater than the sum of its parts.

The widespread practice of designating special conservation areas, which did not of course extend to Ceauşescu's Romania, reflects .an awareness of the value of groups of buildings as well as the importance of spaces around and between buildings and, more generally, the integrity of whole quarters. Underlying this policy is the belief that the integrity and character of an area are worth protecting and enhancing without necessarily preserving everything or discouraging new building. This approach has been carried into effect successfully at Covent Garden in London and the Marais district in Paris, both areas which have been rejuvenated by a sensible balance of conservation, re-use and redevelopment. Such a policy, which is not incompatible with improving the infrastructure and services, was never given the consideration it deserved by the authorities in Bucharest.

Unbelievably, the demolition required to provide a tabula rasa for the new centre caused the loss of fourteen churches and two monasteries, one of which, as has already been observed, was the famous Mihai Vodă Monastery. It caused the loss of a number of nineteenth-century public buildings such as the Brâncoveanu Hospital, the George Călinescu Institute of Literature and the Bellio House, first home of the Romanian Academy. The demolition also caused four churches to be moved to new sites, such a move inevitably causing damage to the masonry and inevitably changing the setting of the church for the worse. Some of these churches have been moved to sites which are so inappropriate that it will tax the ingenuity of the very best architects to provide them with a worthy setting. The architectural competition, 'Bucharest 2000', barely touched on this problem.

Competitors were more concerned with the main objective of the competition, that of urban reintegration, of making two cities again into one. The competition conditions required competitors to show how they would heal the fractures caused by wholesale destruction and how they would at best blur the new centre's overwhelming totalitarian image, for it was a requirement that both Boulevard and Palace be retained. This meant in effect denying the Palace its singularity and isolation, and finding a way of reducing the powerful axial effect of the Boulevard and Palace together. It meant building up the shattered area around the edge and somehow tying the old to the new by a gradual change of scale in both street pattern and buildings. It meant, above all, validating the old urban structure where it survives by using it to provide the genesis for that transitional zone without which the new centre will always remain divorced from the rest of the city.

The difficulty of integrating the new centre is compounded by the uniformity of its architectural style, whereas the architecture of the old city is infinitely variable. Add this uniformity to the fact that the units of building in the new centre are far fewer and larger, and the shock experienced when entering the new centre becomes understandable. With regard to town-planning and urban design Ceaușescu is known to have been impressed by the capital of North Korea, Pyongyang, rebuilt after the Korean War in the image of Kim Il Sung's particular brand of tyranny, which was, if anything, more extreme than Ceaușescu's. With regard to architecture, Ceaușescu admired the Classical style favoured by the pre-war Fascist dictatorships – Albert Speer's architecture for Hitler or Piacentini's for Mussolini. He also admired the Stalinist architecture of Moscow, with which he would have been more familiar as a result of his stay in Moscow when he was attending the Frunze Academy in the early 1950s. It so happened that when he was building the new centre in Bucharest thirty years later, architects in western Europe and America were toying with so-called Post-Modernist styles and, in order to do so, were examining both Speer's and Stalin's architecture. It is one of the ironies of history that the architecture of Ceaușescu's new centre should have been built in what was perceived by many westerners as the latest and most fashionable Post-Modernist style.

Having described the new centre – the city within a city – the damage and the problems it has caused Bucharest as a whole, what of the other city, the old city? The art historian, Dana Harhoiu, in her remarkable study of Bucharest, *București, un Oraș între Orient și Occident* (Simetria, 1997), has identified a Byzantine inheritance post Byzantium within the present structure of the city. The first documentary evidence of Bucharest dates from 1459, six years after the Fall of Constantinople, three years after the Siege of Belgrade and two years after the accession to the throne of Moldavia by Ștefan the Great, who fought valiantly

191

throughout his long reign (1457-1504) to check Ottoman expansion. Already in the early part of the century in Wallachia Mircea the Old (1386-1418), whose capital was Târgovişte, had rebuilt the fortress called Dâmboviţa after the river on which it stood, renaming it Fortress Bucharest and using it as a base from which he could quickly reach his castles on the Danube to confront the Ottoman armies.

Vlad the Impaler, three times reigning prince of Wallachia (1448, 1456-62, 1476) and owner of large estates in the Bucharest region, enlarged the fortress, and it is in a document ordering some local boyars to fortify their houses, 'written on 20 September in Fortress Bucharest in the year 1459', that the city is first mentioned by name. If the main purpose of the larger fortress was to assist Ştefan the Great in his fight against the Turks, its very presence attracted merchants and artisans, so that a population of some 2,000 was soon gathered there. The main commercial artery was called Main Street (Uliţa cea Mare) and is the same street which since 1589 has been called Strada Lipscani because of its associations with merchants who imported goods from Leipzig. The oldest arteries of the city, which are known to have been in existence at this time, are Main Road (Podul Uliţei Mari), today Strada Iuliu Maniu, which came right up to the fortress; and Outer Market Road (Podul Târgu-lui de Afară), today Calea Moşilor, which led northeast to the Obor market place.

Both Ştefan the Great and Vlad the Impaler set themselves up as heirs to Byzantium and last defenders of the Orthodox Christian faith against the Infidel. In the first half of the sixteenth century the fight was continued against greater odds by Petru Rareş in Moldavia (1527-38, 1541-46) and Neagoe Basarab in Wallachia (1512-21). A more sophisticated way of opposing the Turks, and perhaps more durable in its results than giving battle, was to support the Orthodox Church in the Balkan peninsula by founding monasteries and churches. Vlad the Impaler had built a monastery on an island in the Lake of Snagov north of Bucharest and, according to tradition, the Monastery of Comana south of Bucharest, rebuilt in 1588 by Radu Şerban, reigning prince from 1602 till 1611, and again in 1699 by a nephew of Şerban Cantacuzino who bore the same name and was cupbearer (*paharnic*) to Constantin Brâncoveanu. Neagoe Basarab, who was the author of *Instructions to his Son Theodosius*, in which he set down, among much else, the Byzantine doctrine of absolute monarchy, rebuilt Snagov and founded the monasteries of Curtea de Argeş and Căluiu. These monasteries were surrounded by high walls and watch-towers, and formed, together with the fortresses of Bucharest and Tărguşor, a line of out-posts protecting the princely residences at Tărgovişte, Curtea de Argeş and Câmpulung. Later, at the beginning of the seventeenth century, when the Turks had taken control of the Danubian fortifications, the line of defence moved into the Wallachian plain, and we find Matei Basarab, an officer under Mihai the Brave and later reigning prince (1632-54), founding the monasteries of Maxineni, Slobozia, Negoieşti, Sadova and, closer to Bucharest, Căldăruşani, Plumbuita and Plătăreşti.

Bucharest in the sixteenth century was one of the few towns in Wallachia which continued to grow apace, spreading on to the right bank of the Dâmboviţa and tak-ing in that section of Calea Rahovei which Ceauşescu's new centre succeeded in cutting off. To the west it reached the marshy area of Cişmigiu and to the east it extended to the intersection of Calea Moşilor and Strada Hristo Botev. It is not sur-prising, therefore, that the first known delimitation of the city dates from the reign of Mircea V the Shepherd (1545-54, 1556-59). A charter states that the territory of the city was deemed to consist of the property belonging to its citizens and the area lived in, and that one of its limits was where it met the territory belonging to the vil-lagers of Văcăreşti.

Mircea the Shepherd also built the princely residence, the Old Court (Curtea Veche) as it came to be called much later after the Phanariot princes had moved to the New Court on Spirea Hill (1776). The Old Court, which replaced Mircea the Old's fortress, occupied a quadrilateral defined by the streets Iuliu Maniu, Şelari and Bărăţiei and by Calea Moşilor. It comprised residence, chancellery, guard-house, stables, pleasure pavilion, garden and church. This last, with the exception of the vaulted cellar of the residence revealed in recent archaeological excavations, is the only building which has survived. The whole was surrounded by high walls on three sides and protected by the river on the fourth side.

The new princely court attracted merchants and artisans, so that during the sec-ond half of the century the population of Bucharest rose to ten thousand and the number of guilds to forty. The Court also attracted traffic, which gave rise to a net-work of radial roads converging on to it. At the same time the buildings of the merchants and artisans – shops, workshops, living quarters – grouped themselves tightly around the Court in narrow streets which took the name of the trades prac-tised in them: furriers, ironmongers, cobblers, milliners, saddlers – all street names which survive to this day in the Old Court quarter.

By this time the majority of towns had become permanent centres of exchange where the produce from the boyars' estates was sold at better prices. So the boyars, who until the sixteenth century had had only indirect links with the towns, through their agents coming regularly to town to sell the estate produce and buy goods brought by merchants from abroad, started buying land in towns with princely courts such as Bucharest and developing it not only with houses for themselves, but with churches and monasteries, and with their own shops in the commercial centre and around the market places.

One of Mircea the Shepherd's boyars, Governor Bălăceanu, built in 1562 on a site off Calea Moşilor, St George's Church, which came to be known as Old St George's when Constantin Brâncoveanu founded in 1707 New St George's in its vast caravanserai. The Radu Vodă Monastery was built on a hill situated in a bend on the right bank of the river during Alexandru Mircea's reign (1568-77) and forti-fied in 1595 by the Turkish commander, Sinan Pasha, in anticipation of an attack by Mihai the Brave which never materialized. Before withdrawing from Bucharest the

Turkish army blew up the monastery, which remained in ruins until 1614, when Radu Mihnea began restoring it. On another hill on the right bank of the river, a mile or so upstream, on the site of an earlier wooden church, Mihai the Brave founded in 1589, when he was governor of Craiova, the imposing Mihai Vodă Monastery, which, as has already been noted, was demolished in 1984, the hill on which it stood razed and the church and gate-tower moved to a new site.

Until about 1600, when the battles with Mihai the Brave decided the Turks to forbid it, Wallachian towns were fortified, but with palisades of tree trunks and a deep ditch, not with stone walls and watch towers or bastions, as in Transylvanian towns. The ditch, cut out of the earth and defining territorial limits, has always had a greater symbolic importance for the Romanians than the palisade. From time immemorial the Romanian village was surrounded by a ditch, and the Romanian for village, *sat*, is derived from Latin *fossatum*, meaning a ditch. The French lawyer, Pierre Lescalopier, who visited Bucharest in 1574, saw the palisade erected by Mircea the Shepherd in 1545 and described it as 'made of large tree trunks, driven into the earth tightly one against the other, and held together by cross-beams fixed to the trunks with long, large dowels'. Some eight years later Paul of Aleppo, who travelled extensively in Wallachia and Moldavia with the Patriarch Macarie of Antioch between 1653 and 1658, visited Târgovişte, which had clearly ignored the Turkish edict (the Turks in fact ordered the Metropolitan Palace to be demolished only in 1659), finding the city 'as large as Aleppo and Damascus, very spread out, crossed by a number of streams and surrounded by a palisade and deep ditch'.

Until 1827, when stone paving was introduced, the main streets of the city were paved with wooden planks, which prompted Gheorghe Crutzescu's remark in his *Podul Mogoşoaei* (Bucharest, 1987) that Bucharest was 'a city totally devoid of stone and surrounded by unlimited forests'. Sir Robert Ainslie, who visited Bucharest in the first years of the nineteenth century, described the streets as a 'continued bridge, being floored from side to side with massy planks of ten or twelve yards long, and as many inches thick, which are continued through a considerable part of the town, for some miles in extent.' This accounts for the use of the old word *podul* ('bridge') to denote some streets and roads, e.g. Podul Tîrgului de Afară, now Calea Moşilor, Podul Calicilor, now Calea Rahovei, and Podul Mogoşoaei, now Calea Victoriei.

With the principal roads and some of the churches and monasteries in place, it becomes possible to identify the Byzantine inheritance in the city's structure. For a long time it has been assumed too readily that, unlike Roman or medieval European towns, Bucharest had no structure but developed as a loose aggregate of monasteries, churches and markets, separated from each other by wide open spaces, with an organic road pattern and irregularly grouped houses with extensive gardens and orchards, giving the city as a whole the look of a large village. Dana Harhoiu's analysis begins with the complementary effect of people's movement against natural features – commercial and political routes against the tortuous Dâmboviţa river

The Church of the Greeks, a 19th-century lithograph

valley with its corniches and hills. Of particular importance was the trade route between the German cities and the Ottoman south, passing through L'viv, Moldavia and Bucharest, which developed when the Ottoman conquests of the Genoese cities on the north coast of the Black Sea blocked the route via these cities. This Moldavian road, none other than Calea Moșilor, formed a right angle with the river, its axis when projected southwest cutting through the hill on which in 1655 the Patriarchal Church was erected.

Another route, parallel to the axis of the river, had provided connections since the fourteenth century between the princely courts of the sub-Carpathian zone and the fortifications on the Danube. Bucharest's development in the seventeenth century and the choosing of it to be the capital of Wallachia around 1660 (it had competed with Târgoviște for the best part of a century) should also be related to a new road along the Prahova Valley to Brașov, which served the large estates of the rich and powerful Cantacuzino family and, around 1700, Constantin Brâncoveanu's Palace of Mogoșoaia.

Laying out cities and ordering urban space have possessed since the earliest times an all-important sacred and religious dimension. It is therefore not surprising that the urban structure of Bucharest should incorporate such a dimension. Hills and similar eminences may have had a strategic role to play, but they were regarded above all as holy places on which only temples or churches should be built.

Churches and mosques are the only buildings the orientation of which is sacred. The use of astrology and astronomy in the siting and orientation of buildings, and in the way they relate to one another, places the city and its creation within a larger cosmic framework. The structure of Bucharest is concentric and radial, with the *axis mundi*, the road to Moldavia, passing through the centre of the circle, Old St George's Church, and through the Patriarchal Church on the hill. The circle is divided by six radii, two of which (northeast and southwest) form the *axis mundi*, and another two (south and northwest) pass respectively through the hill monasteries of Radu Vodă and Mihai Vodă.

The circle consists of a series of concentric rings representing the growth of the city through its churches. Thus the first ring contains the sixteenth-century churches of the Old Court, Old St George and Răzvan Stelea; the second and third ring contain the early seventeenth-century churches of St Nicolae Jicniţa, St Dumitru and Ghiormea Banul, later to be known as the Church of the Greeks; and the fourth ring, which in turn generated the development of the Phanariot city, contains the Patriarchal Church (1654-58), Batiştei (1660), Oţetarii (1681) and the Armenian Church (1685).

The central importance accorded to Old St George's Church by such a diagram is in no way incompatible with the church standing on the site today, which dates from 1880 and replaces a church built in 1724 and destroyed in the great fire of 1747. Its importance lies in the fact that the original church of 1562 functioned as the Patriarchal Church until Constantin Şerban built his church on the Patriarchate Hill nearly a century later; that here stood also the first Princely Academy and subsequently Şerban Cantacuzino's Slavonic Academy; and that the parish of St George had by far the highest density of population, with twice as many houses as any of the other parishes.

The concept of sacred space and the quest for a celestial geometry in city planning faded during the eighteenth century in the face of increasing pressure from a growing population and a great expansion in commercial activity brought about by the many Greeks who came to both principalities during the period of Phanariot rule.

While the memory of Byzantium was preserved, as Dana Harhoiu has remarked, in the sacred space of its churches, Bucharest in the eighteenth century became, also under the influence of Constantinople, a city of the urban caravanserai. A decline of the sacred and religious in all aspects of life, moreover, was inevitable with the influence of the Enlightenment filtering through, this time from western Europe, its rational approach to social and political problems undermining the authority of Church and State as well as the belief in such concepts as absolute monarchy.

A survey carried out at the beginning of the nineteenth century identified 43 caravanserais, which in Romanian are called *han*. Fifteen of these were large, and seven had a church in the middle of their courtyard, just like a monastery. There were three kinds of han. One was a simple rectangular two-storey structure with between twenty and forty merchants' setts: of this type no examples survive. A larger kind consisted of a courtyard surrounded by ranges on three sides, such as the early nineteenth-century Red Han (Hanul Roşu), which still stands near the intersection of Strada Şelari and Strada Iuliu Maniu on land formerly occupied by the princely residence: or the nearby Han cu Tei (lime tree), built in 1833, which is reached through the Pasai Blănari (Furriers' Passage). The third type of caravanserai was very large and monastic in plan, with a single gated entrance, sometimes in the form of a tower. The only example of this kind which survives is the Han of Manuc (Hanul lui Manuc) in Strada Iuliu Maniu.

One of the oldest and largest of this type was the Han Şerban Vodă, built between 1683 and 1686 in the reign of Şerban Cantacuzino, after whom it was named. It stood on the site of the present National Bank (1883-85, architects Cassien Bernard and Albert Galleron). In 1670 the same Şerban Cantacuzino, when he was prefect of the city, began the construction of the largest of all the Bucharest caravanserais, the Han of St George, which was only completed thirty years later in the reign of Constantin Brâncoveanu. It consisted of a vast courtyard with the grand New St George's Church in the middle, surrounded on all four sides by two-storey ranges, which accommodated some two hundred merchants' setts. For a century and a half this han played host to all the leading merchants, coming with the most expensive and desirable goods from Leipzig, Constantinople and Galaţi. Both han and church suffered greatly in the 1847 fire, and the demolition of the han followed. The church was restored immediately after the fire by the Catalan architect Xavier Villacrosse in the neo-Romanesque style, but on the old ground plan. Destroyed a second time in the 1940 earthquake, it was restored to its original form in 1988-92 by Ştefan Balş.

There was a concentration of caravanserais in the area of Strada Lipscani and Strada Stavropoleos, which provides an idea of the character of commercial Bucharest in the eighteenth and early nineteenth century. Walking down the last section of Calea Victoriei between its intersection with Bulevardul Regina Elisabeta and the river, we can imagine both sides of the street lined with the high and largely blank walls of caravanserais for almost its whole length between the junctions of Lipscani and Iuliu Maniu. On the west side, where the imposing neo-Baroque Savings Bank (1896-1900, architect Paul Gottereau) now stands set back palace-like, was the large Han of St John, while on the opposite side of the street, on either side of the Stravropoleos junction, stood the Zlătari Han and the Constantin Vodă Han. There were massive han walls on both sides of Stavropoleos for most of its length: the Zlătari Han and the Han of the Greeks on the north side, and the Constantin Vodă Han and Stravropoleos Han on the south side. Extending well into the south side of Lipscani, the Han of the Greeks faced the Şerban Vodă Han on the north side of the street.

Hanul lui Manuc, lithograph, 1841

Continuing east along Lipscani and crossing both Strada Smârdan and Strada Şelari (Street of the Saddlers), we find two examples of surviving hans: on the north side at nos. 63-65, the Han cu Tei built in 1833, whose long and narrow courtyard extends to Strada Blănari, and on the south side, at no. 86, the sixteenth-century Han Gabroveni, which extends to Strada Gabroveni. If we continue further east along Lipscani, crossing Bulevardul Bratianu, we find New St George's Church which, with its wide open spaces around it, is easily imagined standing in the very large courtyard of the former Constantin Vodă Han. Finally, by descending Brătianu, we may reach via Strada Şepcari (Street of the Milliners), the Han of Manuc, the Church and ruins of the Old Court (Curtea Veche) and the Han Roşu, all in Strada Iuliu Maniu.

The only one of its kind to survive and so unable to bear any comparison, the Han of Manuc must have ranked highly, even when it had grander rivals, on account of its consistent and unified design, all four sides of the courtyard consisting of a masonry plinth supporting two floors of open timber galleries with three-cusped arches spanning between elegantly carved columns and over continuous balustrading, which every so often cascades down in a staircase. Built in 1808, the han played host four years later at the end of the six-year Russo-Turkish War to the delegation that drew up the Treaty of Bucharest, which, among other things, ceded Bessarabia to Russia. Around 1865 the han was converted into an hotel, which it has remained to this day, though not without a further major conversion and restoration in 1969-70 (architect Constantin Joja), which revealed that the han had incorporated two earlier buildings of the Old Court.

By the end of the seventeenth century Bucharest had become the most important city of Wallachia and one of the principal urban centres of southeast Europe. To the Lower Market (Târgul de Jos) around the Old Court were added first the Upper Market (Târgul de Sus) and then the Cuckoo Market (Târgul Cucului) around New St George's Church. In the course of the century the number of guilds had doubled to eighty. Antonio del Chiaro, the Italian secretary of Constantin Brâncoveanu, whose *Storia delle moderne rivoluzioni di Vallachia* was edited by Nicolae Iorga and published in 1914, described Bucharest as having 'an almost circular form, with a very large circumference'. Although the inhabitants numbered some 50,000 according to a contemporary census, the city had a large spread and a low density, its houses being 'isolated one from the other like islands, each with courtyard, kitchen block, stables and orchard, lending the place a very agreeable aspect and plenty of life'. Thomas Thornton at the beginning of the nineteenth century found Iaşi and Bucharest to be 'more like large villages than what they are meant to be, that is seats of government. In one as in the other the most representative buildings are the churches and monasteries: as for the boyars' palaces, surrounded by courts and large gardens, they provide a painful contrast with the dwellings of the common people, which have a most miserable appearance.' In addition to the princely court, the three market areas and the grand boyars' houses, Bucharest contained many monasteries and churches, caravanserais, public baths and water-mills along the river. Because the Turks forbade the construction of city fortifications, defensive features in the form of high surrounding walls and watch-towers were the privilege of the prince's palace, monasteries and caravanserais.

New St George's Church, a lithograph of 1837

*The Church of St Spiridon (1852-58),
watercolour by Carol Pop de Szathmary,
1868*

Seventeenth-century engravings of Bucharest, generally seen from the Spirea Hill south of the city, show a large river in the middle distance and the city on the far bank depicted in a fanciful manner, which tells us more about the way a medieval city was perceived than about the city itself. One seventeenth-century engraving entitled 'Prospekt der Stadt Bukarest in der Wallachey' (p. 186) shows a compact city of buildings with high-pitched roofs, out of which spring a multitude of tall slender towers with conical roofs, like some northern San Gimignano. A more dominant and denser mass of buildings, with a square tower reminiscent of the Campanile of St Mark's in Venice, indicates the princely Court, while a very tall octagonal watch-tower, part of the defensive system of ramparts and bastions which surrounds the city, suggests that the greatest and most persistent threat lay with the Turks in the south and, sure enough, we find in the foreground of the engraving a Turkish army encampment. Most fictitious of all is the background landscape north of the city, which is depicted as a range of barren mountains where there is in fact a second river valley.

Another early eighteenth-century engraving shows the city entirely circumscribed by castellated walls and towers, crowded with buildings, of which rows of gable-ended houses, three to four storeys high, and minaret-like towers crowned with the Islamic crescent moon are the most persistent. More credible are the two approach roads quite close to one another, each crossing the river by means of a simple wooden bridge and leading to a city gate. There were in fact two main approaches from the south: Calea Rahovei leading to the Old Court, and Calea Şerban Vodă leading to Old St George's Church. The latter was always used by the Phanariot rulers and by the sultan's emissaries arriving in Bucharest from Constantinople.

Until Calea Victoriei came into existence, Calea Şerba Vodă was the most important street and one of the five principal arteries of old Bucharest. Still to be seen along the first section of this road are two churches of historical rather than artistic importance. St Catherine (Sfânta Ecaterina) stands on the site of a sixteenth-century monastery near the place where in 1631 Aga Matei from Brâncoveni defeated the boyars of the reigning prince, Leon Tomşa, and assumed the throne as Matei Basarab. The present church was built in 1774 by the reigning prince, Alexandru Ipsilanti's wife, Ecaterina, and restored after the great fire of 1847. Nearby, on the east side of the street, set back among trees, is one of the largest churches in Bucharest, New St Spiridon (Sfântul Spiridon Nou) built between 1852 and 1858 in the neo-Romanesque style. It stands on the site of an earlier church built by the reigning princes Scarlat Ghica (1758-61 and 1765-66) and his son Alexandru Ghica (1766-68). Scarlat Ghica and three other Phanariot princes are buried in the church: Nicolae Mavrogheni (1786-90), Constantin Hangerli (1797-99), both put to death on orders from Constantinople, and the last Phanariot reigning prince, Alexandru Soutzo (1818-21).

The typical reign of a Phanariot prince was generally too short for him to carry out a substantial building programme. The shining exception is Nicolae Mavrocordato (1715-16 and 1719-30), who built the monastery of Văcăreşti some five kilometres south of the city, and in whose reign were constructed the Creţulescu Church (1724) in Calea Victoriei and the Stavropoleos Church (1724) in Strada Stavropoleos. The Văcăreşti Monastery, which was demolished in 1985 on the orders of Ceauşescu under the pretext of wanting the site for a new 'law courts' building, has been described as the greatest eighteenth-century monastic complex in southeast Europe. It was built in two stages because of the 1716-18 Austro-Turkish war. Begun in 1716, work was interrupted for three years when the Austrian army under General Stainville marched into Bucharest and carried off Mavrocordato to prison in Sibiu. Reinstated in 1719, Mavrocordat continued the work for another three years and in 1722 completed the monastery, which consisted of an immense courtyard surrounded by ranges of monastic and secular buildings, including a residence for the prince in the northeast corner. The monastery's dominant axis originated at the entrance gate situated in the western range, passed through the free-standing church in the middle of the courtyard and extended to the chapel in the eastern range. Although in use as a prison for over a hundred years, the monastery buildings had been restored before the final demolition order was given.

Before Nicolae Mavrocordato, the Cantacuzino family and Constantin Brâncoveanu, whose mother was a Cantacuzino, had been great builders. Şerban

Cantacuzino built himself a palace in 1678, the year of his accession as reigning prince, on land which he owned in the Upper Market around Strada Doamnei and Calea Victoriei. It was his favourite residence and was in constant use throughout his ten-year reign, but soon fell into disrepair after his death. Restored and transformed many years later, it became the Russian Legation after the War of Independence and once again the scene of glamorous political and social events. Abandoned at the Russian Revolution, it was eventually sold by the government of the USSR and finally demolished in 1935 to allow for the extension of Strada Doamnei.

Of more lasting value was Şerban Cantacuzino's reorganization of the hundred-year-old Slavonic Academy at Old St George's, making it into one of the most important centres of learning in the Balkans, and his revival and patronage of the capital's printing presses, the most important result of which was the publication in 1688 of the first Bible in the Romanian language. The re-animated Slavonic Academy was soon to be overtaken by Constantin Brâncoveanu's Greek School at St Sava's Monastery situated on the present University Square. This monastery, which was rebuilt by Brâncoveanu on the site of a sixteenth-century foundation named after the monastery near Jerusalem to which it was dedicated, became famous because of the school which was attached to it and in which it was possible to study Greek, rhetoric, philosophy, logic, the physical sciences, astronomy, geology and foreign languages. The school, which did not acquire a Romanian language course until 1818, despite Alexandru Ipsilanti's reorganization in 1776 in the spirit of the Enlightenment, was finally demolished in 1855 to make way for the University building (architect Alexandru Orăscu) and the projected boulevard and square.

Şerban Cantacuzino's greatest foundation, begun in 1679, was undoubtedly the Monastery of Cotroceni, situated on a hill forming part of the southern corniche of the River Dâmboviţa, some three kilometres west of the city centre in what at the end of the seventeenth century were still forests, covering most of the right bank of the river. Today it is called the Palace of Cotroceni, having become, since the Union, the summer residence, and in more recent times the permanent residence, of the head of state. From the very beginning the monastery incorporated a princely residence whither the reigning prince and his retinue would repair for rest or refuge, or because the princely courts in the city centre were no longer habitable. Both Alexandru Ioan Cuza (1859-66), the first prince since Mihai the Brave to reign over the United Principalities of Moldavia and Wallachia, and his successor, Prince, later King Carol I (1866-1914), until the completion in 1880 of Peleş Castle at Sinaia, used Cotroceni as a summer palace. After 1888 the monastery became the permanent home of Crown Prince Ferdinand, and it was for him and his wife, the future Queen Marie of Romania, that the old Princely Residence was demolished and replaced with a grander building designed in a Venetian Classical style by the French architect, Paul Gottereau. A few years later the Romanian architect, Grigore

Biserica Doamnei, and detail of stucco image of palace on its outside wall

Cerchez, remodelled the north wing in the National-Romantic style, adding a large hall with a terrace on top and two delightful colonnaded belvederes, one of which was a replica of the famous belvedere at Hurez Monastery, Brâncoveanu's great foundation near Râmnicu Vâlcea.

Until 1984, in the second courtyard of Cotroceni Monastery, stood the church which, together with some of the surrounding buildings incorporating the old kitchen and a range of vaulted cells, was all that was left of the old monastery. The plan of the church combined a trefoiled nave surrounded by a central domed tower with a spacious rectangular narthex, within which twelve ornately carved stone columns supported a second lower tower. An arcaded porch extending the full width of the narthex formed the entrance to the church. Orders went out on 25 April 1984 for the demolition of the church. No explanation was given, but it was known that Cotroceni was one of Ceauşescu's palaces and that he disliked churches. Fortunately, there was an architect in charge who dismantled the church with the greatest care, numbering and storing all the stonework, so that it could be rebuilt and still retain a fair degree of authenticity.

In 1683, the year of the Siege of Vienna, Şerban Cantacuzino's wife, Maria, founded the Princess's Church (Biserica Doamnei), which survives to this day in Strada Doamnei, near the site of the Princely Residence and opposite the National-

Romantic pile of the Marmorosch-Blanck Bank (1915-23, architect Petre Antonescu), now the Investment Bank. The beautiful columns of the porch and the two larger columns which separate the narthex from the nave are very like the columns of the demolished Cotroceni Church. With the exception of the bell-tower over the narthex which has long since disappeared, and the interior frescos of which only fragments survive, the church is well preserved and, with its remarkable porch and well-proportioned interior, highly characteristic of its time.

One of Şerban Cantacuzino's brothers, Mihai, who was commander-in-chief of the army, built the monastery at Sinaia (1690) as a thanksgiving for his, his mother's and his sister's safe return from a journey to the Holy Land and to the Monastery of St Catherine on Mount Sinai, after which the new monastery and later the town which developed around it were named. In Bucharest he founded in 1695 the Colţea Hospital and Church in Bulevardul Brătianu (formerly Colţea) and in 1699 the extraordinary Fundenii Doamnei Church in the village of Fundeni on the eastern shore of Lake Pantelimon, seven kilometres northeast of the city. The hospital church, built on the site of an earlier wooden church, is one of the most beautiful examples of seventeenth-century Wallachian architecture, with a remarkable Baroque portal and a particularly fine porch, in the domes and arches of which some interesting frescoes survive. The hospital buildings which we see today, grouped around a vast courtyard, are the result of the reconstruction and enlargement in 1888 of the original hospital. It was then, too, that the Colţea Tower (Turn Colţei), a much illustrated Bucharest landmark which had lost its upper part in the 1802 earthquake, was demolished to make way for the new boulevard, part of the north-south axis consisting of four boulevards, Lascăr Catargiu, Magheru, Bălcescu and Brătianu, which was not completed until after the First World War.

The Fundenii Doamnei Church is extraordinary – and probably unique – because of the seventeen stucco relief panels which decorate the external walls, the panels on the north wall having barely survived the intemperate weather conditions. Though impossible to explain, the influence is undoubtedly Persian, as can be seen in the flowers, birds, fountains and especially the singular palace which form the subject matter of the panels.

It is supposed that the stuccatore who worked at the Fundenii Doamnei Church was also responsible for the stucco decoration of floral motifs at the Palace of Potlogi, one of a number of country houses built in the environs of Bucharest by the team of building craftsmen which Constantin Brâncoveanu set up for this purpose. Ever since the early seventeenth century the grander boyars had taken to building themselves country houses. One of the earliest is that of Udrişte Năsturel, Matei Basarab's brother-in-law, at Herăşti, some forty kilometres south of Bucharest, part of which can still be seen. It was described by Paul of Aleppo, who saw it when it was new, as 'a palace without equal in the world except perhaps in France, built inside and out in dressed stone'. Constantin Cantacuzino, lord chamberlain (*mare postelnic*) and father of Şerban and Mihai, had a large estate at Filipeşti de Târg, west of Ploieşti. Its splendour astonished Paul of Aleppo, who found the house, today a mere vestige of a ruin, 'more beautiful than anything in the city', its many rooms 'planned and decorated in the manner of palaces at Constantinople', with the possibility of 'taking wonderful hot baths in beautiful marble', the water being brought from the river by means of wheels and a system of canals with which the orchards and vegetable gardens could also be watered. Nearby at Măgureni, around 1670, Constantin's grandson, Pârvu, who had been educated at Constantinople, also built a family house of considerable dimensions; but this, too, is now in ruins.

In Bucharest, Constantin Brâncoveanu's alterations and extensions to the Old Court were much admired by his contemporaries. Antonio del Chiaro, perhaps not unsurprisingly, writes proudly that 'the palace was built entirely of stone, with the principal staircase of marble'. It contained several large vaulted halls, one of which, the throne room, had a row of columns down the middle. Outside the palace there was a large garden, which del Chiaro described as 'very beautiful, square in shape and designed with the good taste of an Italian'. The great change which came about under Brâncoveanu's rule was the application of classical principles in planning and design. This influence may have come via the France of Louis XIV, through the Russia of Peter the Great, or direct from Italy. It is most evident in the symmetry and order found in the palaces of Potlogi, Doiceşti and Mogoşoaia.

Of all Brâncoveanu's palaces, Mogoşoaia, the construction of which was begun in 1700, is the only one that has survived more or less complete. It is the first such palace to be built in the middle of what was originally a vast rectangular court enclosed on three sides by high walls (the side to the lake being left open); previously the princely residence had always been part of the surrounding structures. Not only is the palace now free-standing, but one of its long sides faces and relates to the distant landscape via a series of terraces which step down to the lake. Brâncoveanu lived barely twelve years in his sumptuous new palace before he was deposed and taken to Constantinople where, on 15 April 1714, he, his four sons and his chancellor, Ienache Văcărescu, were all beheaded. For a while Mogoşoaia became a caravanserai. In the 1769-74 Russo-Turkish War, it was badly damaged when Russian troops occupied Bucharest. A first restoration was attempted after 1860 by the reigning prince, Gheorghe Bibescu, who had inherited the property through his marriage to a Brâncoveanu. Continued with the help of a French architect by his son Nicolae, the restoration was finally completed, with the help of the Venetian architect, Domenico Rupolo, by Georges and Marthe Bibesco after the First World War, and the palace became once again a home as well as a centre of social and political activity. After the Second World War, the property was seized by the Communist government and the palace turned into a museum.

Although Bucharest at the end of its medieval phase ran true to form in so far as 'religion', as Lewis Mumford wrote in *The City in History*, 'gave way to commerce, "faith" to "credit"', the spiritual substance tending to disappear with the very growth of the city, new churches continued to be founded under the Phanariots, but by boyars, merchants or priests rather than by reigning princes, and often in places that in the eighteenth century were still outside the city's limits. There is, for example, the Mântuleasa Church at the junction of Strada Negustori and Strada Mântuleasa, a small but well-proportioned edifice with an elegant belfry and good interior frescos, built in 1734 by Manta Procupeţul, whose surname may well denote a mercantile function which has long since disappeared. There is the charming little Stejar Church near the intersection of Strada Câmpineanu and Strada Luterana behind the former Royal Palace, built in 1743 by Tânase Căpitanul and restored by King Carol I with the intention of making it the Chapel Royal, and in Calea Griviţei there is the Manea Brutaru Church with its separate bell-tower, built in 1777 and named after its founder, the Master of the Corporation of Bankers.

Of the churches built outside the city's limits, three deserve to be mentioned: Old St Eleutheria (Sf. Elefterie Veche), halfway to Cotroceni on the right bank of the Dâmboviţa, built between 1741 and 1744 by the Metropolitan Neofit with money left for this purpose by the merchant, Maxim Lupetu; Mavrogheni Church in Strada Monetăriei off Şosea Kiseleff, built together with a princely residence and a beautiful garden, of which nothing remains, by the reigning prince, Nicolae Mavrogheni in 1789, the year in which Austrian troops, under Prince Frederick of Saxe-Coburg, occupied Bucharest; and the Church of St Nicholas at Băneasa, which is all that survives of the illustrious court of the poet-boyar, Enăchiţă Văcărescu, begun in 1755,

The Stavropoleos Church, 19th-century engraving

The Bucur Church in the foreground, with the Radu Vodă Monastery behind,
19th-century watercolour

twice delayed by Russo- and Austro-Turkish wars, and eventually completed in 1792 as the private chapel of the court.

The best loved and the most ornate of the eighteenth-century churches in Bucharest was and is Stavropoleos Church in the street of the same name. Built to a rectangular plan in 1724 by the Greek monk, Ioanikie, as a chapel for his han, it was enlarged in 1730 by the addition of an elaborately decorated porch and lateral apses. The church best loved by the aristocracy was Domnița Bălașa, situated in a large garden at the eastern end of what is now Strada Sfinții Apostoli, but what used to be, before the construction of Ceaușescu's new centre, the beginning of Calea Rahovei. The church we see today, the fourth building on the site, is a tall brick edifice with five towers, built in the National-Romantic style between 1881 and 1888 by Alexander Orăscu, the architect who was also responsible for the University building, but which he designed, not inappropriately, in the Palladian manner. The first church on the site, however, was built in 1751 by Brâncoveanu's daughter, Bălașa: it was rebuilt in 1831 by the governor, Grigore Brâncoveanu, but, having collapsed in the earthquake of 1838, was rebuilt a third time by Grigore's wife, Safta.

It would be inconceivable in an essay on Bucharest to omit the Bucur Church, if only because of its association with the shepherd Bucur, who, according to legend, founded Bucharest in the late fourteenth century, building this church in the place where he took his sheep to graze. Dana Harhoiu has pointed out that it was nineteenth-century Romanticism that connected this legend with the pastoral life of the Romanians and that it needed Mircea Eliade's mythopoeic and religious perspective to re-establish the mythic dimension of this tradition and consider 'Bucur as precursor, endowed with the knowledge of signs, destined to see the materialization of some superior energy in the cosmic becoming of the place'. The little church, which seems to belong more to a village than to a capital city, was in fact built in 1743 as the cemetery church to the adjacent Radu Vodă Monastery.

The finest of the eighteenth-century churches are also the earliest: Antim Monastery Church, founded in 1714 by the metropolitan Antim Ivereanu, and the Creţulescu Church, built between 1720 and 1722 by the governor, Iordache Creţulescu. Despite the loss of the western range and most of the northern range, where an excessively bulky synodal house was built in the second decade of the twentieth century, and despite the irreparable damage to its setting caused by Ceauşescu's new centre, Antim Monastery, with its imposing belfry entrance gate and church aligned on a central axis, its chapel and symmetrically disposed cells and kitchen, and its superlative stone carving, remains a monument of outstanding artistic quality. The Creţulescu Church is exceptionally well-proportioned, with a grand porch, two towers and brick walls gracefully decorated with panels and blind arches. The church was not built in conjunction with a han, but the founder erected some houses nearby which enabled the church to become a monastery forty years later. In 1822 the Prussian consul in Bucharest, Ludovic Kreutchely, found the church surrounded by a great han, part of which survived until 1939.

The Creţulescu Church was built at what was then the northern 'gate' into the city in a place called Puţul cu Zale, recalling the presence of an earlier well. Bucharest, with its river valleys, the Colentina and the Dâmboviţa, both well-endowed with springs, has never been short of water. Indeed it is axiomatic that a city can only survive and prosper if it has access to an adequate supply of pure water. Bucharest's abundance is reflected in the many place names which include the words for water, well, source, spring and especially fountain in the sense of a structure for the constant supply of drinking water. One of the churches destroyed by Ceauşescu was called Fountain of Healing (Izvorul Tămăduirii) and it was in the Street of the Well with Cold Water (Puţul cu Apă Rece). There is the Street of the Flowing Waters (Apele Vii), of the Small Fountain (Fântânica), of the Stone Well (Puţul de Piatră), of the Well with Poplars (Puţul cu Plopi), and there are many others with similar names. The modern fountain in front of the Military Circle (Cercul Militar) building on the corner of Bulevardul Regina Elisabeta and Calea Victoriei, a monumental neo-Classical pile erected in 1912 to the designs of D. Maimarolu, V. Ştefănescu and E. Doneaud, which replaced the famous Sărindar Church built in

Matei Basarab's time, is the site of one of the oldest fountains in Bucharest, 'with spring water brought from afar at great cost', as Gheorghe Crutzescu put it.

In 1786 the reigning prince, Nicolae Mavrogheni, put a fountain in front of the Izvorul Tămăduirii Church, which he had built, and brought water to some of the boyars' houses. Another fountain, Cismeaua Roşie (Red Fountain) was erected in 1800 at the junction of Calea Victoriei and Strada Nuferilor (Street of the Water Lilies) whose original name was Strada Fântânei (Street of the Fountain). Piped water was installed after the War of Independence by the Swiss engineer, B. Urelly Ziegler, the works beginning in 1884 and finishing in 1888, which is also the year when the canalization of the Dâmboviţa inside the city was begun. The section between Piaţa Naţiunile and Piaţa Unirii was put underground before the Second World War, eliciting Gheorghe Crutzescu's comment that 'this wretched little stream, which in its time has been a mirror to the Old Court, the Burnt Court, Brâncoveanu's Court and so much princely pomp and circumstance, will remain from now on and for evermore a collector-canal'. Under the post-war Communist regime, however, the Dâmboviţa was dammed and a lake formed some five kilometres upstream; and the central section, which had been put underground, was again exposed, but in a canalized form. There is now the possibility, encouraged by the 1996 Architectural Competition 'Bucharest 2000', that the section across Piaţa Unirii, which has remained underground, may also be exposed.

The valley of the Colentina River north of the city has provided a green belt and set a natural limit to expansion northwards. This river valley has in fact been transformed, starting before the Second World War and continuing after it, into a chain of lakes – Mogoşoaia, Stăuleşti, Griviţa, Băneasa, Herăstrău, Floreasca, Tei, Pantelimon and Colentina – which provides a vast and wonderful area for leisure, recreation and sport.

Wars, like fires, earthquakes and epidemics, have been regular events in Bucharest's history. In the 200 years between the Second Siege of Vienna in 1683 and the War of Independence in 1877-78 there were, if we include the 1848 Revolution with its 'bloodbath of Bucharest' as Karl Marx called it, no fewer than ten wars involving Turkey, Russia, Austria and one or both of the principalities in some combination or other. But wars sometimes have a positive side and, in the case of Bucharest, it was Austrian and Russian engineers and cartographers, in occupation of the city with their respective armies, who surveyed it and drew the early plans, the Russians being the first in 1770 and the Austrians second in 1789. Not only did these and later more detailed plans, such as Major Borroczyn's of 1852, provide an invaluable record, but they also laid the foundations for town-planning in Bucharest.

There had been two previous Russian occupations, in 1769 and 1808, but it was the Russo-Turkish War of 1828-29 and the Russian occupation and administration of both principalities from 1828 to 1834 that had the most positive and lasting effect.

Under the terms of the Treaty of Adrianople of 1829, regulations known as the Organic Law (Règlement Organique) were introduced. These were, in effect, a constitution which remained in force in both principalities, except for a brief moment during the 1848 Revolution, until 1858, when they were replaced by a political, social and administrative statute for the use of the United Principalities of Moldavia and Wallachia, which were about to unite under the reigning prince, Alexandru Ioan Cuza. This constitution remained in force until 1923, when a new constitution, based on the Belgian constitution of 1831, was introduced. The Russians in 1830 thus unwittingly encouraged both union and independence.

The Règlement Organique determined a clear separation of powers into executive, belonging to the reigning prince, who was elected for life, and legislative, belonging to the General Assembly, whose chairman was the metropolitan. It established the general competence of central bodies; created public and specialized services with well-defined tasks; separated justice from administration; abolished the monopoly of the guilds, thus protecting the development of industry; and set up a single tax-action system, the poll-tax. It could be said that town-planning proper in Romania dates from the Règlement Organique, which required towns to set up administrative organs that would control development. The requirements included the preparation of cadastral plans and setting limits to the growth of the town, cutting new roads (usually parallel to existing arteries) to ease the growing volume of traffic, and, most significant of all, the use of durable building materials such as brick or stone instead of the light inflammable materials of which most of the old buildings in Bucharest were constructed. Finally, anyone wishing to build had to obtain a permit from the town administration. The new controls over building materials and the further requirement to demolish wherever possible old buildings which were a fire hazard did not prevent the Great Fire of 1847, when Bucharest burnt for three days and nights and half the city was destroyed.

If the Russian occupation strengthened among Romanians the idea of union and independence, it also opened the door, paradoxically, to the full force of western influence. In 1832, General Count Pavel Kiseleff, the president plenipotentiary of the Divans of Wallachia and Moldavia, whose policies reflected those of his late tsar, the liberal and reformist Alexander I, laid out Şosea Kiseleff, which extends Calea Victoriei northwards through woods to today's Piaţa Presei Libre (Free Press Square) with its monumental and alien-looking Stalinist pile, to the lakes of Herăstrău and Băneasa. Unlike the Stalinist pile, it was a fine present to Bucharest from the Russians, which was to be enhanced in the 1840s and 50s by the reigning princes Gheorghe Bibescu and his brother Barbu Ştirbey, with extensive gardens planned on either side of the long avenue by the German landscape architect Wilhelm Meyer, who from 1850 to 1852 also laid out in the English Romantic style the beautiful Cişmigiu Gardens. A few years later in 1859, the year of the union of Moldavia and Wallachia, the first and largest of eighteen cemeteries, the Bellio

The destruction of St George's Church in the great fire of 1847

Cemetery, was opened at the southern end of Calea Şerban Vodă.

Public gardens, parks and cemeteries were all essential elements in what in the middle of the nineteenth century was perceived as a modern city. In addition to Şosea Kiseleff and the Cişmigiu Gardens, there was the Carol I Park in the southern part of the city, designed in 1903 by the French landscape architect Redont and created to accommodate the exhibition commemorating forty years of the king's reign; the Botanic Gardens at Cotroceni, laid out in the 1890s and made into a public garden by the architect Octav Doicescu between the wars; and the Carol II Park on the banks of the Herăstrău Lake, laid out in 1936 for the exhibition 'Luna Bucureştilor', part of which, the Village Museum, became a permanent fixture, expanding considerably, with its many genuine peasant houses and farmsteads and the fine wooden church of Dragomireşti in Maramureş moved from their place of origin and re-erected in idyllic surroundings.

It was also in the nineteenth century that the concept arose of the infrastructure of a city – roads, bridges, sewers, water etc – and that the connection was made between a sound infrastructure and the health of citizens. Haussmann's operation in Paris had a direct influence on the planning of Bucharest. If the 1850s mark the beginning of the history of the centre of modern Paris, 1857 is the year in which in Bucharest a start was made with the cutting of Bulevardul Carol I, part of that east-west artery starting in University Square, which continued westwards with Bd. Regina Elisabeta in the 1870s and eastwards with Bd. Pake Protopopescu in 1890. A similar north-south artery, running roughly parallel with Calea Victoriei, was begun in 1894 with the straight northern section between Piaţa Romana and Piaţa Victoriei, called Bulevardul Lascăr Catargiu, and continued in 1906 with the middle and southern sections, Magheru, Bălcescu and Brătianu boulevards, which were only completed after the First World War in time to benefit from the inter-war building boom. As a result of this boom, the Magheru and Bălcescu boulevards presented at the end of this period, and still present today, a unique array of 1930s Modern Movement architecture.

If the Règlement Organique of 1831 laid the foundations of town-planning, the Great Fire of 1847 required Bucharest to be largely rebuilt and provided the opportunity of creating a capital city worthy of the United Principalities (1859), an independent sovereign state (1877) and a kingdom (1881). Some of the grander houses built of masonry survived the fire. One of these was the house of the court equerry (*stolnic*) Dinicu Golescu (1812-15), which stood on the site of the south wing of the former Royal Palace, today the Palace of the Republic and National Museum of Art. Two-storeys high and neo-Classical in style, the house had at least 25 rooms, of which one, the saloon, was very large indeed for Bucharest at that date. Acquired by the state in 1832, the house became the palace of the reigning prince, Alexandru Ghica, whose successors, Gheorghe Bibescu and Barbu Ştirbey, used it for ceremonial purposes only, preferring to go on living in their own houses. Both Alexandru Ioan Cuza and Carol I made the house their palace, though Carol I, after becoming king, found it necessary to build the first Royal Palace (1882-85, architect Paul Gottereau), linking it to the house with a domed structure containing a circular saloon. After a fire in 1927 the Royal Palace was totally rebuilt between 1930 and 1937 on a U-shaped plan, to the grandiose Palladian design of Nicolae Nenciulescu.

Dinicu Golescu's house became the reigning prince's palace more because of its location than because of its grandeur. Larger and much grander, but located on the

The house of Mihai Ghica, 1850

A Bucharest street in the 19th century

borders of Lake Tei outside Bucharest, was Grigore Dimitrie Ghica's palace, built in 1822, the year Ghica ascended the throne of Wallachia as the first native reigning prince after more than a century of Phanariot rule. Like the Golescu house, the Ghica-Tei Palace, as it came to be called, is a full-blooded Classical design with a rusticated ground-floor podium carrying a piano nobile divided into bays by Corinthian pilasters supporting a cornice, and pediments over the side wings. Towards the end of his reign, in 1833, Ghica added a chapel, the plan of which is an oval with four deeply rounded niches, supporting a circular drum and dome. Both buildings are western imports planted on Wallachian soil and part of the western-ization process which was a reaction to the predominant Greek influence of the Phanariot period.

A house in the very heart of Bucharest which survived the fire was that of Governor Slătineanu on the corner of Calea Victoriei and Strada Edgar Quinet, today the Restaurant Capşa. It was in this house in 1871, in the renowned Slătineanu Hall, that the German colony in Bucharest, celebrating the victories of the Prussian army over the French, had stones hurled at them through the windows by pro-French student demonstrators, after which the Prussian Prince Carol I threatened to abdicate. Three years later Grigore Capşa, who had learnt the culinary arts from Boissier in Paris, bought the house and converted it into a confiserie, *salon de thé*, restaurant and hotel, the confiserie and salon de thé becoming not only the very best of their kind, but a fashionable meeting-place, both of which they remained, as readers of Olivia Manning's *The Balkan Trilogy* will know, well into the Second World War.

Other houses of note which survived the Great Fire include the neo-Gothic Soutzo Palace, today the History Museum of the Bucharest Municipality, built in

213

1833 to the designs of Konrad Schwinck and Johann Veit on a site opposite Colțea Church in Bulevardul Brătianu; the elegant neo-Classical Știrbey Palace in Calea Victoriei, built in 1835 to the designs of the French architect Charles Sanjouand, and restored in 1881 by the Austrian architect Hartmann, who added the picturesque corner tower, its well-preserved interiors being ransacked in 1950 by an insensate, Communist-inspired mob; and, built about the same time as the Știrbey Palace, the Crețulescu House at 4 Strada Fundației, now the Museum of Romanian Literature.

It was the street-fronted shops, cafés and eating houses, of which Bucharest at the beginning of the nineteenth century boasted some 1500 and which proliferated as the century progressed, as well as the development of the wax, cloth and paper industries on the periphery of the city, that led to the decline and eventual disappearance of the caravanserai. An example from the very first years of the nineteenth century which survives is the fragile-looking Cafeneaua Veche (The Old Coffee House) on the corner of Strada Șelari and Strada Covaci. On the other hand, the Brasserie Carul cu Bere in Strada Stavropoleos, built in 1875 to the designs of Zigfrid Kofczinsky, an architect of Polish origin, is a robust neo-Gothic building with remarkable and well-preserved contemporary interiors.

The introduction of street lighting, an essential part of modernizing the city, created a dramatic change in the appearance of the streets at night. The first public lighting with oil lamps was inaugurated in 1857, and the first gas lamp standards date from 1861, earlier than Paris or Berlin. Gas lighting was fully introduced in 1871 and electricity in 1881, the year Carol I was crowned. It does not need too much imagination to appreciate the difference the introduction of oil lamps must have made to the setting of the recently completed and very popular National Theatre. Begun in 1846, on the west side of Calea Victoriei between Strada Matei Milo and Câmpineanu, its construction was delayed first by the Great Fire and then by the 1848 Revolution, so that it was not completed until 1852, marking the start of development in a city which is well known today for its lively and creative theatre.

Romanian theatre has dual origins in the itinerant players of the eighteenth century, a kind of commedia dell'arte, and in the court theatre of the Phanariot princes, who in 1818 built the first theatre a little further north in Calea Victoriei near Cismeaua Roșie. Performances, which were at first in Greek, were also given in the Greek School of St Sava Monastery and in the Slătineanu Hall. Given legitimacy by the founding in 1833 of the Philharmonic Society and School of Music and Dramatic Art, the theatre flourished, so that the spaces in which performances took place soon became inadequate. The new theatre, designed by the Viennese architect, Josef A. Heft, in the Italian Baroque tradition, with a horseshoe plan and several tiers of boxes, also provided a capital aspiring to modernization with its first cultural status symbol. The architect and art historian, Grigore Ionescu, in his *București, ghid istoric și artistic* (Bucharest, 1938), described the old National

Theatre as 'pleasing to look at with its simple architectonic lines, yet in its proportions and beauty, providing a marked contrast with the uniform and cold
architecture of the two giant buildings which frame it, the Telephone Building on
one side and the Adriatica Company Building on the other'. The theatre survived a
few more years, until damage from the 1944 bombardment of Bucharest became the
excuse for its total demolition after the war, and its eventual replacement in the
1970s by a new theatre in Piața Teatrului Național. The buildings framing it, which
were constructed in the 1930s, are still there.

Other necessary cultural symbols were related to higher education and included
university buildings and museums. The construction between 1856 and 1869 of the
University and its relation to the formation of the new square and east-west artery
have already been noted. Alexandru Orăscu's imposing 'palace' was extended by
Nicolae Ghica-Budești between 1912 and 1926 to include the faculties of letters,
philosophy, theology, pharmacology and the sciences. The Faculty of Medicine,
also created in 1856, only acquired its own fine building, designed by the French
architect Louis Blanc, on the corner of Bulevardul Carol II and Strada Carol Davila
(named after the famous French doctor who founded the faculty) in 1903. The
training of architects was also envisaged in Alexandru Ioan Cuza's law of 1864
which established the University. Between 1892 and 1897 there was a private school
of architecture in Bucharest, after which architecture became part of the curriculum
of the Academy of Fine Arts until 1904, when the Academy of Architecture was set
up as a separate and parallel institution, for which Grigore Cerchez designed a monumental building in the National-Romantic style in Strada Biserica Enei, begun in
1912 but not completed and occupied by the Academy until 1927.

The oldest museum in Bucharest dates from 1836 and is the National History or
Antipa Museum (named after the distinguished natural historian and sometimes
director of the museum, Grigore Antipa). Founded by Alexandru Ghica and his
brother Grigore, it began life in the School of St Sava, transferring, when this was
demolished, to the new university building until 1906, when it finally moved into a
white-stuccoed neo-Classical building in Piața Victoriei at the start of Șosea
Kiseleff. However, no building or institution in Bucharest was more representative,
or more fully the embodiment of national cultural aspirations than the Romanian
Athenaeum (Ateneul Român), built in 1886 to the designs of the French architect
Albert Galleron, on a site in Calea Victoriei, which had belonged to the Văcărescu
family and on which had stood a church erected by General Mihai Cantacuzino and
given by him to the see of Râmnicu Vâlcea. With the church gone, the site had come
to be known as the Bishopric Garden (Grădina Episcopiei) and it was at the back of
this garden, on the foundations of a circus building which the Romanian Equestrian
Company had started in 1874 but had been unable to finish, that the Athenaeum
with its grand Ionic entrance portico and ornate Second Empire dome was built. It
is best known today for its delightful concert hall (in which the first Parliament of

215

*Bucharest City Hall,
designed by Petre
Antonescu, 1906-10*

Greater Romania ratified the union with Bessarabia, Transylvania and Bucovina in 1919), but it was designed also to contain a library and the national collections of art, which have long since been moved to other premises.

It would be impossible to leave the world of culture without mentioning the National Museum Carol I, the great National-Romantic pile of red brick next to the Antipa Museum in Şosea Kiseleff. Designed by Nicolae Ghica-Budeşti, the museum was begun in 1912 with the intention of housing all the collections of Romanian popular art from prehistoric times to the present day. With the museum still unfinished in 1939 (three of the four projected wings had been built), completion was only achieved in the 1960s by reverting to a simpler and more modern style of architecture. Changed under the Communist régime to the Museum of the History of the Communist Party, it has recently been restored to its original purpose and renamed Museum of the Peasant.

As a result of the union of Moldavia and Wallachia, and with the establishment in 1862 of a parliamentary democracy, new buildings were required to house the burgeoning institutions of government – parliament, ministries, law courts, town hall – and the new service industries – postal services, telephones, hotels and railways, gas and electricity companies. The Patriarchate Hill, as we have already seen, was a holy place. It had been the exclusive domain of the Patriarchal Church and of its palace, a straggling building the oldest part of which dated from the late seventeenth and early eighteenth century (including the private chapel of the patriarch with its well-preserved frescos), and to which major extensions were added between 1850 and

1875, and again between 1932 and 1935 in the National-Romantic style (architect George Simotta). To the church and early palace Constantin Brâncoveanu had added in 1698 a gate-tower and belfry. There is no better example of the decline of the sacred and spiritual than the admission to the holy site of the Patriarchate Hill of a temporal power, first in the shape of the princely Divan, where on 24 January 1862 Alexandru Ioan Cuza proclaimed before the Moldavian and Wallachian Assemblies the definitive union of the two principalities and declared Bucharest the capital of the new state, and outside which on 8 June in the same year, Barbu Catargiu, leader of the Romanian Conservative Party, was shot dead as he was leaving the Assembly; and second, in 1907, in the shape of a grand parliament building, designed by the architect Dimitrie Maimarolu, which survives to this day, but since 1996 has had no function as a result of the move of both Houses of Parliament to the Casa Republicii in Ceauşescu's new centre.

Some new ministries moved into grand boyars' houses as they became available, such as the Sturdza Palace in Piaţa Victoriei (Ministry of Foreign Affairs) and the Gheorghe Vernescu house at 154 Calea Victoriei (Ministry of Industry and Commerce), built to the designs of Ion Mincu, the leading advocate of the National-Romantic style. The Sturdza Palace was a building of no beauty, but of the utmost fantasy and a true rarity. It was demolished in 1938 as part of a grandiose scheme for Piaţa Victoriei, which has never been realized, to make way for a new Ministry of Foreign Affairs designed by Duiliu Marcu. This building was damaged by bombs in the Second World War, repaired and completed after the war, and subsequently became the Presidency of the Council of Ministers. Other ministries had new 'palaces' purpose-built for them, such as the vast Ministry of Finance on the corner of Calea Victoriei and Griviţei (1883), and the French Renaissance-style Ministry of Agriculture on the corner of Bulevardul Carol I and Brătianu (1896, architect Louis Blanc). Also in Renaissance style, but more severe, are the Law Courts (Palatul de Justiţie) on the quays of the Dâmboviţa, built between 1890 and 1895 to the designs of the French architect Albert Ballu, son of the great eclectic, Théodore, whose masterpiece was the Trinité Church in Paris. Far more original and one of the most interesting buildings erected during these years was the City Hall built between 1906 and 1910 by Petre Antonescu, a staunch advocate of the National-Romantic style and an influential architect who later became rector of the Academy of Architecture, where he was able to educate a whole new generation in his manner of thinking.

The union of the two principalities not only increased their economic potential, but provided a powerful incentive to development and expansion, in other words to what was perceived as progress. This development was most conspicuous in the fields of industry and commerce, and in the establishment of the most modern methods of transport and communication. With the official registration of crude oil production in 1857 (the year which also saw the installation near Ploieşti of the first

217

*The General Post Office, 1894-1900,
now the National Museum of History*

Romanian oil refinery), Wallachia became the first country in the world with an industrial oil production, crude oil extraction rising from a mere 275 tons in 1857 to nearly two million tons in 1914. Other industries which experienced considerable growth included mining, timber, leather, paper, building materials and, most important of all in a country with a predominantly agricultural economy, food. The Chamber of Commerce was established in 1864, a new monetary system introduced in 1868 (Romanian thus acquiring its own currency, the leu) and the State Mint inaugurated in 1870. The National Bank was founded in 1880, acquiring magnificent bespoke premises in Strada Lipscani five years later, and was followed by the establishment of some 170 banking organizations over the next thirty years, two of which, the Savings Bank in Calea Victoriei and the Marmorosch-Blank Bank in Strada Doamnei, have already been noted. One other deserves to be mentioned, the Chrissoveloni Bank, with façades in Strada Lipscani and Stavropoleos, built after the First World War to the robust Palladian designs of G. M. Cantacuzino.

In matters of communication, the year 1853 saw the inauguration of the telegraph line between Iaşi and Vienna, and the following year the start of the construction of telegraph lines between Bucharest and Ruschuck (Russe), Bucharest and Braşov, Timişoara and Braşov, and Timişoara and Orşova. In 1862 an agreement regarding the international telegraphic service was concluded between the United Principalities and Austria, Turkey and Serbia. This was followed by a series of postal conventions stipulating that postal services on Romanian territory were to be effected only by the Romanian post, in 1867 with Russia and in 1868 with Austria-Hungary and Germany. These extraordinary and exciting developments in communications were marked by one building, the General Post Office. No budding European capital could afford to be without one, and Bucharest built its imposing 'palace' (architect, Alexandru Săvulescu) between 1894 and 1900 in Calea Victoriei (converted after the Second World War into the National Museum of History), on the site of the Constantin Vodă Han, which had been largely destroyed in the fire of 1847 and replaced by a large wooden structure housing a circus, Circul Suhr, which performed there for the best part of fifty years.

The second half of the nineteenth century saw the growth of traditional means of transport – the intensification of river and maritime navigation, the reorganization of river ports and, on land, the construction of over 27,000 kilometres of roads – as well as the development of a totally new means of transport, the railway. The very first railway line on Romanian territory was laid in 1857 between Timişoara and the Serbian frontier town Jimbolia. In 1866 a British company, John Trevor Barclay and John Stainforth, was licensed to build the railway from Bucharest to Giurgiu, its inauguration being held three years later with the completion of Gara Filaret, Bucharest's first railway station. In 1868 a law was passed licensing an Anglo-Austrian and Prussian consortium to build railways linking all the principal towns from Suceava and Botoşani in northern Moldavia, via Ploieşti and Bucharest, westwards to Craiova and Turnu Severin. In 1872 Romania signed an agreement with Russia to connect the railway systems of the two countries, and similar conventions followed with Austria-Hungary, Serbia and Bulgaria. Also in 1872 Bucharest's main railway terminus, Gara de Nord (North Station) in Calea Griviţei, a structure of little distinction, which has suffered many alterations and additions, was inaugurated on the occasion of the opening of the Bucharest-Ploieşti railway, and of the official start of work on the Piteşti-Bucharest-Buzău-Galaţi-Roman line.

The 25 years preceding the First World War were characterized by an extraordinary freedom of movement. It was possible with only a passport, and without the need of visas, to travel comfortably by rail almost anywhere in Europe. Not surprisingly, hotels sprang up in profusion not only following, but often in anticipation of, the construction of railway stations. We have already observed how the Han of Manuc was converted into the Hotel Dacia around 1865. Typical of this early period was the Hotel Boulevard in Calea Victoriei, completed in 1867 to the designs of Alexandru Orăscu, who also designed the University building and who is generally recognized as the first truly Romanian architect. The much later Athénée Palace Hotel (1912), Bucharest's Ritz, built to the designs of the French architect Théophile Bradeau, has the distinction of having been the first building in Bucharest to make use of a reinforced concrete structure. The hotel was enlarged in the 1930s and again in the 1960s, and has recently been restored to something like its original splendour.

The population of Bucharest rose threefold in the hundred years before the First World War, from 100,000 in 1821 to 300,000 in 1918, a relatively steady increase compared, say, with Budapest, which rose from a mere 36,000 in 1813 to 930,000 in

Postwar flats on Golescu Boulevard

1920. With the creation of Greater Romania in 1918 and the period of prosperity which followed, the rate of increase accelerated, and by 1945 the population of Bucharest was close to one million. To cope with this increase, between the wars some public and a great deal of private housing was built, mainly in the form of two- and three-storey houses and small apartment blocks, often imaginatively designed. There are whole quarters of such housing, and they are invariably well laid out with plenty of open space generously planted with trees – an extension of the true garden city that Bucharest has always been.

Over the fifty years after 1945 the population of Bucharest more than doubled to

2.25 million, an increase which occurred mainly at the expense of the countryside, as is made clear by the rise in the percentage of the total population of Romania living in towns, from 21% in 1930 to 45% today. It is hardly surprising that the post-war Communist governments made housing a priority and built a vast number of apartment blocks in satellites or along the main arteries of the city, as a result of which Bucharest suffered a considerable expansion to the east and west. In general this housing was poorly built and has been even more poorly maintained, leaving the democratic and market-oriented governments of the post-Communist era with a difficult problem, not unlike that of London with its 1960's council blocks or Paris with its HLMs (*habitats à loyer moyen*). Because there is so much of it, demolition, except in a few isolated instances, is not an option. A better way forward would be to make it possible for tenants to buy their apartments and to encourage the formation of tenants' associations to look after the communal areas inside and outside the building, as these establish the image and are generally in desperate need of improvement.

Housing, mainly on the periphery of the city, is just one of the many problems – perhaps the most visible – that constitute the legacy of the Communist era. Industry is another, but this, too, lies at the periphery and does not have a direct impact on the city itself. It is the making good of the enormous damage to the old city caused by the construction of Ceaușescu's new centre, which was noted at the beginning of this chapter, that remains the most important and urgent of the many tasks confronting the people of Bucharest. In this task it will be necessary to have a vision of the future city, of a sustainable city, which is clean and pleasant to walk in, which espouses the principle of 'greening' its buildings while continuing the tradition of greening its open spaces, which appreciates the importance of daily care and maintenance, which respects, restores and re-uses its old buildings, and, above all, a city which has the imagination and wit to patronize the best artists, urban designers and architects.

Twentieth Century Painting and Sculpture

by John Villiers

At the end of the nineteenth century both music and the visual arts in Romania were still deeply imbued, as they had been for centuries, with the spirit of traditional folk art, both with regard to their subject matter and to the media that the artists employed, whether textiles, ceramics, woodcarving or painted icons. However, this long tradition was already beginning to be overlaid and to a great extent superseded by a process of what may loosely be described as Westernization. During the second half of the nineteenth century knowledge of Western art became more widespread in Romania through the creation of art museums in several cities and the formation of private art collections by wealthy Romanians, among whom King Carol I was prominent, while opportunities for the study of Western art were created through the foundation of art schools and academies, notably in Craiova and in Bucharest, where Theodore Aman (1831-91), generally considered to be the father of modern Romanian painting, was director. More importantly, for the first time study in France, Italy or Germany became possible for gifted young Romanian artists. Among the first of these were Nicolae Grigorescu (1838-1907) and Ion Andreescu (1851-92). Grigorescu, who like El Greco had begun his career as a self-taught painter of icons, studied at the École des Beaux Arts in Paris, where he attended the workshop of Sébastien Cornu with Renoir, and subsequently worked with Millet, Corot, Courbet and Rousseau at Barbizon and became a leading exponent of the Impressionist style in Romania, where he returned to live permanently in 1890. Among his most important successors were Theodor Pallady (1871-1956), who studied in Dresden and in Gustave Moreau's studio in Paris with Rouault and Matisse and was strongly influenced by the latter, Ştefan Luchian (1869-1916), Gheorghe Petraşcu (1872-1949), Jean Steriadi (1880-1956), Iosif Iser (1881-1958), Nicolae Tonitza (1886-1940), Dimitrie Ghiaţă (1888-1972), Lucian Grigorescu (1894-1965) and Ion Ţuculescu (1910-62). Most of these painters studied at various times in France or Germany, and several of them lived abroad for long periods, but by using the Romanian rural landscape and scenes of Romanian peasant life as the

*I am grateful to the late Paul Neagu for supplying me with some of the information for this chapter.

Brâncuşi, The Gate of the Kiss, Târgu Jiu

Self-portrait, Ion Ţuculescu

principal subject-matter for their paintings, which they executed in a variety of post-Impressionist and semi-abstract styles, they brought Romanian painting into the mainstream of European art. Petraşcu was one of the most cosmopolitan of these painters and often chose romantic and exotic subjects, such as moonlit scenes, views of Venice and other urban landscapes, ruins and interiors.

In the field of sculpture the work of Frederick Storck (1872-1942), who is generally considered to be the father of Romanian sculpture, was soon overshadowed by Constantin Brâncuşi (1876-1957), whose work is discussed on pp. 226-227 and who revolutionized the art of sculpture not only in Romania but throughout Europe and beyond. Meanwhile, a number of Romanian architects who had trained abroad were transforming the urban landscape of Bucharest and other Romanian cities, among them G. M. Cantacuzino (1899-1960), for whom architecture was closely linked to the other arts and who was also an accomplished watercolour painter of the Moldavian landscape and a prolific writer about Romanian folk art, Horia Creanga (1892-1943) and the Jewish architect and painter Marcel Iancu (1895-1984), who later emigrated to Israel.

During the First World War and the years that followed a number of talented Romanian artists were active in Germany, France and elsewhere in Western Europe, notably in Zurich, where Marcel Iancu was one of the founders of the Dadaist movement before he returned to Romania in 1920. An important member of the group of artists associated with the Expressionist journal *Der Sturm*, founded in Berlin in 1910, was the Transylvanian painter and sculptor Hans Mattis-Teusch (1884-1960), who, after many years in Munich, returned to Romania and produced a number of works that showed the influence of Kandinsky, the Jugendstil and the Vienna Secession; he was also a regular contributor to two avant-garde art journals, *Integral* and *Contemporeanul*, the latter edited by Marcel Iancu. On the other hand, despite the emergence of Constantin Brâncuși as a sculptor of quite startling originality, such artists as Dimitrie Paciurea (1873-1932) and his pupil Ion Jalea (1887-1983) maintained a more traditional, classical style in their official and public sculpture. One of Paciurea's most gifted pupils, Gheorghe Anghel (1904-66) spent the years 1924 to 1937 in Paris, and his sculpture clearly shows the influence of Rodin, as well as certain elements derived from folk art and Byzantine art, which are revealed in his statues of Theodor Pallady (Craiova Museum) and the poet Mihai Eminescu (in front of the Ateneul Român, Bucharest).

During the first decade of Communist rule after the Second World War, only those artists who were willing to toe the official party line imposed from Moscow and who were deemed to express revolutionary socialist and working-class ideals

Chimera, Dimitrie Paciurea

Constantin Brâncuşi

Constantin Brâncuşi, one of the greatest European sculptors of the twentieth century, was born in 1876 in the small village of Hobiţa, one of the seven children of a ploughman and his spinner wife. As a child he worked in a cooper's shop and tended flocks in the meadows by the Bistriţa River, though he had a smattering of primary education. He repeatedly ran away to nearby towns, working variously as a dyer, a shop assistant and a waiter in an inn; but in 1893 he was taken on by a general store in in Craiova whose owner recognized his remarkable talents and arranged for him to go to school. In 1898 Brâncuşi gained a place in the Academy of Fine Arts in Bucharest, where he remained until 1902. Within a few weeks he produced a bust of the Emperor Vitellius (Craiova Museum), which, although

described as a '*bust dupa antic*', is no mere copy, but already a work of great power and originality. Other portrait busts followed. In 1901, Brâncuşi's studies of anatomy came to fruition in his *Ecorşeul* (*The Flayed Man*), which shows exceptional mastery of form and of the plaster medium but, with its almost clinical attention to the detailed rendering of every muscle, gives little hint of how Brâncuşi's work was later to develop.

In 1903 Brâncuşi left Romania, going first to Munich, and then to Paris, where he was to remain for the rest of his life (though he travelled widely and often returned to Romania). From 1906 he was working in the studio of Auguste Rodin, who exercised a powerful influence. Yet already by about 1907 Brâncuşi's work began to take an entirely new and original direction. 'I studied anatomy

Brâncuşi in his studio

for ten years,' he wrote, 'and I learnt how to model from corpses. When I had learnt this skill to perfection, I put it all to one side and wrestled directly with the material, forgetful of everything I had learnt.' He decided to abandon realism altogether and to try to achieve as great a degree of objectivity in his work as possible by means of reduction and simplification of form. This aim was at variance with the ideas of the Expressionists, whose preoccupation with artistic subjectivity was then fashionable.

Cubism had also gained many adherents in Paris at that time, and the Cubist painters were strongly attracted to primitive, non-European, especially African, art. Like Picasso and other contemporaries, Brâncuşi found in African art a demonic and maleficent quality that greatly appealed to him, and a 'primitive vitality' that prompted him to abandon modelling in favour of carving and to begin working in wood, thus placing himself firmly in the tradition of Romanian folk sculpture. In 1909 in Paris he became friendly with Modigliani, whose subsequent work, especially his mask-like stone heads in African style and the elongated ovoid heads of his portraits, clearly show Brâncuşi's influence. Some of Brâncuşi's own finest work belongs to this period, notably the beautiful marble head entitled *Sleep* (1908, Bucharest Museum).

Brâncuşi's first important essay in reduction and simplification was *The Kiss*, of which he made at least eight versions (one of the earliest, dating from 1907, is in the Craiova Museum). From 1910 Brâncuşi began his long series of nearly abstract sculptures of animals, fish and birds, and he achieved almost total abstraction in his smooth egg-shaped sculptures, such as *Sculpture for the Blind* (1916), *The Newborn* in steel (1923) and the very similar *The Beginning of the World* in polished bronze (1924). But it was perhaps in his portrait busts that his desire to represent living forms in ever more abstract terms is best illustrated.

Another important strand in Brâncuşi's art was his representation in wood of themes from myth and legend, such as his *Sorceress* (1916), *King of Kings* (1920) and *Adam and Eve* (1921) (all Guggenheim Museum, New York).

In 1935 Brâncuşi received a commission from Aretia G. Tătărăscu, president of the National League of Women in his native Gorj *judeţ*, to create a votive and funerary monument in the Târgu Jiu Public Gardens to the Romanian soldiers who had fallen in the First World War. In response, Brâncuşi produced a group of three large monumental sculptures, which were formally inaugurated in 1938. The most important of the three is the *Endless Column*, composed of iron beads on a steel core and almost thirty metres in height. The other monuments in the complex are *The Gate of the Kiss*, which marks the last stage in Brâncuşi's long process of stylization and abstraction of this subject, and *The Table of Silence*, which consists of twelve circular stools shaped like hour-glasses round a circular table, suggesting an enormous stone clock, and thirty more stone stools, also hour-glass shaped, but square, arranged in

The Endless Column

groups of three in five recessed niches on each side of the path leading from the gate to the table.

Brâncuşi continued to work throughout the Second World War, dying in Paris in 1957. In spite of his relatively small output, amounting to only some 215 sculptures, with a further fifty that have been lost or destroyed, Brâncuşi's work has been enormously influential and he is considered by many to be the father of modern sculpture. He was also a fine photographer, chiefly of his own sculptures.

and aspirations in their art found favour with the authorities, but a number of artists, among them Mircea Teodorescu (1900-71), Doru Bucur (1922-69), Ion Bițan (1924-97), Brăduț Covaliu (1924-91), Ion Pacea (1924-99) and Sorin Dumitrescu (b. 1926), contrived to do this at the same time as they also produced innovative work in defiance of the official line. During the first phase of Ceaușescu's regime, from 1965 to 1971, cultural links of all kinds with the West were tolerated, if not positively encouraged, and such painters as Vasile Grigore (b. 1935), who is both a collector and a painter and draughtsman of exceptional talent and whose work is characterized by a palette of great richness and vibrancy, Paul Neagu (1938-2006), who, however, moved to London in 1969, and Horia Bernea (1938-2000), and the sculptors George Apostu (1924-86) and Ovidiu Maitec (1925-2007), whom the Romanian historian Mircea Eliade described as the 'true successor to Brâncuși' and who, like Brâncuși, worked chiefly in metal and wood, were not subject to any serious restrictions and were allowed to travel and to exhibit their work abroad.

After 1971, however, the atmosphere changed, the regime became ever more repressive and the personality cult of Ceaușescu and his wife ever more exaggerated. Artists who showed any signs of a more radical, experimental or innovative approach risked earning the condemnation of the Artists' Union, which exercised a rigid control over their work. In Transylvania, Magyar artists were able to find an outlet and to cultivate links in Hungary, where the arts were less rigidly censored, and groups of artists in Transylvania began to experiment in performance art, conceptual and land art until the 1980s, when they too incurred official displeasure and suffered repression.

After the revolution of 1989 a number of artists who had earlier established themselves under Communist rule, such as Sorin Dumitrescu, Horia Bernea and Ovidiu Maitec, gained benefit from their new freedom, although even they were still starved of international recognition, while others only came to the fore after a long period of transition during the 1990s. These latter include Napoleon Tiron (b. 1936), a sculptor who works in wood, bronze, string and glue, and several artists working in a variety of new and experimental media, such as kinetic art, video art and installations. Of these some of the most interesting are based in Timișoara, where such artists as Constantin Flondor (b. 1936), Ștefan Bertalan (b. 1930), Sorin Vreme (b. 1963) and Alexandru Patatics (b. 1963) have produced interesting and innovative work.

The textiles of Romania

by Sheila Paine

The traditional rural home of Romania may be simple, but it is transformed by the wealth of textiles displayed in every room. Beautiful kilims cover bench and bed or hang on walls. Shaggy blankets add warmth, while woven and embroidered pillows are piled almost to the ceiling. White towels, decorated by weaving or embroidery, are draped over windows, icons and ceramic plates. The floor, of wood or earth, is usually left bare, though sometimes a striped rug lies beside bed or table. On a rod above the stove, or by the bed or bench, hangs the clothing of the family: shifts, shirts and woollen or sheepskin vests and coats. To step into such a house is to be made instantly aware of the profound significance of textiles in Romanian life.

Most will have been made by the woman of the house, usually as her dowry. She was – and in some areas such as Maramureş still is – expected to make ten large pillow cases, ten to fifteen kilims, ten deep pile blankets and countless numbers of towels. Clothing has never been considered part of the dowry, but she would also embroider five to twelve blouses or shifts, or even more.

At her marriage, the bride's textiles were formerly paraded round the village by horse and cart to show to all her skill and qualities as a prospective wife. Many of her towels were offered to the wedding guests.

In almost every home, both rural and urban, there was a loom, and in many cases there still is. On this the woman would weave for all her family's needs, though in the case of more specialized work, such as the heavy woollen jackets, one woman would work for the whole village. Traditionally everything was home-produced: wool from the people's own sheep, hair from their goats, hemp and linen they had grown, spun and woven themselves. Silk was also produced in the south. Now wool, still often handspun, and cotton are the fibres most often used.

Kilims (kelin) The kilims of Romania are little known outside the country but, particularly the older ones of Oltenia, deserve more acclaim. They were made, not only in rural homes, but also in cooperatives and nunneries, or, in the case of Oltenia, in specialized workshops in Craiova and elsewhere. They were woven not only for domestic use, but also for the benches and walls of churches.

The designs of each region are very different, though the kilim weaving technique leads to naturalistic and fluid motifs. The patterns of Oltenia are pictorial: women in full-skirted dresses, often with small fashionable accessories such as sashes, hats and umbrellas; birds such as parrots or the local hoopoes, geese and turkeys; animals of

Spinning, Calineşti

Oriental or Turkish influence such as camels, horses and lions. Flowers fill deep borders and also the field. The kilims of Multenia, in contrast, are dramatic and much like Navajo rugs, while those of Moldavia have narrow borders and repeat motifs of the tree of life, and those of Maramureş are woven in squares, rather like a patchwork.

The warp is always of hemp or cotton and the weft of wool. Dyes used to be of vegetable origin in villages and commercial in factories. Now the skill of making natural dyes is being revived, especially in the village of Botiza in Maramureş, and in Moldavia where traditional patterns are woven in natural pastel colours.

Hand-knotted pile rugs are also still made in cooperatives, for example in Braşov.

Woollen blankets (tol): These shaggy pile bedcovers are woven in the home, often by one woman working for the whole village. The handspun, local wool produces a rough fabric in which short cut pieces of tapering wool are inserted to form a pile several centimetres deep. When the weaving is completed it is taken to a fulling mill, where pounding with hammers in water produces a dense, heavy and virtually waterproof fabric. A few of these wooden water-mills are still worked by hand, the weaving being placed in a slatted wooden tub over a stream, and beaten. The thick woollen fabric of men's and women's coats and waistcoats is made in the same way. That such hand methods of fulling died out in most of Europe in the Industrial Revolution imbues their survival in Romania with a value not only ethnographic but also emotional.

Towels (cingeu): The techniques of towels and pillows are the same. Home-grown, handspun and handwoven white linen or hemp, replaced later by cotton, is used in loom widths for towels and joined to make pillows. Decoration is more often woven than embroidered, and is almost without exception in red and black, with occasional touches of blue. Green, yellow and light blue are later additions. While woven decoration is mainly striped, embroidered motifs of cross-stitch are generally symbolic versions of the tree of life and stylized solar patterns or flowers.

The towels are not only important textiles in the home, but also in church where they are always hung over icons. For these a religious scene or saint is often embroidered. The old wooden churches of northern Romania are warm with towels and kilims that focus the faith of the people.

Costume: The glory of Romanian textile art is the intricately embroidered costume. It has a uniformity of style, within which are great regional differences in decoration that serve to identify people, especially women, and can also indicate social and economic status.

The basis of women's costume is a white linen shift or blouse. The shift, *camesoi*, is straight in cut, employing loom widths supplemented by gussets so that the fabric is used in the most economical way possible. In the case of the blouse, *brezarau*, the

Maramureş peasant men at the beginning of the 20th century

231

Left: peasant woman from Haţeg, Transylvania; right, costumes from the Bucovina; both first quarter of the 20th century

loom widths form the body and sleeves are gathered into a round neckline. Linen is no longer cultivated and has been replaced by cotton, but the cut and the white colour remain the same. The most important embroidery is on the sleeves, especially with the blouse, where a wide band of embroidery on the shoulder, *altiţă*, is separated by a narrow band, *încret*, usually pastel or neutral and often in drawn threadwork, from the vertical or diagonal lines of embroidery, *riuri*, that decorate the rest of the sleeve to the wrist. Particularly fine examples come from Bucovina.

With this white shift or blouse three different kinds of skirt or apron are worn. One is the apron, *catrinţa*, a rectangular piece of cloth worn hanging from the waist at the front, or in two sections from both back and front. Another is the *fotă*, a straight or pleated cloth wrapped round the body below the waist. The third is the *valnic*, a short pleated or gathered skirt.

A white linen or cotton shirt is also the main item of men's costume, usually worn with a wide decorative belt over white trousers of linen or cotton for summer, or fulled wool for winter.

A complex range of headgear includes the *maramă*, a long fine silk women's scarf found particularly in the south; the small beribboned straw hats still worn every day by men of the Cosau Valley of Maramureş; and the extraordinary black felt hats adorned with beading and a high cockade of peacock feathers, flaunted for special occasions by the young men of Nasaud.

Most costume is embroidered in threads of silk or cotton, predominantly in red and black. Metal thread features in the costume of Muscel and silver plate in the aprons of Mehedenti. Patterns are mainly geometric or stylized floral, and there is always an æsthetic balance between areas of plain white and of decoration.

The textiles of the ethnic minorities of Romania are equally significant in people's lives, but different in execution. In particular, the Magyar people of Kalotaszeg in Transylvania wear costume that is Hungarian. The women's dress consists of a series of petticoats and aprons, though still with a white blouse, but it is more floral and colourful than Romanian dress, adorned with scarlet brocaded ribbons, orange pompoms and sparkly beads. Men wear the *cifraszur*, the white fulled wool coat of Hungarian shepherds. In Hungary its embroidery is mainly floral and red, in Romania it is of geometric black wool appliqué.

The Calvinist churches of the Magyars are festooned with white cloths worked in heavy red cotton or wool thread, sometimes in cross-stitch, but more often in the open chainstitch known as *irasos*. Designs are floral combined with religious texts.

Costumes from Oltenia; first quarter of the 20th century

Family from the Banat, first quarter of the 20th century

Other minority groups include the Saxon, most of whom have now left for Germany, but whose influence remains. The costume of the various Germanic settlers of the region around Sibiu and also Bistriţa is decorated soberly in stylized cross-stitch motifs, usually in black, while the fortified Saxon churches, if they have any textiles at all, are merely hung with a few inscribed banners. Romanian costume of these regions is, under Saxon influence, discreetly black and white.

The costumes of Romania, though vibrant and rich, nevertheless have a controlled beauty. Red, black and white are artistically balanced. Fripperies such as straw hats adrift with flowers and mirrors, or bonnets of coins; magnificently colourful sheepskin vests of appliqued leather discs and embroidery; ornate belts of leather studded with copper, or of velvet punched with beads, merely highlight the basic dignity of dress.

The finery of village costumes, once worn every day before being confined to Sundays and festivals, must have been sensational. In a setting of dirt streets, trampled by homecoming cows, goats and sheep, by horses and carts, by pigs and geese, the splendour of the people's dress must have been akin to the effect of a cathedral on a medieval town of wooden huts, a powerful statement of faith and beauty.

Traditional costume is still worn in many villages in Romania. In Maramureş the

Couple from Sincraiu, Transylvania

women have kept the woollen waistcoat, apron, and the wrapped leggings, *obiele*, worn with the soft leather shoes, *opincă*, of Dacian origin. In other villages entire costume is worn, but there is a subtle difference in the way this is done. For some, costumes made by grandmothers are treasured and brought out of trunks for Easter, New Year, dance festivals and other special occasions. They are worn with pride, but almost as fancy dress. But there are other villages where the old, men and women alike, walk to church every week in their 'Sunday best' simply because that is what they have always done. For them, church and costume are inextricably linked, and this is the role of textiles in Romania that will inevitably be lost. The costumes will survive in museums, but the life that gave rise to them and the context in which they were worn sadly will not.

Romanian Glass Icons

by John Villiers

The art of painting icons on glass was practised by the Romanian peasantry at least from the early 18th century and continued to flourish in Transylvania and to a lesser extent also in northern Moldavia until the early 20th century. Many icons painted on glass are still to be found today in village churches as well as in some of the older and more richly decorated peasant houses.

Painting on glass is an ancient technique, probably first adopted as a peasant craft in 17th-century Tyrol and Bohemia. It seems to have been established in Transylvania some time before the Miracle at Nicula in 1699 (when an icon of the Virgin was seen shedding tears), after which the production of glass icons became a small industry in the area. Glass had been available locally since the 16th century from primitive manufactories (*glăjării*), while woodcuts of religious subjects had started to circulate at the same time, ideal models for the peasant craftsmen to copy. Exposure to wider art currents increased after Transylvania was incorporated into the Habsburg Empire in 1699, a development that also encouraged them to find their own means of artistic expression, however modest (unlike painting on wood, painting on glass does not require any specialized training). In the 18th century several centres for painting icons on glass also seem to have come into being in northern Moldavia, probably as a result of links with northern Transylvania and of influences from Galicia in Poland (after 1772 an Austrian possession), where there was already a tradition of icon painting on glass.

At the end of the eighteenth century glass paintings, initially used only as icons in churches, began to be mass produced and find their way into the homes of the peasants, where they were used to decorate the interior in combination with drinking cups and porringers, wall-hangings and cloths. In this way, glass icons served both as ornaments and as devotional objects, and this, combined with the peasant artists' natural inclination to simplify, led to the rapid development of this remarkably expressive art form.

Glass both serves as a support for the painting and does away with the necessity of using varnish. It lends great luminosity and transparency to the colours, but also has drawbacks, notably its fragility and the difficulty of making the paint adhere to it. Moreover, the painter has to remember that the picture will appear inverted on the other side of the glass and that no corrections can be made subsequently.

Black paint, made from soot mixed with glue, alcohol and usually also egg yolk, was used for drawing the outlines. The other colours were mixed with oil and a little turpentine, and lead acetate was added just before the colour was applied to the glass to ensure quick drying. The most frequently used colours were red, yellow, bluish-purple, green, white, brick-red, carmine, bronze and silver-grey, but the tonality and depth achieved varied from centre to centre and artist to artist.

The icons were almost always copied from a model. The outline was first traced in black or white with a brush or pen. Next, the inscription was written, usually in Cyrillic, but sometimes in Roman or Greek script. Mistakes often occur because many of the painters, particularly those from Nicula, were illiterate. The colours were then added, and turpentine was applied over the whole icon. Bronze or gold leaf was used for the saints' haloes and sometimes even for the whole background. Repeated copying of tracings made from a single model would often result in variations in the original design occurring between one icon and another, and these were made greater by differences in the personal style of individual artists and, in some cases, by their clumsiness and uneven workmanship. The icons were set in wooden frames made generally

Adam and Eve, glass icon, northern Transylvania, late 19th century (Folk Art Museum, Cluj)

of fir-wood and painted to match. Some icon painters, for example those working at Laz, used carved frames ornamented with a twisted rope pattern. A piece of paper was often placed between the glass and the wooden back of the frame to give additional protection; and sometimes the paper also served as a background, in which case it would usually be silver-grey.

The subjects most commonly chosen by these village icon painters are of local patron saints, scenes from the Life of Jesus and the Blessed Virgin and from the Apocalypse. Elements taken from folk literature, folklore and everyday life also appear. Some saints were particularly popular: St George and St John were believed to protect livestock, Elijah to fend off lightning, St Haralambos to guard against the plague (shown as a woman, a skeleton or a dragon) and other diseases. St Nicholas brought good luck, and was often portrayed in the setting of a south Transylvanian village with the three maidens whom he has saved from dishonour. St George on horseback slaying the dragon was another favourite subject, often painted with many details and decorative motifs taken from local models. In some icons St George is accompanied by his fellow dragon-slayer St Tiron, also on a horse. These saints were also patrons of the different seasons, and the peasants tilled their fields and tended their vineyards under their protection: St George for spring, the Virgin Mary for summer, St Demetrius for autumn and St Nicholas for winter.

Icons of the Virgin Mary and the Nativity were considered to be symbols of fecundity and therefore formed part of many bridal dowries. The Virgin is frequently portrayed holding the dead Jesus in her arms, sometimes, particularly in icons from the Sibiu area, wearing a necklace of three rows of gold coins, formerly a common adornment among Romanian peasant women. In Nativity scenes the background is always white and a stylized star hangs in the night sky above, while a shepherd clad in a long-haired sheepskin cloak similar to those worn in the Făgăraş Mountains plays a flute as he watches over his flock grazing among the rocks.

Another favourite subject is Elijah. In one version he is shown ascending to Heaven in a a peasant cart drawn by two horses and throwing down to Elisha a sheepskin cloak like those worn by the shepherds in Poiana Sibiului, while nearby a peasant ploughs and a woman spins near a cradle on the bank of a stream full of fish. In another, Elijah's chariot is drawn by four horses, which he urges on with a three-thonged whip, while Elisha stands beneath, framed in clouds. Again, a peasant is shown at a plough, drawn by two white oxen and a horse, in defiance of the Old Testament injunction against the yoking together of animals of different species.

Icons of the Last Supper, showing Jesus and the twelve apostles, (Judas shown without a halo), often either demonstrate the influence of the Italian Renaissance, notably Leonardo, or are painted in a more hieratic style derived from Byzantine models. Depictions of the Crucifixion, on the other hand, are generally in the style of folk woodcuts, and contain a number of details derived from folklore and other non-biblical sources. Icons of the Resurrection also often include elements derived from western models, such as the depiction of the angel lifting the tombstone (in the Eastern Church the tomb is normally shown still sealed). Christ is also often portrayed giving His benediction or holding a vine branch, although in some icons, particularly those of the Nicula and Schei-Braşov schools, He is shown with a vine growing from the wound in His side, an ancient motif adopted from early Slavonic Christian iconography.

The subject of Adam and Eve in the Garden of Eden is usually treated in a naive but highly decorative style. Adam and Eve are shown near the forbidden tree round which the serpent is coiled. The tree is usually portrayed in the form of a decorative arch and the rest of the garden is composed of repeated floral motifs, as in a tapestry. Above the tree can be seen the sun and moon, representing the forces of nature. Some icons show the creation of Eve from Adam's rib, the serpent tempting

*The Prophet Elijah borne up to
heaven in the fiery chariot,
Făgăraş,
mid nineteenth century
(Braşov Museum)*

Eve to eat of the forbidden fruit, and Eve spinning and Adam ploughing after their expulsion from the Garden of Eden.

Subjects varied greatly from centre to centre. In some places, patterns were copied so often that they were completely transformed, as happened in the nineteenth century at Nicula; in others, both the subject and its treatment varied considerably. In many centres there were genuinely creative artists who became dissatisfied with merely copying the same model over and over again and began to consult books of folklore and religion, and even secular literature in search of new themes, as well as making use of subjects and motifs taken from illuminated manuscripts and other forms of book illustration. All that they took from these sources, however, they interpreted in an individual way, and the more gifted among them usually introduced elements from local life into their work..

It is difficult to trace the history of the development of the glass icon in Romania, partly because, as we have already noted, so few of them are signed and dated, partly because so many of the old centres of production have disappeared, and partly because not only were the icons sold by pedlars travelling over wide areas, but the models for them were equally widely circulated, so that icons produced in different centres at a considerable distance from one another are often found together in the same area, so that caution needs to be exercized before attributing any icon to a particular centre. Furthermore, recent researches have revealed that there were some places that specialized in the sale rather than in the production of icons, such as the village of Vlădeni near Braşov, where in the nineteenth and early twentieth centuries icons painted at Schei-Braşov were transported and sold by the peasants throughout southeast Transylvania.

The Music of Romania

by Robert Matthew-Walker

Yehudi Menuhin wrote in his autobiography *Unfinished Journey* that 'The strength of Romania's musical traditions, even in our urban, streamlined, computerized international civilization, is something to marvel at and offer up thanks for.' The music of Romania is an extraordinary amalgam of various elements derived from varied regions and ancient influences. Until the mid-nineteenth century the Romanian principalities remained somewhat apart from the direct influence of European arts and sciences, but the court of Carol I, the first king of united Romania, became a central focus for all the arts under the direction of the highly cultivated Queen Elisabeta. From that time, the development of Romanian art music as a part of European culture can truly be said to have begun.

As it happened, Queen Elisabeta's considerable and very welcome influence was exerted when opportunities were just beginning to appear for gifted Romanians to study European music in their own country. Royal support and encouragement for music gave the fledgling institutions the best possible status. State conservatoires for music were established in 1860 in Iaşi and in 1864 in Bucharest. In 1868 they were joined by the Romanian Philharmonic Society, the first established symphony orchestra in the country, and in 1877 by the first permanent opera company, the Romanian Opera, was also established in Bucharest, although western opera had been performed in the capital fairly frequently – even if almost invariably by touring companies from abroad – since 1847.

One of the more far-reaching developments in music that took place in the last quarter of the nineteenth century was the rise of nationalism, a movement which seemed at one level to parallel the political demands of the day, but which also had a specifically aesthetic purpose, namely to throw off the then all-pervasive Germanic influence. In countries as far apart as Ireland, Norway, Finland, Russia, Poland, Italy and Spain, some composers, although not all, were ready to learn the essential features of composition – structure, fugue, counterpoint, orchestration and so on – either in Germany or through German models, and yet, once past their student years, were keen to seek fresh inspiration from the folk-music of their native countries.

In this regard, the young musicians of Romania were singularly well placed to achieve their aims. On the one hand, they had established conservatoires and enjoyed royal patronage, in Bucharest and elsewhere; in addition, they were geographically closer to Russia and thus far removed from the immediate influence of German music colleges. On the other hand, they had the extraordinary diversity and richness of Romanian folk-music on which to draw for their nationalist compositions – a diversity and richness that reflected the unique combination of ethnic elements which had gone to make up the people of Romania, as well as the culturally diverse mix of older European musical influences with those of more eastern provenance that existed in the main cities throughout Romania.

One distinctly eastern aspect was the absence of musical instruments in Orthodox worship. What one might call the evolving harmonic basis of much European music, that of the Christian churches – be they Catholic or Protestant – did not form part of the everyday musical experience of all Romanians. One should not labour this point; the Romanian tradition glories in unaccompanied choirs singing in rich harmony, as elsewhere in Orthodox Christendom including, of course, Russia, Bulgaria and Greece – but the absence of an organ was the most obvious instrumental difference, and the organ brought music from outside the religious celebration into the churches.

In this way, therefore, the evolving development of harmonic and contrapuntal writing characteristic of western music was largely absent in Romania and, at least up to about 1860, musically gifted Romanians therefore had to study music abroad, which meant the great conservatoires of western Europe. Paris (the cultural centre of Europe in the early nineteenth century), Berlin and, to a lesser extent, Vienna, were all considered to be 'second homes' for musical Romanians.

Even if we consider the absence of a Western European harmonic tradition to be a disadvantage in Romanian church music, we must not forget that music in Orthodox worship has its own unique and vital tradition. Founded upon the ancient modes, but allied to older, eastern musical scales, which may initially sound strange to western ears, Orthodox church music has a character and a deep-rooted basis which is just as viable, just as capable of artistic revivification, as any other. It is also in many ways more flexible, for it permits quarter-tones and elisions from note to note, and a harmonic foundation which does not necessarily adhere to the rules of western harmony, and yet is not entirely based upon Byzantine modes. These qualities can be discerned even in the earliest surviving written music of Romania, the hymns composed in the Cozia Monastery by Filothei in the fourteenth century. The result is music that in many ways is fresher, freer and more responsive to the momentary demands of the musician than we often find within the more structured western tradition. A further source of inspiration was the introduction of the Romanian language into church music at the end of the seventeenth century and the beginning of the eighteenth. The Romanians themselves had recognized the unique aspects of this musico-religious branch of their culture: in 1928 a school of Romanian church music was founded in Bucharest to ensure its continued study and survival, and although the thirty-odd years of Communist rule caused much of this music, and its attendant study, to fall into disfavour, it did not – indeed, could not – wholly disappear. In quite recent years there has been a most encouragingly strong revival of interest in the subject of Romania.

There is one other equally vital and important strain in Romanian music, which tragically was virtually stamped out. By the mid-1930s, Bucharest had become one of the great Jewish cities of Europe, offering refuge to over 200,000 Jews fleeing from capture and persecution, not only in Romania but in the neighbouring countries. Many of them only settled there temporarily and were soon to seek permanent residence in Israel or elsewhere; Romania was the only socialist country to maintain good relations with Israel. However, the largely temporary nature of the Jewish population in Bucharest (there were upwards of one million throughout the whole of Romania) meant that their musical contribution to the life of Romania would be confined mainly to support for western art music; nonetheless, there has existed in Bucharest, as in most European capital cities, a significant Jewish population which kept its own musical traditions.

Such an environment, which so readily embraced the best of east and west in its music, would be perfectly capable of producing a dynamic and exciting art, as indeed proved to be the case in the work of one wholly exceptional musician. However, this claim has to be considered alongside the fact that western musical teaching on a systematic basis has been established in Romania for rather less than 150 years.

Nevertheless, although the influence of the early conservatoire composers such as the Wachmanns (Edourd and his son Anton) was a vital development, there had been composers of merit in Romania from the sixteenth century onwards, notably Hieronymus Ostermayer (1500-1561) and, a century later, Reilich, Croner, Bakfark, Caianu and the remarkable Prince Dimitrie Cantemir. This exceptional man, who spoke eleven languages, lived from 1673 to 1723 and was for a short period ruler of Moldavia under Turkish suzerainty; he introduced musical notation to Turkey and wrote, in Turkish, a musical treatise which is thought to be the first work of its kind to be produced in Romania. He also wrote, in Romanian, an introduction to Turkish music.

Later still, in the mid-eighteenth century, significant contributions were made to secular music by Johann Sartorius and Filothei sin Agai Jipei. In 1838 Prince Alexandru Ghica, governor of Wallachia, intent upon restructuring the music of his court along western lines, brought the Viennese musician, Ludwig Weist, to Bucharest. Soon after Weist's arrival, the prince dismissed his Turkish band. Turkish music had enjoyed a considerable vogue in the musical capitals of western Europe in the closing decades of the eighteenth century, and had attracted, in varying degrees, Haydn, Mozart, Beethoven and Weber; but by the time Weist arrived in Bucharest in the late 1830s, the fashion for Turkish music had begun to wane in Vienna and Paris.

Weist, however, was not only a reorganizer, but also a gifted violinist and conductor, and he not only established a good western type of orchestra at the

Wallachian court, but also wrote a number of successful orchestral fantasias on Romanian airs. Although Weist was not himself of Romanian stock, we can sense in these works, almost wholly forgotten today, the planting of the first seeds of a national Romanian school, based upon folk-music.

The seed may have brought forth early fruit in the publication, in 1852, of a study of many rural Romanian ballads and popular songs by the poet Vasily Alexandri (1821-90). This was, of course, only a few years before the election of Alexandru Ioan Cuza as prince of both Moldavia and Wallachia, which led directly to the unification of the country and the consequent establishment of a national dynamic.

'Cometh the time, cometh the man,' as the saying goes, and the myriad influential streams that irrigated the soil of Romanian music were soon to find a genius who was to take the music of Romania to the shores of every civilized country in the world.

George Enescu was said by the great Pablo Casals to be 'probably the most amazing musician since Mozart'. Enescu achieved international renown as a violinist, conductor, composer and pianist, and he displayed genius in every one of these disciplines. He was without question one of the greatest violinists of the twentieth century, he was a conductor of exceptional insight, penetration and technical command, he was beyond doubt the greatest composer Romania has so far produced, and he was a pianist of considerable attainment.

Enescu possessed a phenomenal memory and knew the entire repertoire of classical and romantic music by heart, in addition to many twentieth-century works, towards which we might think that someone of his generation might well have been unsympathetic. Quite apart from these superlative gifts, Enescu was a man of deep humility; he was a most profound teacher,

Georges Enescu as a young man

although he very rarely gave private lessons, and amongst his pupils were Dinu Lipatti and Yehudi Menuhin, who regarded Enescu as the most important single influence on his early life, as much for his humanity as for his musical genius. Enescu impressed every musician who met him, and there were many.

George Enescu was born in 1881 in the Carpathian Mountains. So gifted was the boy that, by the age of seven, his accomplishments as a violinist allowed him to enter not the Bucharest but the Vienna Conservatoire. By then he had already decided to become a composer. His progress was sensational, and although he never forgot his home or his native Romania, he had graduated with distinction from the Vienna Conservatoire before his eleventh birthday. By this time also, Enescu had played on the first desk of an orchestra conducted by Brahms in a performance of the latter's First Symphony and his First Piano Concerto, in which the composer was the soloist. Brahms became Enescu's lifelong hero, together with Wagner. This twofold admiration demonstrates the broad range of Enescu's sympathies. Indeed, it was Wagner's music that Enescu said had become 'part of my vascular system'; later in life, he would play whole acts of Wagner's operas from memory.

In 1892 Enescu entered the Paris Conservatoire, studying composition with Massenet. When Enescu was only thirteen, Massenet wrote to the boy's father: 'Your son is an exceptional individual; his is the most interesting musical constitution there can be.' As a young composer, Enescu showed an astonishing command of large-scale forms; by the age of 16 he had composed four symphonies (called today 'Symphonies d'École', to differentiate them from his three numbered mature symphonies). He was also the soloist in the world premiere of his own Violin Concerto, which he played in Paris at the age of fifteen.

By the time of his eighteenth birthday in 1899, therefore, George Enescu was not only a supremely gifted musician, but a thoroughly trained one. He had also begun his mature list of compositions which, opening with his Opus 1, the magnificent *Romanian Poem* for chorus and orchestra, composed when he was seventeen, was to pay tribute again and again to the homeland from which he had been separated for ten years. By the turn of the century Enescu had written the two works for which, as a composer, he is remembered above all – the Romanian Rhapsodies.

On his return to Romania in 1898, Enescu was struck by the 'gypsy-style' violinists who played in the hotels, restaurants, clubs and cafés of Bucharest. As a man from the countryside, Enescu naturally absorbed the folk-music of rural Romania. His conservatoire years had instilled in him a largely Germanic tradition, and his debts to Wagner and Brahms were balanced by similar debts to French masters, but at heart Enescu remained deeply Romanian. An important consequence of this was his series of works using Romanian folk-song. It is fascinating to compare his early folk-based music with that of his contemporary Bartók, for both began in this field from somewhat similar Lisztian principles, as in the earlier master's 'Hungarian' works. If Bartók found his roots – coincidentally researching Romanian folk-music – in ethnomusicological purity at the zenith of the Austro-Hungarian empire, Enescu created alone an international Romanian 'school'. Between his Opus 1 and his penultimate score, the *Romanian Overture* of 1948, he wrote several nationalist works using aspects of Romanian folk-music: part-modal and part-pentatonic, with richly ornamented tunes of eastern provenance.

Apart from his more overtly 'Romanian' works, Enescu wrote a number of other large-scale compositions, including the three symphonies already mentioned, but above all the four-act opera *Œdipe*, which Enescu himself described as a 'lyric tragedy'. This is undoubtedly his masterpiece, and one of the great operas of the century. It was completed in 1932.

A Romanian Gipsy band,
mid 19th century

As a youth, Enescu was greatly encouraged by the Romanian court, where he met and was adored by members of the royal family. He was appointed court violinist by Queen Elisabeta, and then fell in love with Princess Cantacuzino, an established and married member of the aristocracy. As an adult, his love for her developed: it was returned, and the couple were longtime lovers, although they always retained a veneer of decorum. The princess's husband died in the 1930s; Enescu married her, although by then she was very ill and needed constant nursing. For most of the year he would be on tour, living a performing life that would have felled many less gifted men, but always providing for her. Such was his genius that, for example, at a single concert in 1919, he played the solo parts in both Beethoven's Violin Concerto and in Liszt's Second Piano Concerto.

Through the Second World War Enescu remained in Romania, but when the Communists took power in 1947, he moved to Paris in order to spare his wife. There he died in 1955, but not before making a number of important recordings as a conductor, notably one of Schumann's Second Symphony. After his death, his home village of Liveni was renamed George Enescu.

In 1896, while Enescu was completing his studies in Paris, the government of Romania, prompted by the enthusiasm of Queen Elisabeta, had set up a national subvention for the collection of Romanian folk-songs and dances. This soon became one of the finest such collections in the world, numbering many thousands of recordings, and led to the founding in 1928 of the Folk-music Archive, later renamed the Institute of Ethnography and Folklore. It is thanks to these pioneering efforts that we know as much about Romanian folk-music as we do. The most frequently encountered instruments associated with this music are the *bucium* (a kind of Romanian alpenhorn, mostly found in Wallachia), the *nai* or pan-pipes (famous

Dancing the batuta, c. 1900

worldwide through the success of the Romanian player, George Zamfir), the *cimpoi*, a type of bagpipe, and the violin. Mention should also be made of the Romanian *buhaiu* ('bullock'), a unique percussion instrument said to produce a sound akin to that of cattle lowing.

As we have noted, the provenance of Romanian folk-music is very varied and for this reason, the forms and scales also vary considerably. Yet, in spite of this variety, the result is almost always recognizably Romanian. Exactly why this should be so is difficult to explain; perhaps the main reason is melodic, for, despite the variety, it remains generally true that the overwhelming majority of Romanian folk-tunes have a descending phrase. As with almost all European folk-music, that of Romanis is allied to the seasons, and, consequently, to life and death. But there is another genre of Romanian folk-music, called the *doina*. This does not refer to any specific incident or time of year, but rather to a particular state of mind.

The *doina*, whilst not being intentionally sad or pessimistic in character, tends to express the eternal struggle of life, the darker side of existence. Consequently, the music will often be found to turn in upon itself and will fall chromatically; despite this, there is a moving sense of fulfilment in the *doina*, which can also exist in instrumental forms. Interestingly, in the Wallachian region, there exists a unique type of *doina* which sings of love in all its forms of expression; here, generally speaking, we find that the music conveys a more optimistic state of mind.

It is possible to confuse Romanian songs with ballads, but the latter are historically based, recounting deeds and other events from ancient times. If in Transylvania and parts of Moldavia we still find texts of ballads being sung to certain melodies, this merely proves the practical impossibility of categorizing folk-art too rigidly. The songs proper are almost always much more regular with regard to their strophic texts, even if, as Bartok noted, they can vary considerably from region to region, and we will often find songs with refrains.

Easter is a most important time of the year; the coming of spring finds expression in a wide variety of Romanian folk-music, especially songs and dances for rain-makers and for the fertility aspects of Whitsuntide. The religious festivals themselves, as well as the later harvest, also abound in many varied musical expressions, more obviously in pastoral folk-music. The seasons tend to find their chief expression in the dance, in which Romanian folk-music is particularly rich, especially in the choreography, even if musically almost all Romanian folk-dances are in duple time.

One of the great glories of Romanian folk-music is the carol (*colinda*); here we find a particularly rich repertoire, from all regions and of the greatest variety and subtlety. Often the *colindă* becomes a sung dance with quite involved choreography. There is also another rich seam of folk-music connected with commemorations of birth, marriage and death. The last is quite ritualistic and the folk-music associated with it therefore the more moving for, like the ritual, it is not written down.

Clearly, the almost inexhaustible variety and richness of Romanian folk-music is not only exceptional in itself, but also provides a vast treasure-chest of ethnic material and an immensely fertile musical environment in which gifted Romanian musicians, taking their lead from Enescu, have been able to develop their talents. This has led in turn to a number of later Romanian musicians making international names for themselves: the conductors Sergiu Celibidache and Constantin Silvestri, the singers Ileana Cotrubas and Angela Gheorghiu, the pianists Clara Haskil and Radu Lupu amongst others.

Carol singers, Bucharest, mid 19th-century

Wildlife in Romania

by Dudley Iles

Flying into Bucharest on a clear day, one has the impression that the city is surrounded by small lakes and forests. The journey from the airport to the centre first reveals extensive allotments then wide streets and massive, grim, grey blocks of flats. Only swifts and sparrows and the universal feral pigeon seem to be able to survive this man-made environment. However, a short distance from the city the Village Museum Park contains some familiar garden birds, and the common but less well-known Syrian woodpecker and golden oriole. The lakes are popular with fishermen, but from the attractive Hotel Lebada (Swan), situated on an island, it is possible to hear cuckoo and quail, and to see black-necked grebe on the lake. Many lakes near the capital are popular at weekends but it is worth spending an hour or so on wooded shores and quieter bays looking for birds, butterflies and wild flowers.

The journey eastwards, for some 270 kilometres, to the Danube Delta is on a major road, but it is narrow, bumpy and slow for much of its distance. Instead of the heavy lorries the visitor may be happier to watch for the colourful gypsy caravans and the many mule- and horse-drawn wooden carts. Each village has its flock of noisy geese and, in summer, children selling bright red cherries by the roadside. People walking to the fields, carrying scythes and other long-forgotten implements, remind us of rural life in Constable's England, whilst beyond stretch the gently rolling, seemingly endless fields of wheat, maize or nodding yellow sunflowers. Massive combines line up along the edges like dinosaurs ready to swallow up the harvest. Where stubble lies, flocks of rooks and jackdaws gather and Montagu's harriers quarter the ground, whilst in early summer occasional parties of red-footed falcons search above the stubble for insects exposed by the harvesting. We become increasingly aware of white storks searching the ground for grasshoppers, frogs and mice to be carried back to feed their growing young. Their huge nests can be seen on telegraph poles and churches in almost every village, sometimes as many as twelve or more together. House sparrows take advantage of these stick complexes to build their own nests. Where the grain has not been cut, the fields are often splashed with red from millions of wild poppies, and the roadside, which is rarely

Pelicans in the Danube Delta

sprayed, is blue with larkspur, comfrey, vetches, meadow clary and cornflowers. Melilots, sainfoin and mulleins provide additional colour. Like many continental roads, our route to the east is lined with trees, which provide cover for flocks of tree sparrows descending on the scattered grain left by the combines. Poplar, limes, cherry-trees and false acacia, each trunk painted white, we are told, to alert the sleepy driver to the coming bend. But to the birdwatcher from Britain, the tele-phone wires provide a test of quick identification, as many birds use these vantage points to drop on unsuspecting beetles below, or to capture flying insects above, or simply to rest. Every few hundred metres lesser grey shrikes, rollers and bee-eaters, kestrels, finches, swallows, house martins and others make use of the wires. Lakes and marshy ground are frequent along the way, and here wading birds can often be seen in large numbers. Black-tailed godwits, avocets and smaller waders come here on their way to the east and north in spring after their winter in the south, or on their return once more in late summer.

Just before Hârşova, the road crosses the Danube flowing north towards Galaţi, where it turns at a right angle to begin its final passage to the Delta. This area is interesting to the naturalist, but time and military control usually discourage too long a stop.

Dobrogea is the most thinly populated province in Romania and, apart from the famous Black Sea holiday complexes to the south, is little known to most tourists. It is dominated by the low but very old Măcin Hills diverting the Danube to the north. To the east of these hills lie the plains and marshes of the Delta and the Sinoe-Razim complex of shallow lakes and wetlands forming the western shore of the Black Sea.

This region supports extensive broadleaf forests. Topalog Forest has a variety of vegetation where red-backed shrikes take over from lesser greys, and black and middle spotted woodpeckers, wryneck, nightingale and hawfinch are to be found. Bee-keepers with their brightly painted carts and hives use the woods in summer. The extensive woodland, rolling hills and open plains beyond provide ideal condi-tions for birds of prey. Short-toed eagle may be watched hovering over the hills, and the rare eastern race of the Imperial eagle occasionally soars on thermals over the plains. In the woodland honey buzzard and sparrowhawk can be seen. Butterflies use the fringes of the wood, where white umbelliflorae attract red admi-ral, peacocks, marble whites and silver-wash fritillaries.

To the naturalist the Danube Delta is the jewel in the crown of Romania. Just above Tulcea the river splits into two channels. The Chilia Channel winds its way north and then east bordering the Ukraine, whilst the southern channel shortly divides to produce the commercially important Sulina Channel, straightened and widened between 1880 and 1903 for shipping, and the narrower Sfântu Gheorghe Channel, which meanders its way to the south of the Delta. Within these waterways is a vast wetland equal in area to the Rhône Delta in France and the Guadalquivir

Delta in Spain put together. The waters of this great river and the millions of tons of silt it carries find their way to the Black Sea through a myriad of levéed streams which support willows and alders, their roots bathed by the river and their branches often touching to form delicate natural green tunnels. Beyond stretch open lakes, phragmites-fringed, and with delightful displays of yellow and white water-lilies. The vast vista of the sky and the flat, open, wooded and wet landscape give an ethereal atmosphere to this wild and primitive region.

The vast reed-beds have their own ecology. Peat formed from the remains of dead reeds and bulrushes creates a micro-habitat. Flowering rush, purple loosestrife, ferns and mosses contribute to these floating reed-islands (*plauri*), which assist in the distribution of many water plants. Marsh frogs, in particular, and edible frogs have their territories along the waterways and reed-beds, whilst grass snakes are frequently seen swimming the channels. Coypu and musk-rat have also established themselves as part of the delta community.

Apart from the landscape, birds must remain the most lasting memory for those who visit this wilderness. As you slip quietly along, be it in a local rowing boat or a launch, there are continual reminders that this is a European stronghold for many waterbirds. Squacco and night heron, great white and little egret, little bittern and purple heron, glossy ibis and cormorant are frequently seen on shore or on floating islands, whilst overhead sudden flashes of brilliant white draw your attention to the soaring flocks of white pelicans turning in unison as they gain height. It is possible to count as many as 2000 planing in from their feeding grounds in the evening. Long lines of cormorants, sometimes the rarer pigmy cormorants, continually cross the sky like flighting geese. Deep in a secret place in the Delta, is one of the largest colonies of cormorant in Europe; they nest in low trees, accompanied by a few glossy ibis, whilst below, amongst the water-lily pads, black-necked and red-necked grebe sit on their floating nests, and whiskered terns use the leaves to support their eggs. On one occasion our boat surprised one of the few remaining white-tailed sea eagles as it plucked a newly killed coot on the bank.

The willows along the bank support many smaller birds, including grey-headed and Syrian woodpeckers, garden warblers and penduline tits, whose nests hang precariously from the ends of the willow branches. Surprisingly, magpies and cuckoos seem well adapted to this extensive wetland.

Since prehistoric times the Danube has continually deposited sediment along the edge of the Delta into the Black Sea, so that the Delta region has greatly increased in area and many old sandy shores and islands are now several kilometres inland. The two largest of these sandy islands, Grindul Caraorman and Grindul Letea, contain picturesque villages with wooden, reed-thatched cottages and fences enclosing tiny farmyards with vegetable patches and cherry orchards bright with flowers. But for an occasional tractor, there are no vehicles to disturb the geese and brindled pigs which roam the broad sandy streets. Storks nest on many of the telegraph posts;

starlings, occasionally rose-coloured starlings, feed in the cherry-trees; a red-backed shrike nests in the honeysuckle above a cottage door. A small boy proudly displays a racoon dog that he has just caught.

Beyond the village are wet meadows and spacious broadleaf woodland composed of oak, ash, poplar, alder, crab-apple and wild pear, which can be reached by tractor, and where there are sunny glades that make good picnic sites. Letea Forest has a rich small bird population: golden oriole, hoopoe, thrush, nightingale, Icterine warbler, wood warbler, and collared flycatcher. In winter, we are told, elk and even wolves may move down from Russia to join the resident roe-deer, fox and wild cat which inhabit the woods. Much of the Delta to the south of the Sulina Channel is remote and full of *grinduri*, extensive reed-beds and scattered lakes where pelicans and cormorants share with the fishermen the aquatic bounty of this unique ecosystem. A journey from Tulcea southeastwards along road 222c offers an interesting cross-section of Dobrogea. There are many good stopping-places along the road, such as the hill just south of Tulcea where not only herons, spoonbills, ibis, garganey and visiting waders can be seen with ease, but also breeding bee-eaters, an occasional hobby and a colony of ground squirrels (*suslek*) on the sandy slope overlooking the river. The road to the north runs through several villages, each with its marshes. To the south grain fields stretch into the distance, and at Beştepe an arm of the Măcin Hills provides updraughts for soaring birds where once griffon vultures could be seen, whilst nearby a colony of red-footed falcons sometimes rear their young in magpie nests after the owners have gone. Near Murighiol, where a pleasant hotel complex has been developed, a small lake provides good viewing of breeding common terns, black-headed gulls, a few Mediterranean gulls, black-winged stilts and three species of grebe.

Babadag Forest is well worth a visit. It has a wide variety of habitats and open views of the plain on the southern edge, and it leads on towards Histria, the well-preserved Graeco-Roman port. The road once more crosses grain fields with calling quail and occasionally corncrake, then passes between the phragmites-lined lakes of Nuntaşi and Istria, and opens into a flat region of brackish grassland with shallow pools that vanish in the heat of summer. To the northeast lies the 'port' where hoopoes and tree sparrows nest in the ancient walls and roe deer occasionally appear on the edge of the adjoining reed-beds. Cleopatra butterflies, swallowtails and clouded yellows are attracted to the many wild flowers on the site.

The western edge of the Black Sea, with its complex of brackish mud flats, lakes and marshes, is a major migration route for many thousands of wading birds. Parties of little stint, ruff, spotted redshank and marsh sandpiper feed alongside locally breeding avocet and black-winged stilts. Other breeding birds include pratincoles, Kentish plover and shelduck – the latter a long way from their counterparts in Western Europe. This exciting area always has something to interest the observer; whether it is Dalmatian pelicans, black storks, or little gulls and little terns. Singing tawny pipits, sky and Calandra larks are often to be seen in the sky on sunny days.

The road south eventually leads the visitor away from the rural countryside of Dobrogea and into the holiday resort towns and oil refineries of the Black Sea coast, but a few kilometres inland the familiar open fields bright with poppy and corn-flower reappear. Some 12 kilometres west of Mangalia lies a delightful little reserve: Hagieni is an island of woodland, limestone slopes and a marshy stream within a sea of cultivation. The sunny slopes support the growth of lady's bedstraw, scabious, thyme, bird's-foot trefoil, milkwort and many more, attracting small coppers, bluespot hairstreaks, chalkhill blues and common blue butterflies. The wooded hill-sides are the home of nightjar, red-backed shrike and ortolan bunting, whilst birds of prey soaring overhead can pose problems of identification.

Much further west, from Băneasa to Giurgiu, 64 kilometres south of Bucharest, the Danube once more exerts its influence. Its periodic flooding revives many shal-low lakes and encourages the growth of lush vegetation. This region records most of the birds of the Delta, as well as some with a more southern distribution. Lake Oltina supports one of the largest colonies of sand martins in Europe. The same sandy cliffs provide nesting sites for bee-eaters and occasional pied wheatears.

In contrast to the steppes and Danube lowlands of the east and south, to the north and west stretches the rugged splendour of the Carpathian Mountains. This moun-tain massif rises to over 2,000 metres. It is drained by many swift-flowing stony streams, which flow through deep, youthful valleys, often with spectacular views. Local villages with characteristic architecture nestle amongst the lush meadows, where cattle graze and hay-making in the old style can be seen. The meadows before cutting are rich in wild flowers: viper's grass, bistort, lady's mantle, cranebill, yellow rattle and clovers.

Above the fields, old beech woods occupy the steep slopes. An early morning walk along one of the many woodland paths may provide sightings of redstart, red-breasted flycatcher, greater spotted woodpecker, blackcap and hawfinch. On path edges, yellow foxglove, deadly nightshade, dusky cranesbill and bellflowers provide colour.

Nestling deep in the mountains, Poiana Brașov lies only 14 kilometres from the historic town of Brașov, at the foot of Mount Postavarul. Despite its popularity with local people and tourists, and the less than attractive hotels that have been built to accommodate them, Poiana Brașov is a good centre for the naturalist. The hotels are surrounded by mature pine and spruce and scattered mountain meadows. Small colonies of fieldfare breed in the evergreen trees on the edge of the meadows, where mistle thrush, song thrush and ring ouzel hunt for food amongst the cattle. It is pos-sible to see nutcrackers, crossbills, crested and willow tits from almost any hotel window.

The cable car allows a quick ascent to the mountain top. A check before the pic-nickers arrive may disclose a wall-creeper on the cable-car station wall. The slopes below, in their season, display alpine flowers, lousewort, alpine lady's mantle, and saxifrages. The three-hour walk down the mountain passes through tall, quiet ever-green forests, where fallen trees are left to fungi and the beetle. The avifauna of robins, dunnock and siskin reflect a temperate climate, but the holed rotting tree stumps are the work of three-toed woodpeckers, and Ural owls are known to breed here. These forests are sanctuaries for fox, badger, roe-deer and bear. The latter for-age in the hotel dustbins at night, much to the chagrin of the local dogs. These magnificent creatures, which often have cubs, add to the atmosphere of the vast, dark forests which are so characteristic a feature of the Carpathian Mountains.

Gazetteer

Abrud (Abrudbánya) Transylvania
Town in western Transylvania about 65 km
northwest of Alba Iulia, a goldmining centre
from antiquity to the early 20th century. It
has a castle on the site of a Roman fort and
numerous old wooden houses. Its neo-
Baroque buildings are clad in floral stucco
and incorporate stones from earlier Roman
structures. Many are covered with plaques
commemorating notable visitors who came
here when Abrud was the Moţi capital. The
town has a faded elegance, and there are
churches of many denominations here – two
Protestant, one Catholic, one Orthodox and
one Uniate – a testament to the town's former
vibrancy, due mainly to its once-flourishing
mines. (There have recently been controver-
sial proposals to revive opencast mining
here, particularly for gold.) **Roşia Montana**,
a few km northeast, has a museum illustrating the history of mining in this area.
Bucium, a village 13 km east of Abrud, was
also a gold town, whose inhabitants still
wear a distinctive local costume. Nearby are
some spectacular basalt rock formations
known as the **Detunata**, which can be
climbed in about an hour.

Adamclisi Dobrogea
Attractive village in southern Dobrogea, site
of the celebrated Tropaeum Traiani, a monument dedicated to Mars, that was erected by
the Emperor Trajan in 109 AD to commemo-

rate his victory over the Dacians in 101-2
AD. Most of the monument, which is 30 m
high, is in fact less than 50 years old: a
polygonal base supporting a martial figure
rests on a gigantic cylinder, only the very
bottom of which is genuine. The original
metopes and cornice carvings showing
scenes from the campaign, bound captives
and some scenes of everyday life can be seen
in the museum inside the village, which also
represents other periods of the area's history. Remains of the Roman town, including
fortifications and early Christian churches,
can be seen to the west. See pp. 32, 47ff.

Adamclisi: section of the Tropaneum Traiani,
showing the extent of the original monument
under the modern cladding

Agapia Moldavia

Two convents in a beautiful location 12 km southwest of Târgu Neamț. The church of the main convent, Agapia din Vale ('Agapia in the Valley'), is dedicated to the Archangels Gabriel and Michael, and was built in 1644-47. After restoration, the interior was decorated *c*. 1860 by the young Nicolae Grigorescu, who went on to become Romania's foremost Impressionist painter. He came to live in Agapia in 1901-2, and his work can also be seen in the museum outside the monastery dedicated to Alexandru Vlahuta (1858-1919), one of the writers and artists (including the poet Mihai Eminescu) who lived in the village. The museum also displays icons and vestments from the 17th and 18th centuries.

The older Agapia din Deal ('Agapia on the Hill'), or Agapia Veche ('Old Agapia'), is a smaller, more remote convent high up a wooded slope about half an hour's walk from Agapia din Vale. It was founded in the 14th century by a hermit named Agafie.

Agnita (Szentágota/Agnetheln)
Transylvania

Old Saxon village 30 km southeast of Mediaș, with modern textile factories. The Gothic fortified hall church was built in 1409 on the walls of a Romanesque church. The Museum of the Hârtibaciu Valley (closed Mon.) displays Saxon remains. The 16th-century ring-walls are fortified with four towers, named after the guilds charged with maintaining them: the Coopers', Tailors', Smiths' and Shoemakers' Towers.

Aiud (Nagyenyed, Strassburg)
Transylvania

Pretty town, 25 km north of Alba Iulia, where Celtic weapons have been found, dating from the 2nd century BC. It was an important cultural centre from the late Middle Ages to the 18th century. Its German and Hungarian names hint at its cosmopoli-

tan heritage. It has a 15th-century fortified Protestant church, as well as an impressive citadel, one of the oldest in Romania, dating from 1302. It now contains two Hungarian churches and a museum of history. The baroque interior of the Gábor Bethlen College (1796) is now a science museum. Aiud's prison was used to hold Soviet spies during the Second World War and Iron Guardists after the Communist takeover.

Alba Iulia (Gyulafehérvár, Weissenburg)
Transylvania

Built on the site of a Roman fort, the city, with its towers, domes and bastions, is dominated by a massive fortress. It lies in the valley of the river Mureș, flanked by vineyards. Although today something of a backwater, Alba Iulia was formerly one of the most important towns in Transylvania. In its time it has been a capital, a religious centre, a Habsburg fortress and the site of the unification of Transylvania with the rest of Romania in 1918.

In the 2nd century BC there was a Thracian settlement here called Apoulon, which became in the 2nd and 3rd centuries AD the important Roman *municipium* of Apulum, the administrative centre for the gold mines in the Apuseni mountains. From the end of the 9th century it was known as the 'White Town': the Slavs called it Bálgrad (a name also used by the Romanians), the Hungarians Gyulafehérvár ('White Castle of Gyula'), the Romanians Alba Iulia, and the Transylvanian Saxons Weissenburg. After the Battle of Mohács, Alba Iulia became the capital of the principality of Transylvania. It was briefly captured by Mihai the Brave in 1599 and was sacked by the Turks in 1658.

In the 18th century, after the Habsburg annexation of Transylvania, the name was changed to Karlsburg (Romanian: Alba Karolina) in honour of the Emperor Charles VI (1716-35). The rebuilding of the original

Renaissance citadel took place during his reign. Set on its high terrace, this contains most of the town's interesting buildings. It was commissioned by Prince Eugene of Savoy and constructed between 1715 and 1738 to designs by Giovanni Morando Visconti, following an 18th-century plan made famous by the French architect Vauban. It is constructed in a seven-pointed star pattern, a shape which affords maximum visibility and protection to its defenders, while its exterior walls are built with a plethora of casemates, tunnels and other passages. It is the most complete Baroque monument in Transylvania.

The equestrian statue of Charles VI, which stands above the Third Gate of the citadel, has lost its head, and its arms are damaged, but the emperor's horse still tramples Turkish prisoners beneath its hooves, and a bas-relief shows the emperor handing a banner and sword to Prince Eugene of Savoy with the inscription *In hoc signo vincis*: 'by this sign, you conquer', the words that accompanied the Emperor Constantine's vision of the Cross before the Battle of the Milvian Bridge in 312.

Inside the gateway are the cells where the captured leaders of the 1784 uprising were held until their execution the following year. Pieces of the rebels' bodies were displayed around the streets as a warning to others. The martyrs are commemorated by a granite obelisk (1965) just outside the gate. This is the most splendid of the citadel's three Baroque gates, adorned with scenes from Greek mythology and the Habsburg coat of arms. They were created by a workshop led by Master Johannes König. The palace within the citadel was begun in the 14th century for the bishop and was later extended and decorated for Queen Isabella (d. 1559) and became the residence of Mihai the Brave. In the 18th century it was used as barracks by the Austrians. The Academy founded by Gábor Bethlen in 1622, where

the poet Martin Opitz briefly taught, was also converted to a barracks.

The Roman Catholic Cathedral of St Michael combines elements of Romanesque, Gothic and Renaissance styles into a harmonious whole. Parts of a 10th-century rotunda and fragments of the church founded by the Hungarian king Stephen I in the first half of the 11th century have survived, including a magnificent sculpture of Christ in Majesty above a blind door in the south aisle. Most of the present church is late Romanesque and was begun during the reign of Andrew II (1205-35). A basilica with an apsidal east end, a transept with eastern apses and two west towers, it is notable for its fine late Romanesque sculpture, including the south portal, which has a tympanum with Christ flanked by the Apostles Peter and John and animal carvings on the transept apses (the carving of a man's head in the south apse is said to represent the architect). The choir was lengthened and given a Gothic vault and pointed windows in the early 14th century.

In 1512 an elaborately decorated Renaissance chapel was built at the north entrance by the provost János Lázói, dedicated to the souls of the faithful. Its Italianate façade is the earliest example of Renaissance architecture in the region and is decorated with figures from pagan mythology and biblical history, including Hercules and a centaur, Moses, Judith and St. Sebastian. Lázói himself kneels before the Virgin Mary. The interior has a superb late Gothic net vault.

Work on the southwest tower lasted for about four centuries and was completed by Italian masons during the rule of Prince Gábor Bethlen. The northwest tower was blown up in 1603, when it was being used as an ammunition store. From 1605 until 1715 the church was in Protestant hands, first Lutheran, then Calvinist. The Baroque statues of saints on the western gable were added in 1727-37. The interior has Baroque doors, altarpieces and pulpit. The tombs of

Alba Iulia: the Orthodox Cathedral

the Hunyadi family are on the right of the entrance. The effigy of the greatest of Transylvania's warlords, Jancu of Hunedoara (Janos Hunyadi), carved in 1456, is badly worn, but the equestrian groups on the base can still be seen. (Jancu's bones were dug up and scattered by the Turks.) Here too are the tombs of Queen Isabella, which has a bas-relief showing the story of the Good Samaritan, and of her son John Sigismund (d. 1571), prince of Transylvania. Several of his successors, including Gábor Bethlen and György I Rakoczy (r. 1630-48) were also buried here. Having been neglected for much of the 20th century, the cathedral is now being restored.

Beside the cathedral stands the Bishop's Palace, formerly the princes' residence. It was here that Mihai the Brave made his triumphant entry in 1600, and here that the magnificent Gábor Bethlen held court.

The Regional Museum (closed Mon.) is housed in the building opposite, a former officers' mess built in 1908. It contains the 'Hall of Unification' where the incorporation of Transylvania was declared on 1 December 1918, creating modern Romania

The Battyaneum Library was founded in 1794 by Bishop Ignatius Batthyány in the town's former Trinitarian monastery, where he also established the oldest observatory in Romania. Behind its restrained exterior are 60,000 or so books, including 609 incunabula and an important collection of historical documents. Its greatest treasure is part of the Lorsch Gospels (late 8th century), with gold calligraphy and illumination, a masterpiece of Carolingian art. It also has a copy of the earliest translation of the Bible into Romanian (1582). The two fine 17th-century patrician houses near the library were built by Count Nikolas Bethlen and Count Apor.

South of the Battyaneum is the Deal Furcilor, where Horea and Cloşca, two of the leaders of the 1784 Peasants' Revolt, were put to death on the wheel.

The oldest surviving Orthodox church in Alba Iulia is Holy Trinity in the Maieri district of the town. It was erected in 1713 using stone from the old Orthodox Cathedral of Mihai the Brave, which was destroyed in the construction of the citadel. After the First World War a new Orthodox Cathedral of Reunification, set in an arcaded courtyard, was built in the citadel in 1921-2 by the architect V. Stefănescu, who took the Byzantine cross-in-square churches of Târgovişte as his model. The wall paintings include portraits of King Ferdinand and Queen Marie, who were crowned here in 1922.

Albac (Albák) Transylvania
Attractive village 20 km northwest of Câmpeni, a centre for traditional crafts such as wood- and stone-carving. It is first

recorded in 1688, and by 1782 there were two villages and four churches here. Albac is famous for its connections with Horea, one of the leaders of the 1784 rebellion.

Albeşti (Fehéregyháza, Weisskirch) Transylvania
At the east end of this village is a small museum commemmorating the life of Hungary's national poet, Sándor Petőfi, who was trampled to death by Russian Cossacks in 1849.

Alexandria Wallachia
Alexandria is the capital of the *judeţ* (district) of Teleorman, southwest of Bucharest. Teleorman means 'Forest of Madness'; in the early medieval period it was an area of dense oak woods. The town holds a music festival every November.

Almaş (Nagyalmás) Transylvania
Medieval citadel overlooking the Almaş Valley. It was founded as a fortified Benedictine monastery in the 13th century, when the Magyars were trying to bring Catholicism to Transylvania. In 1249 King Bela IV of Hungary gave the estate to his magistrate in recognition of his help in fighting the Tatars. A fortress was built on the hill, and for 400 years it protected the surrounding plain and provided refuge in times of war. The village, the name of which comes from the Hungarian word for 'apple', benefited from this protection. It lay on one of the main salt-trading routes, and its inhabitants grew wealthy as fruit-growers and shopkeepers. Today, all that remains of the fortress are some broken walls, a tower and a bastion.

Apold (Apoldya, Trappold) Transylvania
Village 15 km south of Sighişoara with a Late Gothic hall church situated on a hill in the middle. This replaced an earlier, aisleless Romanesque structure. It was fortified in 1504-7, when the walls of the chancel and nave and the west tower were raised and galleries were built. The outer ring wall has five towers. The chests along the walls of the chancel and aisles were for storing clothes to be worn at festivals. A beautiful late Gothic sacrament house stands on the north side of the chancel. The fronts of the galleries are painted, and the elegant neo-Classical altar comes as a surprise in this village church. At the top of the bell tower is a wooden statue known locally as Bogdan Mischi.

Arad (Arad) Banat
A fine city 50 km northeast of Timişoara, on the Mureş River. It is dominated by a huge six-pointed star-shaped Vaubanesque citadel (1762-83; not open to the public), built by the Habsburgs across the river from the city centre to withstand the Turks. By the time it was finished, however, the Turks, who had destroyed Arad and massacred its inhabitants in the 16th century, had long gone, and the citadel was used as a prison.

The main street, Bulevardul Revoluţiei, has impressive 19th- and early 20th-century public buildings, including a large turn-of-the-century Roman Catholic church, and the imposing Town Hall by the brilliantly original Hungarian architect Ödön Lechner. Many buildings along the boulevard are adorned with fine wrought-iron balconies and balustrades, a legacy of the metalworking foundry established in the 1780s by the Emperor Joseph II. At No. 98 is the Hotel Mureşul, built in 1841. It is now a cinema, but was once the city's most glamorous hotel. Romanian and Hungarian writers stayed here, and Bartók, Brahms and Liszt performed in its concert hall.

The Palace of Culture on Piaţa Enescu designed by Lajos Szántaj was finished in 1913 and is a hybrid of neo-Romanesque, Gothic and Classical styles. It houses a County History Museum, a theatre and a

*The painted church
at Arbore*

concert hall. The Art Museum on Str. Gheorghe Popa 2-4 houses contemporary Romanian art, Biedermeyer furniture and works by minor European masters from the 17th century onwards. There is a market nearby, on Piaţa Viteazu.

On Str. Goldiş is the Romanian Orthodox Cathedral (1865), and next to it is Arad's main market square. On the corner of Str. Stefan Cicio Pop and Str. Mihai Eminescu is Farmacia Grozănescu, a pharmacy with a striking Secessionist interior. Arad's Jewish quarter, near Str. Lazăr, has several interesting old buildings and two synagogues. Piaţa Veche (Old Square) is the heart of Arad's oldest district and has several elegant but abandoned 18th-century houses. At the southern end is the Serb district, with its Orthodox Church, the oldest in Arad, built in 1702.

Arbore Moldavia
Village 33 km northwest of Suceava. The church was built in 1502 by Luca Arbore, the lord of the village and an important general. The church has spectacular, though badly decayed, paintings on the outer walls. Those on the southern and western sides are better preserved and are painted in a combination of Renaissance and Byzantine styles.

Scenes include a Feast of St George, with figures daringly painted with their backs to the viewer; scenes from Genesis; Lives of the saints; a Last Judgement; scenes from the Gospels; scenes from the Life of the Virgin and the Life of Moses, and a dramatic Siege of Constantinople.

In the churchyard are stone slabs which were used as palettes by the artist, who took 40 years to complete the project. Restoration work inside the church has recently uncovered paintings that were badly damaged by fires in the 17th and 18th centuries. The tombs of Arbore and his Polish wife can be seen in the narthex of the church.

Archita (Erked, Arkeden) Transylvania
Village 25 km east of Sighişoara with an
imposing fortified church, which stands on
the east side of the market square. Its
Baroque altarpiece was installed after a fire
gutted the church in 1748.

Arcuş (Árkos) Transylvania
Here, five km northwest of Sf. Gheorghe,
stands the late 19th-century Szentkereszti
Castle, set in landscaped grounds with speci-
men trees.

Arieşeni (Lepus) Transylvania
Ski resort 43 km east of Ştei, with a notable
wooden church (1791), now overshadowed
by a newer stone church.

Arnota Monastery Wallachia
Monastery in the village of Costeşti (56 km
west of Râmnicu Vâlcea) founded in 1633 by
Matei Basarab, prince of Wallachia. He built
it as a thank-offering to God after he managed to escape the Turks by hiding in caves
nearby, and he is buried here, surrounded by
fragmentary murals of his wife. The 18th-
century porch and tower are by Constantin
Brâncoveanu.

Aţel (Ecel, Hetzeldorf) Transylvania
Village 10 km west of Mediaş with a Gothic
church (c. 1380). Its plan, with transept and
west tower, is similar to Sibiu. The splendid
west portal was added in the second quarter
of the 15th century. At the end of that century the tower and chancel were extended
and the rib-vaults constructed. The church is
particularly rich in architectural sculpture,
including an early Gothic south portal and a
late Gothic sedile attributed to Andreas
Lapicida. The intarsia choir-stalls (1516) are
by Johannes Reichmuth. A double ring-wall
was built in the 15th-16th century and
linked by a covered entrance gate. Part of the
outer ring and a tower of the inner ring still
survive.

Avram Iancu (Felsővidra) Transylvania
Village 25 km southwest of Câmpeni, named
after the leader of a revolt in 1848 against
Habsburg rule whose birthplace is preserved
here. On the nearby **Găina Mountain**, a
folk festival known as the 'Girl Fair' takes
place each year on the Sunday before 20
July, the feast day of the Prophet Elijah. The
Girl Fair is the region's largest festival; it was
inaugurated in 1816 as a way of introducing
lonely shepherds to girls from the nearby
villages. Nowadays it is a festival of folk
music and dancing, and attracts the finest
folk musicians in Romania. The festival
begins at dawn, with an alphorn chorus on
the hill. Nearby is **Dealul cu Melci**, where
thousands of fossilized snails have been
excavated.

Babadag Dobrogea
Historic town near the lake of the same
name, surrounded by wooded hills.
Although no longer of great distinction,
Babadag was an important Turkish settlement even before the Ottomans conquered
Dobrogea. It is mentioned by the 14th-
century traveller Ibn Battuta. There is still a
large Muslim community and a beautiful,
recently restored mosque complex containing the oldest mosque in Romania, dating
from 1522. It is named after Ali Gaza Pasha,
who is buried here, and there is a small
museum of Islamic art nearby.
Unfortunately, the industry on the outskirts
of the city is in steep decline.

Numerous archaeological remains dating
from Dacian times to the Middle Ages have
been found at **Enisala**, 7 km to the east,
where there is also a 13th-century citadel
and a folk museum in a restored peasant
house.

Bacău Moldavia
Town 58 km southeast of Piatra Neamţ.
Here Ştefan the Great had a court, of which
a few ruins remain, together with the

261

Precista Church (1490), founded by Ştefan's son Alexandru. Ştefan also founded the monastery at **Buhusi** (1457), northwest of Bacău.

Baia Mare (Nagybánya, Frauenbach) Maramureş
The principal town of Maramureş, at the foot of the Gutâi Mountains, formerly a regional capital and from the 14th to the 17th century a thriving centre of gold mining and industry. At Piaţa Libertăţii 18 is the Casa Elisabeta, the house of Iancu of Hunedoara, voivode of Transylvania, regent of Hungary and victor over the Turks at Belgrade in 1456. Nearby is the 15th-century Stephen's Tower (Turnul Ştefan) and the Baroque Church of the Holy Trinity (1717-20). To the south are remains of the medieval city walls. The town's museums include the Museum of History (Muzeul de Istorie), the Ethnographic Museum (Muzeul de Etnografie) and the Art Museum (Muzeul de Artă), which displays works by painters of the Baia Mare School. This was a late 19th-century movement of Hungarian artists whose founder, Simon Hollósy (1857-1918), established a summer school here and pioneered the *en plein air* style of painting. The movement became known as the 'Hungarian Barbizon', and a community of artists gathered in the town.

The open-air Village Museum (Muzeul Satului) is a ten-minute walk north of the town and contains numerous reconstructions of the traditional architecture of Maramureş.

About 20 km to the southeast of Baia Mare are the adjacent villages of **Şurdeşti** and **Plopiş**, and further to the southeast is **Rogoz**. All three villages have exceptionally fine wooden churches (*see separate entries*).

Băile Felix (Félixfürdő) Banat
Health resort 8 km southeast of Oradea. Its mineral springs are of great antiquity and

have certainly been known since the 15th century. Two km to the northeast is a smaller spa, **Băile 1 Mai**. The waters support examples of the thermal lotus, a rare species.

Băile Govora Wallachia
Spa town 25 km west of Râmnicu Vâlcea. The nearby monastery of **Govora**, founded by Prince Radu cel Frumos ('the Handsome'), where the first Romanian printed book was published in 1640, has a trefoil church originally built in the late 15th century but restored by Constantin Brâncoveanu in the early 18th.

Băile Herculane (Herkulesfürdő, Herkulesbad) Banat
Spa resort in the Cerna Valley, northwest of Drobeta-Turnu Severin, surrounded by forested hills. It was known to the Romans as Thermae Herculi and to the Austrians as Herkulesbad, on account of the legend that Hercules cured his wounds inflicted by the Hydra by bathing in its nine springs. It was popular with members of the Habsburg imperial family during the 19th century, and although the baths and many of the hotels are now badly decayed, there is still a romantic air of Habsburg elegance in the old town centre, which is surrounded by steep limestone crags and forested cliffs. The History Museum (Muzeul de Istorie) is in the old casino building on Str. Cernei 14, while Roman remains can be seen inside the Hotel Roman on Str. Romana 1.

Băile Olaneşti Wallachia
Spa town 32 km northeast of Băile Govora. It lies at an altitude of 450 m, with gorges and caves in the surrounding hills.

Băile Tuşnad (Tusnádfürdő) Transylvania
Old health spa set amid larch and fir woods, 37 km south of Miercurea-Ciuc, at the foot of the Ciomatul Mare Massif. From here a two-hour walk leads to the Sfânta Ana Lake,

located inside an extinct volcanic crater. Other smaller spas nearby include **Malnaş-Băi**, 18 km to the south, and **Băile Balvanyos**, beyond the Turia Pass to the east.

Băişoara (Jarabany) Transylvania
Resort just over 20 km from Turda offering skiing and sledging in winter and walking in summer. The health spa specializes in herbal teas made from local plants.

Barboşi Moldavia
see Galaţi

Bârsana Maramureş
Village 20 km southeast of Sighetu Marmatei; World Heritage Site. The hilltop wooden Church of St Nicholas has some very fine paintings (by Toader Hodor and Ioan Plohod) and Baroque carvings, made in 1720 soon after the church's construction. The nearby nunnery (1 km) has been expanding since the 1990s, and the new monastic buildings in the Maramureş timber style include a timber spire said to be the tallest wooden structure in Europe (56m).

Basarabi Dobrogea
Port 18 km west of Constanţa, on the Danube-Black Sea Canal, which was constructed with enormous loss of life between 1949 and 1984, in order to connect the Black Sea with the Danube and, ultimately, with Western European waterways. Nearby is a group of extraordinary rock churches, cells and tombs, with intriguing inscriptions and drawings on the walls. This is thought to have been Romania's first monastery, occupied until the late 10th century.

Beia (Homorodbéne, Meeburg) Transylvania
Village 20 km south of Ordorheiu Secuesc. Its church has a very beautiful interior, with painted galleries and furnishings dating from the 17th and 18th centuries. The winged

The monastic complex at Bârsana

altarpiece painted with scenes from the Life of St Ursula is dated 1513 and attributed to Johann Stoss, son of Veit Stoss.

Beiuş Banat
Town 63 km southeast of Oradea, with a museum reflecting the area's rich ethnic diversity. From here one can visit the cave at **Meziad** 10 km to the northeast, and the ski resort of **Stina de Vale** 25 km to the east.

Bicaz Moldavia
Town 3 km south of the lake of the same name, close to the spectacular Ceahlău Massif, where chamois, capercaillie, boars, bears and the Carpathian stag are all found. First recorded in 1616, the town was modernized after 1950, with the construction of a hydro-electric complex at the end of the lake. To the southwest, the Bicaz Gorges lead to **Lacul Roşu** ('the Red Lake'), a health resort.

Bicaz Maramureş
Remote village 45 km south of Satu Mare in the west of Maramureş, with an 18th-

263

century Orthodox church decorated with wall paintings.

Bicaz Ardelean Moldavia
Pretty village, 35 km east of Gheorgheni, nestling in the dramatic Bicaz Gorges, with a wooden church dating from 1829.

Biertan (Berethalom, Birthälm) Transylvania
Village 15 km east of Mediaş containing the best-known and most magnificent of all the Saxon fortified churches, now a UNESCO heritage site. The three encircling walls, with watch-towers and bastions, are linked by secret passages. Within the innermost ring stands a late Gothic hall-church dating from 1522, which contains some outstanding furnishings. The sacristy door (1516) has an impressive late Gothic lock and superb intarsia work comprising Gothic motifs, while the chancel contains a large winged altarpiece dating from 1483. Its style is primitive and, like the altarpiece at Mediaş, the twelve main panels (scenes from the Life of the Virgin) are the work of a painter influenced by the late 15th-century Viennese Schottenstift school.

The panels above and below, showing the Crucifixion and figures of saints, date from the early 16th century, and are by different painters. The stone pulpit was probably made by Master Ulrich of Braşov. The choir stalls (1514-24) by Johann Reichmuth are decorated with intarsia and carvings. The church contains many fine tombs and several Turkish carpets. One of the towers (the Catholic Tower) in the inner ring-wall contains 15th-century wall paintings.

Bilea Transylvania
Mountain resort area, southwest of Făgăraş, with a spectacular lake (Bilea Lac) and waterfalls (Bilea Cascada).

Bistriţa (Beszterce, Bistritz) Transylvania
Town in northern Transylvania, about 80 km northeast of Cluj, which features in Bram Stoker's novel *Dracula*; it was here that Jonathan Harker received the first hints of the danger to come. Although 'modernized' during the Communist period, Bistriţa still has some important medieval buildings.

Visible from afar at the foot of the Borgo Mountains, in the shadow of hills planted with fruit trees and vines, the town was founded during the colonization of the region by the Transylvanian Saxons. In 1353 Louis of Anjou, king of Hungary, granted permission for a 15-day annual fair, the Bartholomew Fair, to be held here every August. The town's seal dates from the same time; it shows the head of an ostrich with a horseshoe in its beak, intended to symbolize the commercial talents of the townspeople. In the 15th and 16th centuries Bistriţa was a thriving centre of trade, as can be seen from the numerous old buildings, including many houses throughout the town that have beautiful medieval carved stone surrounds. The oldest building, which is on the east side of the town, is the former Franciscan church (now Uniate) built in the Cistercian style in the 13th century.

The Cornmarket (Sugălete), a group of 13 arcaded houses, stands on the north side of the main square. The Silversmith's House (Casa Argintarului) at Str. Dornei 5 (now the Historical and Archaeological Museum) probably dates from the second half of the 16th century.

The Lutheran parish church was built in 1560-63 to replace a smaller 14th-century church. It was renovated in 1560 by Petrus Italus, an architect from Lugano who introduced the Italian Renaissance style into Moldavia. The Renaissance door and window-frames date from this time. The tower was built between 1487 and 1519, but the four statues in the corner niches of the fourth storey seem to be older, probably dating from the 15th century and taken from the previous church.

The former Domus Consistorialis was the seat of the Bistriţa Council, a body of 100 high officials and 12 jurors who governed the region. There are remains of the town walls along Str. Kogălniceanu, Str. Ekaterina Theodoroiu and Piaţa Petru Rareş, but the only tower remaining is the Coopers' Tower.

Bistriţa Moldavia
Monastery 8 km west of Piatra Neamţ. Founded in 1407, it contains an icon donated by the Byzantine Emperor. The church was rebuilt in the mid-16th century and has been considerably restored. There is a museum.

Blaj (Balaszfálva, Blasendorf) Transylvania
Town 42 km northeast of Alba Iulia, at the confluence of the Timava Mare and Timava Mica rivers. The town's Historical Museum, housed in a 15th-century mansion in the Avram Iancu Park, is the principal attraction of the town and tells the story of the demonstration by Romanian nationalists, led by Avram Iancu, that took place during the Hungarian revolt against Habsburg rule in 1848.
The Uniate Cathedral of the Holy Trinity (1738-65) is by A. E. Martinelli. To the south of the town, the Field of Liberty (Campul Libertăţii) is a sculptural complex which commemorates the 1848 uprising.

Bogdand (Bogdánd) Banat
Town about 60 km south of Satu Mare with a small museum, housed in a 19th-century farmhouse, dedicated to the history of Magyar culture in the area. Off the main road a kilometre south is a 15th-century church with a beautiful coffered ceiling and a pulpit by the Transylvanian sculptor Dávid Sâpos.

Bonţida (Bonchida, Bonisbruck) Transylvania
Ruined palace 27 km north of Cluj. Formerly a seat of the Banffy family, it dates from the 15th-19th centuries. The 18th-century sections are by Fischer von Erlach. It was destroyed by the Germans in 1944 in retaliation for attempts by Count Miklós Banffy (author of the Bánffy Trilogy, more properly *The Writing on the Wall*) to negotiate peace with the advancing Soviet army; its treasures were removed and destroyed in later bombing in Germany. It is now being used as a training centre for architectural restoration by the Transylvania Trust.

Borşa Maramureş
Town in the Viseu Valley, near the source of the Viseu River. Long-established as a centre of mining and forestry, it has a ski complex nearby. Its wooden church (1700) has notable carved decorations and late 18th-century wall-paintings.

Botiza Maramureş
Village about 60 km southeast of Sighetu Marmaţiei, a centre for agrotourism and traditional crafts, particularly carpets and woodwork. The wooden church is early 18th century.

Botoşani Moldavia
Town northeast of Suceava, first recorded in 1439. Eight km to the northwest is the village of **Ipoteşti**, sometimes known as **Mihai Eminescu** after the famous poet, whose family home is preserved here. There is also a study centre, with a museum dedicated to the memory of the poet.

Brad (Brád) Transylvania
Town 38 km northwest of Deva. Its history as a gold-mining centre is recorded in a museum at Str. Motilor 14. The ethnographic museum (Str. Closca 2) celebrates the culture of the surrounding Zarand region. In the town's environs, at **Crişcior**, there is a local history museum and a 13th-century church founded by Prince Ştefan Balea. It has fine wall-paintings, notably a

15th-century Last Judgement on the exterior. There is also a 14th-century frescoed church at **Ribiţa** (*see separate entry*).

Brăila Moldavia
Port-town on the left bank of the Danube, 32 km south of Galaţi, on the edge of a group of islands close to wetlands of outstanding beauty, which are a haven for birds. This area has been continuously occupied since Neolithic times, but does not enter written documents until the mid-14th century, when it was already becoming an important harbour. In subsequent centuries, during the Turkish occupation, Greeks and Armenians lived here and traded with the native population. The Armenians helped to establish the carpet-weaving industry. The Turks occupied the town for almost 300 years and built a series of concentric rings of walls and ditches.

The town's cosmopolitan heritage is demonstrated by a number of buildings. The Church of the Holy Archangels, near the waterfront, was originally a mosque, and there is an Orthodox church dating from 1872, decorated by Gheorghe Tattarescu, on Calea Călăraşilor. There are also numerous decaying 19th-century villas, testifying to the wealth generated by Brăila's harbour. The waterfront was developed by the great engineer Anghel Saligny (1854-1925). The town has an important archaeological collection in the Brăila Museum (Muzeul Brăilei), Piaţa Traian 3, an ethnographical section in a pavilion in the public gardens, and a good art museum at Str. Belvedere 1.

Bran (Törcsvár, Törzburg) Transylvania
One of the most famous tourist attractions in Romania for its (tenuous) Dracula connections, Bran Castle, 28 km southwest of Braşov, guards an important pass through the Carpathians (ill. p. 20). It was constructed by the Saxons of Braşov in 1377 on the site of the Teutonic castle of Dietrich-stein. It has an irregular plan, with outer fortifications extending across the valley, and an inner courtyard surrounded by three towers. Initially governed by castellans appointed by the princes of Transylvania, in 1498 the city's merchants took control of it and thereafter maintained it at their expense. It was captured in the mid-15th century by Vlad the Impaler, later identified with Bram Stoker's fictional Dracula. Decorated in the early 20th century by Queen Marie, wife of King Ferdinand, it now houses an important collection of furniture from various periods, while its grounds contain a museum of local vernacular buildings. However, it is as 'Dracula's Castle' that it is best known. In 2006 ownership of the castle passed to Queen Marie's grandson, Dominic von Habsburg.

Brâncoveneşti (Marosvécs) Transylvania
Village founded on a Roman site. It has a castle dating from the 14th century which has been turned into an orphanage for handicapped children. On the first Sunday of June a Cherry Fair is held to celebrate the annual harvest.

Braşov (Brassó, Kronstadt)
Transylvania
One of the cities of the Siebenbürgen, picturesquely situated in the Carpathian Mountains. The Old Town was founded in the 13th century by Saxon colonists and knights of the Teutonic Order, who named it Kronstadt (Crown City). The Şchei district to the southwest developed as a settlement for the Romanian population, who were in the minority during the medieval period. The Saxons laid out their town around a market-place. Early documents refer to the town as Corona.

The earnestness of the Saxons seems to have determined the character of the town in the Middle Ages. As farmers, artisans and merchants, they were privileged immigrants.

Craftsmanship and trade flourished. While in Sibiu it was the titled officials who set the tone, giving the town a cheerful and animated character, the solemn burghers of Braşov had a more plodding mentality, which was expressed in their architecture.

A charter of 20 January 1386 confirmed Braşov in 'its old freedoms'. Braşov occupied a key position on the great trade routes and in the 15th century it had more than 30 guilds, who used their wealth to build their own bastions in the town walls. The Bastion of the Weavers (Bastionul Ţesătorilor), with its wooden galleries used to store food for emergencies, can still be seen today. (The museum inside contains a model of the town in 1600.) Remains of the Clothmakers' Tower are at the foot of Tâmpa Mountain. From here it is possible to walk along the town walls and through the Baroque Poarta Şchei, which once separated the German town from the Romanian suburb, or through the less elaborately decorated Catherine Gate (Poarta Ecaterinei, 1559).

Braşov's greatest periods were the 15th century, when much Levant trade passed through the town, and the 16th, when Honterus led the Protestant Reformation here and made the town the leading centre of learning in Transylvania.

The Town Hall (Casa Sfatului), which stands alone in the middle of the triangular market-place, was built in 1420 by the Guild of Furriers, and extended several times since. The Town Hall Tower rises 60 m, with a gallery below the eaves where trumpeters once stood to raise the alarm when there was danger of fire, flood or war. Today the old town hall contains a museum with archaeological collections, old weapons and documents, and paintings by Romanian artists of the 19th and 20th centuries.

About 1550 the diplomat Georg Reichestorffer wrote that the weekly market here was more like an annual fair, so great was the value of the costly merchandise which the townspeople – Szeklers, Wallachs, Armenians and Greeks – bought and sold there. Even today during festivals, especially at Christmas, the square is transformed into a fairground.

One of the oldest houses on the market square is a splendid 16th-century merchants' hall (Casa Negustorilor) which is now a restaurant called Cerbul Carpatin, once reputed to be the best in Romania. Its grand rooms bear witness to the self-confidence of the Saxon merchants. The oldest church in the town is St Bartholomew, begun in 1223 and situated to the north of the old town centre. The style is influenced by the Cistercians. The massive Black Church in the centre of the town is the most striking evidence of the prosperity of Braşov's burghers. It was begun at the end of the 14th century and dedicated to the Blessed Virgin.

The Black Church got its name after a great fire in the city, which broke out on 21 April 1689. The 20th-century Braşov writer Adolf Meschendörfer wrote a vivid description of the conflagration: 'The flames engulfed the grand houses of the rich, as well as the poor folks' shingle roofs, the warehouses of the guilds, the storerooms for half the Orient. Here precious cloths and spices were ablaze, there in flames were the parsonage, weighhouse and the grammar school, with its world-famous library founded by the great reformer Honterus ... the flames played even on the town's greatest treasure, the great parish church; the tower and the roof burned, the vaults burst, the five harmonically tuned bells fell to the ground half-melted, the famous organ from the time of the Reformation, the valuable tapestries, one of which was supposed to have been made by the Apostle Paul, the pulpit of Honterus, the golden altar, the shimmering epitaphs and a hundred other treasures were destroyed in a matter of hours.'

*Braşov, Black Church: head supposed to
be of St Thomas*

A contemporary described it as a 'fire of
wrath, punishment and vengeance' – retribu-
tion, that is, for the uprising of the
townspeople against the 'paternal protection'
imposed by the Habsburg monarchy. The
ringleaders of the uprising were severely
punished, among them the 85-year-old
hatter Stephan Steiner and the goldsmith
Kaspar Kreisch, who were condemned to
death and executed. Only a bronze font survived the fire unscathed. It is shaped like a
chalice and is surrounded by an octagonal
grille. The coat of arms of King Matthias
Corvinus of Hungary (1458-90) and his wife
Beatrice of Aragon also survived, and is
attached to a pier opposite the pulpit. Next
to it is the coat of arms of the town (a crown
on a tree stump, a reference to the town's
German name). Nearby, above the door at
the eastern end of the south side, is a much-
restored fresco of the Virgin Mary adored by
St Catherine and St Barbara (*c.* 1477), an outstanding example of the Italian Renaissance
style fostered by King Matthias.

The church is full of interesting furnishings, among them a 17th-century Baroque
pulpit, which was donated by a master-
butcher and cost the price of a hundred
oxen. The tomb slabs built into the lower
part of the north tower date from the same
period, with figures of town councillors and
pastors carved in relief. There is also a magnificent collection of oriental carpets, said to
be the largest in southeast Europe.

The mighty organ, with its 4,000 pipes, 74
registers and four keyboards, is played once
a week, as has been the tradition here since
the 16th century. The first organist known
by name was Hieronymus Ostermayer, who
also performed at the Wallachian court.
Ostermayer wrote a chronicle of events in
the town and was buried with the following
epitaph:

> *Anno MDLXI ist gestorben Herr*
> > *Hieronymus Ostermayer*
> *Geboren zu Markt Gross-Scheyer*
> *War Organist in der Stadt allhier*
> *Hat nie getrunken Wein und Bier,*
> *War gelehrt, fromb und gut*
> *Nun er im Himmel singen thut.*

> [*In 1561 died Herr Hieronymus Ostermayer*
> *Born in Market Gross-Scheyer*
> *He was organist in the town here,*
> *Never drank wine nor beer.*
> *He was learned, good and pious*
> *Now he's singing in the heavenly choirs.*]

To the south of the church stands a monument to Johannes Honterus (1498-1549), the
humanist and reformer, who was born in
Kronstadt in 1498, studied at Cracow,
Vienna, Wittenberg and Basle and brought
the Lutheran Reformation to Transylvania.

In contrast to the soaring but rather
gloomy Gothic Black Church, the neighbouring Orthodox Church of the Holy
Trinity (1825) is bright and delicate;
behind it, by the town walls, there is a
small Greek cemetery full of old tomb
slabs and crosses.

The narrow alleyways of the quarter called Şchei, southwest of the old town centre, lead to the Orthodox Church of St Nicholas, which was built in 1512-21 for Prince Neagoe Basarab and extended in the 18th century. The neighbouring school, built at the same time as the church, was the first school in which instruction was given in the Romanian language. It is now a museum and contains a small but valuable collection of icons (16th-18th centuries), some illuminated gospel books and liturgical objects from the 16th century, as well as archives, a library and a display devoted to Coresi, the first translator of the Bible into Romanian. The Saxon Protestant reformers promoted the use of the vernacular and sought converts among the Romanian population, and the earliest printed books in the Romanian language using the Roman alphabet instead of the Cyrillic were printed in Braşov.

As well as the museums already mentioned, there are museums of ethnography and art (both at Bulevardul Eroilor 21) containing folk art, glass icons, traditional costume and the work of leading Romanian painters, including Aman and Grigorescu.

Breaza Wallachia
Small town with an 18th-century church of St Nicholas. Its interior is covered in paintings, notably the Last Judgement in the porch.

Breţcu (Bereck, Bretz) Transylvania
Village 16 km northeast of Târgu Secuiesc, on the site of a Roman settlement (2nd century AD). It has an 18th-century Orthodox church. 12 km to the northeast, the **Oituz Pass** leads to Moldavia.

Brezoi Transylvania
An old forestry centre, situated at the confluence of the Lotru and Olt rivers, 67 km southeast of Sibiu.

Bucharest Wallachia
Capital, pop. 2.25 million. The history of Bucharest and its buildings is treated in detail on p. 185ff. This gazetteer entry gives a summary of the major sites, starting at the historic core.

Bucharest owes its historical importance to its position midway between Wallachia's southern border on the Danube and the princely courts of Târgovişte and Curtea de Argeş in the foothills of the Carpathians, and athwart an important cross roads that controlled the main overland trade route between western Europe and Constantinople/Istanbul. The east-west route ran beside the river Dâmboviţa, now canalized and partly built over; the north-south down what is now Bulevardul I. C. Brătianu. Close by this crossroads Vlad Ţepeş ('Dracula'), enlarged the fortress built by Mircea the Old and in the next century Mircea the Shepherd replaced it with his Princely Court (Curtea Veche, see p. 193), of which little remains. The 16th-century Princely Church (Biserica Curtea Veche, 1546 and later) is the only part of the complex still standing, but has been much restored. Nearby are two other historical churches, the 18th-century Stavropoleos church (see p. 207) and the Zlătari church. The latter stands near the neo-gothic Carul cu Bere beer hall (see p. 214), and next to the eclectic National History Museum of Romania (Muzeul Naţional de Istorie a României; see p. 219) which houses important Scythian, Sarmatian and Dacian pieces, a cast of Trajan's Column, and the Tezaurul Român, or Romanian Treasury, with precious exhibits ranging from prehistoric grave goods to more recent coronation regalia.

Just south of the Princely Court is the Hanul lui Manuc (see p. 198) a rare survival in something approaching its original form of the caravanserais that were such a feature of early Bucharest (see pp. 196-8). It is now a hotel and tourist restaurant; a few steps away is the early 19th-century Cafeana Veche,

269

Bucharest's oldest café (see p. 214). A detour over Bulevardul I. C. Brătianu brings one the New St. George's church (Sf. Gheorghe Nou; see p. 197), built by Constantin Brâncoveanu, and his burial site; and a little further south is the Jewish Choral Temple and then Bucharest's Great Synagogue, with a museum of Jewish history.

Returning over Bulevardul I. C. Brătianu we are back in the only quarter of the old city to come through systematization more or less unscathed. Lipscani is today hugely run down, but lively and picturesque. in the northern part of the quarter, interesting buildings include the fine 19th-century arcade Pasajul Vilacros; the Doamnei church (see p. 203) and Russian church on Strada Doamnei; and then, moving towards Piaţa 21 Decembrie 1989, the Colţea church and hospital (see p. 204) and the Museum of the History of the Bucharest Municipality (Muzeul de Istorie şi Artă ai Municipiului Bucureşti), in the ornate Suţu palace (1833, but updated in 1863 by the sculptor Karl Storck).

South of Lipscani, around Piaţa Unirii, some early buildings survived Ceauşescu's onslaught. On Metropolitan Hill (Dealul Mitropoliei) these include the Radu Vodă Monastery (see p. 193), the Patriarchal Cathedral (Catedral Patriarhei, 1658 see pp. 206-7) and Palace (1708), the Bucur church, allegedly founded by the shepherd Bucur (see pp. 207-208), and the Brâncoveanu-style Antim Monastery (1715, see p. 208). More historic buildings were demolished to create the Unirea Shopping Centre, and other elements of Ceauşescu's planned civic centre, and the view from Piaţa Unirii is dominated, as intended, by the monstrous Palace of Parliament (Palatul Parlamentului, also Casa Republicii, see p. 187), which stands isolated in a dog-infested space at the end of Bulevardul Unirii. It can be visited, and contains the Museum of Romanian Folk Costume (Muzeul Costumelor Populare din România) and the National Museum of Contemporary Art (Muzeul Naţional de Artă Contemporana).

Just north of Bulevardul Unirii are the Domniţa Bălaşa church (see p. 207), the Sf. Apostoli church founded by Matei Basarab (1636) and completed by Şerban Cantacuzino (1715), and the Sf. Nicolae Mihai Vodă church (see pp. 187-8) built by Mihai the Brave in 1589 and moved to its present position along rails; other nearby survivors include the rebuilt Sf. Spirea Vechi (1747).

The modern core of the city is the area between the Piaţa 21 Decembrie 1989 and the Piaţa Victoriei. Piaţa 21 Decembrie 1989 is overshadowed by the towering Intercontinental Hotel. The main building is the Teatrul National, the National Theatre of Romania, with a façade designed under the supervision of Elena Ceauşescu, who is said to have ordered it to be rebuilt twice (see pp. 214-215). The square runs into the Piaţa Universităţii, with the University Palace (1857-9, see p. 215) opposite the National Bank of Romania.

Behind the University Palace is the Architecture Faculty, in one of the most characteristic of neo-Romanian buildings; it was the site of student resistance to the miners brought from the Jiu valley by Iliescu. Just to the west is Calea Victoriei, the spine of modern Bucharest; going north we pass the fabled Casa Capşa restaurant (see p. 213), the Art Deco Telephone Palace (Palatul Telefoanelor), the neo-renaissance Hotel Continental, and the Creţulescu church (see p. 208). Calea Victoriei now reaches Piaţa Revoluţiei. At the southern end of the square is the Senate (Senatul), formerly the Communist Party headquarters, with the balcony from which Ceauşescu delivered his last speech, and from which in happier times he had denounced the Soviet invasion of Czechoslovakia.

Piaţa Revolutiei is dominated by the for-mer Royal Palace (Palatul Regal, 1927, see p. 212), which now houses the National Museum of Art (Muzeul Naţional de Artă ai României), with an interesting collection of Old Master paintings (Antonello da Messina, Rembrandt, El Greco, Tintoretto, Bassano etc.) and modern Romanian art. Behind is a Communist-era congress hall, the Sala Palatului; a little further is the charming Stejar church (see p. 206). Opposite the Royal Palace is the University Library, very badly damaged in 1989, on the corner of Strad C. Rosetti, further down which is the attractive Theodor Aman house museum, with late 19th-century paintings.

At the northwest end of the square (here called Piaţa Enescu) is the Ateneul Român, Bucharest's magnificent principal concert hall, built by public subscription (1886, see p. 215), and the Athénée Palace Hilton Hotel (see p. 219).

Beyond the Ateneul, the Calea Victoriei goes north towards Piaţa Victoriei. It passes or goes near a number of interesting sights: the Ceramics and Glass Museum in the for-mer Ştirbey Palace (1856, see p. 214), the Museum of Art Collections (Muzeul Colecţiilor de Artă), the Museum of Romanian Literature in the former Creţulescu House, the Storck museum (sculptures by F. Storck), the George Enescu National Museum of Music, in the exuber-ant Belle Epoque baroque Cantacuzino Palace (1900) where the composer briefly lived. Bulevardul G. Magheru, roughly par-allel to the east, was and remains one of Bucharest's main shopping streets, and still has some grandiose buildings (see pp. 211-212), including Horia Creangă's luxuriously appointed Patria Cinema (1931-5). This area also has some of Bucharest's most appealing pre-war villas.

Piaţa Victoriei, where both streets effec-tively meet, is dominated by the Palatul Victoria (1937-44), one of the main seats of government. More attractive are the Gregore Antipa Museum of Natural History (see p. 215) and the Geological Museum, with fine exhibits (the latter open by appointment only); next to them stands the Romanian Peasant Museum, in an appropriately neo-Romanian building (Muzeul Ţaranului Român; see p. 216). It is the finest collection of its kind, as is the Village Museum (Muzeul Satului) further north at the end of Şosea Kiseleff, beyond the Triumphal Arch (1936), which has some 300 vernacular buildings set over 28 acres within the attrac-tice Herăstrău Park (see p. 211).

Bucharest is exceptionally rich in small, personal collections and artist's studios, often in specially designed buildings. Just to the east of Piaţa Victoriei is the Hrandt Avakian Collection, and especially the Zambaccian museum, with Romanian and French post-impressionists in a building that blends *cula* style with other vernacular influences. Still further north, beyond the monumental Free Press House (Casa Presei Libere) in the square of the same name, and near Băneasa railway station, are two small museums, the Minovici Museum of Folk Arts in a more straightforward version of an Oltenian cula (1905) and the Minovici Museum of Ancient Art, the latter consisting of western Renaissance art in a Home Counties Plantagenet building.

East of Piaţa Universităţii is the Armenian quarter, centred on the Armenian Cathedral (1781) and museum. Nearby is another artist's collection in an attractive 18th-cen-tury hourse, the Pallady Museum, with the paintings of the post-impressionist Theodor Pallady. The eastern part of Bucharest beyond this, though run down, preserves more of the atmosphere of the pre-Ceauşescu city. The eclectic architecture ranges from Parisian classical, through neo-Romanian to uncompromising Modernist.

West of Piaţa Universităţii, Bulevardul Regina Elisabeta leads past the fine neo-classical Cercul Militar on the corner of Calea Victoriei, with the palatial Savings Bank building by the French architect Paul Gottereau (now CEC Palace, Casa de Economii şi Consemnaţiuni) just to the south; the Grădina Cişmigiu, a peaceful park; then at the river the Opera Română (often fine productions and very good value; www.operanb.ro); and the Casa Radio, a vast unfinished building originally intended as a museum of the Romanian Communist Party. Just to the north is the National Military Museum, on Strada Mircea Vulcănescu.

Crossing the river, (and passing another charming small artist's studio, the Dimitrie and Aurelia Ghiaţă Museum just off Bulevardul Eroilor Sanitari) the main sight is the Cotroceni Palace (see p. 202), now a residence of the President. It stands on the site of the monastery founded by Şerban Cantacuzino, of which the surviving chapel was eventually demolished by Ceauşescu. A few of the original cellars etc. remain in the current structure, which was built in a mixed French and neo-Romanian style for Queen Marie. After many vicissitudes it has now been thoroughly restored. Booking advisable. Just behind it are the run-down Botanical Gardens (Grădina Botanică; see p. 211).

South of the city centre is the Parcul Tineretului, hard by the Heroes of the Revolution Cemetery (Eroii Revoluiţiei) and the Bellu Cemetery, with many literary graves, including that of Eminescu. The nearby French-designed Carol I Park (Parcul Carol) contains the former mausoleum of Communist leaders, now re-affected to the Unknown Soldier and First World War heroes originally buried at Maraşeşti.

Excursions from Bucharest include Snagov Monastery (18 km), Mogoşoaia (14 km) and Căldăruşani (35 km), for all of which see separate entries.

Buneşti (Szaszbuda, Bodendorf) Transylvania

The 14th-century village church was fortified in 1505, when the side-aisles were removed. The church and its west tower were surrounded by defensive galleries, which were demolished in the 19th century. The interior has interesting wall-paintings in the chancel, and the folk paintings on the interior galleries by Johann Rössler date from 1680.

Buşteni Transylvania

A small ski resort with a large cross erected in the 1920s as a war memorial. There is good walking, including trails leading to the famous rock formations known as the Sphinx and the Old Ladies.

Buzău Moldavia

Town in southern Moldavia, 115 km northeast of Bucharest. It is renowned principally for its midsummer festival, which takes place on the last Sunday in June. It also has a cathedral (1649), an archaeological and art museum at B-dul Balcescu 50, and an ethnographic museum at Str. Razboieni 8.

At **Sarata-Monteoru**, a spa west of Buzău, Bronze Age, Dacian and Roman remains have been discovered, while **Berca**, 20 km northwest of Buzău, has a monastery dating from 1694.

Călan (Kalán, Kalan) Transylvania

Industrial town, 10 km east of Hunedoara; a spa since Roman times. In the suburbs is the fine Orthodox Church of Strei-Sangeorgiu, with frescoes dating from 1313. Two km south of Călan is another 13th-century church at **Strei** (see separate entry).

Căldăruşani Wallachia

Lakeside monastery 35 km northeast of Bucharest built by Matei Basarab in 1638. From 1787 it contained a school of icon painting, where the 19th-century Romanian Impressionist painter Nicolae Grigorescu was trained. In 1980 it became briefly famous as the location of the wedding of tennis stars Björn Borg and Mariana Simionescu.

Călimăneşti (Kelementelke)
Transylvania
Spa town in the Olt Valley 18 km south of Brezoi. Nearby is the monastery of **Cozia**. Its principal church, modelled on the Serbian triconch basilicas of the Morava Valley, dates from the 14th century and is the earliest example of Byzantine architecture in Wallachia. Inside, the narthex has some fine 14th-century paintings, while those in the nave and altar were added in the 18th century. The monastery houses a museum of religious art. Across the road is the elegant Infirmary Church, which was built in 1542. About 2 km north is the **Turnul Monastery**, which has 16th-century cells carved out of the Cozia massif.

Călineşti Maramureş
See **Cosău Valley**.

Câlnic (Kálnok, Kelling) Transylvania
Village 9 km east of Sebeş, with a magnificent 13th-century Saxon castle, now a cultural centre. It is UNESCO-protected and has been beautifully restored. The chapel has ruined 16th-century frescoes.

Câmpeni (Topánfalva, Topesdorf) Transylvania
Town in western Transylvania, the capital of Ţara Moţilor, the Land of the Moţi, who are traditionally known for their woodwork. A former centre of Romanian nationalism, Câmpeni has a statue of Avram Iancu, the 1848 revolutionary. The town is a convenient base for exploring the Apuseni Mountains.

Câmpina Wallachia
Oil town, 33 km northwest of Ploieşti, incongruously endowed with a refinery, a haunted neo-Gothic castle (**Haşdeu Castle**) and a museum of Romania's most famous painter, Nicolae Grigorescu (1838-1907). The museum (closed Mon.), has a large number of his works on display.

Câmpulung (Muscel) Wallachia
One of the oldest towns in Wallachia, 64 km northwest of Târgoviste, Câmpulung's name means 'long field'. It was occupied by the Teutonic Knights in the 13th century and in 1330 became the first capital of Wallachia. Nearby is the 14th-century Roman Catholic Bărăţiei Church and a Museum of History and Art. There are also two 16th-century churches, the Domnească and the Subeşti. (Nearby is the monastery of **Negru Vodă** *see separate entry*.)

Câmpulung Moldovenesc Moldavia
Market town on the Moldova River in northwestern Moldavia (Bucovina). It lay on an important trade route between

Traditional wooden spoons

Transylvania and Moldavia, and the people of the town grew rich on the profits of trade. It was also the centre of a mini-republic, whose inhabitants had the right to make their own laws. This autonomy ended only with the invasion of Bucovina by the Austrians in 1774. Its heritage as a centre of the timber industry is celebrated in the Museum of Wood Art (Muzeul Arta Lemnului), Calea Transilvaniei 10, and the Wooden Spoon Collection of Ioan Tugui (Colecţia de Linguri de Lemn Ioan Tugui), Str. G. Popovici 1.

Câmpuri Moldavia
Village 30 km west of Tecuci with a museum celebrating the life of the peasant activist and parliamentarian Ion Roată. 14 km to the east lies the village of **Mărăşeşti** with its First World War battle memorial (*see separate entry*).

Caransebeş Banat
Town at the confluence of the Sebeş River and the Banat Timis, 75 km north of Băile Herculane. Despite its historical importance as a judicial centre and garrison town, little remains of Caransebeş' heritage, apart from

The castle at Cetatea de Baltă

the provincial museum on Piaţa Dragolina. 23 km to the southeast is the ski resort of **Muntele Mic**.

Carei (Nagykároly) Banat
Village 34 km southwest of Satu Mare, named after the Károlyi family, whose former home, a neo-Gothic castle (1794), is now a local history museum (closed Mon.). There is also an 18th-century Ruthenian Orthodox church.

Cârţişoara (Strezaercisóra, Oberkerz) Wallachia
Village about 40 km east of Sibiu with a museum (closed Mon.) containing a good display of traditional houses and objects typical of Oltenian village life.

Cernat de Jos (Alsócsernáton) Transylvania
Village 10 km southwest of Târgu Secuiesc with the Bod Peter Museum of Szekler life and culture (open daily), showing an excellent collection of wooden objects and ceramics. The village also has several 18th- and 19th-century manor houses.

Cernavodă Dobrogea
Port at the confluence of the Danube-Black Sea Canal and the Danube itself, which is crossed here by Anghel Saligny's impressive iron bridge of 1895. The area has various other distinctions, ranging from the burial site where the Neolithic 'Hamangia Thinker' – now in the National Historical Museum in Bucharest – was discovered, to the country's sole nuclear power station.

Cernica Wallachia
Monastery 14 km east of Bucharest, on an island in a lake of the same name. Begun in 1608 by Governor Cernica Ştirbei, it contains two 19th-century churches, dedicated respectively to St Nicholas and St George, with frescoes by Gheorghe Tattarescu.

Cetatea de Baltă (Kükülvár, Kockelburg)
Transylvania
Village with a splendid Renaissance castle
built in 1624 and open to the public.

Cetăţuia Moldavia
A monastery on the outskirts of Iaşi, whose
name means 'The Little Citadel'. It was
founded by Prince Gheorghe Duca and
completed in 1672, the year of his death. He
and his wife are buried inside the church,
which is decorated with frescoes of the Last
Judgement on the porch and very dark
paintings inside, as well as beautiful stone
carving. There is a good view from the top of
the hill across the vineyards to Iaşi.

Chioar
see **Lăpuş Valley**

Cincsor (Kissink, Kleinschenk)
Transylvania
Fine aisleless church with defensive walls
that were built round it in the 15th century,
using stone from an old Roman *castrum*.

Cincu (Nagysink, Grossschenk)
Transylvania
Village 15 km northwest of Făgăraş. The
13th-century aisled citadel church has a massive west tower added after the Mongol
invasion. In the 15th century the chancel was
fortified with a double ring wall. The central
panel of the splendid altarpiece is an early
16th-century painting, *The Incredulity of St
Thomas*, from Moşna; the carved surround
dates from the 17th century and incorporates
a late 15th-century predella. The church also
contains several interesting oriental carpets.

Ciprian Porumbescu Moldavia
Village 23 km southwest of Suceava, named
after the 19th-century composer of the
Romanian national anthem, to whom a
museum nearby is dedicated.

Cisnădie (Nagydisznód, Heltau) and
Cisnădioară (Kisdisznód, Michelsberg)
Transylvania
Legend has it that these two villages are
linked by a tunnel. **Cisnădie** is a town
located at the foot of the Cindrel Mountains,
14 km south of Sibiu. Recorded as early as
1204, it was formerly an important wool
town. Its industrial history can be studied in
the Textile Museum at Str. Apărarii 4. The
town's well-preserved fortified church dates
mostly from the 15th century. It has a fine
Romanesque west portal which was part of
the 13th-century church, remodelled and
fortified in the 15th century. At the same
time two oval ring walls, with a moat
between them, were built to defend against
the Turks. Fragmentary wall paintings can
be seen on the north wall of the chancel. In
the sacristy is a small, simple bronze crucifix
on a processional cross, said to have been
brought to Transylvania by the first settlers.

The neighbouring village of **Cisnădioară**
has both a Baroque and a fortified Romanesque church, one of the oldest in
Transylvania, as well as a folk museum. From
1223 the village belonged to the Cistercian
abbey of Cârţa (Kerz). The Gothic church in
the middle of the village was rebuilt in the
18th century, while the old church stands on
a hill some distance away. It has preserved its
Romanesque form: nave and aisles with an
apsidal chancel and smaller apses at the end
of the aisles. The west portal is one of the
earliest pieces of architectural sculpture in
Transylvania, and traces of paintwork can
still be detected. Surrounding the church is a
ring wall with battlements and gallery. The
courtyard still contains a pile of massive
stone blocks, which the besieged villagers
rolled through apertures in the fortifications
down on to the heads of their Tatar attackers.

Cloaşterf (Miklóstelke, Klosdorf)
Transylvania
Village 20 km southeast of Sighişoara. The

stone church and brick-built fortifications (a rectangular defensive wall with corner towers) were erected in 1521. The early Gothic font comes from an earlier building. The gallery panels inside the church were painted by Georgius Rössler.

Cluj-Napoca (Kolozsvár, Klausenburg)
Transylvania

Romania's second city and the capital of Transylvania, situated on the River Someş Mic, Cluj is an important cultural centre and the birthplace of Unitarianism. The city has a history that is convoluted even by Transylvanian standards. The first half of its name, a corruption of the German 'Klausenburg' (Latin: Castrum Clus, 'Closed Camp') reveals its Saxon past: Germanic settlers first arrived here in the 12th century at the invitation of the Hungarian King Geza, and it became a Hungarian provincial capital. Today, one-fifth of the city's population is Hungarian. However, the city's origins lie in the ancient Dacian settlement of Napoca, and this name was revived in 1974 by Ceauşescu in order to emphasize its 'Romanian' identity. The Hungarians call the city Kolozsvár.

In the 16th century Cluj became an important cultural centre. In 1530 a stonemasons' workshop was founded, producing elaborate vegetal and floral decorations that gave rise to a style known as the 'Flower Renaissance'. In 1556, Dávid Ferenc founded the Unitarian sect in Cluj. Its main tenets are a rejection of the doctrine of the Trinity and of Christ's divinity; today there are 250,000 Unitarians in Romania, mainly Hungarian-speakers.

The heart of Cluj's medieval town is Piaţa Unirii. Here is the spectacular Roman Catholic church of St Michael (east end begun 1349), the largest church in Transylvania, which was converted from a basilica into a star-vaulted hall-church in the 15th century. The decoration of its north portal, executed between 1410 and 1430, recalls the town church at Koşice, Slovakia, while its sacristy door (1528), a fine example of the Transylvanian Renaissance style, is surrounded by carvings of putti and a bust of the donor, Johannes Clyn. There are also a Baroque pulpit and altarpiece, added after a fire destroyed much of the interior in 1698, and a 19th-century neo-Gothic bell-tower.

Nearby, the National Art Museum (Muzeul National de Artă) has an important collection of mostly Romanian art from the 16th century to the modern period, although surprisingly there is nothing by Brâncuşi. It is housed in Johann Eberhard Blaumann's Baroque Banffy Palace (1774-85), which has carvings of classical mythology on the façade by Anton Schuchbauer. Piaţa Unirii is also graced by Janos Fadrusz's equestrian statue (1902) of King Matthias Corvinus of Hungary, (r. 1458-90), whose horse is trampling the crescent banner of the Turks underfoot. King Matthias was born in Cluj: his birthplace, a modest two-storey house at Str. Matei Corvin 6, is now an art school. At Piaţa Unirii 28 is the Pharmacy Museum, in the 16th-century St George's Pharmacy.

To the northwest of Piaţa Unirii is Piaţa Muzeului, which has a Baroque Franciscan church and some Roman remains and is named after the nearby National History Museum of Transylvania (Muzeul National de Istorie a Transilvaniei). It is particularly rich in Bronze Age, Dacian and Roman artefacts, including relics of the largest brooch factory in the Roman Empire.

To the south of Unirii, Str. Universităţii (which has a striking Baroque Piarist church, 1718-24) leads to the charming Str. Kogălniceanu. As well as the Babeş-Bolyai University (founded 1872), Kogălniceanu contains the Teleki Palace (1795), now a public library, and the aisleless Calvinist church (Biserica Reformată, 1486-94), formerly part of a Franciscan friary founded by Matthias Corvinus, with original vaulting in the choir and some mid-17th-century alterations and a fine Rococo organ.

To the east, the 15th-century Tailors' Bastion (Bastionul Croiţilor) on Str. Baba Novac is all that survives of the town wall. From here, two squares, Piaţa Ştefan cel Mare and Piaţa Avram Iancu, extend north. They contain early 20th-century public buildings: the theatre and opera house by the Viennese theatre specialists Fellner and Helmer (1906), and the huge neo-Byzantine Orthodox Cathedral (1920-33), built to commemorate the union of Romania and Transylvania; a towering statue of Avram Iancu stands nearby. Cluj-Napoca's attractions are not confined to the historic centre. To the south a distinguished botanical garden, Grădina Botanică 'Alexandru Borza', can be found on Str. Republicii 42, while to the west of the Old Town on Calea Moţilor is the Calvinist 'Cock' Church (1913), (Biserica cu Cocoş, named after St Peter's denial of Christ and decorated with crowing birds) in an elegant vernacular style characteristic of its architect, the Transylvanian Hungarian Károly Kós.

Perhaps the most extraordinary site, however, is in a relatively distant suburb beyond the Someş Mic River. This is the open-air section of the Transylvanian Ethnographical Museum (Parcul Etno-grafic 'Romulus Vuia'), Str. Tăietura Turculuţ, (closed Mon. and 2 Nov-30 April) founded in 1929, containing a remarkable selection of reconstructed village architecture from all over Transylvania, including peasant houses, churches, hydraulic and mining equipment and presses, mostly made of wood. The farmhouses in Romanian, Hungarian, Szekler and Saxon styles are an eloquent testimony to the region's ethnic variety. The main building of the museum at Str. Memorandumului 41 in the city centre has what is arguably Romania's finest collection

The Tailors' Bastion, Cluj

of traditional carpets and folk costumes in a rebuilt 16th-century palace.

Cobia Wallachia
Charming, recently-restored 17th-century monastery church, 22 km southwest of Târgovişte. The exterior walls are decorated with colourful glazed bricks. Around the cornice are signs of the zodiac in ceramic discs.

Comana Wallachia
Village 32 km north of Giurgu with small monastery originally found by Vlad the Impaler and rebuilt in the 17th century by Radu Şerban.

Constanţa Dobrogea
Important Black Sea town and Romania's principal port. Constanţa was originally known by its Greek name Tomis, and was settled in the 6th century BC by Greeks from Miletos. It came under Roman control in the late first century BC. In 8 AD the great Latin

*The Casino,
Constanța*

poet Ovid was exiled here by the Emperor Augustus, on suspicion of intriguing at court. He lived here until his death in 17 AD and wrote two series of mournful poems called the *Tristia* and *Epistulae ex Ponto*, in which he complained bitterly of the cold weather and the privations of his place of exile. The winters, he claimed, were so cold that not only did the wine freeze but the inhabitants, whose own hair 'tinkles with ice', drank it in the form of frozen shards. On the whole, however, he found the citizens kind and hospitable, despite the odd raid by neighbours from beyond the Danube. Today the town remains welcoming, and its patchy economic fortunes are on the rise since Romania's accession to the EU.

There are considerable classical remains on several sites, in particular a fine Roman mosaic (early 4th century AD), ruined baths, port buildings and city walls. The Museum of National History and Archaeology (Muzeul de Istorie Națională și Arheologie)

on Piața Ovidiu has a significant collection of ancient sculptures, most notably the Glykon, a hybrid serpentine monster dating from the 2nd century AD. There are also numerous funerary monuments and sarcophagi outside.

In the 6th century Tomis' name was changed by the Byzantines to Constantiana (after Constantine the Great). After the fall of Constantinople in 1453 to the Ottoman Turks it was renamed Küstendje. There are few medieval remains, although the light house (Farul Genovez, 1860) at the end of the esplanade marks the site of a 14th-century structure built by Genoese merchants. Most buildings in the Old Town date from the 19th or early 20th century, and are constructed in either Classical, vernacular or Art Nouveau styles. There is a spectacular Casino (1909) on the sea-front, which recalls the city's heyday as a fashionable resort, when it was visited by royalty, socialites and literati: Romania's national poet, Mihai

Eminescu, stayed in the nearby Hotel Intim.

Ion Mincu's neo-Byzantine Orthodox Cathedral of SS Peter and Paul (1884-95) is distinguished by the quality of its proportions and wall-paintings. There is also a Roman Catholic Cathedral built of brick in an elegant early Christian style, as well as two mosques, one dating from 1869 and the other, the Mahmudiye, a gift of King Carol, from 1910. The latter has an enormous concrete dome. Perhaps the most touching 19th-century adornment is the statue in Piaţa Ovidiu of Ovid brooding on a column, which was made in Rome in 1887 by Ettore Ferrari and placed above the legendary site of the poet's tomb.

As well as the Archaeological Museum, Constanţa has a number of important collections: the Art Museum (Muzeul de Artă), B-dul Tomis 84, contains Romanian Impressionists and Post-Impressionists; the Museum of Folk Art (Muzeul de Arte Populară), B-dul Tomis 32, has glass icons and exquisite peasant costumes; the Collection of Ion Jalea, an academic sculptor (Colecţia Ion Jalea), Str. Muzeelor 26; the Museum of the Romanian Navy (Muzeul Marinei Romane), Str. Traian 53. There is also a dreary aquarium near the Casino, and a dolphinarium and a planetarium by Lake Tăbăcăriei, in the north of the city.

Corabia Wallachia
Village on the Danube 38 km west of Turnu Măgurele. The site of Sucidava, a Geto-Dacian citadel which was important in Roman times and during the Byzantine era. A museum here tells the story of the area's early history.

Cornet Wallachia
A tiny Orthodox monastery, situated relatively far from the usual tourist routes. It is south of Sibiu, just across the old border between Transylvania and Wallachia in the spectacular setting of the Ciăneni Pass, where the River Olt cuts through the Carpathians. The church, which stands in the middle of a small walled precinct, was built in 1666 on a trefoil ground plan. The walls of alternating ashlar and brick are decorated with coloured glazed tiles. A vertical accent is given by the two elegant towers. The wall-paintings date from the 18th century.

Corund (Korond) Transylvania
Village 26 km north of Odorheiu Secuiesc, famed chiefly for its pottery and handicrafts, notably knitwear and basketwork. Corund pottery is sold in most good craft shops throughout Romania. It is usually either white with cobalt blue patterns, or plain green or ochre. The village has numerous wooden Szekler houses and a small museum. An annual ceramics fair is held here in mid-August.

Cosău Valley Maramureş
Valley south of Sighetu Marmaţiei. The villages and their beautiful wooden churches are here described in the order in which one would encounter them after entering the valley from the north, just south of the village of Berbeşti: **Fereşti** has an 18th-century church of St Nicholas, with wall-paintings by Alexandru Ponehalschi and 18th-century icons. **Corneşti**, on the other side of the Cosău River, also has a church of St Nicholas (early 18th century), with wall-paintings by Toader Hodor (1807) and icons by Alexandru Ponehalschi (1755).

Further south, **Călineşti Susani** and **Călineşti Josani** (Călinesti Caieni) are both dedicated to the Birth of the Virgin. The former (1784) has wall paintings by Nicolae Cepschin; the latter, begun before 1663 and enlarged in the 19th century, has wall-paintings and icons by Alexandru Ponehalschi (see pp. 181-2).

Sârbi has two churches dedicated to St Paraschiva. **Sârbi Susani** (1667) has 17th-century icons and wall-paintings by

Iosip Iacovu, Nicolae Famokevici and Ponehalschi, who also decorated the imperial doors at **Sârbi Josani** (1703), where there are icons by Radu Munteanu. The churches in the unspoiled village of **Budeşti**, which are both dedicated to St Nicholas, have wall paintings by Ponehalschi, as well as numerous icons, manuscripts and printed books. The older of the two churches is **Budeşti Josani** (1643); **Budeşti Susani** dates from 1760, but was enlarged in the 19th century.

Costache Negri Moldavia
Village 50 km northwest of Galaţi, formerly known as Minjina. It is now named after its most celebrated son, a 19th-century politician, who was one of the leaders of the Unionist movement, and whose house is now a museum (closed Mon.).

Costeşti Transylvania
Village close to a ruined Dacian citadel, 17 km south of Orăştie, founded in the 1st century BC and containing remains of perimeter walls, watchtowers and temples. Nearby are the remains of a Roman fort, which was used by Trajan's soldiers when they were fighting the Dacians. **Blidaru**, another Dacian site to the south, can be reached on foot from Costeşti and affords a wonderful view. Costeşti is also the starting point for visiting the site of the old Dacian capital **Sarmizegetusa Regia** 18 km away (*see separate entry*).

Cotnari Moldavia
Town 54 km northwest of Iaşi, established in 1448 and famous for its vineyards. The first Latin college in the country was founded here in 1562 by the Protestant voivode Ioan Iacob Heraclid. A small royal palace built in 1947 is now used by the local winery.

Costeşti Wallachia see Arnota

Covasna (Kovászna) Transylvania
Spa 30 km east of Sfântu Gheorghe, by the Covasna Brook. To the east is the **Valea Zânelor** (Fairies' Valley) and a spectacular late 19th-century railway, which still carries timber by gravity down the mountainside. The road north of Covasna leads through **Zăbala**, 7 km away, which contains a 14th-century Reformed church with Gothic and Renaissance carvings. It also has a late 17th-century palace built by the Mikes family, with gardens and an arboretum.

Craiova Wallachia
Important manufacturing centre on the Jiu River, and Wallachia's second city after Bucharest. It is an old city, originally a Roman camp under Trajan. From the 15th to the 18th centuries it was a regional capital.

Craiova is not particularly beautiful, but it has a number of cultural attractions. These include museums of art, ethnography and history. The Theodor Aman Museum of Art (Muzeul de Artă Theodor Aman), Calea Unirii 10 is housed in a neo-Baroque building by the French architect Paul Gottereau. Theodor Aman was an influential turn-of-the-century painter who helped to found the Academy of Fine Arts in Bucharest. The museum is best known for its collection of early Brâncuşi sculptures, including a version of *The Kiss*. The Ethnographic Section of the Oltenia Museum (Muzeul Olteniei Secţia de Etnografie), housed in a late 17th-century palace at Str. Matei Basarab 14, has a fine collection of traditional costumes, tools and carpets. The Museum of Oltenian History (Muzeul Istorie Olteniei), Str. Madona Duda 44, focuses on the history of the region from Palaeolithic times to the present day. The Church of St Demetrius-Baneasa (1889), by André Lecomte du Noüy replaced an earlier building that collapsed during an earthquake. The municipal park (*Parcul Romanesiu*) is an unusually fine example of turn of the century picturesque planning.

Five km west of the city is the early 16th-century monastery of **Bucovăţ**, which contains important frescoes.

Criş (Keresd, Kreisch) Transylvania
Village southwest of Sighişoara. The Renaissance castle in the centre of the village is a good example of the castles built by the great Hungarian aristocratic dynasties of Transylvania. It was the seat of a branch of the Bethlen family, and was begun in the mid-14th century. It was extended and remodelled in the Renaissance manner at the end of the 16th century. The prominent round tower with figures of warriors in relief on the upper storey was built in 1598. The courtyard has arcaded galleries. The castle was allowed to fall into disrepair after 1947, but is now being restored.

Cristian (Keresztényfalva, Grossau) Transylvania
Village 10 km west of Sibiu, with a museum and a citadel containing a 15th-century Gothic hall-church. The Romanesque church was remodelled in the 14th century and then converted by Andreas Lapicida in the later 15th century into a three-aisled hall church. The interior was given its present appearance in the 18th century, when the altarpiece (1719), organ (1775) and galleries (1795) were built. An unusual feature is the so-called 'Plague House', an oriel with very small windows through which the pastor could preach during a plague epidemic. The double ring wall has five towers. Next to the store-rooms stands the Speckturm ('Bacon Tower').

Curtea de Argeş Wallachia
Charming town 36 km northwest of Piteşti, which became the second capital of Wallachia in the 1350s. It has ruined court buildings and a princely church (Biserica Domnească Sf. Nicolae) of *c.* 1352 (*see p. 123*), with frescoes of a similar date. The monastery or Episcopal Church, begun in 1512 (*see p. 124*), was clumsily restored by André Lecomte du Noüy in the 1870s. The original architect, Master Manole, is said to have been imprisoned on the church roof so that he could never again create anything so beautiful. A well marks the spot where he fell to his death, attempting to fly with the aid of wings made from two roofing shingles. Kings Carol I and Ferdinand, the first monarchs of modern Romania, are buried here, together with their queens.

The Transfăgăraşan Highway, only open in the summer, is a magnificent scenic route built by Ceauşescu to counter possible invasions from the north.

Dârjiu (Székelyderzs) Transylvania
Unitarian Szekler village 15 km southwest of Odorheiu Secuiesc with a fine fortified church containing a coffered ceiling and frescoes of 1419. Hams and grain are still stored inside the church, a custom dating back to the time when the threat of a siege was ever-present.

Dej (Des, Desch) Transylvania
Town 46 km north of Cluj, with a Gothic Reformed church built between 1453 and 1536, and rebuilt in the 18th century. There is a Baroque Franciscan church (1730), a Municipal Museum and a Military Museum, with exhibits ranging from the Roman to the Communist period.

Dealu Frumos Transylvania
Village with an impressive and well-preserved fortified church: the 13th century basilican church, which was remodelled in the early 16th century as a hall-church, with fortified towers at the west end and over the chancel. The rectangular ring-wall has five towers. The name of the village means 'the beautiful hill'.

Densuş (Demsus, Densdorf)
Transylvania
Village with one of the region's most extraordinary buildings. The present church was erected in the 13th century on the ruins of a 4th-century predecessor. The square *naos* is surmounted by a pyramidal stone roof which supports a tower with a pointed spire. The semi-circular eastern apse was added in the 14th century, and various rooms (now roofless) were added on the north side. The church is built of Roman stones from the Dacian-Roman town of Ulpia Traiana Sarmizegetusa, including tomb slabs, inscriptions, fragments of statues, columns and the two lions on the roof of the apse. Inside are mid-15th-century wall paintings by Master Ştefan. The most recent restoration of the building took place in 1961-1964.

The Orthodox church, Densuş

Deseşti Maramureş
Wooden church in the Mara Valley, built in 1770, with a clerestory. Inside are wall-paintings by Radu Munteanu and Gheorghe Zugravul (1780), with figures of saints a nd martyrs, together with Turks, Jews, Germans and Franks, and geometric and floral motifs and Cyrillic inscriptions.

Deva (Déva, Diemrich)
Transylvania
Town on the River Mureş in western Transylvania. Deva is dominated by a citadel, which was founded in the 13th century on top of an extinct volcano, and is still impressive, despite having been damaged by a magazine explosion during the Hungarian uprising of 1848-9. The hill is a rich nature reserve. Although much modernized, Deva has a long history, which can be studied in the Museum of Dacian and Roman Civilization (Muzeul Civilizaţiei Dacice şi Romane) in the 17th-century Magna Curia Palace at B-dul 1 Decembrie 39, once a seat of the Bethlen family (closed Mon.). It contains a superb collection of Dacian and Roman statuary, jewellery and artefacts. There is also a Catholic church (18th century), a Reformed church (14th and 15th centuries) and an Orthodox church with an 18th-century tower.

   Lesnic, 10 km west of Deva, has a 15th-century Orthodox church, with wall-paintings showing battles against the Turks. Slightly further (25 km west of Deva) is **Gurasada**, with an interesting church (see separate entry).

Dintr'un Lemn Wallachia
Carved wooden monastery church, south of Râmnicu Vâlcea. Its name means 'from one piece of wood' and recalls its legendary foundation by a shepherd, who is supposed to have built it out of a single tree trunk. Originally erected in the early 17th century, it was rebuilt after fire damage in the 19th

Carved wooden gate

century. Nearby is a stone church and attractive balconied abbot's lodgings.

Dobrovăţ Moldavia
Monastery about 40 km south of Iaşi, now housing a community of Romanian monks. The date of the monastery's original foundation is unknown, but Ştefan the Great endowed a church here and dedicated it to the Holy Spirit in 1503-4. The church has a rectangular plan, with blind arcading and niches along the top of the walls.

Internally, the church has three lateral walls including a wooden iconostasis. The frescoes, commissioned by Ştefan's illegitimate son Petru Rareş in 1529, cover the walls from top to bottom. Many are badly faded, but among the subjects depicted are scenes showing the Passion of Christ, including the Betrayal, Trial, Crowning with Thorns and Crucifixion. In the sanctuary are scenes from the Last Supper, and on the east wall is a votive scene showing Petru beside

his father and his brother, both former voivodes of Moldavia. This was an attempt to demonstrate the legitimacy of Petru's claim to the throne.

In the *pronaos* is a fine example of the Ladder of St John Climax ('of the Ladder') and scenes of the Life of Christ and of St George. Beside the church is a winter chapel of the same period, and an 18th-century watch-tower, containing a chapel.

Dragomirna Moldavia
Fortified monastery 12 km north of Suceava. Its name means 'love of peace'. It was founded by Metropolitan Anastasi Crimca, a highly educated man who designed the church himself and established an icon-painting school here. The church was completed in 1609. It is an astonishingly tall, slender Renaissance building, 42 m high and only 9.6 m wide. The sheer walls and blind arcading add to the impression of height, but the sternness of the plain white façade is offset by

Gothic detailing and floral stonework in the Moldavian style. The carved rope encircling the building consists of three strands, representing the Trinity, and is repeated round the window frames and arches (see p. 132f).

Crimca is buried in the nave of the church, and his portrait can be seen on the pillar to the left as you walk through. The lofty nave is star-vaulted and covered in blue, red and gold frescoes. The Baroque iconostasis comes from the medieval church at Solca. Today, the monastery houses a community of nuns. Dragomirna also has a museum containing some of the illuminated manuscripts produced at Crimca's school and a smaller church in the Wallachian style.

Drăuşeni (Homoróddaróc, Draas)
Transylvania
The easternmost of the free Saxon villages of the Königsboden, about 25 km south of Odorheiu Secuiesc. The Saxon population left in 1944, and the inhabitants are now mainly Szekler. Until recently the church was neglected. The late Romanesque basilica (1224) with a west tower, which has unusually rich carved decoration and an apsidal east end, was altered in the 16th century, when the side aisles were removed and the building was fortified with external galleries. Inside, the nave walls are painted with scenes from the Life of St Catherine (1375). The painted galleries (1637) have been removed for safekeeping, and the roof has recently been repaired.

Drobeta-Turnu Severin Wallachia
Industrial town founded in 1833, 113 km west of Craiova, at the entrance to the Danube Gorges ('Iron Gates'), on the Serbian border. (The Danube passes through four spectacular gorges here, the grandest of which is the Kazu Gorge.) Known to the Dacians as Drobeta, the town was fortified by the Romans. The grounds of the Museum of the Iron Gates (Muzeul Porţilor de Fier),

Str. Independenţiei 1, contain the ruins of the great bridge built by Apollodorus of Damascus in 104-105 AD and portrayed on Trajan's Column. The bridge, the largest yet built, allowed Trajan's men to cross the Danube extremely quickly, thus giving them a crucial advantage over the Dacians. Hadrian dismantled the bridge, as he feared that it might afford too easy a passage to barbarians crossing the frontier into the Empire. Nonetheless, two of its piers have survived. There are also remains of the Roman fort (2nd-6th century AD) and the 14th-century Severin church. Further west, to the south of B-dul Republicii, are the remains of a medieval citadel. There is an attractive Art Museum (Muzeul de Artă) in Str. Rahovei with 20th-century Romanian work.

Cerneţi, a village 5 km to the east of the town, has a museum dedicated to Tudor Vladimirescu, the leader of the Revolution of 1821.

Durău Moldavia
Resort close to Lake Bicaz, with a hermitage (1835) decorated in the 1930s with frescoes by Nicolae Tonitza. A shepherds' festival takes place here on the second Sunday of every August. It is a good base for hiking in the **Ceahlău Massif** (see Bicaz). Only 2 km away is a popular waterfall, Cascada Durvitorarea.

Eforie Nord Dobrogea
Resort 17 km south of Constanţa, famed as much for the delights of its mud-bathing as for its beach. The mud, from nearby Lake Techirghiol, is said to be effective against rheumatism and polio. Eforie Nord has two elegant 1930s buildings by G. M. Cantacuzino: the Villa Aviana and the Bellona Hotel. Such distinction cannot be claimed for the town of **Eforie Sud** (also known as **Carmen Sylva**), 4 km to the south, which is far less appealing.

Făgăraș (Fogoras, Fogarasch) Transylvania
Industrial town lying north of the Făgăraș Mountains, about 60 km northwest of Brașov. Saxons were settled here in the 13th century. In 1369 the town came into the hands of Romanian princes from Wallachia. The castle in the town centre was originally built in the early 14th century and was destroyed by Vlad the Impaler. It acquired its present appearance in the 17th century, when it was enlarged and its fortifications strengthened with a moat and outer wall. In the castle courtyard there is an interesting and well-arranged museum of antiquities. The Transylvanian Diet met in the Knights' Hall on the first floor. The Church of St Nicholas has a fine set of carved 17th-century doors.

About 20 km west of Făgăraș is the monastery of **Sâmbăta** (see separate entry) famous for glass icon painting (see p. 236). Another glass icon centre in the Făgăraș area is **Avrig**, which has a Lutheran church dating from the 13th and 16th centuries, and the 18th-century Baroque palace of Samuel von Brukenthal, now a sanatorium. The 'Flowers of the Olt' folk festival takes place here on the second Sunday in April.

Feldioara (Földvár, Marienburg) Transylvania
Site of a 15th-century stronghold north of Brașov. It was built by local peasants to withstand attacks by the Turks, perhaps on the site of a citadel constructed by the Teutonic Knights in the 13th century. There is a 15th-century Lutheran citadel church close by.

Feleac (Szász-Fellak, Falk) Transylvania
Village with a 15th-century church commissioned by the Moldavian voivode Ștefan the Great. On the west door is an inscription in Old Slavonic dating from 1516. From Feleac

there is a panoramic view over the valley to Cluj.

Fildu de Sus (Felsófüld) Transylvania
Extremely picturesque village in western Transylvania, 55 km west of Cluj, with a beautiful early 18th-century timber church and many attractive buildings in traditional style – cottages, thatched barns and farmhouses with carved wooden gates. The interior of the church, which stands to the south of the village, is decorated with 19th-century frescoes, including scenes of Daniel in the Lions' Den, and figures in traditional costumes.

Focșani Moldavia
Principal town of the Vrancea *județ* in southern Moldavia. Although it already existed in the 13th century, almost all its present buildings are modern. There are archaeological and historical collections in the District Museum (Muzeul Județean), at B-dul Garii 5, and the neighbouring History and Archaeology Section (Secția de Istorie si Arheologie). **Petrești**, 7 km to the northeast, has a fascinating open-air museum of local vernacular architecture.

Galați Moldavia
Port on the left bank of the Danube, at its confluence with the Siret and Pruth rivers. Galați was developed after the devastation of the Second World War as a steel-producing town, but a few earlier monuments still survive, including the 17th-century churches of Precista and Mavromol and Ion Mincu's City Hall of 1911. There is also a Museum of Visual Art (Muzeul de Arte Vizuale), Str. Domneasca 141, and a District Museum of History (Muzeul Județean de Istorie), Str. Cuza 80.

The area around Galați has two interesting archaeological sites. The Roman camp of Tirighina is at the nearby village of **Barboși**. It was built c. 113-117 AD, under Trajan, as a frontier post. During the reign of Hadrian, Trajan's successor, it played an important role in Rome's defence of the Danube. The citadel at **Garvan**, 14 km to the southeast, was used intermittently from the 1st century BC until the 12th century AD.

Gârda de Sus Transylvania
Village in the Apuseni Mountains, 30 km northwest of Câmpeni, with traditional houses and a timber church (1792). From here it is possible to hike up to **Pestera Gheţarul**, the ice cave of Scărişoara, near the village of **Gheţari**. The ice in the cave is 15 m thick. Beyond is the **Padiş Plateau**, which culminates in the strange-looking karst **Pomor Citadels** (Cetăţile Pomorolui).

About 18 km from Câmpeni is the village of **Albac**, an important centre for traditional crafts. At **Horea**, 10 km north of Albac, is a monument to the eponymous hero of the peasants' uprising of 1784.

Geoagiu-Bai (Ferodőgyogy) Transylvania
Village at the foot of the Metaliferi Mountains, 58 km west of Alba Iulia. Known as Thermae Dodonae in Roman times, it still functions as a spa. Its 13th-century church was built with Roman bricks.

Ghelinţa (Gelence) Transylvania
Village 10 km south of Târgu Secuesc. It has a church built before the Tatar invasions of 1241 and reconstructed in the 14th century, which contains a series of wall-paintings showing stories from the Life of St Ladislas.

Gheorgheni (Gyergyószentmiklós) Transylvania
Town 57 km northwest of Miercurea-Ciuc, first recorded in 1332 and settled by Armenians in the 17th century. It has an Armenian Catholic church (1730-33), as well as a 14th-century Roman Catholic church and a county museum on Piaţa Petófi Sandor.

6 km north of here is the village of **Lăzarea** with its castle (*see separate entry*).

From Gheorgheni a spectacular mountain road leads to **Lacul Roşu** ('the Red Lake'), a resort 26 km to the northeast.

Gherla (Szamosújvár, Neuschloss) Transylvania
Town 45 km northeast of Cluj-Napoca, formerly known as Armenopolis on account of its large Armenian community. It has a Baroque Armenian Catholic cathedral (1748-98), the Renaissance castle of George Martinuzzi, Bishop of Oradea (1551), as well as a Museum of History (Muzeul de Istorie) at Str. Mihai Viteazul 6, which contains a collection of Armenian manuscripts and icons.

Giurgiu Wallachia
Industrial town on the Danube, 64 km south of Bucharest, with little of interest to see other than the Turnul Ceasornicului, a fire-tower 22 m high built by the Turks in the 18th century, which is now a clock tower. There are also military relics of Mircea the Old, who fought the Turks in the 1390s.

Goleşti Wallachia
Village about 100 km northwest of Bucharest belonging to the Golescu family, one of the leading families of 19th century Wallachia (contributing no fewer than three prime ministers). Their attractive summer residence has been turned into the open-air Museum of Viticulture and Fruit Growing (Muzeul Viticulturii şi Pomiculturii, closed Mon.), with tools, traditional buildings and a wooden church on display.

Gurahonţ Banat
Village on the Criş Alb River southeast of Sebiş, in an area inhabited since Paleolithic times. A monument here commemorates Ion Buteanu, a revolutionary of the 1848 uprising, who was executed here.

Gura Humorului Moldavia
Town 36 km southwest of Suceava, with an ethnographical museum. This is a good base for visiting the famous painted churches at **Voroneţ** and **Humor** (*see separate entries*).

Gurasada Banat
Village on the Maroş River, west of Deva, with a late 13th-century Orthodox church combining Byzantine and Gothic elements. Inside are 15th-century Byzantine frescoes depicting sinful women.

Hălmagiu Banat
Village with medieval origins, northwest of Brad. It is celebrated for its 'Kiss Fair', which takes place in March each year.

Hărman (Szászhermány, Honigberg) Transylvania
Village 12 km northeast of Braşov, with an impressive fortified church, which stands in the middle of the village and is entered by a drawbridge across a moat. The massive ring-walls have three galleries. Within the inner wall are four storeys of chambers where the villagers could live in times of danger, using food stored there. The style of the church shows Cistercian influence, but it was considerably remodelled in 1595 after a devastating fire in 1593. Wall-paintings in the International Gothic style, dating from around 1400 and whitewashed over in the Reformation, were uncovered in a side chapel which the villagers had been using as a smokehouse for curing bacon. Subjects include the Crucifixion, St Peter, Paradise and the Last Judgement.

Hărniceşti Maramureş
Village in the Mara Valley. The 17th-century Church of the Birth of the Virgin (before 1665) has some fine 17th-century icons and early printed books. The museum is in a building said to be the only 19th-century nobleman's house left in Maramureş.

Haţeg (Hátszeg, Wallenthal) Transylvania
Settled by Walloons in the 13th century when it was under Hungarian rule, this is a good place from which to explore Transylvania's Roman remains at **Ulpia Traiana Sarmizegetusa** (*see separate entry*), and the **Retezat** National Park. There is a bison reserve 3 km to the north and some interesting Romanesque churches survive in the area, including the 13th-century church at **Santamaria-Orlea**. 15 km north of Haţeg is the **Prislop Monastery**, founded in 1400 and one of the oldest religious houses in Romania.

Histria Dobrogea
Sometimes known as 'the Romanian Pompeii', Histria was founded by Greeks in the 7th century BC. Situated on Lake Sinoe, originally close to a mouth of the Danube, its harbour eventually silted up. Rediscovered in 1914, most of Histria's visible remains are Roman, with a forum, impressive fortifications, baths and an early Christian basilica, although there are also traces of far more ancient Greek temples. The museum covers all stages of the city's development.

Hobiţa Wallachia
Village west of Târgu Jiu, where the great sculptor Constantin Brâncuşi was born in 1876. His birthplace has been turned into a memorial house (closed Mon.). (*See p. 226*)

Homorod (Homoród, Hamruden) Transylvania
Village 4 km east of Rupea. The church here dates from 1270 and in the 15th century was surrounded by two rows of earthworks. A new chancel was built in 1792. The church is now orientated to the south because the east chancel of the old Romanesque church was converted into a defensive tower *c.* 1500. The rather faded pre-Reformation wall-paintings in the old choir and in the west porch are

considered to be the earliest surviving frescoes in Transylvania.

Horaiţa Moldavia
Monastery 20 km north of Piatra Neamţ, founded in 1725. The church was rebuilt in 1867 with eight spires. **Horaicioara Hermitage** is 1 km away.

Horezu Wallachia
Town 70 km northeast of Târgu Jiu, set amid fruit orchards and lilac trees. It is famous for its ceramics, especially plates, which are traditionally handed out after funerals. The Cocoşul de Horezu pottery fair is held on the first Sunday of June. 4 km to the northeast, is the village of **Romani de Jos** and the frescoed **Hurez Monastery,** which is the largest and most impressive of the religious foundations of Prince Constantin Brâncoveanu in Wallachia, and the site of the school that established the Brâncoveneanu style. The Great Church, completed in 1693, has a ten-pillared porch and carved wooden doors. Inside are frescoes darkened by smoke from the fires lit by Turkish troops who camped here. They include portraits of Brâncoveanu and his family. The complex also contains the chapel of St. Michael, hermitages of the Holy Apostles (1698) and St. Stephen (1703), and a fire tower, which dates from 1753. Overnight accommodation available.

A few km to the north is **Bistriţa Monastery,** which was founded in the 15th century, although most of the buildings, which include three churches as well as a nearby cave enclosing two chapels, were constructed much later. **Arnota Monastery** is another 4 km to the northeast (*see separate entry*). To the west of Horezu in the Olteţ Gorges is **Polovragi,** a monastery dating back to the late 15th century and rebuilt by Constantin Brâncoveanu. Nearby **Bolniţa** has a church (1736) with exceptionally fine frescoes. At the mouth of the Olteţ Gorges is the Polovragi Cave, which was sacred to the ancient

Dacians and said to be the abode of Zalmoxis, their chief deity. It is now open for guided tours; the stalactites in the 'Candlesticks Gallery' are the most popular sight.

Of particular interest are the two *cule* or fortified manors at **Măldăreşti,** 4 km south of Horezu *(see p. 138)*. These were built in the early 18th and 19th centuries, and contain a museum of icons (closed Mon.)

Hosman (Holczmány, Holzmengen) Transylvania
Village about 30 km northeast of Sibiu set against the backdrop of the Făgăraş Mountains. The fortified church was remodelled in the 18th century, but the bell-tower has preserved its sculptured Romanesque doorway. The gate tower in the ring-wall still has its portcullis.

Huedin (Bánffyhunyad) Transylvania
An extensively modernized town, 46 km west of Cluj. Its 15th-century Gothic Reformed church has a wonderful coffered and tiled ceiling dating from 1780, decorated with plants, animals, emblems and inscriptions. To the southeast is the village of **Mănăstirene,** which has a Calvinist church, originally built in the 13th century in the Romanesque style and much altered in the 15th century.

Humor Moldavia
Monastery 5 km north of Gura Humorului. Its church has fine external wall-paintings dating from 1535. The Siege of Constantinople, on the lower half of the west end of the south wall, is particularly dramatic. It shows the Byzantine capital's miraculous liberation from the Persian siege of 626, but the city is depicted as a medieval Moldavian town under fire from Turkish cannon. The frescoes in the interior are also very fine, and there is an iconostasis with four 15th-century icons *(see p. 102)*.

Hunedoara (Vajdahunyad, Eisenmarkt)
Transylvania
Town 19 km south of Deva. As its German
name indicates, its history is linked to the
mining and processing of iron ore. The
town's most famous monument, the moated,
towered and ramparted Corvin Castle
(Castelul Corvinilor), stands in striking contrast to the surrounding industrial bleakness.
Founded in the 14th century on Roman fortifications, the castle was mostly built by
Iancu of Hunedoara in the mid-15th century, with subsequent additions by his son
Matthias Corvinus. Further alterations were
made by Prince Gábor Bethlen in the 17th
century. The castle was restored after
destruction by fire in 1854 and now contains
a museum devoted to Iancu of Hundeoara. It
also has a 15th-century Orthodox church
which contains wall-paintings dating from
the 17th century.

Interior of the Monastery Church, Humor

Hurez Monastery Wallachia
See **Horezu**

Iacobeni (Jakabfalva, Jakobsdorf)
Transylvania
Village about 25 km south of Sighişoara
with an exceptionally beautiful and well-
preserved fortified church set on a hill. The
sandstone fortified tower was built on to the
church at the end of of the 15th century. The
inner ring-wall has a three-storey residential
tower, and the entrance gate on the north
side has a portcullis.

Iaşi Moldavia
The most important and most sophisticated
city in Moldavia, and second largest city in
Romania, Iaşi was the capital of the principality of Moldavia from the 1560s until the
creation of the state of Romania in 1859, and
indeed shared capital status with Bucharest
until 1862. Romania's first university was
founded here in 1860, and the city is still
today the region's cultural centre.

The unification of Wallachia and Moldavia
was inaugurated by Alexander Ioan Cuza in
what is now Piaţa Unirii, and the event is
marked every 24 January. Cuza's palace at Str.
Lăpuşneanu 14 is now the Union Museum.

The city's spine is Bulevardul Ştefan cel
Mare, which runs southeast from Piaţa
Unirii. Here is the Hotel Traian, which has
an iron frame constructed in the early 1880s
by Gustave Eiffel. Along the boulevard,
which has many ugly Communist-era
buildings, are a number of impressive
churches, in particular the neo-Baroque
Orthodox Cathedral (1884), the largest
Orthodox church in Romania, with frescoes
by Gheorghe Tattarescu. It contains the
relics of St Paraschiva, the patron saint of
Mol-davia, as well as of households, har-
vests, traders and travellers. Her feast day, 14
October, can attract up to a million pilgrims
to Iaşi. The cathedral's precinct (1950s) is by
G. M. Cantacuzino. Opposite is the vast
City Hall.

A little further south are the 18th-century
Catholic Church and the monastic Church

University buildings, Iaşi

of the Three Hierarchs (Trei Ierarhi), commissioned in 1637 by Prince Vasile Lupu, one of the ablest and most cultivated of Moldavia's rulers. The present structure is a rather heavy-handed 19th-century reconstruction by André Lecomte du Noüy of the original Mannerist building by the Greek architect Ienache Etisi.

At the far end of the boulevard, in Piaţa Palatului, is the French-inspired neo-Gothic Palace of Culture (Palatul Culturii). Designed by I. D. Berindei as the town hall and law courts and completed in 1926, it contains museums of science, ethnography, history and art (closed Mon.), while the 17th-century Casa Dosoftei nearby displays incunabula and manuscripts in the former home of a great scholar, the Metropolitan Dosoftei. Between these two buildings is the ancient church of St Nicolae, rebuilt by Lecomte du Noüy between 1884 and 1904

on the site of a late-15th-century church commissioned by Ştefan the Great.

To the east of B-dul Ştefan cel Mare are buildings that testify to Iaşi's formerly mixed population of Orthodox and Armenian Christians, and Jews. The Armenian church and the synagogue date from the early 19th and 18th centuries respectively, but are on the site of much earlier foundations. The Orthodox churches in this area include St Sava (late 16th and 17th centuries), the mostly 17th-century Golia Monastery and the Barnovschi Church (1628).

Near the Golia is the splendid Vasile Alecsandru National Theatre (Teatrul Naţional Vasile Alecsandri) by the Hapsburg theatre specialists Fellner and Helmer. It also houses the Romanian National Opera House (Opera Naţională Română din Iaşi).

To the north of the town centre is B-dul Independenţei, which has two important 18th-century buildings, the monastery of St Spiridon (c. 1750) and the slightly later Old University (Universitatea Veche) in an 18th-century palace. Much further north, the suburb of **Ticău** has museums dedicated to the writer Ion Creangă (Str. Simion Barnutiu) and the prime minister Mihai Kogălniceanu (Str. Kogălniceanu 7a), while the Copou Park (Parcul Copou) next to the botanical gardens in the northwest contains a museum devoted to Mihai Eminescu, Romania's national poet (1850-89). An avenue of giant busts commemorates members of Romania's foremost 19th century literary circle, the Junimea.

Another suburb worth visiting is **Nicolina** in the south of the city, which contains three monasteries: the neo-Classical Frumoasa (18th and early 19th centuries); the Galata (1583), built in the classic Moldavian style, but with two towers instead of one and the Wallachian cord motif around the body of the church; and the fortified Cetăţuia (c. 1670). **Bârnova**, 13 km south, has a fortified monastery (1620-65) begun by Prince Miron Barnovschi, who also commissioned the Barnovschi Church inside the city.

Isaccea Dobrogea
River port on the Danube, 11 km northwest of Niculitel. Founded by the Dacians, it was known to the Romans as Noviodunum. At **Tichileşti**, a few km to the west, is Europe's last leper colony.

Iza Valley Maramureş
Valley running eastwards from **Vadu Izei**, a village 6 km southeast of Sighetu Marmaţiei. A centre of folk art, Vadu Izei has a village museum and attractive timber architecture, as well as a tourist office.

15 km further east, the village of **Bârsana** has a monastic complex with several wooden churches (*see separate entry*).

A further 20 km to the east is the village of **Glod**, with an early 18th-century wooden church which has a beautiful 19th-century iconostasis.

The wall-paintings at the village of **Rozavlea** a further 6 km on, are by Plohod and Filip Şantner and date from 1720. There are also 18th-century wall-paintings in the Church of the Birth of the Virgin (1760) in **Şieu**, further to the southeast.

In **Poienile Izei**, 12 km southwest of Rozavlea, is the 17th century timber church of St Paraschiva (*see separate entry*).

The valley ends at **Bogdan Vodă**. Formerly known as Cuhea, this village was renamed in 1968 in honour of the 14th-century prince of Maramureş, who marched from here to become voivode of Moldavia in 1359. The village has ruined 14th-century fortifications and an elaborately painted and carved church of 1718.

The oldest wooden church in Maramureş, dating from 1364, is at **Ieud**, a highly traditional village 2 km southwest of Bogdan Vodă. This has paintings by Ponehalschi (1782) and formerly contained the earliest known document written in Romanian (a text of ecclesiastical law composed in 1391-2), now in the National Museum in Bucharest. Here also is a Uniate church of 1717, with a large collection of glass icons.

Jurlovica Dobrogea
Fishing village on Lake Goloviţa, 53 km northeast of Histria, with a population composed chiefly of Lipovani, descendants of Russian religious dissidents known as 'Old Believers'. Many of the houses here are made from dried peat bricks. The museum tells the story of the village's varied population.

Lăpuş Valley and **Chioar** Maramureş
The Lăpuş Valley in southern Maramureş is a beautiful region with many villages containing wooden churches built in a distinctive style, including the following:

Lăpuş, Dormition of the Virgin, before 1661, wall-paintings 1697, icons by Radu Munteanu.

Ungureni, Holy Archangels, before 1733, wall-paintings by Radu Munteanu.

Cupşeni, idyllic village with two churches, St Elias (before 1733, wall-paintings 1823), and Sfânţii Arhangeli, before 1733, wall-paintings 1848, 17th-century imperial doors.

Libotin, Holy Archangels, 1671, beautiful wall-paintings by Radu Munteanu.

Rogoz, Holy Archangels, 1661-1701, restored 1960-61, some of the most beautiful wall-paintings in Maramureş and icons by Radu Munteanu and Nicolae Man (1785), and carved horses' heads on the roof. Also the Uniate Church of St Paraschiva, 1695.

Dobricu Lăpuşului, Virgin Mary, c.1701, wall-paintings and icons by Radu Munteanu. Also Holy Archangels, 17th century, wall-paintings and icons by Radu Munteanu.

Răzoare, before 1730, wall-paintings by Petru Diacul of Preluca (1759).

Drăghia, 1706, imperial doors by Petru Diacul of Preluca (late 18th century), wall-paintings 1857.

Stoiceni, Holy Archangels, late 18th century, with wall-paintings by Toader Tecariu (1872).

Costeni, St Nicholas. Late 18th century.

Fânaţe, 1840.

Cărpiniş, Assumption, early 18th century.

Şurdeşti, Holy Archangels, 1738, (*see separate entry*). There is a fine view over the valley from its 54-metre-tall tower.

Plopiş, Holy Archangels, early 19th century.

Cetăţele, Wall-paintings by Ştefan Zugravul of Şişeşti.

Săcălăşeni, Dormition of the Virgin, 1442, with fine 19th-century wall-paintings (*see separate entry*).

Vălenii Şomcutei, Holy Archangels, 17th century, enlarged 19th century, with 19th-century wall-paintings on canvas.

Remetea Chioarului, St Demetrius, c. 1800, wall-paintings 1839.

Coruia, Holy Archangels, before 1794.

Culcea, 1721, restored 1860 and 1900.

Lăzarea (Gyergyószárhegy) Transylvania
Village 6 km northeast of Gheorgheni. Lăzarea Castle, built for the Lazar family, is a half-ruined 15th-century Renaissance building with a magnificent hall and frescoed façade. It is currently being restored, and a gallery (closed Mon.) exhibits the work of artists engaged on the restoration. Close by are a 16th-century Franciscan monastery and a fortified church.

Lipova Banat
Attractive town on the south bank of the River Mureş, 33 km southeast of Arad. Lipova was recorded as early as the 12th century. It has an interesting museum, and a 14th-century church, the Orthodox Church of the Annunciation, which contains the most important murals in the Banat, painted in the 15th century in the Byzantine style. One km to the south is the spa of **Lipova Baó** and 3 km to the northeast are the ruins of **Şoimoş Castle** (13th-15th centuries).

Livezile (Jád, Jaad) Transylvania
Old Saxon village 6 km northeast of Bistriţa, whose name means 'the Orchards'. The *judeţ* museum, housed in the Saxon House (Casa Săsească, no. 152, closed Mon. and Tues.), is kept as if it were still a working farmhouse, and contains displays of Saxon utensils and domestic objects. Across the street is the Colecţie Ion Rus, another collection of Saxon furniture and objects.

Lugoj Banat
Peaceful town 63 km east of Timişoara, with an 18th-century Baroque Orthodox Church of the Assumption by Fischer von Erlach the Younger on Piaţa Victoriei. The museum (closed Mon.) on Strada Andrei Mocioni has

displays of ceramics, costumes and weaponry.

Lupşa (Lupsa) Transylvania
Village in the Arieş Valley, 15 km east of Campeni. Although Roman remains have been discovered here, the village's main distinction is its excellent ethnographic museum (Muzeul Etnografic Pamfil Albu) and its 15th-century timber monastery church with wall-paintings.

Macin Dobrogea
River port on the Danube, 40 km southwest of Isaccea. The walls of the Roman town of Arrubium can still be seen. To the south is **Greci**, from where it is possible to climb the peak of **Tutuiatu** (467 m).

Măgura Moldavia
Village 27 km northwest of Buzău, with a sculpture park nearby. In the neighbouring village of **Tisău** is the Ciolanu Monastery (1560), which has a museum of arts and crafts.

Mahmudia Dobrogea
Settlement on the Sfântu Gheorghe arm of the Danube Delta, 28 km southeast of Tulcea, on the site of Salsovia, an ancient city originally dedicated to sun worship. Traces of late Roman fortifications can still be seen.

Mălâncrav (Almakerék, Malmkrog) Transylvania
Village about 25 km southwest of Sighişoara, with a fortified Lutheran church on a hill outside. The ring-walls built in the early 15th century formerly had towers and bastions, of which only the gate-tower survives. The Church of St Mary, dating from the 14th century, is impressively large and has some of the best medieval frescoes in Transylvania. The chancel was remodelled at the end of the 14th century, when it was decorated on the walls and vaults with wall-paintings in the International Gothic style. The Passion scenes on the north wall are particularly striking, and their colours are well-preserved, but the colours of the biblical scenes uncovered beneath Reformation whitewash in the nave are now less brilliant. The funerary vault of the Apafi family is in a chapel near the church.

Mamaia Dobrogea
Coastal resort 6 km north of Constanţa, now somewhat past its prime. Its name is supposed to recall the cries of a girl calling out for her abducted mother. Much frequented in winter by stray dogs, the town cheers up somewhat during the summer, and the white sandy beach is a draw. The seafront has an Art Deco casino. There is also a lake nearby, with an island named after Ovid. To the north lies **Navodari**, which also has a lovely beach, but has been spoilt by a phosphates factory.

Mangalia Dobrogea
The ancient Greek port of Callatis, founded in the 6th century BC, is now a small seaside resort, spa and port, just north of the Bulgarian border. The town has been thoroughly modernized, and its public buildings are adorned with heroic Socialist Realist decoration. However, a charming mosque (Moschee Sultan Esmahan, Str. Oituz), built in 1525 and surrounded by a graveyard, survives. It still serves the large Muslim community of Turkish and Tatar extraction.

There are also substantial ancient remains: Sarmatian and Hellenistic burial grounds; Roman city walls dating from the 3rd century AD, with an adjoining 5th-century Syrian basilica; and, inside the Hotel President (Str. Teilor 6), layers of excavated streets from different periods. Artefacts from these sites, including ceramic figurines and jewellery, can be found in the museum (Str. Constanţei 23). Sadly, the ancient port is now under the sea.

Around Mangalia there are a number of interesting caves, notably at **Limanu** to the southwest and **Movile** to the northeast. The latter possesses a unique ecosystem consisting of organisms that exist in total darkness.

Mara Valley Maramureş
Valley in central Maramureş, south of Sighetu Marmaţiei. At the northern end of the valley is **Berbeşti**, which has a notable late 17th-century Calvary, a carved wooden crucifix with mourning figures, standing by the side of the road (*see p. 166*). Such wayside crucifixes were once common in Moldavia and offered protection to travellers. Further south, at **Sat-Şugatag**, is the Church of St Paraschiva (1642), with icons by Gheorghe Visovan.

Mănăstirea Giuleşti, 1 km to the east, is a monastery in a tiny village with a church founded in 1653, decorated with 17th- and 18th-century paintings, and late 18th-century icons by Ponehalschi. Three km to the south is the spa of **Ocna Şugatag**. A little further on is **Harniceşti**, with a 17th-century wooden church (*see separate entry*).

Another attractive wooden church in the region is the Holy Virgin at **Deseşti** (*see separate entry*).

Mărăşeşti Moldavia
Small industrial town about 20 km north of Focşani with an impressive circular memorial (1938) to a crucial battle won by the Romanians against the Germans in 1917 (*see p. 77*). There is also a small museum (closed Mon.). **Panciu**, 16 km to the northwest, is an important wine-growing centre.

Marginea Moldavia
Village in Bucovina, 9 km southwest of Rădăuti, famous for its black ceramics decorated with patterns based on ancient Dacian designs. The pottery workshops are open to visitors Mon. to Fri., and there is a gift shop next door.

Medgidia Dobrogea
Port and industrial centre on the Danube-Black Sea Canal, 22 km northwest of Basarabi. Although significant Neolithic finds have been made here, the town's principal cultural interest lies in its mosque and Islamic seminary.

Mediaş (Medgyes, Mediasch)
Transylvania
Medieval town, 44 km east of Blaj, on the Timava Mare River. Although originally occupied by Hungarian-speaking Szeklers, it was taken over in the 12th century by German settlers. In the central square, Piaţa Republicii, is a fortified Gothic church complex comprising two ring-walls, with four towers and a gate-tower, enclosing buildings of various dates: the old Town Hall, the pastor's house (1513), the chaplain's house, and a school (next to the Speckturm). The Church of St Margaret, built in 1488 on the foundations of an early Gothic predecessor, has a beautiful net-vault with bosses painted with coats of arms and heads of saints and apostles. The winged altarpiece (*c.* 1485), possibly painted by a Viennese master of the Schottenstift school, has scenes of the Passion, with a silhouette of the city of Vienna in the background. Turkish carpets, presented by merchants in lieu of tax, are suspended from the galleries.

There are also two surviving gate-towers, as well as the Town Museum (Muzeul Orăşenesc) in a former Franciscan monastery at Str. Mihai Viteazul 46, which contains archaeological remains, some from the second millennium BC (closed Mon.).

From Mediaş it is also possible to visit the spectacular fortified churches at **Biertan** and **Richiş** (*see separate entries*).

Miercurea Ciuc (Csikszereda, Szeklerburg)
Transylvania
Industrial town near the source of the River Olt, at the eastern edge of Transylvania. Its

German name reveals the ethnic identity of many of its citizens, while its Romanian name recalls the Wednesday (Miercuri) markets that used to take place here. Although heavily modernized, Miercurea still has a number of churches, and an Italian Renaissance-style citadel, built by Ferenc Mikó in the early 17th century, which houses a museum of Szekler life (Muzeul Secuiesc, closed Mon.). The most celebrated church is a Franciscan foundation of 1442 (rebuilt 1804) at **Sumuleu**, 2 km to the east. There is a pilgrimage here on Whit Sunday.

Miercurea Sibiului (Szederhely, Reussmarkt) Transylvania
Village 22 km southeast of Sebeş, named after the market which still takes place every Wednesday (Miercuri). It also possesses a 13th-century church, surrounded by 15th-century fortifications.

Mogoşoaia Wallachia
Beautiful and important palace 14 km northwest of Bucharest, built by Prince

Constantin Brâncoveanu for his son Ştefan in 1698-1702. Badly damaged later in the 18th century, it was restored by Princess Marthe Bibesco (1886-1973), historian, novelist and socialite. After scandalous neglect during the Ceauşescu regime, it has recently been renovated. Its architecture mixes Renaissance, Islamic and vernacular Romanian elements and motifs. There is a museum, and outside a small collection of rescued statues of Communist leaders.

In the grounds is the tomb of Prince Antoine Bibesco (d. 1951), Proust's intimate friend Ocsebib, model of Robert de St Loup in *Swann's Way*, and his wife Elizabeth (d. 1945), daughter of the British prime minister H. H. Asquith. A church dedicated to St George of the Meadow (1688) lies outside the palace gates; the frescoes include portraits of Brancoveanu and his family.

Moldoviţa Moldavia
Monastery dedicated to the Annunciation, 22 km north of Câmpulung Moldovenesc, near the Moldoviţa River. The church,

*Monastery
Church of the
Annunciation,
Moldoviţa*

founded in 1532, is decorated with especially fine external frescoes, painted in 1537. The scene showing the Virgin's miraculous deliverance of Constantinople from the Persian siege of 626 reflects 16th-century concerns about Ottoman power: it features Christians attacking Turks with arrows and exploding cannons. Above is a depiction of the Acathistic Hymn to the Virgin, and further along is a Tree of Jesse. In the porch is a Last Judgement.

Inside, there are frescoes of military saints, including St George, and the Emperor Constantine at the Council of Nicaea, and narratives of saints' lives and ecumenical councils. In the nave, the founder of the monastery, Petru Rareş, standing with his wife and children, is shown giving a model of the church to Christ as a votive offering. There is also a small museum of monastic treasures (closed Mon.).

Moneasa Banat
Spa 18 km northeast of Sebiş, in the valley of the Moneasa River. From here it is possible to hike into the Codru-Moma Massif. There are also facilities for winter skiing.

Moreni Moldavia
Monastery founded in 1540. The last monk died in 1883, and the monastery was deserted until the 1930s, when a small community of monks re-established itself there, but after a few years it was again deserted. In 1958 the Communist government closed Moreni, together with most of Romania's other monastic institutions. However, in recent years it has been re-established. It has a small 19th-century church, and now houses a community of about 50 nuns, who cultivate the farm land and create beautiful hand-sewn ecclesiastical vestments. They welcome visitors, and there is excellent guest accommodation. Moreni makes a good base for exploring eastern Moldavia, and is a peaceful haven for those looking for a retreat.

Moşna (Szász-Muzsna, Meschen) Transylvania
Village 10 km south of Mediaş, with a late Gothic, three-aisled hall church, built by the Transylvanian architect Andreas Lapicida and completed at the end of the 15th century. The church was fortified with defensive galleries, and towers were built over the north and south portals. The five-towered ring-wall was built in the late 15th and early 16th century. Inside are some fine Gothic carvings: a tall tabernacle, pulpit and an elaborate doorway to the sacristy (1500-2). The town hall is built on to the five-storey gate tower.

Movile Wallachia
Impressive fortress near the Olt Valley. The fortified church stands on a hill in the middle of the village. The west tower, built after the Mongol invasion, contains medieval bells with inscriptions. A second tower was built over the chancel in the 15th century. The defensive ring-wall has galleries and three towers.

Mugeni (Bögöz) Transylvania
Village 11km southwest of Odoreiu Secueisc with a 14th-century church containing a coffered ceiling and interesting frescoes.

Murighiol Dobrogea
Settlement by the Sfântu Gheorghe arm of the Danube Delta, 45 km southeast of Tulcea, renamed **Independenţia** during the Communist era. Some Roman fortifications dating from the 2nd century BC can still be seen, although Murighiol's main attractions are the ornithologically rich lakes and wetlands nearby.

Nadăşa (Gorgényados) Transylvania
Village with a small 19th-century wooden church that has been converted into a museum, containing icons, statues, carvings and manuscripts.

Năsăud (Naszód, Nussendorf)
Transylvania
Town 20 km northwest of Bistriţa, with a
museum and a large Orthodox Church of
the Archangels (before 1735, restored 1970s).
Five km south is the village of **Liviu
Rebreanu**, named after its most famous son,
a distinguished novelist (1885-1944).

Neamţ Moldavia
Fortified monastery 17 km northwest of
Târgu Neamţ, the oldest and one of the
largest in Moldavia. Although founded by
Petru I Muşat in the 14th century, most of
the complex was built by Ştefan the Great in
1497, after defeating the Poles at Suceava.
The architecture combines Byzantine and
Western elements, including Gothic windows (*see p. 99*). Neamţ contains a remarkable library of illuminated manuscripts
made at the monastery, some of which are
displayed, while artefacts from the church at
Secu (*see separate entry*) are kept in another
museum on the site. There is also a small
19th-century church behind the main
medieval structure.

The Church of the Ascension, Neamţ

Negreşti-Oaş (Avasfelsöfalu)
Maramureş
Town on the Tur River, 50 km northeast of
Satu Mare. Its Municipal Museum (Muzeul
Orăşenesc, closed Mon.) has important
ethnographic collections, including reconstructions of local buildings, such as the
wooden church brought here from the
village of Lechinţa-Oaş.

Negreşti is the centre of the Oaş
Depression, which has its own distinctive
folklore and costumes. These are fully displayed at the annual festival (1 September),
and can also be seen in places such as
Camarzana, 20 km to the northwest.

Negru Vodă Wallachia
Monastery in Câmpulung founded in 1215
by Radu Negru, voivode of Wallachia, and

completed in the 14th century. It was
largely rebuilt in the 19th century, incorporating stonework from the original. The
gate tower is 17th century, with a 12th-
century carving of a deer. Inside the church
is a 13th-century tomb of a Western
knight.

Neptun-Olimp Dobrogea
The most exclusive among a series of beach
resorts between Eforie and Mangalia,
Neptun-Olimp boasts two lakes and a number of smart hotels, as well as villas formerly
reserved for the elite of the Communist
Party. Less pretentious are **Costineşti**, 6 km
to the north, with a fine beach, and, south of
Olimp, the unappealing concrete jungles
known as **Jupiter, Aurora, Venus** and
Saturn.

Nicula (Füzesmikola, Nickelsdorf)
Transylvania
Small village 35 km northeast of Cluj dating
from the 14th century, where a miracle is said
to have taken place. In 1694 a group of
Austrian army officers came to Nicula and
claimed that, when they went into the church,
they saw an icon of the Virgin Mary weeping
real tears. Eventually 27 eye-witnesses testified
that they had seen the icon crying day and
night for 26 days. Today, tall wooden crosses
stand beside the road to commemorate the
miracle.

Outside the village, **Nicula Monastery**,
founded in 1326 and rebuilt in the 17th century, is an important centre of glass icon
painting. Examples can be seen in the icon
museum here. The original miraculous icon is
housed in the the monastery's 19th-century
church. There is also an 18th-century timber
church brought here from Bistrița.

Niculițel Dobrogea
Town 31 km west of Tulcea, situated on a
brook of the same name. Originally a Dacian
settlement, it contains a ruined 4th-century
Christian basilica, with 5th-century alterations; there are martyrs' remains preserved
in the crypt. Seven km to the west, the
Cocos Monastery (1838) has a collection of
medieval books and icons.

Ocna Sibiului (Vízakna, Salzburg)
Transylvania
Spa 18 km northwest of Sibiu. Salt was
mined here from Roman times, and there are
saline lakes used for bathing.

Odobești Moldavia
Village 12 km northwest of Focșani. Like the
nearby villages of **Cotești, Panciu** and
Nicorești, Odobești has been associated
with wine-making since Ștefan the Great's
time. 24 km to the west, at **Andreiasu de
Jos**, combustible gases are emitted from the
earth's crust, creating tongues of 'living fire'.

Odorheiu Secuiesc (Székelyudvarhely,
Odorhellen) Transylvania
Town 44 km southeast of Sovata, with the
remains of a Roman camp, a citadel dating
from the 16th century, three 18th-century
churches and a museum. The 13th-century
Jesus Chapel is in the south of the town.

23 km to the west is **Cristuru Secuiesc**,
which has a fine ceramic museum and a frescoed 15th-century church. Also nearby are
the villages of **Mugeni** and **Dârjiu**, both
with frescoed medieval churches (*see separate entries*).

Oradea (Nagyvárad, Grosswardein)
Banat
Town in Crișana, on the Criș River close to
the Hungarian border. The best view of
Oradea is from the bridge over Crișul
Repede (the 'Swift Criș'). It has the air of a
western European town, with yellow Baro-
que houses, gardens and brick fortifications.
Historically a Hungarian-populated town, it
is now 65% Romanian.

The city was founded in the late 11th
century, and the Citadel, now a UNESCO
World Heritage Site, dates from that period.
Oradea's golden age, however, started from
the date of its cession to the Hapsburgs in
1692.

In the north of the city is the Roman
Catholic Cathedral designed by Franz
Anton Hillebrandt, the largest Baroque
church in Romania, erected under Habsburg
rule between 1750 and 1780. The main
façade is flanked by two towers set at an
angle to add movement to the architectural
composition. The ceiling paintings inside are
by Johann Nepomuk Schopf of Prague. The
former Archbishop's Palace, also known as
the 'Palace of 365 Windows', is arguably the
finest Baroque building in Romania and certainly one of the largest. It was also designed
by Hillebrandt along the lines of the
Belvedere Palace in Vienna, with a frescoed
great hall, a chapel, the Schönbrunn Hall and

long enfilades. Until recently it housed the Crişana Museum (Muzeul Tării Crişurilor), with paintings by the Surrealist Victor Brauner and European art from the 16th century onwards.

On the far side of the river is the late Baroque Orthodox Cathedral (1784-6), which was built after the Habsburg Emperor Joseph II's Edict of Toleration of 1781. The exterior walls of the plain rectangular building, with its single west tower, are articulated by elegant pilasters. In the gable below the tower a clockwork mechanism installed in 1794 displays the phases of the moon and has given the cathedral its popular name of 'the Moon Church'. To the east of the Orthodox cathedral is the citadel, which was rebuilt in 1570 and remodelled in the 18th century in a Vaubanesque style.

Oradea also possesses much fine neo-baroque and Secessionist architecture, such as Pasajul Vulturul Negru (1909, by Marcel Komor and Dezsö Jakab). The City Theatre (Teatru de Stat) is by the metropolitan specialists Fellner and Helmer.

According to some traditions Albrecht Dürer's father was born in Oradea.

Orăştie (Orest, Broos) Transylvania
Town 29 km east of Deva. Founded in the 12th century, Orăştie has had a violent past, to which its medieval fortifications bear witness: it was sacked by the Tatars in the 13th century and by the Turks in the 15th. It was, however, the site of an important Romanian-language printing house during the Renaissance: one of the first printed books in Romanian, the *Palia*, was produced here in 1582. Moreover, it is the birthplace of the humanist Nicolas Olahus (1493-1568).

As well as possessing its own attractions, which include a folk-art museum, Orăştie is also close to the Dacian citadels of **Costeşti** and **Sarmizegetusa Regia** (*see separate entries*) and **Blidaru**.

Typically eclectic 19th-century building, Oradea

Oraviţa (Oravicabánya) Banat
Town 62 km south of Reşiţa, near the Serbian border. For centuries an important mining and industrial centre, it had a railway as early as 1849. Its history is recorded in a museum housed in the foyer of the neo-Classical Teatrul Vechi (Str. Eminescu 8), the country's oldest theatre (1789-1817). To the south are the **Nera Gorges** (Cheile Nerei).

Orşova Wallachia
Town at the confluence of the Cerna and the Danube, about 30 km northwest of Drobeta-Turnu Severin. This once hazardous stretch of the Danube, known as the Iron Gates, was tamed by the construction of a new channel in 1896 and more recently by a vast hydroelectric dam (1956-71), built jointly by Romania and Yugoslavia. The project submerged old Orşova, near the spot where the Hungarian patriot Kossuth buried the crown of St Stephen after the failed revolution of 1848. The new town has little architectural interest, but 9 km to the west is the spectacular gorge of **Cazanele Mici**, where there is a

tablet commemorating Trajan's construction of a road in 104 AD. Another gorge, **Cazanele Dunarii**, is 7 km further west.

Pâclele Maci and **Pâclele Mici** Moldavia
12 km north of Berca. A lunar landscape of 'muddy volcanoes' *(vulcanii noroioşi)* with bright mineral colours, and rare flora.

Păltiniş (Hohe Rinne) Transylvania
Romania's first ski resort, founded in 1894, in the Cindrel Mountains, southwest of Sibiu. It also attracts summer hikers.

Pâncota (Pankota) Banat
Market town 33 km north of Lipova, with a ruined 14th-century citadel. A colourful parish fair is held here on 1 February each year.

Pătrăuţi Moldavia
Painted monastery 10 km northwest of Suceava, built by Ştefan the Great in 1487 and currently under restoration.

Petroşani (Petrozsény, Petroschen) Transylvania
Mining town in southwestern Transylvania, north of Târgu Jiu. In 1990 and 1991 the miners marched on Bucharest from here and from Târgu Jiu to secure Iliescu's regime against right-wing challengers.

As well as having a mining museum (closed Mon.), Petroşani is close to the beautiful West Jiu (**Jiul de Vest**) Valley. Particularly fine hikes in the Retezat Massif can be made from **Câmpu lui Neag**, 33 km to the southwest.

Piatra Fântenele Transylvania
Ski resort near the Tihuta Pass between Bistriţa and Vatra Dornei in Moldavia. Ski competitions were held here as early as 1921. Here also are the remains of a 2nd-century Roman road.

Piatra Neamţ Moldavia
Town near the Transylvania-Moldavia border and one of Romania's oldest settlements. It was a centre of Neolithic, Bronze Age and Dacian culture. Its name means 'Rock of the Germans', which probably refers to the German merchants who once traded here.

The town's principal church, the Church of St John the Baptist, is one of the many foundations of Ştefan the Great. The region is still rich in legends of this king: how he founded a monastery for every victory he won and how, when he shot from his bow, he built a church wherever his arrow fell. St John's, founded in 1497, stands in Piaţa Libertăţii in the centre of the town, near the stone clock tower (Turnul lui Ştefan) which is almost all that remains of his residence (now a museum). The simple rectangular exterior looks more like a windowless patrician house than a church, and gives no indication of the domed interior. The plain rubble-stone façade has blind niches on its outer walls and is decorated with the green and yellow ceramics characteristic of Moldavian architecture.

In the same square are two museums, of art and ethnography, while nearby is the house of the writer Calistrat Hogas (1874-1917). The historical museum on Str. Mihai Eminescu 10, has a remarkable archaeological collection. (All museums closed Mon.) A rare survival is the wooden synagogue, built in 1766. Eight km west is the monastery of **Bistriţa** (see separate entry).

Piteşti Wallachia
Industrial town 38 km south of Curtea de Argeş, first recorded in 1388. There is a County Museum, a Gallery of Modern Art (Galeria de Arte Modernă) and a Gallery of Naive Art (Galeria de Arte Naivă) in the town (all closed Mon.). The Piteşti Experiment Monument Complex (Complexul Monumental Experimentul Piteşti) commemorates the prisoners of the

Communist dictatorship on the site of a former prison camp.

Ploieşti Wallachia
Oil-refining town 60 km north of Bucharest, which was heavily bombed in the war on account of the importance of its oil to the German war effort. Despite suffering much destruction then, the town's Princely Church (1639) is still worth seeing. There are also several museums of interest (all closed Mon.): the Oil Museum (Romania's oil industry is said to be the oldest in the world); the Museum of Human Biology, which has interesting displays on anatomy and evolution; the History and Archaeology Museum; the Art Museum and the rich Clock Museum.

Poiana Braşov Transylvania
Attractive and popular ski resort, especially good for beginners, at an altitude of 1000 m, 12 km southwest of Braşov.

Poiana Sibiului (Polyána) Transylvania
Village located on the slopes of the Cindrel Mountains, with an interesting museum.

Poienari Castle Wallachia
Castle on a crag in the north of the village of Arefu, 18 km north of Curtea de Argeş, said to be the real castle of Vlad the Impaler, who is often identified, without any evidence, with Dracula. It can be reached by climbing 1,400 steps. At the summit there are the remains of a citadel, two towers and residential buildings, from where Vlad's wife is said to have hurled herself out of a window as the Turks approached the castle. Vlad himself is believed to have escaped capture by the Turks by riding over the mountains on a horse that had been shod back to front to fool his pursuers.

Poienile Izei Maramureş
Village 12 km southwest of Rozavlea, with

the exceptionally fine wooden church of St Paraschiva (1604). The interior is painted with scenes of Hell (1794): sinners being tortured, goat-like devils and the damned being led into the mouth of Hell, all set against a vivid red background.

Potlogi Wallachia
Fine palace and church 40 km west of Bucharest, built by Prince Constantin Brâncoveanu in 1698.

Predeal (Predéal) Transylvania
Mountain resort situated at an altitude of 1060 m on the heights between the Prahova and Timiş valleys, south of Braşov. Lying near the border between Transylvania and Wallachia, Predeal was an important frontier town before the incorporation of Transylvania into Romania after the First World War. It has some fine wooden houses, the earliest of which were built in 1830 around an 18th-century hermits' settlement. The Orthodox church (2000) is a striking modern addition to the town, with an eclectic mix of Byzantine, Secessionist, modernist and folk elements.

Prejmer (Prászmár, Tartlau) Transylvania
Town 18 km east of Braşov, with a 13th-century fortified Gothic church, originally built by the Teutonic Knights. From 1240 the church, which rises from a fertile plain, belonged to the Cistercian abbey of Cârţa (Kerz) and, like the abbey, was destroyed by the Mongol invaders. (The ruined abbey is located between Făgăraş and Sibiu.)
The present, heavily restored, fortifications (closed Sun. and Mon.) were built in the 15th century, when a great number of chambers were constructed to house the population in time of siege. There are 275 of these miniature dwellings, fitted in wherever possible in the inner courtyard, the outer courts, the exterior walls of the church, above and below the stairs. The chambers

Coat of arms on the entrance tower, Putna

attached to the church open into the interior through small doors. Inside the church, attached to one of the side walls, is an altarpiece with pictures of Christ's Passion, including a painting of the Three Maries at the Sepulchre, wearing characteristic Saxon headdresses.

Probota Moldavia
Monastery near the town of Dolhasca, about 35 km southeast of Suceava, built by Petru Rareş in 1530 as his family mausoleum, with recently-restored wall-paintings on the exterior and interior, including a Last Judgement, a Siege of Constantinople and a Tree of Jesse.

Prundu Bărgăului (Borgóprund)
(Transylvania)
Village 21 km northeast of Bistriţa, with a paper-mill established in the mid-18th century. It is famous for its folk festivals in spring and autumn.

Putna Moldavia
Monastery 20 km west of Rădăuţi, with a church (see p. 100) founded in 1466 by

Ştefan the Great, who is buried here together with his two wives. The church, unpainted inside, is decorated instead with stained glass windows. The monastery was an important centre for manuscript illumination and embroidery, and the museum (closed Mon.), contains an excellent collection of religious artefacts, including a portrait of one of Ştefan's wives, a Tatar princess named Mary. Nearby is a 14th-century wooden church and a hermitage hollowed out of a rock by Ştefan's spiritual adviser, Daniel the Hermit.

Rădăuţi Moldavia
Market town 43 km northwest of Suceava. There was a princely court here during the 14th century, when the Church of St Nicholas was founded by the Voivode Bogdan I (1359-65). The town's most important industry is pottery, fine examples of which can be seen in the Museum of Applied Folk Art of Bucovina (Muzeul Tehnici Populare Bucovinene) at Piaţa Unirii 63 (closed Mon.). On the southern edge of the town is a famous stud farm, **Herghelia Rădăuţi**, founded by the Habsburgs. It breeds Arab and Ghidran horses.

Râmnicu Sărat Moldavia
Monastery complex founded by Constantin Brâncoveanu and dedicated to the Dormition of the Virgin. Inside are 17th-century frescoes. There is also a Museum of Art and Ethnography at Str. Primaverii 4.

Râmnicu Vâlcea Wallachia
Town in the Olt Valley 50 km northwest of Piteşti, first recorded in 1388. It contains several interesting churches, including the 15th-century Cetăţuia Church, the 16th-century Church of St Paraschiva and the 19th-century Cathedral, which has murals by Gheorghe Tattarescu. There is also a historical and art museum, as well as a museum dedicated to the writer and musician Anton Pann (1796-1854). 5 km from the town is a

fine open-air museum (Muzeul Satului Vâlcean) containing examples of traditional local architecture.

Râşca Moldavia
UNESCO-protected monastery dedicated to St Nicholas, 20 km northwest of Târgu Neamţ. It was founded in the 14th century, but rebuilt by Bogdan III (the One-eyed) in 1510, after the Tatars destroyed it. It was further fortified and endowed by Petru Rareş in 1542, and in 1552 the exterior was decorated with a series of frescoes by a Greek artist. These include depictions of the Last Judgement, scenes from the Life of St Anthony, and the Ladder of St John Climax. Inside, the frescoes have been repainted but still retain some of their former richness, including patches of gold leaf. In the sanctuary are scenes from the Life of St Nicholas.

Răşinari (Resinár, Städterdorf) Transylvania
Village 12 km southwest of Sibiu, with a large Roma population. There is a painted Orthodox church (1752) and a museum (closed Mon.). Răşinari was the birthplace of the poet and nationalist politician Octavian Goga (1881-1938), whose house has been turned into a memorial museum.

Râşnov (Barcarozsnyó, Rosenau) Transylvania
Small industrial town 11 km northeast of Bran, founded on the site of Dacian and Roman settlements by the Teutonic Knights c. 1225. The 13th-century Lutheran church contains attractive 17th-century ceiling paintings. It was never fortified, but is overlooked by a picturesque citadel originally built by the Teutonic Knights in the 13th century on a hill above the village.

The citadel, now partly ruined, became a characteristic Transylvanian *Bauernburg*, or 'peasants' castle'. It was strengthened c. 1500 and again after its capture in 1612 by Prince

Gabriel Báthory. The ring-wall contains no keep or great hall, but has 25 small dwellings for the villagers, together with storerooms, a small chapel, schoolhouse and a pastor's house. There is a well 146 m deep, which was dug in 1623-40 by Turkish prisoners. There is also a small museum. The citadel commands a fine view over the surrounding countryside.

Rasova Dobrogea
Port on the Danube. Roman and Byzantine fortifications have been discovered on Muzait Hill nearby.

Reghin (Szászrégin, Regen) Transylvania
Town 30 km northeast of Târgu Mureş, with a 14th-century Lutheran church, Baroque houses, a timber Orthodox church (1744) and an ethnographic museum. It is also celebrated for its brewery. To the east are the traditional villages of the **Gurghiu Valley**. In **Gurghiu** itself is the castle of the Bornemisza family, which was converted in the 19th century into a hunting lodge by the heir of the Austrian Emperor Franz Josef, Crown Prince Rudolf: it is now a forestry school and hunting museum.

Reşiţa (Resicabánya, Reschitz) Banat
Town 105 km southeast of Timişoara. An important iron-working centre for over two centuries, it has a museum devoted to this industry at Str. Valiugului 103. Reşiţa is also useful as a base for exploring the Semenic Mountains to the south. **Semenic**, 33 km to the southeast, is a ski resort; **Caraşova**, 16 km to the south, is close to a series of gorges containing remarkable grottoes.

Ribiţa Transylvania
Village 10 km north of Brad, with Roman origins and an ancient stone church, with interior paintings thought to be the oldest Byzantine-style frescoes in Romania.

Richiş (Riomfalva, Reichesdorf)
Transylvania
Village 6 km from Biertan. The fortified
Lutheran church (15th and 16th centuries)
has remarkable architectural carvings. The
portal (1400) depicts scenes from the
Crucifixion. Inside are capitals and bosses
sculpted with plant, animal and human
figures, and a fine pulpit.

Rimetea (Torockó, Eisenburg)
Transylvania
Picturesque village 22 km northwest of
Aiud. A centre of iron-mining since the 13th
century, it has a museum with displays relating to this industry, as well as a collection of
local folk art (closed Mon.). Many of the
Saxon farmhouses here have been restored in
recent years, and there is a small but fascinating village museum (Muzeul Satului). The
surrounding countryside offers excellent
hiking.

Rogoz Maramureş
Prosperous village in the **Lapuş Valley,** with
a large modern church and two 17th-century
churches (see p. 292).

Roman Moldavia
Industrial town 49 km east of Piatra Neamţ.
According to legend, Roman was founded
by the Emperor Trajan in the early 2nd
century. Little survives from its illustrious
past, although the 16th-century episcopal
church has some of its original frescoes.

Săcălăşeni Maramureş
Village 10 km south of Baia Mare, with a
church dating from 1442, but rebuilt in the
17th century. It has exceptionally fine woodcarving and outstanding wall-paintings by
Paulu Weissu of Baia Mare (1865).

Săcele (Hétfalu, Siebendörfer) Transylvania
Small town 5 km southeast of Braşov, with
an interesting museum (closed Mon.). Forty

km southeast along the 1A road is **Cheia,** a
resort in the Teleajen Valley, close to the
Ciucas Mountains, founded in 1864. The
Suzana Monastery, to the south, has paintings by Gheorghe Tattarescu.

Sălişte (Szelistye, Grossendorf)
Transylvania
Town situated on the banks of the Sălişte
River west of Sibiu. It is famous for its folk
choir and its embroidered textiles, some of
which are displayed in the local museum.

Sâmbăta Transylvania
20th-century copy of a 17th-century monastery founded by Constantin Brâncoveanu
in the hills south of Sâmbăta de Sus. The
monastery was completed in 1698, razed to
the ground by the Habsburgs sixty years
later, and rebuilt as an exact copy of the
original in the 20th century, complete with a
celebrated glass-icon workshop.

At Sâmbăta de Jos the Baroque palace
(1770) built for Joseph von Brukenthal has a
famous Lipizzaner stud farm (Herghelia
Sâmbăta de Jos) which is open to visitors
(except Sat. and Sun.).

Sândulești (Szind) Transylvania
Village 5 km west of Turda, with a 14th-
century Orthodox church which, most
unusually for Orthodox churches in this
region at that time, is built of stone.

Sângorz-Băi (Oláhszentgyörgy)
Transylvania
Dilapidated spa town, base for fine hiking in
the Rodna Mountains. The attractive nearby
village of **Şanţ** is famous for its exuberant
and picturesque wedding ceremonies.

Sânmihaiu Almaşului Transylvania
Village on the Almaş River, 54 km northeast
of Cluj-Napoca, with a beautiful carved
wooden church.

Săpânţa Maramureş
Village, 15 km northwest of Sighet, famous for its Merry Cemetery (Cimitrul Vesel) with its wooden headstones carved and painted with portraits and scenes from the lives of the deceased, and inscribed with aphorisms and witty epitaphs. The idea came from a local woodcarver, Ion Stan Pătraş, in 1935.

Sarmizegetusa Regia Transylvania
18 km southeast of Costeşti, this Dacian settlement, 1,200 metres above sea level and covering 3.5 hectares, is a World Heritage site. It was the Dacian capital from the 1st century BC to 106 AD and contained four sanctuaries dedicated to sun worship, a citadel and residential quarters. Today, only stumps of pillars and low walls remain (*see p. 47*) but it is a peaceful and attractive spot.

Sarmizegetusa Ulpia Traiana *see* **Ulpia Traiana Sarmizegetusa**

Saschiz (Szászkézd, Keisd) Transylvania
Village 20 km west of Sighişoara, with an aisleless church on the south side of the market square, which was built in 1493, replacing an earlier, Romanesque building (some Romanesque sculpture survives). The church earthworks and its bell-tower were fortified in *c.* 1500. A defensive storey was added so that the nave and chancel form a massive block. The exterior walls are supported by 23 buttresses, linked by blind arcades supporting a defensive gallery. The outer fortifications were demolished after earthquake damage. On the impressive bell-tower a figure known as Bogdan strikes the quarters. A Turkish helm adorns the font.

Satu Mare (Szatmár Németi, Sathmar) Maramureş
Town 63 km west of Baia Mare, near the Hungarian border. It was ceded to Romania in 1920 by the Treaty of Trianon, but still has a considerable Hungarian population. The Hotel Dacia (originally Pannonia) in Piaţa Libertăţii is a characteristic Secessionist work by the Hungarian architect Ödön Lechner (1902). Opposite, at Piaţa Libertăţii 2,1 is the Art Museum (Muzeul de Artă), with paintings by Aurel Popp. The ethnographic and historical collections of the Provincial Museum of Satu Mare (Muzeul Judeţean Satu Mare) are at Str. Lucaciu 21. (Both museums are closed Mon.).

Sebeş (Szászsebes, Mühlbach) Transylvania
Town lying on the Sebeş River, south of Alba Iulia. Founded by Saxons in the 13th century, it lies on the site of prehistoric, Dacian and Roman settlements.

An important leather-working centre, Sebeş was sacked jointly by Vlad the Impaler and a Turkish force in 1438. Turnul Studenţului (The Student's Tower) is named after the town's most famous inhabitant, a scholar known as 'Georg of Transylvania' or 'the student of Rumes', who was punished for his resistance to the invaders by being sent in captivity to Istanbul, from where he eventually escaped. He recorded his experiences in a book entitled *De Ritu e Moribus Turcorum* ('Of the Religion and Customs of the Turks'), published in Swabia in 1481. It was eagerly read and became a bestseller; Martin Luther was one of its many admirers.

Another survivor of the Turkish invasion is the church. Its nave and aisles were built in the mid-13th century, and the rib vaulting, strongly influenced by Cistercian architecture, was added at the end of that century. In the prosperous mid-14th century, the townspeople set about rebuilding the church on a grander scale, beginning with a new hall choir (1361-82). The architectural carving, some of the finest in Transylvania, is related to the work of the Parler workshop at Prague Cathedral. The nave was never rebuilt: the town's fortifications were given priority in response to the Turkish raids.

Sebiș (Borossebes) Banat
Town on the Criș Alb River 45 km northeast
of Pincota. Formerly a metal-working
centre, it has an open-air theatre and an
ethnographic and historical museum. 10 km
to the northeast is the 13th-century citadel
of **Dezna**.

Secu Moldavia
Monastery 16 km west of Târgu Neamț. It is
dedicated to St John the Baptist and has four
churches, the main one dating from the early
17th century, with later alterations. The
other churches are from the 17th, 18th and
early 19th centuries. There is also a museum
of religious artefacts.

Sfântu Gheorghe Dobrogea
Small village on one of the three main
branches of the Danube Delta; good centre
for bird watching on Lake Razim and Lake
Sinoie.

Sfântu Gheorghe (Csapószentgyörgy)
Transylvania
Industrial town 30 km northeast of Brașov, a
cultural centre of the Szeklers. The oldest
quarter, to the north of Piața Libertății, has a
mid-16th-century Reformed church. In the
south of the town is a historical and ethnographic museum (Str. Kós Károly 10), built
in 1910 by the Hungarian nationalist
architect Károly Kós.

Five km north of Sfântu Gheorghe is the
village of **Arcuș** (see separate entry), while at
Reci, to the east of the town, there is a
nature reserve.

Sibiel (Szibiel, Budenbach) Transylvania
Charming village 11 km southwest of
Cristian, ideally situated for hiking in the
Cindrel Mountains. Remains of Geto-
Dacian fortifications have been found here,
but the main cultural attraction is the impor-
tant collection of glass icons in the museum,
next to the 18th-century Orthodox church.

Sibiu (Nagyszeben, Hermannstadt)
Transylvania
Important centre on the Cibin River founded by German and Flemish settlers in the
12th century. Some buildings from this
period still survive on Str. 9 Mai.

Sibiu retains the atmosphere of a
Transylvanian Saxon town as it was during
Habsburg times. The medieval centre has
three squares with Gothic and Baroque
houses, protected by fortifications, parts of
which survive (the Haller and Soldisch
Bastions, the Powder Tower and the
Tanners' Towers). Thanks to its recent stint
as European City of Culture, Sibiu's historical centre has rarely been in better condition.

The recently restored Împăratul
Românilor Hotel (Str. Nicolae Bălcescu 3)
takes its name from the Emperor Joseph II,
who stayed there.

The great square (Piața Mare) lies at the
centre of the Upper Town (Orașul de Sus).
In the 15th century witches were burned
here; in the 16th century the great patricians
built their houses around the square, and
conspirators suspected of fomenting revolt
against the Hungarian kings were executed
here. No. 10 is the house of Petrus Haller,
the Burgomaster and Saxon count, whose
influence was decisive in converting the
townspeople to Lutheranism. The square is
famous for its picturesque mansard windows, known as 'the city's eyes'.

The Brukenthal Palace, built in 1785, is
the most impressive of the buildings in the
square. It houses the Brukenthal Museum
and Library (Piața Mare 4-5), the oldest and
one of the most important art galleries in
Romania. Samuel von Brukenthal (1721-
1803), governor of Transylvania under the
Habsburg Empress Maria Theresa, was a
famously handsome man, much admired
by the empress. A Transylvanian Saxon by
birth, Brukenthal was a great connoisseur of
art and left his collection of Old Master
paintings and small personal altarpieces to

the town. The museum contains remarkable late medieval and Renaissance works, in particular Caracciolo's *Mary Magdalene Reading* and works by Veronese and Cranach, as well as illuminated manuscripts and early printed books. (Brukenthal's country seat, at **Avrig**, 26 km east of Sibiu, can also be visited; see p. 284.)

The most magnificent Baroque building in Sibiu is the Roman Catholic Church, built by the Jesuits in the 18th century (with fine decorations and notable Hungarian glass of 1901). With a medieval tower which now houses the Town Museum, it separates Piaţa Mare from a smaller square that is now called Piaţa 6 Martie.

The Gothic Town Church dominates Piaţa Griviţa. Built *c.* 1320 as a basilica with a transept, it became Lutheran at the Reformation, when the southern part was remodelled into a Late Gothic hall church (finished 1520), while the northern section remained a basilica. On the north side of the chancel is a huge wall-painting of the Crucifixion by Johannes von Rosenau, dated 1455. The fine bronze font was made in 1438, and the organ was built in 1672 by Johann Fest. Funerary monuments to Saxon counts, town dignitaries and pastors line the walls. The church contains some works from other Transylvanian churches, including a 16th-century sculpture of Christ with Angels from Copsa Mare and a 17th-century winged altarpiece from Dobărca.

A narrow alley with steps (Pasajul Scărilor) to the right of the church leads under the buttresses down to the Lower Town (Oraşul de Jos), where the streets take their names from the trades once practised there. Many of the houses are reminiscent of the architecture of Westphalia and Franconia, and their peaceful courtyards are often decorated with flowers. The old Transylvanian Saxon dialect can still be heard here, more often than in the rest of Transylvania.

Orthodox Cathedral, Sibiu

Despite this lingering Saxon presence, Sibiu is now undeniably a Romanian town, whose grand Orthodox Cathedral (1906), with its impressive interior modelled on Hagia Sophia in Istanbul, can be found to the southwest of the main squares, on Str. Mitropoliei.

As well as its fine architecture, Sibiu also has museum collections of international importance. These include, in addition to the Brukenthal Museum and Library, the Museum of History (Muzeul de Istorie), Str. Mitropol 2, in the 16th-century former town hall; the Exhibition of the History of Pharmacy (Exposiţia de Istoria Farmaciei), also in a 16th-century building at Piaţa Mica 26; and the Natural History Museum (Museul de Istorie Naturală), Str. Cetăţii 1. Also of note is the ASTRA Museum, an interesting ethnographical collection on two sites, the main building at Piaţa Mica 11-12 and the open-air section at **Padurea Dumbravii** (to the south of the city). The latter contains over 300 reconstructions of traditional rural architecture and machinery. There are restaurants and even accommodation available for an extended visit.

Sic (Szék, Marktstuhl) Transylvania
Town northeast of Cluj, famous for its Hungarian and gypsy bands. A salt-mining centre until the 18th century, it has a 13th-century Reformed church and an 18th-century wooden Orthodox church. The gypsy houses in Sic are thatched and painted blue, and the town is an important centre for Hungarian folk culture: the Magyars here still wear traditional costumes, and folk music is still a part of everyday life.

Sighetu Marmaţiei (Máramarossziget) Maramureş
Town in the Tisa Valley close to the border with Ukraine, famed for its winter carnival, which takes place just after Christmas. First documented in 1326, the town has two ethnographic museums, including an open-air village museum to the east of the town centre, and an art gallery (all closed Mon.). Its attractions also extend to a building on Str. Barnuţiu, which formerly housed a notorious political prison, much used in the Communist era and now the Memorial Museum of the Victims of Communism and Anti-Communist Resistance (closed Mon.) with a striking sculpture by Aurel Vlad (1997) in its courtyard. A reminder of the Jewish presence here before the Second World War is the childhood home of the writer Elie Wiesel in Str. Tudor Vladmirescu, now a museum of Jewish life (closed Mon.)

Sighişoara (Segesvár, Schässburg) Transylvania
Spectacular hilltop city 37 km northeast of Mediaş. Despite periodic calamities, including the Tatar invasion of 1241-2 and the Great Fire of 1676, it contains the most com-

plete ensemble of medieval architecture in Romania. Legend has it that this is where the Pied Piper brought the children of Hamelin. For most visitors, however, the greatest attraction of Sighişoara is its connection with a creation of 19th-century fiction: Count Dracula. The author Bram Stoker never visited Transylvania, but he found the inspiration for his story in the tales told by the Transylvanian Saxons about Vlad Ţepeş, 'the Impaler', voivode of Wallachia (1456-62). Thirteen editions of such stories, published as far afield as Nuremberg, Augsburg, Lübeck, Bamberg and Strasbourg can be seen in the Historical Museum in Bucharest. Vlad Ţepeş killed such large numbers of Turks, and in such an extraordinarily gruesome manner, that Sultan Mehmed II found it necessary to lead a campaign against him in person.

Tourists flock to the town to see the house of the Draculeşti family (Str. Cositorilor 5), supposedly the Impaler's birthplace, which is one of about 150 well-preserved houses of the 16th and 17th centuries, painted red, green and ochre yellow, that enhance the town's romantic character.

A large section of the town's medieval fortifications survive, including nine towers, the biggest of which is the Great Gate Tower (the Stundenturm, or Turnul cu Ceas). This massive clock tower on the town's eastern wall is Sighişoara's most prominent landmark. It was built as a gatehouse and until 1556 was the seat of the Town Council. It now houses a small history museum. In 1677 it was repaired after fire damage by Veit Grueber (from the Tyrol) and Philipp Bonge (from Salzburg). The corner turrets on the tiled roof are said to signify that the townspeople had the right to bear swords. Every night at midnight a figure seven metres high, representing the day of the week, emerges from the door beside the clockface.

The earliest parts of the massive Church of St Nicholas, known as the Bergkirche

Sighișoara

(Biserica din Deal) and formerly the parish church, including the crypt and west tower, date from the 13th century, but it was altered in the mid-14th century. The Gothic hall church was built in 1429-83. Inside are several fine late 15th-century wall-paintings, some heavily restored, including a Last Judgment around the choir arch. The tall tabernacle on the north wall of the choir dates from the same period. The 16th-century winged altarpiece in the north aisle depicting St Martin and St Dominic is said to have been painted by Johann Stoss, a son of the great sculptor Veit Stoss, who settled in Sighișoara. (Two sons of Stoss are mentioned as having been in Transylvania, but it is not stated whether they were stone carvers or painters.) The inlay decoration of the choir stalls (1520) is by the woodworker Johann Reichmuth; and there are some fine wooden chests. The church won the European Cultural Heritage prize for restoration in 2004.

The former Dominican Church (now the Lutheran parish church) was built in 1492-1515 and rebuilt after a fire in 1676, with a Baroque altar, pulpit and organ by Johann Fest and the painter Jeremias Stranovius of Sibiu. The bronze font (1411) comes from the old parish church. There is a notable collection of oriental carpets.

Other interesting churches include the Roman Catholic Church (1894) on Str. Bastionul; the 17th-century Lepers' Church to the west of the railway station; and the Romanian Orthodox Cathedral (1937) on the other side of the Tîrnava Mare River. The School on the Hill (Școala din Deal) in its 18th-century building can be reached up the picturesque Scholars' Stairs.

Many Szeklers live in the villages around Sighișoara. The tall, brightly painted gateways to their houses contrast with the simplicity of the churches (mostly Roman Catholic). Southeast of Sighișoara, the ruins of a 12th-century castle survive near the village of **Rupea**.

Simeria (Piski) Transylvania
Town 15 km west of Orăştie, where Daco-Roman remains have been discovered.

Şimleu Silvaniei (Szilágysomlyó) Transylvania
Town 28 km west of Zalău. It contains the ruins of a castle built in the 16th century by the Hungarian Báthory princes. **Boghiş**, a small spa with thermal mineral water, is 15 km to the south.

Sinaia Wallachia
Town spectacularly situated among the Bucegi Mountains, between Ploieşti and Braşov; a hugely popular holiday destination in both winter and summer, with some fine Belle Epoque architecture (especially in the Dimitrie Ghica Park). Sinaia is celebrated for its monastery, founded by Mihai Cantacuzino after his pilgrimage to the Holy Land in 1682: hence the name of the town, which recalls St Catherine's Monastery on Mount Sinai. The complex contains two churches (the older one dates from 1695, the

The mountains above Sinaia

other is 19th-century) and a museum.

To the northeast of the town is **Peleş Castle** (1878-1914), built for King Carol I by Wilhelm Doderer, Johannes Schulz and Karl Liman in a bewildering variety of styles, but predominantly German neo-Renaissance (closed Tues.). The rooms are decorated in various regional and period styles, including Florentine, Gothic, Turkish and Moorish; a theatre was decorated by the young Gustav Klimt. Nearby are **Foişor**, a hunting lodge used for state guests, and **Pelişor**, a smaller palace built for Queen Marie in a lighter art nouveau vein.

Şiria Crişana
Site of castle built by Matthias Corvinus. Fine 19th-century neo-baroque Bohus Castle houses a museum of local writers and musicians.

Slănic Wallachia
Town 6 km west of Valenii de Munte. Recorded as early as 1532, Slănic has impressive salt workings, a spa (at **Muntele de Sare**) and a salt museum (Muzeul Sălirii).

Slănic Moldova Moldavia
Popular health resort, with mineral waters recommended for the treatment of infections of the alimentary canal, liver and bile ducts, ENT disorders and neurological ailments. **Târgu Ocna**, 18 km to the northeast, is also a spa and has a fine monastery, built in 1664.

Slatina Wallachia
Industrial town on the River Olt, 50 km northeast of Craiova. Recorded in documents dating from 1368, Slatina also has Neolithic and Bronze Age remains, an aluminium factory and a power station.

Slimnic (Szelindék, Stolzenburg) Transylvania
Village 16 km north of Sibiu. The impressive ruins of fortifications on the hill above con-

tain the fragments of an unfinished church. The Gothic parish church in the village (*c.* 1400) has an attractive interior. Its outer fortifications were partly destroyed in 1706.

Snagov Wallachia
Monastery, built in 1519, situated on an island in a lake just north of Bucharest (good skating in winter). It occupies the site of earlier churches, including one built in the 1450s by Vlad the Impaler, who is said to be buried here. Ruins of the prison that he founded next to the church still survive. The present church, a UNESCO World Heritage Site also has exceptionally fine 15th-century carved wooden doors. The early 20th-century Italianate palace nearby is now an hotel. Plans to build a Disney-style Dracula theme park were fortunately cancelled.

Solca Moldavia
Early 17th-century monastery 22 km south of Rădăuţi, fortified with arrow slits in the walls and cellars for storing gunpowder. The brewery next door is of similar date.

Sovata (Szováta) Transylvania
Spa 60 km east of Târgu Mureş, close to a salt lake, Lacul Ursu. Although it is recorded as early as 1597, Sovata mostly dates from the 19th century. **Praid**, 7 km to the southeast, has ancient salt mines and an underground treatment centre for asthmatics.

Soveja Moldavia
Attractive health resort, with a church and ruined monastery, dating from the mid-17th century. There is also a mausoleum, built in 1927, for soldiers who fought in this area during the First World War.

Stănă Banat
Small village with an interesting 17th-century church; the porch has a small verandah and a highly decorated entrance, and the door has an unusual arched lintel.

Ştei (Vaskohsziklás) Banat
Industrial town, 62 km northwest of Brad. From 1958 to 1990 it was renamed after Dr Petru Groza, leader of the Peasants' Party during the 1930s. The remains of about 140 Neolithic bears have been discovered in the Pestera Urşilor (Bears' Cave), with its impressive rock formations, at nearby **Chişcău**. There is also a mid-18th-century wooden church at **Rieni**.

Strei (Zeykfalva, Zeikdorf) Transylvania
Village 5 km south of Călan, with a rare 13th-century stone Orthodox church, decorated with Byzantine frescoes. Outside, there are Roman inscriptions on some of the stone slabs.

Suceava Moldavia
Industrial city in northwestern Moldavia (Bucovina). It was the capital of Moldavia from 1388 to 1566 and has a number of buildings from this period. The Citadel, to the east of the city centre, was founded in the late 14th century by Petru I Muşat, as was the Mirăuţi Church, a little to the northwest, where the coronations of medieval Moldavian princes took place. Nearer to the city centre, north of Piaţa 22 Decembrie, is a ruined 15th-century princely court and a frescoed church, St Demetrius (1534-5), commissioned by Petru Rareş; the frescoes, by the court artists Toma of Suceava, include portraits of Rareş and his family. In the southeast of the town is the Monastery of St John the New (1522), founded by Bogdan III, which has a monumental church dedicated to St George, with remnants of external wall-paintings. It contains the relics of St John the New, a martyr who was killed by Muslims for preaching in Turkish-occupied Moldavia.

Suceava once had large Armenian and Jewish communities. There is still a working synagogue dating from 1870 on Str. Firma, while at **Zamca** in the northwest of the city is a ruined, moated Armenian monastery (1606), which combines an eastern architectural style with some Classical and Gothic elements.

The city's museums include the Ethnographic Museum (Muzeul Etnografic) housed a late-16th-century han at Str. Ciprian Porumbescu 5; the Bucovina Village Museum (Muzeul Satului Bucovinean), close to the Citadel; and the National Museum of Bucovina (Muzeul National al Bucovinei), at Str. Ştefan cel Mare 33. The Historical Museum (Muzeul de Istorie Suceava) is housed in a fine secessionist palace.

Ilişeşti, a village 19 km to the west, is famous for its folk festivals, which are held in July and around Christmas.

Suceviţa Moldavia
Monastery set in a magnificent landscape of mountains and forests near the Suceviţa River. The church, which is enclosed within a massive wall with four corner towers, is dedicated to the Resurrection and was founded in the 1580s. Its splendid series of murals was completed in 1596, making it the last of the great Moldavian painted churches. The scenes depicted on the exterior walls include a Deisis, a Tree of Jesse, an unfinished Last Judgement and an exceptionally fine Ladder of St John Climax. Inside are more frescoes, including scenes from the lives of Moses and Christ and from episodes in the Book of Genesis.

Sulina Dobrogea
A decaying free port at the mouth of the widest branch of the Danube Delta, not connected by road to the rest of the country. Occupied by both the Byzantines and the Genoese, Sulina had until recently a significant harbour. The cemetery between the town and the sea is filled with 19th- and early 20th-century graves of Christian,

Abraham and the three angels, Suceviţa

Jewish and Muslim foreigners. Some were the passengers and crew of passing ships, others were members of the International Danube Commission, which once controlled these waters. The lighthouse built in 1870 by the Commission is now a small museum.

The port has suffered a dramatic decline, recently aggravated by the wars in Yugoslavia. During the Ceaușescu regime efforts were made to revive it by establishing a disposal unit for chemical waste, but this has not been beneficial. A few buildings on the waterfront give some sense of the city's former importance, but cows now wander freely along the unpaved side-streets.

Șurdești (Dioshálom) Maramureș
Village with the magnificent Uniate wooden Church of the Holy Archangels (1738). Its 52-metre-high wooden spire was once the tallest in Europe, but is now overtopped by Bârsana. Inside are remarkable early 19th-century frescoes and some 18th-century icons.

Târgoviște Wallachia
Town on the Ialomița River 50 km west of Ploiești. Between 1415 and 1659 it was the seat of the voivodes of Wallachia. Their mostly ruined princely court (Curtea Veche, closed Mon.) contains a museum in the Chindia tower devoted to the life of the 15th-century voivode Vlad the Impaler ('Dracula'), who ruled from here, and the 16th-century Princely Church, which has later wall-paintings commemorating the life of the voivode Matei Basarab (r. 1632-54). On Str. Nicolae Bălcescu are the Art Gallery, History Museum and Museum of Printing and Local Writers, as well as the 17th-century Stelea Monastery, which has both Gothic and Wallachian features. Târgoviște is now more gruesomely famous as the place of execution of Nicolae and Elena Ceaușescu on Christmas Day 1989.

Eight km to the northeast is the monastery of **Dealu** (1500), which, with its fine stonework and elaborate narthex, influenced later foundations in Wallachia (*see p. 126*). It contains the head of Mihai the Brave, murdered in 1601. There are other royal tombs, as well as fine paintings by the local painter Dobromir.

Târgu Jiu Wallachia
Industrial town in the Jiu Valley mining region, famous for a complex of monumental abstract sculptures created by Constantin Brâncuși in 1937-8 as a memorial to the heroes of the First World War (*see p. 227*). Most of the sculptures are in the park at the west end of an avenue called Calea Eroilor, although the totem-like *Endless Column* is at the opposite end. The Art Museum (Muzeul de Artă) on Str. Stadion has photographs relating to Brâncuși's life, and sculptures by Popescu.

The Casa Memorială Ecaterina Teodoroiu (B-dul E. Teodoroiu 270) commemorates a First World War heroine who fought as a man. Her monument (near the Prince's Church) is by Milița Petrașcu, a celebrated female pupil of Brâncuși. Nearby are the church and house of Cornea Brăloiu, a 17th-century *ban* of Oltenia.

The town's prison has housed two of Romania's most notorious Communist leaders, Gheorghiu-Dej and Ceaușescu, as well as Ion Iliescu, who succeeded Ceaușescu as president of Romania in 1990. Iliescu relied on miners from the Jiu valley to break up student protests in Bucharest in 1990s.

Târgu Mureș (Márosvásárhely, Neumarkt) Transylvania
Town in central Transylvania. First mentioned in 1332 and made a royal free town in 1482, this was a Szekler town, the capital of the *sedes* of Máros. It was an important centre of Calvinist learning in the 16th century. Much of the town's old character has been

313

lost through modernization. However, its main square, Piaţa Trandafirilor, remains an impressive space, dominated by grand public buildings. These include the Palace of Culture (Palatul Culturii, 1911-13), an elaborate Art Nouveau edifice by Marcel Komor and Dezsö Jakab containing the history museum and art gallery; the Baroque Ethnographic Museum (Muzeul Etnografic); and the large Orthodox Cathedral (1925-34), which superseded an 18th-century timber church, still standing on Str. Doiceşti. Also on Piaţa Trandafirilor is the Roman Catholic Church, built by the Jesuits between 1728 and 1750.

On Piaţa Bernady György there is a 15th-century Protestant church (reconstructed after damage in 1601-2) that was used for 37 Transylvanian Diets. Built on the site of a Franciscan and a Dominican friary, it stands next to the remains of the medieval fortifications, built by Stephen Bathory in 1492. Originally pentagonal, they were enlarged and strengthened by the town guilds in the 17th century.

Several significant buildings and institutions were established by the Magyar nobility. Count Samuel Teleki, chancellor of Transylvania 1791-1820, founded the Teleki Library in 1802, and a theatre, now the Apollo Palace, in 1820. (The former now also houses houses the Bolyai Library, founded in 1955.) The Royal Table of Judgment, the highest court in Transylvania under Habsburg rule, was convened in Târgu Mureş, and the Baroque building of 1789 where it met was presented to the Table by the widow of Elek Kendeffy. The magnificent Toldalaghy Palace was built in 1759-1762 by the French architect Jean Luidor.

Târgu Neamţ (Németvásár) Moldavia
Industrial town in northern Moldavia about 50 km south of Suceava. Its name means 'German Market' and recalls the presence

there of the Teutonic Knights in the 13th century. The town's most notable monument is Moldavia's finest ruined castle, the impregnable late 14th-century citadel situated 2 km to the north of the town centre. It survived two major sieges before being dismantled in 1717 on the orders of the sultan. There is an ethnographic museum at Str. Ştefan cel Mare 37 and a museum dedicated to the poet Veronica Micle, the lover of Mihai Eminescu, at Str. Ştefan cel Mare 34. Another member of Eminescu's circle, Ion Creangă, is commemorated in a museum at **Humuleşti**, to the south of Târgu Neamţ.

Târgu Secuiesc (Kézdivásáhely, Szekler Neumarkt) Transylvania
Now a quiet town, 50 km northeast of Braşov, this was a major trading centre in medieval times. Its name means 'Szekler Market', and it is still a stronghold of Szekler culture. Its Thursday market is popular, and its Museum of the Guilds (Muzeul de Istoria Breslelor, closed Mon.) tells the history of the local guilds. It also has a museum dedicated to Aron Gabor, a blacksmith who played a heroic role in the 1848 Revolution.

Târpeşti Moldavia
Village near Târgu Neamţ with a private ethnographic, art and archaeological collection, the Popa Museum (open daily). It was amassed by the sculptor Nicolae Popa in the 1960s and contains some interesting and idiosyncratic exhibits.

Tebea Banat
Village northwest of Brad, with monuments commemorating Horea, one of the leaders of the Romanian peasant uprising in 1784, and Avram Iancu, a revolutionary of 1848, who is buried in the nearby church.

Tilişca (Tilicske, Telischen) Transylvania
Village west of Sibiu, built on the site of a

Dacian settlement, with ruined fortifications on a nearby hill.

Timişoara (Temesvár, Temeschburg)
Banat
Historically one of the most prosperous and cosmopolitan cities in the Balkans, Timişoara was the first town in southeastern Europe to have gas and electric lighting and the telephone. Plays in Romanian, German and Hungarian are still performed in its theatres. A. Lancelot, the French traveller who visited Timişoara in 1860 on the way from Paris to Bucharest, described his impressions of the city. The buildings he found grandiose, while the international hubbub in the market place amazed him: Romanians, Hungarians, Germans, Serbs, Ukrainians and Bulgarians all doing business peacefully together. Around 75,000 Germans, mostly from the Rhine and Mosel regions (although they became known as 'Swabians') arrived in the Banat in three waves during the reigns of Charles VI, Maria Theresa and Joseph II.

Timişoara was founded (by Serbs) in the 13th century, and soon became a major power centre for the Kingdom of Hungary. Its monumental architecture, ringed by spacious parks, mostly derives from the Habsburg period. As well as its numerous Secessionist palaces, such as László Székely's Dauerbach Palace (1913), the city is richly endowed with Baroque monuments. The Roman Catholic Cathedral in Piaţa Unirii was built in the Viennese Baroque style by Fischer von Erlach the Younger in 1736-73, while the Plague Column nearby, which is reminiscent of a similar structure in Vienna, was carved in sandstone by the Bavarian sculptor Gustav Major and shows the Holy Trinity and the Virgin surrounded by the plague saints, St Sebastian and St Roch, with St Charles Borromeo and St John Nepomuk. The contrast is strong with the post-Trianon Orthodox Cathedral, a vast neo-Byzantine edifice dating from 1936.

The town's ethnic and religious diversity is reflected in two other churches dating from this period: the Serbian Orthodox Cathedral (1734) and the Franciscan Church (1733-36). The Baroque Old Town Hall (Primarie Veche, 1731-1734) stands on the site of a Turkish bath, but there are virtually no Ottoman remains left in the city, even though Timişoara was occupied by the Turks for more than 200 years. The Old Town Hall now houses the Timişoara Art Museum (temporary exhibitions).

The principal medieval monument is the Castel Huniazilor, which now houses the fascinating historical section of the Banat Museum (Muzeul Banatului). This was first fortified in the mid-14th century by Iancu of Hunedoara, voivode of Transylvania, then in 1522 by the Turks and again in 1718 by the Austrians.

The open-air Ethnographic Museum at Aleea CFR 1, is in a northeastern suburb of the city. On the opposite side of the Bega Canal, in B-dul 6 Martie, is a Gothic dungeon where the peasant leader Dózsa was tortured in 1514 on the orders of the Hungarian King John I Zapolya. Dózsa was known as 'King of the Serfs' and led an uprising that swept across Hungary and Transylvania. Once captured, he was sentenced to a gruesome death by being forced to sit on a red-hot 'throne' and to wear a red-hot 'crown'. Some of his followers were forced to eat pieces of his charred body before they themselves were executed.

Timişoara is also remembered as the city where the Revolution of 1989, which led to the overthrow of Ceauşescu, began. These events are commemorated by a memorial and research centre at Str. Emanuil Ungureano 8.

Tismana Wallachia
Village 40 km west of Târgu Jiu, with a working monastery set in a beautiful location on the side of a cliff and surrounded by waterfalls. The monastery was founded

by the monk Nicodem in 1375, and is therefore one of the oldest in Romania. It has a Serbian-style church (1377), with striking 16th-century murals by Dobromir of Târgoviște covering the entire narthex wall. The frescoes in the main body of the church are 18th-century. There is also a museum of artefacts made over the centuries by the monks, including some of Romania's oldest embroideries. An annual music and craft festival takes place here on 15 August.

Toarcla (Kisprázsmár, Tarteln) Transylvania
Village, about 40 km east of Sibiu, with a 13th-century Romanesque basilica with a round apse. The carved stonework of the west portal is badly weathered. Attached to the church tower are storerooms for provisions. Only the lower courses of the ring-wall remain.

Toplița (Maroshévíz, Töplitz) Transylvania
A spa town associated with the Dacian settlement of Sangidava, northeast of Târgu Mureș, on the Mureș River. Its monastery of Sf. Ilie has a 19th-century timber church and museum. From here a mountain pass leads to **Borsec**, another spa and resort, 25 km to the northeast.

Tulcea Dobrogea
River-port and industrial centre, situated on the edge of the Danube Delta, near the beginnings of its main branches, Chilia, Sulina and Sfântu Gheorghe. A cosmopolitan town, with a large Ukrainian community, Tulcea is architecturally undistinguished. Much of the town centre and the waterfront suffered 'systematization' under Ceaușescu, although a few 19th-century streets remain towards Citadel Hill, at the eastern end of the town.

Danube Delta vegetation

Crowned by an Independence Monument (1904), Citadel Hill also contains the History and Archaeology Museum (Muzeul de Istorie şi Arheologie), which contains an important collection of artefacts from excavations in Dobrogea, among them some remarkable Dacian remains, including reliefs of the so-called 'Thracian Horseman' and helmets decorated with warlike motifs. Outside the museum, ruined walls, amphorae and sculpture testify to the importance of the ancient Dacian and Roman town of Aegyssus, which impressed even Ovid, then exiled in Tomis (now Constanţa).

The Catholic church, Turda, site of the Diet that proclaimed the Edict of Turda

Other museums in Tulcea include the Ethnographic Museum (Muzeul de Etnografie), Str. 9 Mai 2, showing the cultural diversity of Dobrogea; the Natural History Museum (Secţia de Stiinţele Naturii), Str. Progresului 32; and the District Art Museum (Muzeul Judeţean de Artă, Str. Grigore Antipa 2), which has paintings by the Romanian Jewish artist Victor Brauner.

The town is also a natural starting-point for anyone wishing to explore the Delta area. The Danube Delta Biosphere reserve Administration (ARBDO) is based here, and should be a first port of call for any visitor. During the summer, accommodation is available at the comfortable Lebada Hotel near **Crişan**, on the Sulina branch of the river. Like much of the Delta, **Mila 23**, a nearby village, is inhabited by Lipovani, the descendants of Russian Old Believers, exiled from their homeland because they refused to accept reforms of the Russian Orthodox Church made in 1653. The Slavic origins of much of the Delta's population may explain their prodigious consumption of vodka and *ţuica* (plum brandy).

Turda (Torda, Thorenburg) Transylvania
Town on the Arieş River, 88 km northwest of Medias. Originally settled by Dacians and Romans, it subsequently became an impor-

tant salt-mining centre. The salt mine on Str. Salinelor 54 is now open to the public and is worth a visit. The remains of the Roman castrum are particularly extensive.

The Transylvanian Diet frequently met at Turda, most notably in 1568, when it issued the Edict of Turda granting religious freedom within Transylvania. Now heavily industrialized, Turda still contains some interesting buildings on Piaţa Republicii, especially the Roman Catholic Church, built in 1498-1504, with Baroque decoration inside. The nearby Calvinist Church has a Gothic portal dating from 1400, while the rest of the building is of a later date. There is also an archaeological museum in the 16th-century palace built by the Báthorys (B-dul Hasdeu 2, currently closed for restoration). From Turda it is possible to hike into the spectacular Turda Gorge (**Cheile Turzii**), 10 km to the west.

Ulpia Traiana Sarmizegetusa
Transylvania
Site of the Roman town of Colonia Ulpia Traiana Augusta Dacica, founded by the Emperor Trajan in 108-110 AD, 15 km off the Hateg-Caransebeş road. The town was renamed after the old Dacian capital (*see*

separate entry) by Hadrian. The site contains the remains of a 2nd-century forum, temples, an amphitheatre, private houses and aqueducts, as well as an archaeological museum.

Zeicani, 6 km to the west, is the entrance to the narrow mountain pass known as **Poarta de Fier a Transilvaniei** (the Iron Gate of Transylvania), the site of battles between Dacians and Romans (106 AD) and Turks and Transylvanians (1442).

From Ulpia Traiana Sarmizegetusa there is also a road south to the unspoilt **Retezat Massif.**

Valea Gurghiului Transylvania
The Gurghiu Valley has long been a place where ethnic Romanians fled persecution by the Magyars, Szeklers and Saxons who colonized Transylvania from the 10th century onwards. Consequently, the inhabitants of the valley have retained many of their ancient traditions and still live in relative isolation from the modern world.

Valea Viilor (Nagybaromlaka, Wurmloch) Transylvania
Saxon wine-growing village, 10 km south of Mediaş, which has a massive Gothic fortified church, built after 1359. It is aisleless, with a long chancel, which was raised to form a defensive tower with tall buttresses, a lookout gallery, arrow slits and galleries. The bell-tower at the west end was also fortified. The surrounding walls have four towers and a gallery. The church contains a stone font from an earlier building, a fine tabernacle and carved and painted choir stalls (1528).

Vălenii de Munte Wallachia
Town located between Ploieşti and Braşov. As well as a monastery church (1680), it contains a museum devoted to the life and work of the distinguished historian, writer and politician, Nicolae Iorga, who was murdered by the Iron Guard in 1940.

Vama Veche Wallachia
Unspoilt beach resort near the Bulgarian border, popular with intellectuals since the Communist period, and still retaining Bohemian charm.

Văratec Moldavia
Convent 12 km south of Târgu Neamţ, in a pretty setting surrounded by forests of cedar trees, with a lovely garden. It was founded in the 17th century, but was largely reconstructed between 1808 and 1812. It has a simple, neo-Classical church built in 1808, with cylindrical twin towers, and a porch surmounted by an onion dome. With over 600 nuns now living here, it is one of the largest convents in the world. The nuns are renowned for the quality of their carpet-weaving, embroidery and icon painting. There is a museum of icons and carpets, a small shop and studios where the nuns work. The poet Veronica Micle, Eminescu's lover, who committed suicide after his death in 1889, is buried in the cemetery.

Vatra Dornei Moldavia
Spa and ski resort in beautiful countryside in northwestern Moldavia, about 80 km northeast of Bistriţa. It has two museums dedicated to natural history and ethnography respectively, but its principal attractions are the surrounding mountains, especially the Zugreni Gorges 20 km to the northeast. The Mestecanis Pass, leading to Câmpulung Moldovenesc, contains Ukrainian-style wooden churches, while the houses in Ciocaneşti, 22 km northwest of Vatra Dornei, are decorated with geometric and floral motifs similar to those seen on the peasant costumes of the area.

Vidra (Alsóvidra) Transylvania
Village 12 km west of Câmpeni. One of the oldest settlements in the Moţi territory, it has a 13th-century church and a 16th-

century bell-tower. The frescoes inside the church date from the late 17th century.

Vinţu de Jos (Alvinc, Alwitz) Transylvania
Ancient settlement mentioned by Herodotus, in which many Neolithic, Bronze and Iron Age remains have been found. The ruins of the Renaissance palace (1550) are said to be haunted.

Viscri (Szaszfehérygyháza, Deutsch-Weisskirch) Transylvania
Village with a fortified Gothic church. The original small white church ('Alba Ecclesia'), built here by Szeklers in the 12th century before the arrival of the Saxons, was remodelled and enlarged in the 14th century. Although the church is not large and has no outstanding architectural quality, Dr Hermann Fabini, the leading expert on Saxon churches, suggests that it is one of the most characteristic of the Transylvanian fortified churches. The font comes from the earlier church, while the choir-stalls date from 1694 and the coffered ceiling from 1743. The inner ring-walls around the church have four towers. An additional outer ring-wall was added in the 18th century. The defensive galleries were removed from the church in the 19th century.

This is one of the Transylvanian Saxon villages which the Mihai Eminescu Trust is working to repair and preserve. Several of the traditional farmhouses have been converted to guesthouses.

Vişeu Valley Maramureş
The principal town in this valley is Borşa (*see separate entry*), to the east of which is the spectacular **Prislop Pass** leading into Moldavia.

To the northwest, between Borşa and Vişeu de Sus, is **Moisei**, a village on the site of a settlement mentioned in the 14th century, which became an important centre of icon painting in the 17th century. It has a wooden church (1672), and a monument (1972) by Vida Gheza, commemorating 29 villagers massacred by retreating Hungarian troops in 1944.

Voroneţ Moldavia
Monastery 4 km southwest of Gura Humorului, founded in 1488 by Ştefan the Great in thanksgiving for his victories over the Turks. The church here is one of the most beautiful painted churches in Moldavia, and its exceptionally fine exterior frescoes, dating from the 1540s, have led it to be called 'the Oriental Sistine Chapel'. The opulent blue pigment used in the background of the paintings is now known as 'Voroneţ blue' and was obtained by grinding azurite and lapis lazuli.

The church was designed to be entered via a door in the southern wall, where there is a Last Judgement containing magnificent beasts, including zodiacal animals, unicorns and bulls with fish-tails, ranged frieze-like above a Christ in Majesty judging the good and the sinners. Among the latter are Turks and Tatars, Persians and Ethiopians. Below is a mass of devils, angels and wild animals. It is perhaps the most spectacular scene to be found in any of the painted monasteries.

There is also a beautifully composed Deisis to the east of the church, a lovely Tree of Jesse showing Christ's ancestors back to Jesse, including various sybils and Greek philosophers, and a series of scenes of the Life of the Virgin, and scenes of the Life and Death of St George. All the figures are finely modelled, with expressive faces and dramatic gestures. High up on the east wall is an unusual series of scenes showing Adam selling his soul to Satan.

The monastery was closed by the Habsburgs in 1785 and only began to admit nuns again in 1991.

Zalău (Zilah, Waltenberg) Transylvania
Town in northwestern Transylvania. Its

319

cultural attractions are limited to the two departments of its museum, the Provincial Museum of History and Art (Muzeul Judeţean de Istorie şi Artă). The historical collection on Str. Unirii 9 includes Dacian remains, while the art section (Galeria de Artă Ion Sima) on Str. Gheorghe Doja 6 has Post-Impressionist paintings by local artists, including Ion Sima, who studied in Paris at the end of the 19th century.

At **Jibou** 20 km northeast of Zalău the 24 ha park of the imposing Wesselény Palace (1779-1810) is one of Romania's finest botanical gardens with many exotic trees and shrubs housed in geodesic glasshouses, and a Roman garden.

A few km south of here the ruins of the Roman fort known as **Porolissum**, which include fragments of a temple and an amphitheatre, can be seen near the village of **Moigrad**.

Zombor (Magyarzsombor) Transylvania
Village 49 km from Cluj-Napoca, on the road to Zalău, with a 16th-century wooden church and the Sombori Palace of the same period, now a sanatorium.

Practical information

Romania in brief

Geography

Romania covers an area of 237,500 sq km (UK: 224,103 sq km), extending for approximately 480 km north to south and 640 km east to west. It borders Ukraine to the north for 362 km and to the east for 169 km. The border with Moldova to the east is 450 km long, with Bulgaria to the south 608 km, while the Black Sea coast extends for about 220 km. In the southwest the border with Serbia is 476 km long, and in the west with Hungary 443 km. The country is divided into 40 administrative districts (*judeţe*) and one municipality, Bucharest.

The Carpathian Mountains form the predominant geographical feature of the country, running in an arc across the centre and north, and separating the Transylvanian plateau from the populous plains of the east and south and the Danube Delta. They are divided into the Eastern Carpathians (containing 40% of Romania's forests), the Southern Carpathians (also known as the Transylvanian Alps) and the Western Carpathians. Their highest point, Mount Moldoveanu (8,346 ft, 2,544 m), is found in the Făgăraş Massif in the Southern Carpathians. The Western Carpathians comprise the Apuseni Mountains, which have numerous glaciers, gorges and falls.

The Danube runs for 2,850 km through nine countries into its delta, a swampy triangle on the northern edge of the Dobrogea tableland. The delta covers some 1,750 sq miles in Romania and is uniquely rich in plant and animal life. Most of the rivers of Romania are tributaries of the Danube and, by draining towards it, provide routes linking the hills and plains.

The plains cover a third of the country, hills and tablelands another third, and the Carpathians the remainder. Earthquakes are common in the south and southwest of the country.

Climate: The climate of Romania is temperate-continental, with a wide diurnal and seasonal range of temperature. Summers are very hot in the plains and on the Black Sea coast, where the temperature in June, July and August reaches 24°-30°C, while the highest peaks remain snow-covered. Early autumn is warm, with temperatures around 18°C (64°F), and at this time harvesting and harvest festivals occupy many villagers. Winter lasts from late November to late March, with a northeast wind, the *crivăţ*, bringing severe weather conditions from the Russian steppes and temperatures in the mountains falling to below -15°C. Spring, between April and June, brings torrential rain to the Carpathians, while the Danube Delta has the lowest rainfall.

Average air temperatures in °C and °F

	January	July
The Banat	-2°C/28°F	20°C/68°F
Bucharest	-3°C/27°F	23°C/73°F
The coast	-1°C/30°F	26°C/79°F
The mountains	1°C/34°F	21°C/70°F

Flora and Fauna (see pp. 249-253 and Nature Reserves, pp. 338-9): The Carpathian forests are among the least spoilt in Europe. Between April and July, the alpine forests and sub-alpine pastures at the highest levels display many kinds of flowers and plants, including fritillary, yellow poppy, gentian, saxifrage, and, in the Southern Carpathians, edelweiss. In the warmer regions of the southwest rare plants are found in the Retezat Mountains. There are many rare species of mammals in the forests, including chamois, wild boar, Carpathian stags and moufflons (large-horned wild sheep). Wolves, brown bears and lynx are protected species.

The lower course and delta of the Danube has over 1000 plant species and a rich fauna. In the delta there are important populations of native and migratory birds, including Europe's largest colony of white and Dalmatian pelicans, pygmy cormorants and red-breasted geese. Among the many varieties of fish in the Danube, the sturgeon is the most valuable on account of its high-quality caviar.

Demography: The population in 2005 was about 22.2 million (UN estimate), with a density of 98 people per sq km. About 50% of Romanians live in towns and cities, the largest cities being the capital Bucharest (population 2.25 million), Braşov, Iaşi, Timişoara and Constanţa.

The population today is 89.7% Romanian. The 17 ethnic minorities include Roma (gypsies), Hungarians, Germans, Ukrainians, Croats, Serbs, Russians (chiefly in the east), Armenians, Turks and Tatars.

Transylvania has the largest non-Romanian population, which includes over 500,000 Roma, as well a large Hungarian (Magyar and Szekely) minority.

The number of Jews and Germans in Romania, once substantial, greatly declined during the last century. Under the Ceauşescu regime, both groups were allowed to emigrate in return for large cash payments.

Religion: Over 86% of the population belong to the Romanian Orthodox Church, headed by a patriarch in Bucharest; 5% are Roman Catholics; 3.5% are Protestants; and 1% are Uniates (also known as Graeco-Catholics); Judaism is practised by approximately 0.2%; and Muslims, most of whom are ethnic Tatars and Turks living in Dobrogea, constitute 0.3%.

Under Communism, the Orthodox Church was generally subservient to government policies, and other religious groups suffered varying degrees of persecution and harassment. Today the Church maintains its conservative views on doctrinal and moral issues.

Economy: Farmland covers 95 million hectares (about 62% of the total land mass). Of these about 4.6 million hectares are devoted to pasture, 600,000 hectares to vineyards, orchards, and vine and fruit-tree nurseries, and over 3 million hectares are irrigated. Agriculture employs 31.6% of the labour force and contributes 10.1% to the GDP. Programmes designed to improve the quality and efficiency of farm production (particularly livestock breeding) are proving difficult to implement, and capital investment in rural areas is often inadequate. However, production of high-quality wines is flourishing.

Romanian industry accounts for about 34.7% of GDP and employs 30.7% of the labour force. Major industries include machine-building, metallurgy, engineering, manufacture of construction materials, oil production and refining. Priorities of industrial reform in the post-Communist period include liquidating large energy-intensive industries, increasing privatization, encouraging greater foreign investment and modernizing the industrial base. The service sector now contributes 55.2% of GDP.

The unemployment rate in 2005 was 8%, with approximately 19% of the population below the poverty line.

By 2006 the European Union declared itself satisfied with the progress of economic reforms and admitted Romania to full membership on 1 January 2007.

Travelling

Travelling to and from Romania

By Rail Travelling by train to Romania is to be preferred not only on the grounds of CO_2 emissions; it is a journey through some of Europe's most attractive landscapes and, properly planned, can be as efficient as flying as well as very much more comfortable. Currently the most direct route is London-Brussels-Cologne-Vienna-Bucharest. An afternoon train from London will connect with the Cologne-Vienna night-train. You can then spend the day in Vienna, and take another night-train to Romania, stopping at Alba Julia, Sighişoara, Ploieşti, Braşov and Bucharest. An alternative, and slightly faster route, is to carry on to Budapest and change there for a night train to Braşov, Ploieşti and Bucharest. There is also a route via Paris and the (real) Orient Express, but this will be more expensive.

For up-to-date information on routes and ticketing, consult www.seat61.com. Tickets may be bought at:

Rail Europe Travel Centre
178 Piccadilly, London, W1
tel: 0870 584 8848, 0870 837 1371
www.raileurope.co.uk

International Rail Limited
08700 84 14 10
www.internationalrail.com

Eurostar UK. Ltd
Eurostar House, Waterloo Station
London SE1 8SE, tel 020 7922 6180
www.eurostar.com

By Car The best route to Romania from the UK is via Frankfurt, Nuremberg, Regensburg, Linz and Vienna to Budapest, and then either by the E60 to the Borş border crossing or by the E68 to the Nădlac crossing. Both border posts are open 24 hours a day.

Other principal border crossings are: Petea and Varsand (Hungary); Moraviţa and Porţile de Fier (Serbia); Giurgiu and Vama Veche (Bulgaria); and Siret (Ukraine) .

Information about driving in Romania can be obtained from the UK motoring organizations: the AA (tel: 01256 20123; web: www.theaa.com) and the RAC (tel: 0345 333222; web: www.rac.co.uk.)

By Coach There is no direct coach service from Britain to Romania. Travellers from London must change coaches at Cologne. The whole journey takes two days. For booking contact Eurolines (tel 020 7730 3466, www.eurolines.com).

By Air In order to minimize the carbon footprint of your trip, please consider alternative ways of travelling, such as rail, which offers many other advantages.

Tarom flies direct to Bucharest from the UK and the US, and British Airways from the UK. At the time of writing there are some low-cost airline routes also from the UK. Regular flights use Bucharest Otopeni (officially Henri Coanda International Airport, tel: 021 230 0022), about 16 km north of the city centre, reached by taxi or bus. Low-cost airlines use Bucharest Băneasa airport (tel: 021 232 0020), about 10 km from the city centre and reached by bus.

Visas and Travel Documents For visits lasting less than 90 days visas are not needed by citizens of the UK and other EU countries, the USA, Canada, Australia or New Zealand. To extend your stay beyond three months it is necessary to register with the Romanian Authority for Aliens (Autoritatea pentru Străini, web: www.aps.mai.gov.ro).

Romanian Embassies and Consulates
UK: Arundel House, 4 Palace Green
 London W8 4QD, tel: 020 7937 9667
 www.londra.mae.ro
USA: 1607 23rd St NW, Washington DC
 20008 tel: 202/232 4829, 232 4747
 www.roembus.org
Canada: 655 Rideau Street, Ottawa KIN 6A3
 tel 613/789 5345
 www.romaniacanada.com
Australia: 4 Dalman Crescent, O'Malley,
 Canberra, ACT 2606, tel: 02 6290 2442
 www.canberra.mae.ro

Customs Regulations
Romanian customs regulations are similar to those of most European countries. A traveller can enter and leave Romania with up to US$12,000 in cash or travellers cheques. Larger amounts must be declared.
 Import Allowances: 200 cigarettes or 40 cigars, 4 litres of wine or 2 litres of spirits, 20 rolls of camera film, a reasonable quantity of gifts, medicines for personal use. Valuable goods, such as jewellery, art, electrical items and foreign currency should be declared on entry. Endorsed customs declarations must be kept, as they must be shown on leaving the country. Weapons, ammunition, pornography and narcotics may not be imported.
 Export The following may be exported without duty: food and medicine sufficient for a 24-hour journey, and souvenirs bought in hard currency or up to a value of 1,000 lei. Antiques may not be exported.

Travelling within Romania
By Rail Within Romania there is an extensive rail network, run by the state-owned Căile Ferate Române (CFR). The service is generally very reliable and, though trains are often overcrowded, they provide the best way of getting to small towns and villages and seeing the countryside on the way. Fares vary according to the type of train: the most expensive is the intercity. Seat reservations are obligatory for *accelerat, rapid, express* and *intercity* trains, and the charge for this is included in the price of the fare. It is advisable to book in advance for fast services. Tickets can also be bought 24 hours in advance at CFR Agenţia de Voiaj offices. Rail passes may be obtained from stations and provide first-class travel for a total of 5 days within a 15-day period. The CFR timetable *(mersul trenurilor)* is both cheap and useful and available from CFR offices (www.cfr.ro).

By Bus Bus services operate in almost every village and, though infrequent, are useful when visiting rural areas. Many buses do not run on Sundays, and they are not comfortable, particularly in bad weather. Timetables are not very reliable and should be confirmed with the clerk at the office. Private bus services provide intercity connections, and tickets for these must be bought in advance at the appropriate bus station *(autogară)*.

By Cycle Bicycles may be brought into Romania. Cycling in towns and cities is not recommended, but it is an excellent means of exploring the countryside away from major roads. Bicycles can be taken on trains, sometimes on payment of a small fee; if stored in baggage cars they should be labelled with the owner's name, the destination and the weight. Cycle repair shops are rare, and it is advisable to carry a spare tyre and a few spokes. Beware of potholes on the roads.

There are a few companies offering planned cycle tours, particularly in Transylvania, such as Adventure Transylvania (www.adventuretransylvania. com) and Hooked on Cycling (www.hookedon cycling.co.uk)

By Car Driving in Romania can be hazardous and stressful. Romania's road system is in poor condition, although there are some stretches of motorway *(autostradă)*, for example the A1 linking Bucharest and Piteşti (114 km). This is being extended. The A2 motorway is now under construction from Bucharest to Constanţa (completed as far as Cernavodă), and in 2004 construction began on the A3 linking Bucharest and Oradea. Some major roads *(drum naţional)* have been resurfaced, but many are potholed and poorly signposted. Secondary roads *(drum judeţeana)* and forest roads *(drum forestier)* are even less reliable; the latter are often impassable after heavy rain, and many are unlit, with no markings.

It must also be said that drivers in Romania can be aggressive and unpredictable. Many cars do not have headlights, and it is not unusual to see ox- or horse-drawn carts or other obstacles entering roads without warning.

Documents for Vehicles Motorists need a national driving licence, a vehicle registration document and liability insurance. Green Card insurance is valid in Romania. A road toll badge (RoVinieta) must be obtained on entry to Romania (3 euros for one week, 6 euros for a month).

Car Hire Car rental companies such as Avis, Europcar and Hertz have offices in most cities. Touring ACR (Automobil Clubul Român) can also arrange car hire.

Maps Good road maps and road atlases of Romania are available. The Cartographia road atlas (scale 1:300,000) or the road map

by Kümmereley & Frey (scale 1:500,000) can be bought, for example at Stanfords, 12-14 Long Acre, London WC2 9LP (www.stanfords.co.uk). Detailed town plans and regional maps can usually be obtained from local tourist offices.

Petrol Petrol *(benzină)* which is relatively cheap, may be paid for at Peco and Shell stations with Visa or Mastercard. Unleaded petrol *(fără plumb)* is often denoted by the German term, *Bleifrei.*

Traffic regulations The speed limit in built-up areas is 50 kph (31 mph), outside built-up areas 90 kph (55 mph) and on motorways 120 kph. Motor-cycles are restricted to 80 kph (50 mph) on the open road and 100 kph (62 mph) on motorways. The most important rule to observe is to drive on the right and to overtake on the left. Police can make large on-the-spot fines for speeding.

Drink-drive laws are strict: no alcohol may be consumed before driving. The wearing of seat belts is compulsory at the front and back (if the latter are fitted), as is the wearing of motorcycle helmets. Horns may not be used between 10 p.m. and 6 a.m. in Bucharest, and is illegal at all times in some other towns.

Accidents Accidents should always be reported to the police *(poliţie)*, and drivers must wait until they arrive. For insurance purposes it is necessary in an accident to keep a record of the details of the other party involved and of the relevant legal authorities, together with a document from the police.

Breakdowns and garages Members of the AA, RAC and AAA have reciprocal membership facilities with Romania's Automobil Clubul Român (ACR), which has an emergency repair service using patrol cars (24-hour freephone emergency number: 927). The ACR has offices in most cities; the head office in Bucharest is at Str. Tache Ionescu 27 (tel: 01 650 2595).

Repair shops are common, but spare parts

may still be hard to come by for cars other than Renault or Citroën. Punctures can be repaired at small workshops, which are often identified by the word *vulcanizare* and are found even in small villages.

Emergency telephone numbers	
Police	955
Ambulance	961
Roadside Assistance (ACR)	927
Fire brigade	981

Urban Transport

Taxis Taxi fares are generally moderate. Rates (usually between 1 and 1.50 RON per kilometer) must be displayed by law on the vehicle. Western visitors are less frequently fleeced than they were, but it is still best to use a reputable taxi firm. Phoning for a taxi, where possible, is usually cheaper.

Since 2006 taxi journeys from and to Otopeni Airport must be made with the firm

Fly Taxi (tel: 9411) Some other Bucharest taxi firms are:

Cris Taxi:	tel: 9461
Euro Taxi:	tel: 9851
Getax:	tel: 9531
Meridian:	tel: 9441

Maxi-Taxis are white, eight- or ten-seater minibuses that can be hailed like taxis. Tickets are purchased on board. Five Maxi-Taxi routes connect central Bucharest with the city's main places of interest.

Buses, trolley-buses, trams and metro All towns have local bus services, and in the major cities there are trams and trolley-buses (*tramvai* and *troleibuz*). Tickets (generally 1 or 2 RON a journey) are sold in bunches by tobacconists and ITA street kiosks, which always close at about 5 pm and often also at other times during the day. Passengers must validate their tickets in a machine on boarding the vehicle.

Bucharest has a modern metro system with four lines and 45 stations.

A-Z of other practical information

Accommodation

Hotels Hotels in Romania are graded from 1 to 5 stars. There are five-star hotels only in Bucharest, including the Athenée Palace Hilton on Str. Episcopiei 1-3, facing Piaţa Revoluţiei (tel: 021 303 3777). Facilities at the top hotels (3-5 star) include a phone, cable TV and all the other usual facilities. Mid-range hotels often give the impression of having seen better days, although there are some charming new hotels, such as Casa Moraru at Str. Alexandru Vlahuta 11 A in Sibiu (tel: 0269 21 6291).

In general, budget hotels tend to lack character, and sometimes hot water is only available in the morning and evening. A notable exception is the atmospheric Hanul lui Manuc housed in a former caravanserai on Str. Franceza 62-64, Bucharest (tel 01 313 1411). Breakfast is not always included in the price in cheaper hotels.

All charges are in lei (RON). All hotels ask guests for their passports when they check in.

Hostels and Student Rooms There are very few hostels in Romania. The Vila Helga Hostel in Bucharest is open all year round. Hostels in Cluj-Napoca and Sighişoara offer beds in student dormitories in July and August. Most large towns offer student rooms between 15 July and 31 August. The Youth Tourism Company (CTT or BTT) organizes group bookings. Contact CTT Head Office in Bucharest, Str. Mendeleev 7 (tel 021 614 42 00).

Cabins and Mountain Huts In mountain areas, cabins or chalets (*cabană*) provide sim-ple accommodation. They are cheaper than hotels and less comfortable, and most of them are in isolated areas, although some are not far from towns. Many are open all year, and no reservation is needed (although in the popular Făgăraş Mountains it is advisable to book in advance). In very remote areas empty hikers' huts provide shelter.

Private Rooms There has been enormous growth in the private sector, and bed-and-breakfast in traditional farmhouses is available through a number of organizations: ANTREC (National Association of Rural, Ecological and Cultural Tourism) can arrange accommodation and tours. They have headquarters in Bucharest and Bran and many regional offices.

ANTREC,
Str. Maica Alexandra 7,
22-259 Bucharest
Tel: 021 223 7024
www.antrec.ro/

Another organization set up to help the rural economy through agro-tourism is OVR (Opération Villages Roumains www.villages-roumains.be), providing everything from accommodation to traditional entertainment through its network of village offices. Private rooms are more difficult to find, but branch offices of the Centre for Folk Arts (Centrul de Creaţie Populară) can be helpful.

Camping There are over a hundred camp sites all over Romania. A camping map published by the Romanian Ministry of Tourism is available from tourist offices. Most sites have cabins (*căsuţe*) to rent. These sleep 2-4 people and are provided with mattresses, but often with no bedding or sheets. Communal showers are generally basic, and 2nd-class sites may not even have toilets. Camping on the Black Sea coast, once prohibited, can now be overcrowded. Camping is forbidden in the Danube Delta, but camping in the mountains is allowed provided that safety regulations are observed.

Motels Motels are located along main highways and have similar facilities to the hotels but can seldom be reached by public transport.

Electrical Current 220 volts at 50 Hz alternating current. Sockets need a European plug with two round pins.

Embassies and Consulates in Romania
UK
Str. Jules Michelet 24, 010463 Bucharest
tel: 021 201 7200/fax: 021 201 7317
www.britishembassy.gov.uk/romania

Ireland
Str. Buzesti 50-52, Floor 3, 011015 Bucharest
tel: 021 310 2131/fax: 021 310 2285
email: bucharestembassy@dfa.ie

USA
Str. Tudor Arghezi 7-9, Bucharest
tel: 021 200 3300/fax: 021 200 3442
bucharest.usembassy.gov

Canada
Str. Nicolae Iorga 36, Bucharest
tel: 021 222 9845/fax: 021 312 0366

Australia
B-dul General Magheru 29, Bucharest
Apt 45
tel: 021 312 9097

Food in Romania Romanian cuisine consists of rich, tasty and filling dishes which often combine meat and dairy products. This might be expected in a country with very cold winters, where food is still grown organically and fruit and vegetables are gathered in their seasons.

Grilled pork is a special favourite, but there are also good beef and chicken dishes: shepherd's sirloin (*mușchi ciobănesc*), pork stuffed with ham, covered in cheese and served with mayonnaise, cucumber and herbs; and meadow sirloin (*mușchi poiană*), beef stuffed with mushrooms, bacon, paprika and pepper, served in a vegetable purée and tomato sauce.

Another speciality is 'Moldavian stew' (*tocănțiă moldovenească*), a hearty stew of pork in a spicy pepper sauce with a fried egg on top and served with *mămăligă*, a maize polenta with a bland taste which is served, and goes with, practically everything.

Romania has a variety of soups (*ciorbă*). They often have a sharp taste and are served with sour cream (*smântina*). They include a spicy soup with meatballs and vegetables (*ciorbă de perișoare*), a tripe soup with garlic (*ciorbă de burtă*), a vegetable soup made with meat stock (*ciorbă de legume*) and a kosher lamb soup (*ciorbă de miel*) made from leg or shoulder of lamb and eaten during the Easter festival.

Authentic country dishes include stuffed peppers (*ardei umplut*) or cabbage leaves (*sarma*) stuffed with rice, meat and herbs, stuffed vine leaves (*sămăluțe*) served with sour cream, and small grilled sausages (*mititei*) sprinkled with aromatic herbs.

Salads of tomatoes (*salată roșii*), cucumbers (*salată castraveți*) and mixed tomatoes and cucumbers (*salată asortată*) are very refreshing and eaten by many strictly Orthodox Romanians on fast days and during Lent, when it is forbidden to eat meat.

Many Romanians collect mushrooms

(ciuperci) in the woods and fields, and there are various flavourful dishes made with mushrooms mixed with hard, strong-tasting cheese, fresh or sour cream or yoghurt.

There are also numerous dishes of Turkish origin, notably moussaka *(musaca)* and varieties of pilaf rice, while sauerkraut with smoked pork and such dishes as Transylvanian hotpot were brought into Romania by the Germans and Hungarians.

The Danube Delta is, naturally, famous for its fish dishes, such as carp kebab.

Romanian cakes and desserts are sticky and very sweet, and coffee is often drunk black and sweet in the Turkish fashion, with a layer of ground coffee beans at the bottom of the cup.

The ideal way in which to experience these dishes is to eat in the homes of ordinary Romanians. However, the quality of restaurants has greatly improved in recent years, although it is still variable and it is sometimes difficult to find places open late at night outside the big cities. The range of restaurants in part reflects the country's ethnic diversity: Constanţa, for example, has some excellent Turkish food. However, traditional Romanian fare is the norm.

Space does not allow a comprehensive listing for the whole country, but the following are a few of the capital's notable dining spots. Amongst the most sophisticated are Casa Vernescu (tel: 021 231 0220), in an elegant 19th-century villa at Calea Victoriei 133, and Casa Doina (with a garden) at Soseaua Kiseleff 4 (tel: 021 222 3179). More modest, but still of very high quality, is Boema, Str. C.A. Rosetti 10 (tel: 021 313 3783), and Caru' cu Bere, in an atmospheric Gothic Revival building at Str. Stavropoleos 3-5 in the Old Town (tel: 021 313 7560).

Romanian wines are excellent: red wine *(vin negru* or *roşu)*, white wine *(vin alb)*, dry wine *(vin sec)*, sweet wine *(vin dulce)* and sparkling wine *(vin spumos)*. The best vari-eties come from the vineyards of Murfatlar, Cotnari, Jidvei, Delu Mare, Odobeşti and Valea Calugareasca. Delicious unfermented wine is available during the wine harvest. Romanian plum brandy, *ţuică*, is very strong and is chiefly drunk as an aperitif.

Health

Drinking Water Officially the tap water is safe, but it is advisable to drink only bottled mineral water.

Inoculations No immunizations are compulsory, but it is advisable to ensure that those against hepatitis A, polio and tetanus are up-to-date. This is particularly important in remote areas where sanitation may be poor. Similarly, rabies, typhoid and encephalitis vaccinations should be considered as there are many stray dogs in Romania, especially Bucharest, as well as ticks in the forests.

Medical Treatment Comprehensive medical insurance is recommended. For EU citizens it is advisable to obtain a European Health Insurance Card (EHIC) before leaving. The EHIC entitles you to medical treatment on the same terms as Romanian nationals. In Bucharest, the British and American embassies may be able to recommend an English-speaking doctor or dentist. Hospital facilities in smaller towns are often very poor. In emergencies dial 961.

Pharmacies There are pharmacies *(farmacie)* in every town and city, and in theory one pharmacy in every town should be open 24 hours a day. They stock aspirin, insect-repellent, and many sell antibiotics over the counter. Travellers who require a particular medicine should bring adequate amounts, as it may not be available locally. Tampons, sanitary towels and contraceptives are often difficult to buy in Romania. AIDS and STD are serious problems in Romania and precautions against these are advisable.

Money and Exchange The currency is the leu (plural: lei). There are 100 bani (singular: ban) to the leu. In 2005 the old leu (ROL) was replaced by the new leu (RON) at the rate 1 RON = 10,000 ROL. Banknotes come in denominations of 1, 5, 10, 50, 100, 200 and 500 lei, and coins of 1 ban, 5, 10 and 50 bani. Since the end of 2006 the old leu (ROL) has no longer been legal tender.

Foreign currency may be imported in cash, but damaged bank notes are refused at exchanges. Travellers' cheques can be cashed in large banks, some hotels and some exchange offices, but a considerable commission is usually charged. Credit cards are usually accepted in hotels, restaurants and the more expensive shops, and by car rental companies.

Cash can be withdrawn from automatic teller machines, ATMs (*bancomat*), found at main banks and shopping centres.

In rural areas credit cards are of little use, and there are no ATMs, so it is advisable to carry some cash. Low-denomination US dollar notes may be accepted for some purchases, but generally payment should be made in lei.

Foreign currency can be exchanged at hotels, banks and in the many private exchange offices (identified as *casa de schimb* or *birou de schimb valutar*). It is worth looking around for the best deal, since exchange rates vary. Most banks are open on weekday mornings.

Music, Theatre and Film In Bucharest classical concerts are performed at the Romanian Atheneum (Ateneul Român), and operas and ballet at the Opera Română. Iaşi has a classical music festival in May, Constanţa has an opera house, while in Braşov a jazz festival is held in early December. Festivals of folk-music and dancing take place in all regions throughout the year.

Bucharest has many theatres, staging all kinds of productions, including the Comedy Theatre, the Ţăndărică Puppet Theatre, the Ion Luca Caragiale National Theatre, and the Jewish State Theatre. All theatres are closed in July and August.

There are many cinemas. Foreign films are usually shown with Romanian subtitles.

News The leading English-language newspaper is the daily *Nine O'Clock* available free in hotels (www.nineoclock.ro), which incorporates the *Romanian Economic Daily*. There are also several online English-language papers, such as *Romanian Business News* (www.romania.biz).

Information about cultural events in Bucharest can be found in the English-language guide *In Your Pocket* and in *Bucureşti; What, Where, When* published every two months. Also useful are the Romanian-language listings magazines *Şapte Seri* and *Zile şi Nopţi*

Western newspapers can be bought in some hotels or in the main cities.

BBC Bucharest (88.0FM) broadcasts hourly news in English. Elsewhere the BBC World Service can be heard via the Hot Bird 8 satellite (www.bbc.co.uk/worldservice).

Cable television is usually available in the better hotels.

Opening Times
Banks: Mon-Fri 8 am-12 noon
Food Shops and supermarkets: Mon-Sat 8 am-8 pm; Sun 8.30 am-1 pm
Libraries: The British Council Library in Bucharest is open Mondays 3 pm-7 pm, Tuesday to Friday 11 am-7 pm, and on Saturday 10 am-1 pm. (Calea Dorobanţilor 14, 01572 Bucharest tel: 021 307 9600, email: contact@ britishcouncil.ro)
Museums: Usually open Tue-Sun 9 am-5 pm, or 10 am-6 pm. Some museums in Bucharest are also closed on Tuesdays.
Pharmacies: Mon-Sat 9 am-8 pm. There

should be one 24-hour pharmacy in each town.

Post Offices: Mon-Sat 7 am-8.30 pm; Sun 8 am-12 noon.

Restaurants: Lunch from 1 pm; dinner from 6.30 pm.

Shops: Other than food shops, most are open Mon-Fri 10 am-6 pm.

Tourist Offices: Mon-Fri 9 am-4 pm; Sat 9 am-12 noon.

Post Post office *(poştă)* collection times are Mon-Fri 7.30 am-8 pm and Saturday 7.30 am-2 pm. Cards and letters take 4 to 6 days to Western Europe, and 7 to 20 days to North America. All post offices sell stamps *(timbre)*. Letter boxes marked *alte localităţi* are for foreign mail and all places in Romania other than Bucharest. For further information see www.posta-romana.ro.

Public Holidays

New Year	1 and 2 January
Orthodox Easter	(Sun and Mon) variable
May Day	1 May
National Unity Day	1 December
Christmas	25 and 26 December

During the week before Easter, the churches are packed and the celebration culminates with great solemnity at midnight on Easter Sunday. Other Orthodox festivals are now less widely observed.

Aside from national holidays, there are numerous lesser festivals marking rites of passage and events in the agricultural and pastoral calendar. In September there are musical celebrations in honour of the forthcoming harvest: at Leşu, in the northwest, pan pipers – most of whom are shepherds – perform the Rhapsody of the Trişcaşi, and in November at Odobeşti they hold a competition.

Shopping and Souvenirs Typical Romanian craft products include woven rugs, flatweave carpets, embroidered blouses, sheepskin waistcoats, decorated ceramics, glass icons, metalwork and other handmade goods. Romarta stores sell textiles, glassware and ceramics. Folk-art shops are found at the major tourist spots, especially Bran Castle and the monasteries in Bucovina (northern Moldavia). Most of Bucharest's art galleries and antique shops are in and around Str. Jean Louis Calderon in the east of the city.

Spas Romania is the source of one third of Europe's mineral and thermal water, with over 160 spas, many treating specific health complaints. Among those recommended are Băile Felix on the thermal Lake Felix, used to treat rheumatic ailments, Sovata for gynaecological problems, Covasna and Buziaş for cardiovascular complaints, Slănic Moldova for digestive disorders and Moneasa for nervous complaints. The main health centres in Bucharest are at the Flora Hotel and the Otopeni Clinic, 2 km from the airport.

Telephones Public phone boxes for international calls are orange in colour. The direct dialling country code for Romania is +40, and the outgoing code is 00 followed by the relevant country code (e.g. 0044 for the UK, 001 for the USA and Canada). Cellphone coverage is reasonably good, except in mountainous regions.

Codes for some Romanian cities:

Alba Iulia	0258	Constanţa	0241
Bucharest	021	Iaşi	0232
Braşov	0268	Sibiu	0269
Cluj	0264	Timişoara	0256

Emergency Telephone Numbers	
Police	955
Fire brigade	981
Accident Rescue Service	961

Time Romania is 2 hours ahead of GMT, 7 hours ahead of Eastern Standard Time and 10 hours ahead of US Pacific Standard Time. At the end of March clocks are put one hour forward and at the end of September one hour back.

Tipping Service is included in the bill at hotels and restaurants, but a 10% tip is still appreciated.

Tourist Information and Agencies ONT (Carpaţi) is Romania's only state-owned tourist office. It has offices abroad, as well as in the larger Romanian cities, from which maps, brochures and special interest booklets in many languages can be obtained. Romanian tourist offices abroad often provide better information than those in Romania itself.

ONT addresses abroad:
UK: 22 New Cavendish St, London
    W1G 8TT, tel 020 7224 3692
    www.romaniatourism.com/
USA: 355 Lexington Avenue, 19th Floor
    New York NY 10017
    tel: 212 545 8484; fax: 212 251 0429

In Bucharest the main tourist office is at
    B-dul Magheru 7, Bucharest 70165.
    tel: 021 314 5160; email: office@ont.ro.
    Opening hours: Mon-Fri 8 am-8 pm; Sat
    and Sun 8 am-3 pm.

Many of the provincial tourist offices (OJT) are in private hands and provide good information. The opening hours are Mon-Fri 9 am-4 pm and Sat 9 am-noon, but are often unreliable. Tourist offices and hotel reception desks all over the country will provide tourists with a free town plan *(plan oraşului)* or map of the district *(hartă judeţean)*, arrange city tours or excursions to other places.

There are other agencies, including the Romanian Automobile Club (ACR), which will arrange trips, caravan tours and hotel reservations, book private accommodation, arrange car rentals and provide free city maps.

ACR (Automobil Clubul Român) office:
    Str. Tache Ionescu 27, Bucharest 010353
    tel: 021 650 25 95, fax 021 312 04 34
    www.acr.ro
Touring ACR:
    Str. Stanislav Cihovschi 2, Bucharest
    tel: 021 104 10, fax: 021 143 66
Consus Travel, Cluj-Napoca:
    Str.Gh.Şincai 15, 3400 Cluj-Napoca
    tel/fax: 064 193044,
    email: consus@mail.dutcj.ro.

In addition to the services provided by these bureaux, useful publications about Romanian tourist destinations can be bought from art galleries, museums and good bookshops.

Museums

There are art and/or ethnographic museums in all the major towns, as well as many specialist collections. These are listed in the gazetteer entries. The following list gives details of the major museums and galleries.

Museums are open from 9 am to 5 pm or from 10 am to 6 pm. They are closed on Tuesdays in Bucharest and on Mondays elsewhere. Admission charges are in general very low.

Some useful general websites include www.cimec.ro, www.ici.ro/romania/en/cultura/muzee.html, and www.museum.ici.ro.

Arad
Arad Museum Complex (Complexul Muzeal Arad)
Piaţa George Enescu 1, 310131 Arad
tel: 0257 281847
e-mail: office@museumarad.ro
www.museumarad.ro

Baia Mare
Historical Museum (Muzeul de Arheologie şi Istorie Baia Mare)
Str. Monetăriei 1-3, 430406 Baia Mare
tel: 0262 211927
email: office@maramuresmuzeu.ro
Muzeul Judeţean de Etnografie şi Artă Popular
Str. Dealul Florilor, 430165 Baia Mare
tel: 0262 276895
email: office@maramuresmuzeu.ro
Muzeul de Artă
Str. 1 Mai 8, 430331 Baia Mare
tel: 0262 213964
office@maramuresmuzeu.ro
Mineralogical Museum (Muzeul de Mineralogie)
B-dul Traian 8, 430212 Baia Mare,
tel: 0262 227517
Planetarium
Strada George Cosbuc, Nr. 16

430245 Baia Mare, Maramures
tel: 0262 275206
www.astroclubul.org

Braşov
Ethnographical Museum (Muzeul de Etnografia)
B-dul Eroilor, 21 500030 Braşov
tel: 0268 475 562/0268 476 243
www.etnobrasov.ro

Brebu
Casa Domnească de la Brebu
17th century artefacts in fortified house built by Matei Basarab and finished by Constantin Brancoveanu
tel: 0244 453 7731
www.museum.ici.ro/muntenia/ploiesti/english/fmuzeu.htm

Bucharest
Muzeul Naţional de Istorie Naturala Grigore Antipa
Şos. Kiseleff 1, sector 1, 011341 Bucureşti,
tel: 021 312 88 63; 021 312 88 26
www.antipa.ro
National Museum of Art (Muzeul Naţional de Artă al României)
Calea Victoriei 49-53, 70101 Bucureşti,

tel: 021 314 81 19
11.00 - 19.00 (May-Sept)
10.00 - 18.00 (Oct-Apr)
www.mnar.arts.ro
Museum of Art Collections (Muzeul
Collecţiilor de Artă)
    Calea Victoriei 111, 010071 Bucureşti
    tel: 021 211 17 49; 021 212 96 41
    www.itcnet.ro/museum/museum.html
Pallady Museum (Muzeul Theodor Pallady)
    Str. Spătarului 22, 020772 Bucureşti
    tel: 021 211 49 79
    Collection of paintings and furniture in
    one of Bucharest's oldest houses
    www.itcnet.ro/museum/museum.html
Zambaccian Museum
(Muzeul K. H. Zambaccian)
    Str. Muzeul Zambaccian, nr. 21 A,
    011871 Bucureşti
    tel: 021 230 19 20
    Romanian and French paintings collected
    by Krikor Zambaccian (1889-1962) in
    their original setting.
    www.itcnet.ro/museum/museum.html
National Museum of Romanian History
(Muzeul Naţional de Istorie a României)
    Calea Victoriei, nr. 12, sect. 3,
    030026, Bucureşti
    tel: 021 315 82 07
    www.mnir.ro
Romanian Peasant Museum (Muzeul
Ţâranului Român)
    Şos. Kiseleff 3, Sector 1, 011341 Bucureşti,
    tel: 021 317 96 60
    email: info@muzeultaranuluiroman.ro
    www.muzeultaranuluiroman.ro
National Village Museum (Muzeul Naţional
al Satului Dimitrie Gusti)
    Şos. Kiseleff 28, sector 1, 011342 Bucureşti
    tel: 021 317.91.10
    email: contact@muzeulsatului.ro
    www.muzeul-satului.ro
Museum of Romanian Literature (Muzeul
Literaturii Romane)
    B-dul Dacia nr. 12, sector 1, Bucureşti

tel: 021 212 58 45; 212 58 46
email: info@mlr.ro
www.mlr.ro
National Museum of Contemporary Art
(Muzeul Naţional de Artă Contemporană
MNAC)
    Str. Izvor 2-4, Bucureşti
    tel. 021 318 91 37
    www.mnac.ro
Jewish History Museum (Muzeul de Istorie a
Evreilor din România Dr Moses Rosen)
    Str. Mămulari 3, Bucureşti
    tel: 021 311 0870
    www.romanianjewish.org
    In the 19th-century Great Synagogue.
Muzeul Naţional Cotroceni
    B-dul Geniului 1, sector 6,
    060116 Bucureşti
    tel: 021 317 3100
    www.muzeulcotroceni.ro
Muzeul Naţional de Geologie
    Şos. Kiseleff 2, sector 1, Bucureşti
    tel: 021 212 8952
    Interesting collections in fine eclectic
    building (1907). Open by appointment.
    www.geology.ro

Câmpulung Moldovenesc
Museum of Wood Art (Muzeul Arta
Lemnului)
    Calea Transilvaniei 10,
    Câmpulung Moldovenesc
    tel: 0230 311378
Wooden Spoon Collection of Ioan Tugui
(Colecţia de Linguri de Lemn Ioan Tugui)
    Str. G. Popovici 1,
    Câmpulung Moldovenesc

Cluj-Napoca
Muzeul Naţional de Artă
    Piaţa Unirii 30, Cluj-Napoca
    tel: 0254 596 953
    www.macluj.ro
National Musem of Transylvanian History
(Muzeul Naţional de Istorie al Transilvaniei)

Str. Constantin Daicoviciu 2,
400020 Cluj-Napoca
tel: 0264 595 677
email: secretariat@mnit.museum.utcluj.ro
www.mnit.museum.utcluj.ro
*Ethnographic Museum of Transylvania
(Muzeul Etnografic al Transilvaniei)*
Str. Memorandumului 21,
400114 Cluj-Napoca
tel: 0264 592 344
www.muzeul-etnografic.ro
*Romulus Vuia Ethnographic Park
(Parcul Etnografic Romulus Vuia)*
tel: 0264 592344
Open-air section of the ethnographic
museum

Craiova
Muzeul de Artă
Calea Unirii 15, Craiova
tel: 0251 412342
Romanian art in magnificent French
château
museum.ici.ro/oltenia/dolj/romanian/
muzeul_de_arta_craiova.htm
Oltenia Museum (Muzeul Olteniei)
Str. Popa Sapca 8, Craiova
tel: 0251 411906; 0251 411674
email: office@muzeulolteniei.ro
www.muzeulolteniei.ro
Secția de Historie
Str. Madona Dudu 44, Craiova
tel: 0251 418631
Secția de Etnografie
Str. Matei Basarab 14, Craiova
tel: 0251 417756
Secția de Științele Naturii
Str. Popa Sapca 8, Craiova
tel: 0251 411906

Drobeta-Turnu Severin
Art Museum (Muzeul de Artă)
Str. Rahovei 3, Drobeta-Turnu Severin
tel: 0252 317 377
www.ccm.ro/muzeu/

*Museum of the Iron Gates Region (Muzeul
Regunii Porților de Fier)*
Str. Independen,ei 2,
Drobeta-Turnu Severin
Remains of the Roman bridge and large
scale model
tel: 0252 312177
www.cimec.ro/Muzee/MuzeulRegiunii
PortilordeFier/Index.htm

Golești
*Museum of Viticulture and Fruit Growing
(Muzeul Viticulturii și Pomiculturii)*
Str, Banu Radu Golescu, Golești
tel: 0248 266364
www.cimec.ro/Muzee/golesti/
index.htm

Iași
Moldovian National Museum Complex
Palatul Culturii Iași
Piața Ștefan cel Mare și Sfant 1, Iași
The building contains four museums:
*Moldavian History Museum (Muzeul de
Istorie a Moldovei)*;
*Science and Technology Museum (Muzeul
Științei și Tehnicii Ștefan Procopiu)*
Art Museum (Muzeul de Artă)
*Moldavian Ethnographical Museum
(Muzeul Etnografic al Moldovei)*
www.muzeul-moldova.ro
*Museum of Romanian Literature
(Muzeul Literaturii Romane)*
Casa Vasile Pogor
Str. V. Pogor 4, Iași
tel: 032 213210
The museum consists of several memorial
houses of writers in the city.
www.cimec.ro/Muzee/fier/frame.htm

Măldărești
Museum Complex (Complexul Muzeal)
Măldărești
approx. 3 km from Horezu
tel: 0250 861510

Comprises two well-preserved 18th-century manor houses *(cula)*
www.muzee-valcea.ro

Miercurea Ciuc
Szekler Museum (Muzeul Secuiesc al Ciucului)
Piaţa Cetăţii 2, 530132 Miercurea Ciuc
tel: 0266 372024
e-mail: miko@csszm.ro
www.csszm.ro

Râmnicu Vâlcea
Vâlcean Village Museum (Muzeul Satului Vâlcean)
Calea lui Traian 302, Bujoreni
tel: 0250 738 121
Large open-air museum (8 hectares) with houses, churches, farm buildings, workshops. www.muzee-valcea.ro

Sibiu
Muzeul Naţional Brukenthal
Piaţa Mare 4-5, 550163 Sibiu
email: info@brukenthalmuseum.ro
www.brukenthalmuseum.ro
A fine collection of old master paintings in an imposing 18th-century palace
Complexul Naţional Muzeal ASTRA
Piata Mica 11, 550182 Sibiu,
tel 0269-218195
email: office@muzeulastra.ro
Sections on Transylvanian, Saxon, and Roma ethnography; Franz Binder Ethnographic Museum of African and other art
www.muzeulastra.ro
The museum's open-air section, the largest in Romania, is at Dumbrava Sibiului:
ASTRA Museum of Traditional Folk Civilization (Muzeul Civilizaciei Populare Traditionale ASTRA)
Calea Rasinari, Sibiu
tel 0269-242599; fax 0269-242419
email: muzeuldumbrava@clicknet.ro

Sighetu Marmaţiei
Maramureş Museum (Muzeul Maramureşului)
Piaţa Libertăţii 15, Sighetu Marmaţiei
tel: 0262 311 521
Includes several sections, including an open air museum, *Muzeul Satului Maramuresan*; and the *Muzeul Etnografic al Maramuresului* at Bogdan Voda, nr. 1
Memorial to the Victims of Communism and to the Resistance (Memorialul Victimelor Comunismului şi al Rezistentei)
Str. Corneliu Coposu 4, Sighetu Marmaţiei
tel: 0262 319 424
www.memorialsighet.ro
Elie Wiesel House Museum (now Jewish Culture and Civilization Museum)
Str. Tudor Vladimirescu 1, Sighetu Marmaţiei

Sinaia
Muzeul National Peleş
Str Peleşului 2, Sinaia
tel: 0244 310918
email: museum@peles.ro
www.peles.ro

Timişoara
Banat Museum (Muzeul Banatului)
Piaţa Huniade 1, 300002 Timişoara
tel: 0256 491339
email: muzeul.banatului@yahoo.com
www.muzeulbanatului.ro
Banat Village Museum (Muzeul Satului Banatean)
Aleea CFR 1, Timişoara
tel: 0256 225588
www.msbtm.ro

Nature reserves

Nature Reserves Romania has over 500 nature reserves (covering 4.8% of the country's territory). The mountainous Retezat and Pietrosul Mare reserves and the whole of the Danube Delta are protected as part of UNESCO's network of biosphere reserves. Tourist facilities are relatively well developed in the Delta, but are more limited in the other reserves.

The most important nature reserves are:

The Apuseni Mountains in the Western Carpathians, southwest of Cluj-Napoca. This large area, of 37,900 hectares, is endowed with peaks rising to over 1800 m, as well as forests, gorges, waterfalls and underground waterways. Its most remarkable section is the Padişă Plateau, a karst landscape (formed by the erosion of limestone by rain-water) with caves and subterranean rivers; the most impressive features are perhaps the Ponor Citadels, Cetaţile Ponorolui. This area can be reached from the beatiful Arieş valley, to the south, which contains the celebrated Ice Cave (Pestera Gheţarul), accessed via the village of Gârda de Sus. Another spectacular formation, the Bears' Cave (Pestera Urşilor), named after the remains of bears discovered there, lies further west, near Ştei. Still further south are the gold-bearing Metaliferi Mountains: a rewarding hike leads from the village of Bucium, near Abrud, to the Detunata Peaks (1200 m). At the eastern end of the Aries Valley is the dramatic Turda Gorge (Cheile Turzii), 10 km west of Turda.

The Bucegi Mountains, an area of 35,700 hectares on the eastern side of the Southern Carpathians, are west of the Prahova Valley between Sinaia and Predeal. There are hiking trails from Sinaia, although the most interesting, if tougher, treks are from Buşteni, leading towards the Bucegi Plateau, which is famous for rock formations eroded into strange, suggestive shapes, such as the Sphinx and the Old Women. The spring flowers are magnificent.

The *Ceahlău Massif* in the eastern Carpathians, west of Lake Bicaz, is a national park of 17,391 hectares, whose highest peak, Ocolasu Mare, rises to over 1900 m. The scenery is rugged and superb, and the Massif has some of the richest flora and fauna in Romania, including lynx and chamois as well as bears. The best hikes begin at the resort of Durău, from which it is possible to reach the magnificent Duruitoarea Waterfall, which falls 25 m in two stages. To the south of the massif lie the spectacular Bicaz Gorges.

The *Danube Delta*'s protected area (including the buffer zones) covers 580,000 hectares of open wetland and ancient deciduous forest. Its colony of pelicans, the largest in Europe, is one of many important bird populations fully described in pp. 249-254.

The gateway to the Delta area is Tulcea, a river port from which boats ply the three main channels of the Delta. The Sulina branch, which was made navigable to larger shipping in the late 19th century, is flanked to the north and south by the Chilia and Sfântu Gheorghe channels. The areas that are most rewarding for naturalists are around the smaller waterways. The necessary permits can be obtained in Tulcea at the Delta Hotel on the waterfront (Str. Isaccei 2, tel 040 515753). Trips can be organised by Ibis Tours (Str. Babadag 6, bl. A4, sc. B. ap. 14; tel 092 381398) or ATBAD (Str. Babadag 11, tel 040 514114). The latter owns floating hotels, as well as the renovated Lebada Hotel on the Sulina Channel, close to the village of Crișan.

The Domogled Mountains, at the western end of the Southern Carpathians, are close to the spa of Băile Herculane. Rising to an altitude of 1100 m, this national park of 60,100 hectares was the first nature reserve of its kind in Romania (1932). It is famous for its astonishing variety of butterflies, as well as rare fauna and even turtles.

The *Făgăraș Mountains* are south of the main road between Brașov and Sibiu, in the Southern Carpathians. They contain Romania's highest peaks, Mount Moldoveanu (2544 m) and Mount Negoiu (2535 m), as well as numerous glacial lakes, such as Lake Bilea (with a nearby waterfall). There are spectacular hikes from the town of Victoria and from the tourist complex in the monastery at Sâmbăta de Suș, 10 km southeast of Victoria. Ceaușescu's Transfăgărașan Highway crosses the long ridge of the Făgăraș at its western end.

The *Iron Gates* (Porțile de Fier), at the Serbian frontier on the Danube, are now dominated by a dam and hydroelectric power station, inaugurated in 1971. However, in the vicinity are biologically significant areas, in particular, to the west, the dramatic gorges known as Cazanele Mici and Cazanele Dunarii.

The *Penteleu Mountain*, in the southeastern corner of the Carpathians, can be reached via the Szekler town of Covasna. Its varied alpine flora include rare orchids and the densest groves of spruce in Europe, in the Milea-Viforita Reserve on the southern side of the mountain.

The *Retezat Mountains*, on the western side of the Southern Carpathians, contain a national park of 35.347 hectares, which was set up in 1935. Remote and unspoiled, the park's alpine landscape has over 100 permanent or temporary glacial lakes, as well as more than 300 species of flora, and mountain fauna such as chamois. Hikes begin at Gura Zlata, (south of Sarmizegetusa), to the west of the massif, or at Câmpul lui Neag, to the east.

The *Rodna Mountains*, at the northwestern end of the Eastern Carpathians include a national park of 55,800 hectares. They are accessible from Borșa in the Viseu Valley, or from the Prislop Pass on the border with Moldavia. The range includes the Pietrosul Mare Massif (2303m), which has numerous glacial lakes, as well as rare fauna and flora, in a biosphere reserve of about 900 hectares.

Language

The Romanian language: The Romanian language developed from the various Latin dialects spoken in the Roman province of Dacia at the time of the Emperor Trajan in the early second century AD. The colonists of Dacia came from all over the Roman Empire, and their lingua franca was therefore based on a simplified form of Vulgar Latin. Because of the subsequent isolation of the whole of the lower Danube region from Western Christendom caused by the Slav and Magyar invasions, it was this form of Latin from which the modern Romanian language evolved and not later medieval Latin, which was to form the basis of French, Italian, Spanish, Portuguese and the other Latin languages of Western Europe.

Although Romanian has maintained its essentially Latin character, there are many Slavonic (Old Bulgarian, Serbian, Polish, Ukrainian and Russian), Albanian, Hungarian, German, Greek and Turkish elements in its vocabulary, and to a lesser extent in its phonology and its syntax and grammar. Many of the loan words from these languages were replaced or supplemented in the nineteenth century by words of Italian or French origin (e.g. *amic* for *prieten*, 'friend') in a deliberate attempt to re-Romanize the language. Of the four major dialects of modern Romanian the most important is Daco-Romanian, which is spoken by 90 percent of the population of Romania today. For a more detailed account of the history of the Romanian language and of some of its distinctive features see p. 19ff.

Pronunciation of Romanian Romanian pronunciation is largely regular, and the pronunciation of most letters is approximately the same as that used in many other European languages which use the Roman alphabet.

The pronunciation of the vowels is as follows:

a   Similar to English 'u' in *cut*.
ă   Similar to English 'ur' in *hurt*.
â   No equivalent in English, but similar to English 'ee' in *deep*, spoken with lips spread and the centre of the tongue raised against the palate. Formerly written as î.
âi   Two separate syllables, as in *pâ-ine* 'bread'.
au   Similar to English 'ou' in *out*.
e   Similar to English 'e' in *red*.
ei   Similar to English 'ei' in *beige*.
i   In the middle of a word similar to English 'ee' in *deep*; at the end of a word (e.g. in plural nouns) a very short 'ee' sound.
î   See â.
ie   Similar to English 'ye' in *yes*.
iei   Similar to English *yea*. *Ei* ('they', 'her', 'its') is also so pronounced.
ii   In the plural form *copii* ('children'), a single long 'ee' sound; otherwise two separate syllables.
îi   See âi.
io   Similar to English 'yor' in *yore*.
o   Similar to English 'or' in *fork*.
oa   Similar to English 'wo' in *won*.
oi   Similar to English 'oi' in *voice*.
u   Similar to English 'u' in *put*.
ui   Similar to English 'ui' in ruin.

The pronunciation of the consonants is as follows:

b As in English.

c As in English *cat* before another consonant or 'a', 'o' and 'u'; as in English 'ch' in *chair* before 'e' and 'i'.

ch As in English *chasm*. Only used before 'e' and 'i'.

d As in English, but with the tip of the tongue against the upper teeth.

f As in English.

g Before 'a', 'o' or 'u' as in English *game*; before 'e' and 'i' as in English *gem*.

gh As in English *ghost*. Only used before 'e' and 'i'.

h Before a vowel as in English *head*; after a vowel similar to 'ch' in Scots *loch*.

j Similar to English 's' in *pleasure*.

k As in English.

l As in English, but with the tongue against the upper teeth.

m As in English.

n As in English, but with the tongue against the upper teeth.

p As in English.

r Trilled as in Scots.

s As in English, but with the tongue against the upper teeth.

ş 'sh' as in *ship*.

t As in English.

ţ As in English 'ts' in *cats*.

v As in English.

x Before a consonant as in English 'x' in extreme, before a vowel as in English 'x' [gz] in *exact*.

z As in English.

Some useful words and phrases

Yes — Da
No — Nu
Please — Vă rog
Thank you (very much) — Mulţumesc (foarte mult)
That's all right/Don't mention it — Nu aveţi pentru ce

I beg your pardon? — Poftim?
Sorry/Forgive me — Âmi pare rău/Scusaţi-mă
Excuse me — Fiţi amabil/Iertaţi-mă
Cheers!/Good luck! — Noroc!
Happy birthday! — La mulţi ani!
Congratulations! — Felicitări!
Kind regards. — Sincere salutări

Good morning — Bună dimineaţa
Good day/afternoon — Bună ziua
Good evening — Bună seară
Good night — Noapte bună
Hullo! — Bună! Salut!
Good bye — La revedere
Bon voyage! — Drum bun!/Călătorie plăcută!

What's your name? — Cum vă numiţi?
My name is.... — Mă numesc .....
May I introduce you to Mr/Mrs/Miss? — Vă prezint pe domnul/ doamna/ domnişoara
Pleased to meet you — Âncântat de cunoştinţă
How are you? — Ce mai faceţi?
I'm very well, thank you, and how are you? — Bine, vă mulţumesc, Şi dumneavoastră?

Do you speak English? — Vorbiţi englezeşte?
Does anybody here speak English? — Vorbeşte cineva aici englezeşte?
I don't understand — Nu ânţeleg
I don't speak Romanian. — Nu vorbesc româneşte
Please speak more slowly. — Vă rog să vorbiţi mai rar
What do you call this in Romanian? — Cum se zice asta ân româneşte?
What does that mean? — Ce ânseamnă asta?
How do you spell that? — Cum se scrie asta?
Please write that down. — Vreţi să-mi scrieţi asta

What do you want?	Ce doriți?	Why?	De ce?
Can you help me?	Puteți să-mi ajutați?	Why not?	De ce nu?
Can I help you at all?	Vă pot ajuta cu ceva?	Who?	Cine?
Can you tell me?	Puteți să-mi spuneți?	How?	Cum?
Can you show me?	Puteți să-mi arăați?	open	deschis
Where are you going?	Unde mergeți?	shut	ânchis
Where can I buy..?	Unde pot să cumpăr..?	beautiful	frumos
What would you like?	Ce doriți?	ugly	urât
I would like...	Aș vrea ...	cheap	ieftin
Please bring me ...	Vreți să-m aduceți ...	expensive	scump
I need ...	Am nevoie de ...	easy	ușor
I am thirsty	Mi-e sete	difficult	greu
I am hungry	Mi-e foame	fast	repede
I am scared	Mi-e frica	slow	âncet
I am tired (male)	Sânt obosit	hot	fierbinte/cald
I am tired (female)	Sânt obosită	cold	rece
I am not feeling well	Nu mi simt bine	old	vechi/bătrân
I am lost	M-am rătăcit	new	nou
I don't like it	Nu-mi place	young	tânar
I like it	Âmi place	small	mic
Please wait	Asteptați, vă rog	large	mare
		a little	puțin
I'll call the police	Chem poliția	a lot, much/many	mult/mulți (m)/multe (f)
Call the police	Chemați poliția!	enough	destul
Police!	Poliția!	some	niște
Stop thief!	Stai! Hoți!	more	mai
Fire	Foc!	only	numai
Help!	Ajutor!	with	cu
Stop!	Stop! Stai!	without	fără
Look out!	Atenție!	nothing	nimic
Leave me alone!	Lăsați-mă ân pace!	only	numai
I need your help		perhaps	poate
	Am nevoie de ajutorul		
	dumneavoastra	*Colours*	
I've lost my bag/wallet		black	negru
	Mi-am pierdut valiza/portmoneul	white	alb
It's an emergency	E o urgență	grey	gri
I'm sick (male)	Sunt bolnav	red	roșu
I'm sick (female)	Sunt bolnova	blue	albastru
I've been injured	Sunt accidentat	yellow	galben
I need a doctor	Am nevoie de doctor	green	verde
Can I use your telephone?		orange	portocaliu
	Pot să utilizez telefonul	mauve	mov
	dumneavoastra?	purple	purpuriu
		brown	maro/brun

Numbers		Time	
1	un,una	when?	cind?
2	doi, doua	What's the time?	Ce oră este?/
3	trei		Cât este ceasul?
4	patru	It is five past two.	
5	cinci		Este ora unu şi cinci minuti.
6	şase	It is a quarter past four.	
7	şapte		Este patru şi un sfert
8	opt	It is half past five.	
9	nouă		Este cinci şi jumatate
10	zece	It is twenty to six.	
11	unsprezece		Este opt fără douazeci
12	doisprezece	It is a quarter to ten.	
13	treisprezece		Este zece fără un sfert
14	paisprezece	The train leaves at 14.05.	
15	cincisprezce		Trenul pleacă la ora pais
16	şaispzece		prezece zero cinci.
17	şaptesprezece		
18	optsprezee	now	acum
19	nouăsprezece	early	devreme
20	douăzeci	after	după
21	douăzeci şi un(a)	soon	curând
30	treizeci	before	ânainte
40	patruzeci	during	ân timpul
50	cincizeci	never	niciodată
60	şaizeci	late	târziu
70	şaptezec	until	până
80	optzeci	yet	âncă
90	nouăzeci	today	azi, astăzi
100	o sută	yesterday	ieri
200	două sute	tomorrow	mâine
500	cinci sute	the day after tomorrow	poi mâine
1000	o mie	morning	dimineaă
2000	două mii	midday	amiază
5000	cinci mii	afternoon	după amiază
1,000,000	un milion	evening	seară
1,000,000,000		night	noapte
half	jumătate	midnight	miezul nopţii
quarter		every day	ân fiecare zi
third		last week	săptămâna trecută
		next week	săptămâna viitoare

What day is it today?	Ce zi este azi/astăzi?	Does this train/bus stop in....?	
Monday	Luni		Trenul/autobuzul ăsta oprește la..?
Tuesday	Marți	When does the train/bus for... leave?	
Wednesday	Miercuri		Când pleacă trenul/autobuzul
Thursday	Joi		spre..?
Friday	Vineri	When will train/bus arrive in..?	
Saturday	Sâmbătă		Când ajunge trenul/autobuzul
Sunday	Duminică		ăsta la..?

January	Ianuarie	Taxi!	Taxi!
February	Februarie	Take me to ..., please	
March	Martie		Conduceți-mă la..., vă rog.
April	Aprilie	How much does it cost to get to..?	
May	Mai		Cât costa pentru a ajunge la..?
June	Junie		
July	Julie	*Directions*:	
August	August	where?	unde?
September	Octombrie	here	aici
November	Noembrie	there	acolo
December	Decembrie	Where are the toilets?	Unde e toaleta?
		Is it far to...?	Este până la...?
spring	primăvară	I want to go to...	Vreau să merg la...
summer	vară	In which direction is..?	In ce direcție se află..?
autumn	toamnă	How do I get to the..?	Cum ajung la..?
winter	iarnă	train station	gara
		bus station	stația de autobuz
New Year	Anul Nou	airport	aeroport
Easter	Pași	town centre	centrul aroșului
Christmas	Crăciun	. hotel	hotelul

Merry Christmas and a Happy New Year
            Crăciun fericit și un an nou fericit
Happy Easter   Pași fericite

the British/American/Canadian/	
Australian consulate	
	consulatul britanic/
	american/canadian/australian
Where are there lots of..?	Unde sunt multe..?
hotels	hoteluri
restaurants	restaurante
bars	baruri
sites to see	locuri turistice
Can you show me on the map?	
	Puteți să-mi arătați pe hartă?

Transport

How much is a ticket to...?	
	Cât costa un bilet până la...
One ticket to..., please	
	Un bilet până la..., vă rog
Where does this train/bus go?	
	Unde merge trenul/autobuzul
	ăsta?
Where is the train/bus to...?	
	Unde este trenul/autobuzul
	pentru....?

street	stradă
Turn left	Âluați-o la stânga
Turn right	Âluați-o la dreapta
left	stânga
right	dreapta
straight ahead	drept ânainte

towards the...	după...
before the...	ânainte de...
Watch for the...	ăşteaptă...
north	nord
south	sud
east	est
west	vest
high up, above	sus
above	deasupra
low down, below	jos
underneath, below	sub/dedesubt
downstairs	la parter
upstairs	la etaj
behind	ânapoi
between	ântre
inside	ânauntru
outside	afară
near	lingă
distant	departe
through	prin
towards	spre

Shopping

How much is this?
            Cât costă asta?
That's too expensive
            Este prea scump.
I need...   Am nevoie de ...

toothpaste	pastă de dinţi
a toothbrush	periuţă de dinţi
tampons	tampoane
soap	săpun
shampoo	şampon
pain killer	anti-inflamator
medicine	medicamente
a razor	o lamă de ras
an umbrella	o umbrelă
sun lotion	bronzator
a postcard	o carte poştală
postage stamps	timbre
batteries	baterii
writing paper	hârtie de sris
a pen	un stilou/un pix

English language books/magazines/
    newspaper   cărţi/reviste/un ziar ân
                limba engleză

Driving

petrol station	staţie de benzină
petrol	benzină
diesel	motorină
speed limit	viteza maximă
no parking	nu parcaţi
one way	sens unic
give way	cedează trecerea

Accommodation

Do you have any rooms available?
            Aveţi camere libere?
How much is a room for one person/
two people?
            Cât costa o cameră pentru o
            persoană/pentru două persoane?
Does the room have..? Exista in camera..?
    another blanket ânca o patură
    a bathroom   baie
    a telephone   telefon
    a TV   televizor
May I see the room first?
            Pot să văd camera ântâi?
Have you anything..? Aveţi ceva..?
    quieter   mai liniştit
    bigger   mai mare
    cheaper   mai ieftin
Fine, I'll take the room.
            Bine. Vreau camera.
I'm staying for one night.
            Eu rămân pentru o noapte.
I will stay for .... nights.
            Eu rămân ... nopţi.
Can you suggest another hotel?
            Puteţi recomanda alt hotel?
Do you have a safe? Aveţi seif?
Is breakfast/supper included?
            Preţul include micul dejun/cină?
What time is breatkast/supper?
            La ce oră este micul dejun/cină?
Please clean my room.
            Curăţaţi camera mea, vă rog.

345

Can you wake me at ... ?
>Puteți să mă treziți la....?

I want to check out.
>Aș vrea să achit nota și să plec de la hotel.

Do you accept credit cards?
>Acceptați cărți de credit?

Can you change money for me?
>Puteți să schimbați bani pentru mine?

Where can I get money changed?
>Unde pot să schimb bani?

Restaurant

breakfast — micul deun
lunch — dejun
supper — cină

A table for one person, two people please.
>O masă pentru o persoană/pentru doua persoane, vă rog.

May I look at the menu, please?
>Pot să văd meniul, vă rog?

Is there a house speciality?
>Aveți o specialitate a casei?

Is there a local speciality?
>Aveți o specialitate locală?

I'm a vegetarian — Sunt vegetarian
I would like... — Ăș vrea...
I want a dish containing...
>Vreau o mâncare care conține...

chicken — pui
duck — rață
beef — carne de vită
fish — pește
ham — jambon *or* șuncă
sausage — cârnați
cheese — brânză

eggs — ouă
salad — salată
fresh vegetables — legume proaspăte
tomatoes — roșii *or* tomate
mushrooms — ciuperci
fresh fruit — fructe poraspete
bread — pâine
toast — pâine prăjită
noodles — tăiței
rice — orez
beans — fasole

May I have some ...? Aș dori niște..?
salt — sare
pepper — piper
butter — unt

Bon appetit — Poftă bună
Waiter! — Ospătar!
I'm finished. — Sunt gata.
It was delicious. — Afost delicios.
Please clear the plates.
>Puteți să strangeti farfuriile.

The bill, please. — Nota de plată, vă rog.

Drinks

May I have a cup of..? Aș dori o ceașcă de..?
coffee — cafea
tea — ceai

May I have a bottle of..? Aș dori o sticlă de..?
juice — suc
water (sparkling/still)
>apă minerală/plată
beer — bere

May I have a glass of..? Aș dori un pahar de..?
red/white wine — vin roșu/alb

A beer/two beers, please.
>O bere / două beri, vă rog.

Further Reading

This is a select bibliography, but it aims to be comprehensive. It does not include any works of fiction or of Romanian literature, or any travel guides. Books which I have found especially useful and/or readable and can therefore recommend to anyone interested in Romania are indicated with a star. Where these exist, titles are given in their English versions.

History and biography
*Almond, Mark, *The Rise and Fall of Nicolae and Elena Ceauşescu*, London, 1992
Antal, Dan, *Out of Romania*, London, 1994
Behr, Edward, *Kiss the Hand You Cannot Bite: the Rise and Fall of the Ceauşescus*, London, 1991
Beza, Marcu, *Roumanian Chroniclers*, London, 1941
*Bobango, Gerald, *The Emergence of the Romanian National State*, Boulder, CO, 1979
*Bodea, Cornelia, *The Romanians' Struggle for Unification 1834-1849*, Bucharest, 1971
Bolitho, Hector, *Romania under King Carol*, London, 1939
Burgoyne, Elizabeth, *Carmen Sylva: Queen and Woman*, London, 1941
Burton, Berry, *Romanian Diaries, 1944-1947*, Iaşi, 2000
Căndea, Virgil and Cornelia, *Transylvania in the History of the Romanians: Heritage and Continuity in Eastern Europe*, 1983
Cantemir, Dimitrie, *The History and Decline of the Ottoman Empire*, 1734
Catchlove, Donald, *Romania's Ceauşescu*, Tunbridge Wells, 1972
Constantinescu, Miron et al., eds, *Unification of the Romanian National State: the Union of Transylvania with old Romania*, Bucharest, 1971
Deletant, Dennis, *Ceauşescu and the Securitate: Coercion and Dissent in Romania*, London, 1996
*Deletant, Dennis, *Communist Terror in Romania*, London, 1999
Deletant, Dennis, *Gheorghiu-Dej and the Police State, 1948-1965*, London, 1999
Dragan, Josif, *Antonescu*, 2 vols, Venice, 1986 and 1988
East, William G., *The Union of Moldavia and Wallachia 1859*, Cambridge, 1929
Eidelberg, Philip Gabriel, *The Great Romanian Peasant Revolt of 1907: Origins of a Modern Jacquerie*, Leiden, 1974
Eliade, Mircea, *The Romanians: A Concise History*, Bucharest,1992
Florescu, Radu R. N., *The Struggle against Russia in the Romanian Principalities 1821-1854*, Munich, 1962
*Florescu, Radu R., *Essays on Romanian History*, Iaşi, 1999
Gallagher, Tom, *Romania after Ceauşescu*, Edinburgh, 1995
Gallagher, Tom, *Theft of a Nation: Romania since Communism*, London, 2005
Julia Gelardi, *Born to Rule: Granddaughters of Victoria, Queens of Europe*, London, 2005
    [Includes biography of Queen Marie]
*Georgescu, Vlad, *The Romanians, A History*, London, 1991

*Glenny, Misha, *The Rebirth of History*, London, 1993
*Hitchins, Keith, *The Roumanian National Movement in Transylvania, 1780-1849*, Harvard, 1977
*Hitchins, Keith, *Romania 1866-1947*, Oxford, 1994
*Hitchins, Keith, *The Romanians 1774-1866*, Oxford, 1996
Hlihor, Constantin and Ioan Scurtu, *The Red Army in Romania*, Iași, 1999
Hoven, Baroness Helena von der, *King Carol of Romania*, London, 1940
Hupchick, Dennis P. and Cox, Harold E., *A Concise Historical Atlas of Eastern Europe*, New York, 1996
*Iorga, Nicolae, *Histoire des Roumains et de leur civilisation*, Bucharest, 1922, English ed., 1925
*Jelavich, Barbara, *History of the Balkans, vol. I: Eighteenth and Nineteenth Centuries; vol. II: Twentieth Century*, Cambridge, 1983
Jelavich, Barbara, *Russia and the Formation of the Romanian National State 1821-1878*, Cambridge, 1984
Jowitt, Kenneth, ed., *Social Change in Romania 1860 -1940*, Berkeley, CA, 1978
Lambrino, Paul, *King Carol II: A Life of my Grandfather*, London, 1988
Lee, Arthur Gould, *Crown against Sickle*, London, 1950
Lee, Arthur Gould, *Helen, Queen Mother of Romania*, London, 1956
Mackenzie, Andrew, *The History of Transylvania*, London, 1983
Michelson, Paul E., *Romanian Politics, 1859-1871: From Prince Cuza to Prince Carol*, Iași, 1998
Michelson, Paul E., ed., *The Revolution of 1848 in the Romanian Lands: An Introduction and Guide*, Iași, 1999
Nagy-Talavera, N. M., *Nicolae Iorga: A Biography*, Iași, 1998
Oțetea, Andrei, ed., *The History of the Romanian People*, New York 1978
*Pakula, Hannah:, *Queen of Roumania: The life of Princess Marie, grand-daughter of Queen Victoria*, London, 1984
*Pavlowitch, Stevan K., *A History of the Balkans 1804-1945*, London and New York, 1999
Pearton, Maurice, *Oil and the Roumanian State 1895-1948*, Oxford, 1971
Pop, Ioan Aurel, *Romanians and Hungarians from the 9th to the 14th Century: The Genesis of the Transylvanian Medieval State*, Cluj-Napoca, 1996
*Porter, Ivor, *Michael of Romania: The King and the Country*, Stroud, 2005
Quinlan, Paul, *Carol II of Romania*, Westport, CT, 1995
*Rady, Martyn, *Romania in Turmoil*, London, 1992
Retegan, Mihai, *In the Shadow of the Prague Spring: Romanian Foreign Policy and the Crisis in Czechoslovakia, 1968*, Iași, 1999
Riker, T. W., *The Making of Roumania: A Study of an International Problem*, Oxford, 1931
Roberts, Henry L., *Rumania: Political Problems of an Agrarian State*, Yale, 1951
*Runciman, Steven, *The Great Church in Captivity*, Cambridge, 1968
*Seton Watson Robert W., *A History of the Roumanians from Roman Times to the Completion of Unity,* Cambridge, 1934
Sweeney, John, *The Life and Evil Times of Nicolae Ceaușescu*, London, 1991
Stavrianos, L. S., *The Balkans since 1453*, New York, 1958
Torrey, Glenn, *Romania and World War I: A Collection of Studies*, Iași, 1998

Treptow, Kurt W., ed., *A History of Romania*, Iaşi, 1997

Treptow, Kurt W., ed., *Vlad III Dracula: The Life and Times of the Historical Dracula*, Iaşi, 1999

Turnock, David, *The Romanian Economy in the Twentieth Century*, London, 1986

Villiers, John, *Romania: Cross-roads of Culture*, Bangkok, 1988

Zub, Alexandru: *Reflections on the Impact of the French Revolution: 1789, de Tocqueville, and Romanian Culture*, Iaşi, 1999

Art and Architecture

Baconsky, A. E., *Dumitru Ghiaţa:*, Bucharest, 1966

Baconsky, A. E., *Ion Ţuculescu*, Bucharest, 1972

Barca, Ana, and Dinescu, Dan, *The Wooden Architecture of Maramureş*, Bucharest, 1997

Beza, Marcu, *Byzantine Art in Roumania*, London, 1940

*Buxton, David, *The Wooden Churches of Eastern Europe*, Cambridge, 1986

Celac, Mariana, et al., eds., *Romania in the 1930s: Architecture and Modernity*, exhibition catalogue, Bucharest, 1996

Comarnescu, Petru, *Art Guide to the Monuments in Northern Moldavia*, Bucharest, 1961

Drăguţ, Vasile, *Moldavian Murals from the 15th to the 16th century* [trans. Andreea Gheorghiţiou], Bucharest, 1982

Drăguţ, Vasile, *Christian Art in Romania 4: The 15th century* [trans. Andrei Bantas], Bucharest, 1985

Frunzetti, Ion, *Dimitrie Pacura*, Bucharest, 1971

*Giurescu, Dinu C., *The Razing of Romania's Past*, London, 1990

Iorga, Nicolae, *L'art populaire en Roumanie*, Paris, 1923

Iorga, Nicolae, *Les arts mineurs en Roumanie*, 2 vols, Bucharest, 1934-6

Machedon, Luminata, and Schoffham, Ernie, *Romanian Modernism: the Architecture of Bucharest 1920-1940*, Boston, 1999

Mulligan, Tom, 'Hungary, Romania, Yugoslavia: the Fine Arts and the Boundaries of Change', in Aulich, James and Wilcox, Tim, eds: *Europe without Walls: Art Posters and Revolution 1989-93*, Manchester, 1993

Musicescu, Maria Ana, *La broderie médiévale roumaine*, Bucharest, 1969

Mândrescu, Anatol, *Theodor Pallady*, Bucharest, 1971

Ogden, Alan, *Revelations of Byzantium*, London, 2001

Oprea, Petru, *Brâncuşi*, Bucharest, 1972

Theodorescu, Răzvan, *Bucovina: The Moldavian Mural Painting in the Fifteenth and Sixteenth Centuries*, UNESCO, Bucharest, s.d.

Treasures from Romania, exhibition catalogue, British Museum, London, 1971

Vătăşianu, Virgil, *La peinture murale du nord de la Moldavie*, Bucharest, 1974

Memoirs and Autobiography

Eliade, Mircea, *Autobiography 1907-37: Vol.1, Journey East, Journey West*, Chicago, 1992

Eliade, Mircea, *Autobiography 1907-37: Vol.2, Exiles' Odyssey*, Chicago, 1988

Goma, Paul, *My Childhood at the Gate of Unrest*, London, 1990

Mandache, Diana, *Later Chapters of my Life: The Lost Memoir of Queen Marie of Romania*, Stroud, 2004
Queen Marie of Romania, *My Country*, London, 1916
Queen Marie of Romania, *The Country that I Love: An Exile's Memories*, London, 1925
Queen Marie of Romania, *Ordeal: The Story of My Life*, New York, 1935

Folklore
Barber, Paul, *Vampires, Burial and Death: Folklore and Reality*, Yale, 1988
Kligman, Gail, *The Wedding of the Dead*, Berkeley, CA,1986
*McNally, Raymond and Florescu, Radu, *In Search of Dracula: a True History of Dracula and Vampire Legends*, London, 1997
Verdery, Katherine, *Transylvanian Villagers*, Berkeley, CA, 1983

Travel
Ascherson, Neal, *Black Sea*, London 1996
Boner, Charles, *Transylvania: Its Products and its People*, London, 1865
Drysdale, Helena, *Looking for Gheorghe: Love and Death in Romania*, London, 1996
Etherton, P. T. and A. Dunscombe Allen, *Through Europe and the Balkans: The Record of a Motor Tour*, London, 1928
*Fermor, Patrick Leigh, *Between the Woods and the Water*, London, 1986
Murphy, Dervla, *Transylvania and Beyond*, London, 1993
Ogden, Alan, *Romania Revisited: On the Trail of English Travellers, 1602-1941*, Iaşi, 1999
*Phillimore, Lion, *In the Carpathians*, London, 1912
Porter, Ivor, *Operation Autonomous: With SOE in Wartime Romania*, London, 1989
Sitwell, Sacheverell, *Romanian Journey*, Oxford, 1992

Latin and Greek Antiquities
Texts
Ovid, *Tristia and Epistulae ex Ponto*, trans. A.L. Wheeler, London, 1924
Herodotus, *Histories, Book VI*, trans. Aubrey de Selincourt, Harmondsworth, 1954
Tacitus, *Histories,* trans. Kenneth Wellesley, Harmondsworth, 1964
Suetonius, *The Twelve Caesars*, trans. Robert Graves, Harmondsworth, 1957
Xiphilinus, *Epitome of Dio Cassius*, French trans. M de Lepesant, 1674
Archaeology and History:
Canarache, V., *The Archaeological Museum of Constantza*, Bucharest, s.d.
Florescu, Radu, *Adamclisi*, Bucharest, 1973
Gibbon, Edward, *Decline and Fall of the Roman Empire, Book I*, best modern edition, London: The Folio Society, 1983
Mackenzie, Andrew, *Archaeology in Romania: The Mystery of the Roman Occupation*, London, 1986
Miclea, Ion, *The Column*, Cluj-Napoca, 1971
Parker, H. M. D, *The Roman Legions*, Cambridge, 1961

Pippidi, D. M., *I Greci nel Basso Danubio*, chapters V and VI, Milan, 1971

Poulter, Dr. Andrew G., 'The Lower Moesian Limes and the Dacian Wars of Trajan', in *Studien zu den Militärgrenzen Roms III [Roman 13th International Limes Congress, Aachen 1983]*, Stuttgart, 1986, pp. 519-528

Richmond, Sir Ian, *Trajan's army on Trajan's Column*, Rome ,1982

Rossi, L., *Trajan's Column and the Dacian Wars*, London 1971

Rossi, L., 'A Historiographic Reassessment of the Metopes of the Tropaeum Traiani at Adamklissi', in *Archaeological Journal*,129, 1972, pp. 56-68.

Taylor, Dr. Timothy, 'Thracians, Scythians and Dacians', chapter 13 of *The Oxford Illustrated Prehistory of Europe*, Oxford, 1994

Various authors, *Cambridge Ancient History, vols. XII & XIII*, Cambridge 2005, 1998

Index

```

ly.
```

PRO PATRIMONIO
FOUNDATION
'a future for our past'

Patron: His Majesty King Mihai I   Member of Europa Nostra

Pro Patrimonio—Romania is a non-government organization whose mission is to identify, preserve, and advocate for the historic and natural heritage of Romania. It restores, rescues and revitalizes endangered buildings and sites for the benefit of future generations.

There is no task more meaningful than the protection of nation's heritage and the transfer of that legacy to a next generation. A nation's identity is mirrored in that legacy which if erased or diminished undermines a people's own self-pride.

Much is at risk in Romania. Inadequate resources, the corrosive policies of the communist era, and the quickening pace of modern life are inimical to the careful nurturing of the nation's fragile heritage.

By rescuing, restoring and conserving endangered buildings, lands and environments of cultural interest and historic significance, Pro Patrimonio will contribute to the present and future well-being of Romanian society.

A primary objective of any single Pro Patrimonio project is to stimulate a productive role for traditional crafts and skills, to invite community pride in its heritage, to offer a memorable cultural experience for visitors, and to stimulate economic development.

Please become involved in our work – current projects include Viscri, Voroneţ, and Banffy Castle Park. Enquiries and donations to:

American Friends of Pro Patrimonio, 149 E 63, NYC, NY 10021
    Tel: (212) 980-6635
Pro Patrimonio UK, P.O. Box 2297, London W1A 5GG
    Tel: 020 7439 4052, e-mail: mail@propatrimonio.org

www.propatrimonio.org

Front cover and front cover flap: Szekler farmhouse in Transylvania (Alexander Fyjis-Walker)
Back cover: Frescoes at Voroneţ (Alexander Fyjis-Walker)
Back cover flap: The castle at Făgăraş (Romanian Tourist Office)
Inside cover maps: Romanian Tourist Office

All colour images courtesy Romanian Tourist Office except for colour illustrations p. 1, 8-9, 10-11,
28, col. plates 8, 9, 12, 11, 14 (Alexander Fyjis-Walker) and p. 18, col. plate 3 (Sheila Paine)
Mono illustrations courtesy of the editors

This book is part of the Pallas Guides series, published by Pallas Athene.
If you would like further information about the series, please write to:
Pallas Athene, 42 Spencer Rise, London NW5 1AP
or visit our website **www.pallasathene.co.uk**

Editor: John Villiers
Editorial assistants: Piers Blofeld, Olivia Humphreys, Ava Li, Lynn Quinlan,
Jenny Wilson and Sebastian Wormell

With particular thanks to Nicolae Ratiu and Stephen Lloyd,
without whom this book could not have been published

Series editor: Alexander Fyjis-Walker
Series designer: James Sutton

This edition first published by Pallas Athene London, 2009

ISBN 1 873429 55 X/ 978 1 873429 55 6

Printed through World Print, China